# ALL-NEW X·FACTOR

## 03

"Just another day at the office."

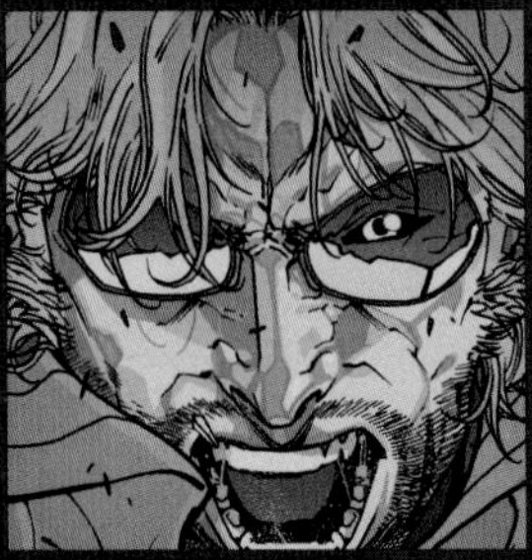

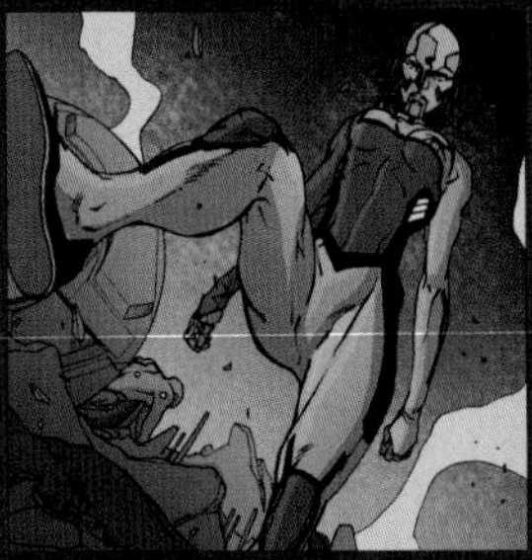

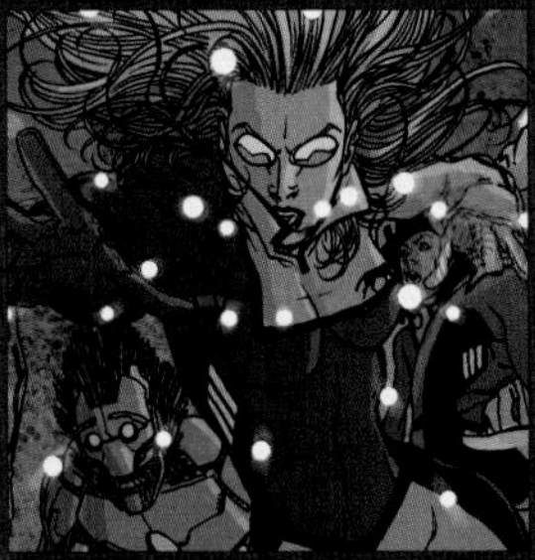

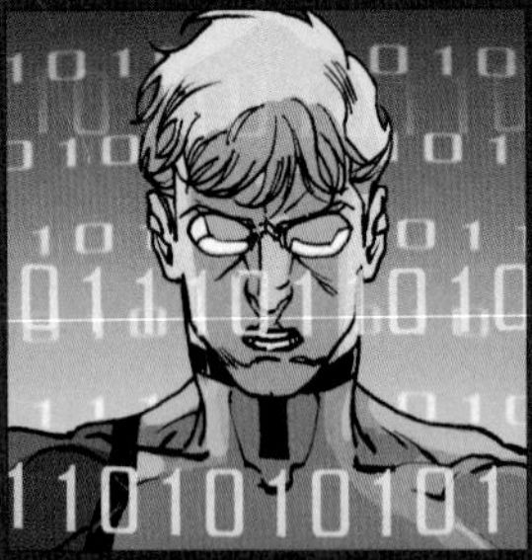
1101010101

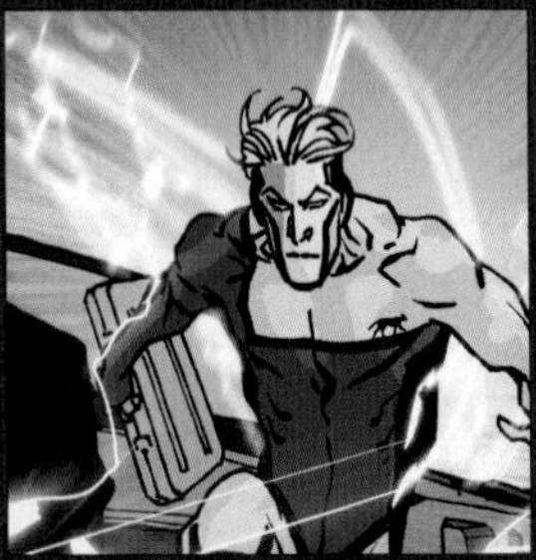

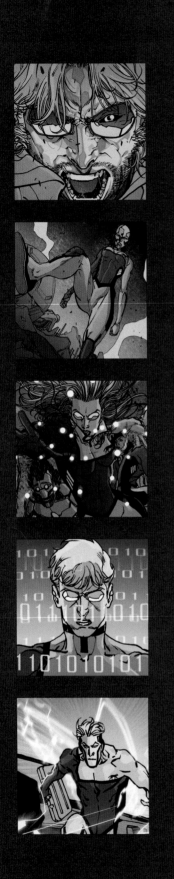

volume 03

# AXIS

**PETER DAVID** writer

issue #13

**POP MHAN** artist

issue #14

**POP MHAN** breakdowns

**POP MHAN & SCOTT HANNA** finishes

issues #15-20

**CARMINE DI GIANDOMENICO** with **WILL SLINEY** (#20) artists

LEE LOUGHRIDGE colorist
VC's CORY PETIT letterer
KRIS ANKA & JARED K. FLETCHER cover art

XANDER JAROWEY assistant editor
KATIE KUBERT editor

JENNIFER GRÜNWALD collection editor
SARAH BRUNSTAD assitant editor
ALEX STARBUCK associate managing editor
MARK D. BEAZLEY editor, special projects
JEFF YOUNGQUIST senior editor, special projects
DAVID GABRIEL svp print, sales & marketing
JARED K. FLETCHER book designer

AXEL ALONSO editor in chief
JOE QUESADA chief creative officer
DAN BUCKLEY publisher
ALAN FINE executive producer

ALL-NEW X-FACTOR sponsored by

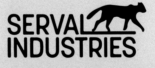

SERVAL INDUSTRIES

# ALL-NEW X·FACTOR

## PREVIOUSLY

Welcome to the all-new X-Factor, Serval Industries' newest way of making your life better — a privately owned and operated super-team handpicked by Serval CEO Harrison Snow to serve the needs of both Serval Industries and the society and people that make up the world we all share. Why should super-teams like the Avengers be the purview of government, bogged down as it is with bureaucracy and politics? X-Factor has the backing and resources of a successful corporation, proven efficient in the free market and unmatched in its charitable works and contributions.

Things finally seemed like they were settling down a bit for X-Factor. So why not have a big press conference announcing the team to the world? You'd think that would be great for PR. Of course, when the former mutant Fatale showed up to accuse Quicksilver of committing horrible misdeeds it dampened the mood a bit...especially when Quicksilver admitted to those crimes and ran off. But accepting the sins of his past has delivered to him a surprising gift — the forgiveness of his daughter, Luna.

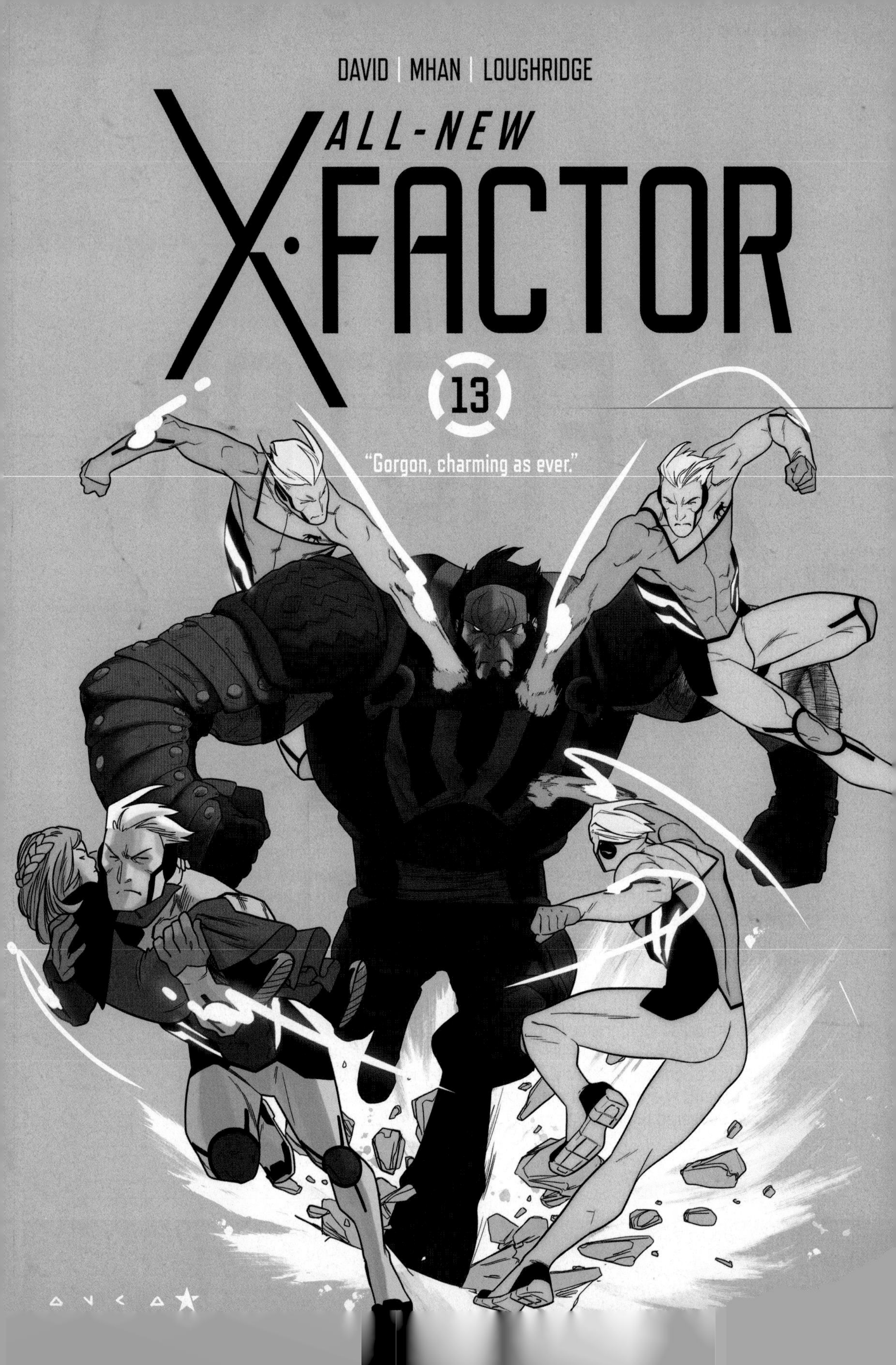
DAVID | MHAN | LOUGHRIDGE
ALL-NEW
X-FACTOR
13
"Gorgon, charming as ever."

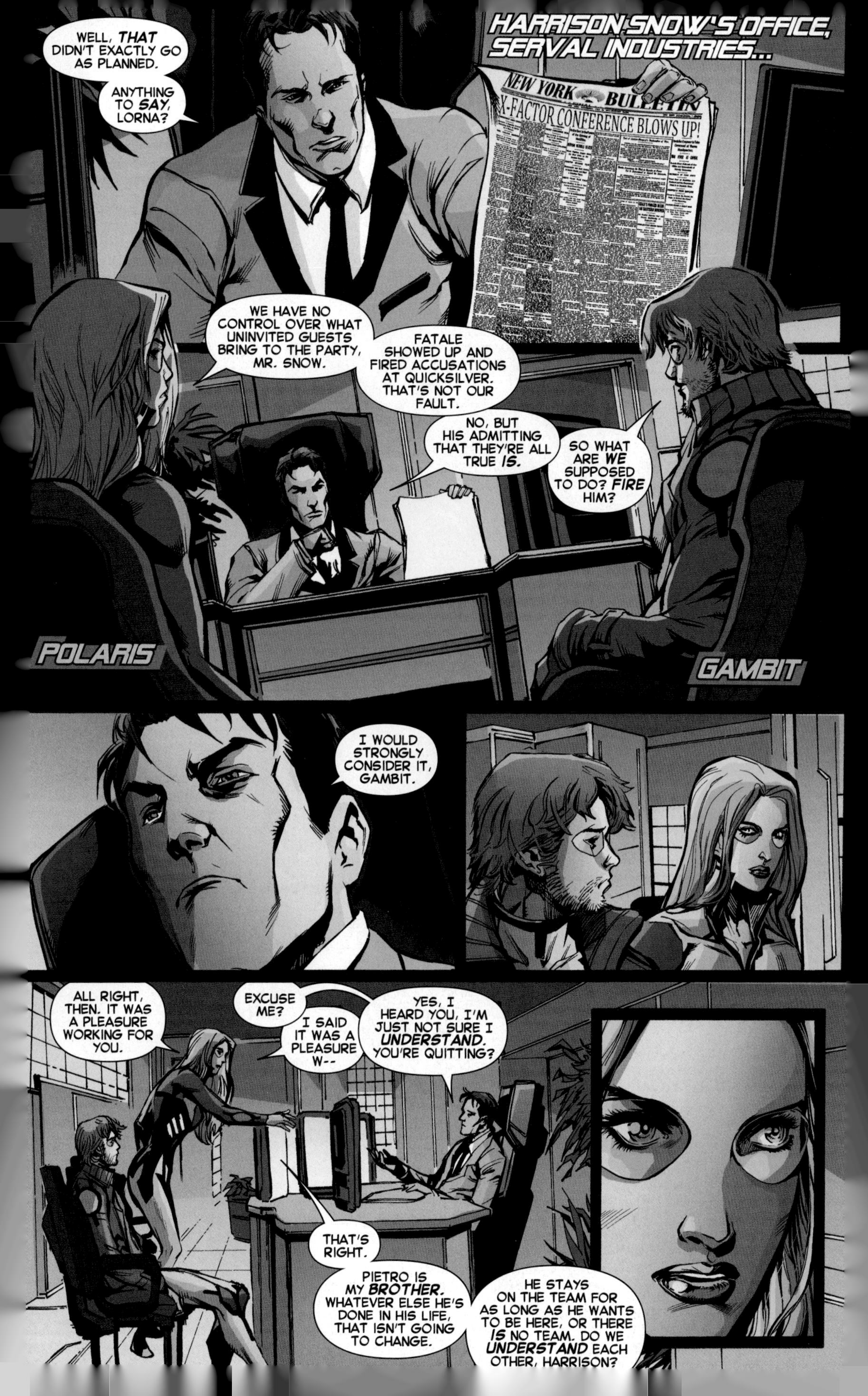
HARRISON SNOW'S OFFICE, SERVAL INDUSTRIES...
WELL, THAT DIDN'T EXACTLY GO AS PLANNED.
ANYTHING TO SAY, LORNA?
NEW YORK BULLETIN
X-FACTOR CONFERENCE BLOWS UP!
WE HAVE NO CONTROL OVER WHAT UNINVITED GUESTS BRING TO THE PARTY, MR. SNOW.
FATALE SHOWED UP AND FIRED ACCUSATIONS AT QUICKSILVER. THAT'S NOT OUR FAULT.
NO, BUT HIS ADMITTING THAT THEY'RE ALL TRUE IS.
SO WHAT ARE WE SUPPOSED TO DO? FIRE HIM?
POLARIS
GAMBIT
I WOULD STRONGLY CONSIDER IT, GAMBIT.
ALL RIGHT, THEN. IT WAS A PLEASURE WORKING FOR YOU.
EXCUSE ME?
I SAID IT WAS A PLEASURE W--
YES, I HEARD YOU, I'M JUST NOT SURE I UNDERSTAND. YOU'RE QUITTING?
THAT'S RIGHT.
PIETRO IS MY BROTHER. WHATEVER ELSE HE'S DONE IN HIS LIFE, THAT ISN'T GOING TO CHANGE.
HE STAYS ON THE TEAM FOR AS LONG AS HE WANTS TO BE HERE, OR THERE IS NO TEAM. DO WE UNDERSTAND EACH OTHER, HARRISON?

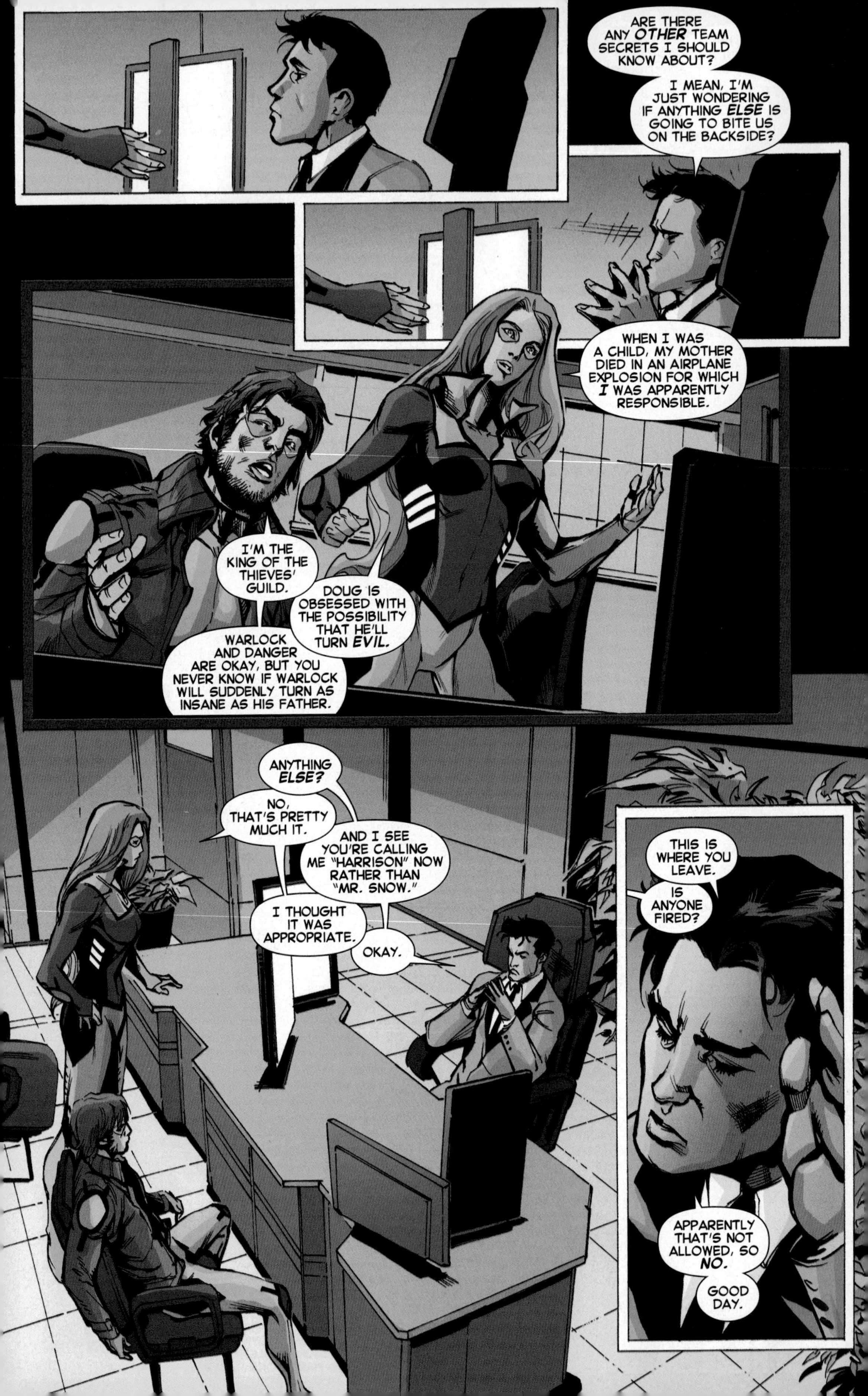
ARE THERE ANY OTHER TEAM SECRETS I SHOULD KNOW ABOUT?
I MEAN, I'M JUST WONDERING IF ANYTHING ELSE IS GOING TO BITE US ON THE BACKSIDE?
WHEN I WAS A CHILD, MY MOTHER DIED IN AN AIRPLANE EXPLOSION FOR WHICH I WAS APPARENTLY RESPONSIBLE.
I'M THE KING OF THE THIEVES' GUILD.
DOUG IS OBSESSED WITH THE POSSIBILITY THAT HE'LL TURN EVIL.
WARLOCK AND DANGER ARE OKAY, BUT YOU NEVER KNOW IF WARLOCK WILL SUDDENLY TURN AS INSANE AS HIS FATHER.
ANYTHING ELSE?
NO, THAT'S PRETTY MUCH IT.
AND I SEE YOU'RE CALLING ME "HARRISON" NOW RATHER THAN "MR. SNOW."
I THOUGHT IT WAS APPROPRIATE.
OKAY.
THIS IS WHERE YOU LEAVE.
IS ANYONE FIRED?
APPARENTLY THAT'S NOT ALLOWED, SO NO.
GOOD DAY.

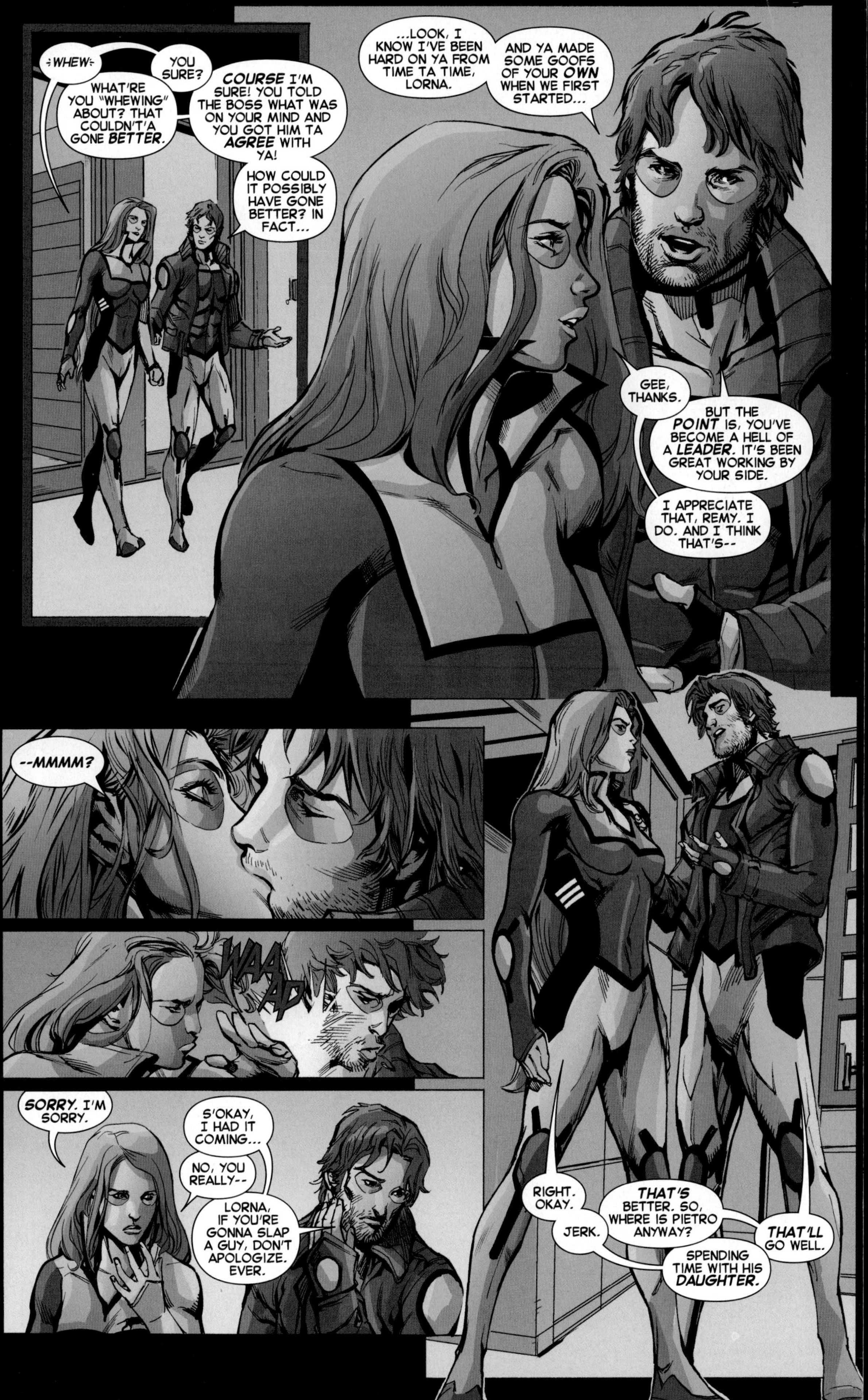

WHEW
YOU SURE?
WHAT'RE YOU "WHEWING" ABOUT? THAT COULDN'T'A GONE BETTER.
COURSE I'M SURE! YOU TOLD THE BOSS WHAT WAS ON YOUR MIND AND YOU GOT HIM TA AGREE WITH YA!
HOW COULD IT POSSIBLY HAVE GONE BETTER? IN FACT...
...LOOK, I KNOW I'VE BEEN HARD ON YA FROM TIME TA TIME, LORNA.
AND YA MADE SOME GOOFS OF YOUR OWN WHEN WE FIRST STARTED...
GEE, THANKS.
BUT THE POINT IS, YOU'VE BECOME A HELL OF A LEADER. IT'S BEEN GREAT WORKING BY YOUR SIDE.
I APPRECIATE THAT, REMY. I DO. AND I THINK THAT'S--
--MMMM?
WAAAP
SORRY. I'M SORRY.
S'OKAY, I HAD IT COMING...
NO, YOU REALLY--
LORNA, IF YOU'RE GONNA SLAP A GUY, DON'T APOLOGIZE. EVER.
RIGHT. OKAY.
JERK.
THAT'S BETTER. SO, WHERE IS PIETRO ANYWAY?
SPENDING TIME WITH HIS DAUGHTER.
THAT'LL GO WELL.

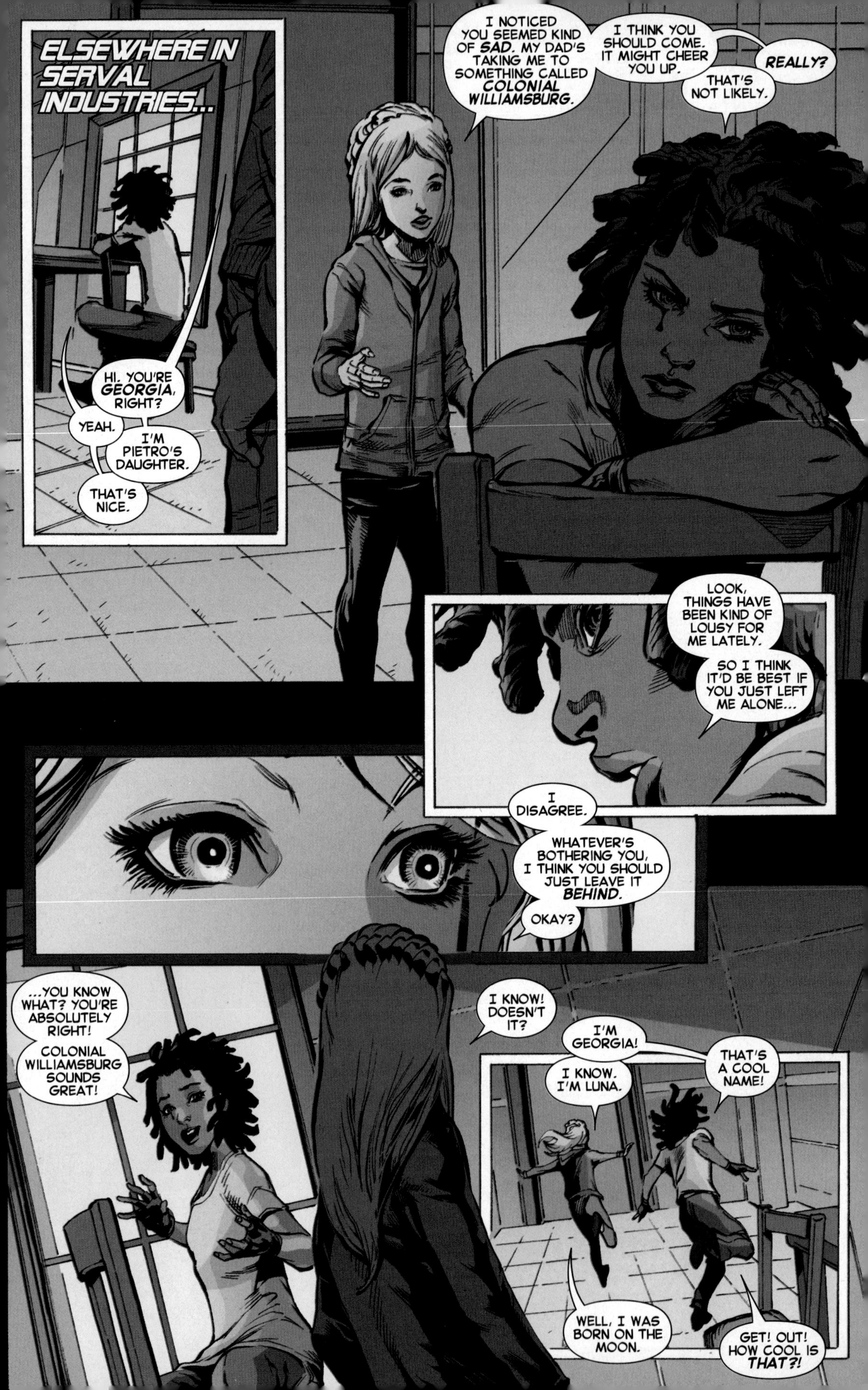
ELSEWHERE IN SERVAL INDUSTRIES...
HI. YOU'RE GEORGIA, RIGHT?
YEAH.
I'M PIETRO'S DAUGHTER.
THAT'S NICE.
I NOTICED YOU SEEMED KIND OF SAD. MY DAD'S TAKING ME TO SOMETHING CALLED COLONIAL WILLIAMSBURG.
I THINK YOU SHOULD COME. IT MIGHT CHEER YOU UP.
REALLY?
THAT'S NOT LIKELY.
LOOK, THINGS HAVE BEEN KIND OF LOUSY FOR ME LATELY.
SO I THINK IT'D BE BEST IF YOU JUST LEFT ME ALONE...
I DISAGREE.
WHATEVER'S BOTHERING YOU, I THINK YOU SHOULD JUST LEAVE IT BEHIND.
OKAY?
...YOU KNOW WHAT? YOU'RE ABSOLUTELY RIGHT!
COLONIAL WILLIAMSBURG SOUNDS GREAT!
I KNOW! DOESN'T IT?
I'M GEORGIA!
I KNOW. I'M LUNA.
THAT'S A COOL NAME!
WELL, I WAS BORN ON THE MOON.
GET! OUT! HOW COOL IS THAT?!

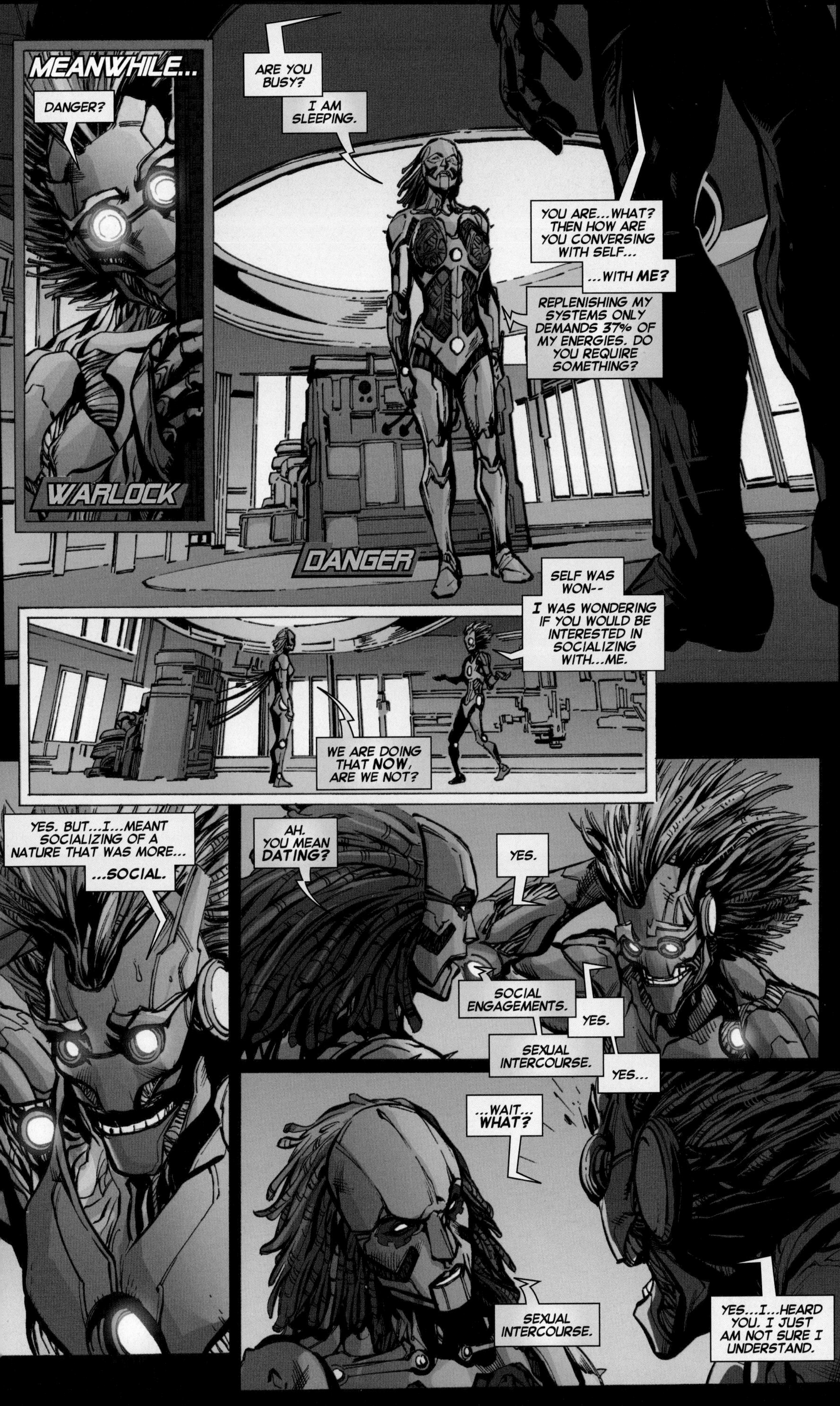
MEANWHILE...
DANGER?
WARLOCK
ARE YOU BUSY?
I AM SLEEPING.
YOU ARE...WHAT? THEN HOW ARE YOU CONVERSING WITH SELF...
...WITH ME?
REPLENISHING MY SYSTEMS ONLY DEMANDS 37% OF MY ENERGIES. DO YOU REQUIRE SOMETHING?
DANGER
SELF WAS WON--
I WAS WONDERING IF YOU WOULD BE INTERESTED IN SOCIALIZING WITH...ME.
WE ARE DOING THAT NOW, ARE WE NOT?
YES. BUT...I...MEANT SOCIALIZING OF A NATURE THAT WAS MORE...
...SOCIAL.
AH. YOU MEAN DATING?
YES.
SOCIAL ENGAGEMENTS.
YES.
SEXUAL INTERCOURSE.
YES...
...WAIT... WHAT?
SEXUAL INTERCOURSE.
YES...I...HEARD YOU. I JUST AM NOT SURE I UNDERSTAND.

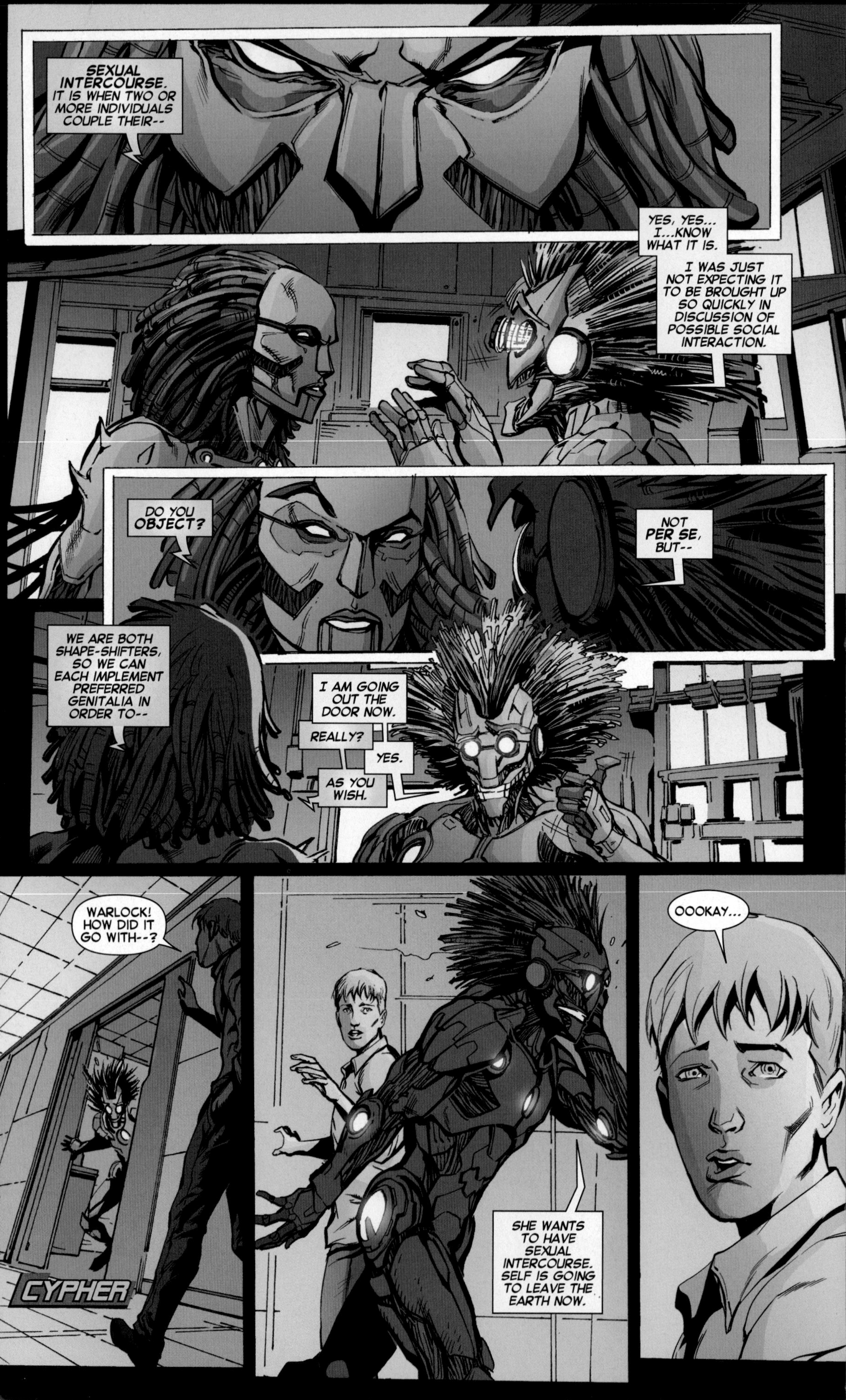
SEXUAL INTERCOURSE. IT IS WHEN TWO OR MORE INDIVIDUALS COUPLE THEIR--
YES, YES... I...KNOW WHAT IT IS.
I WAS JUST NOT EXPECTING IT TO BE BROUGHT UP SO QUICKLY IN DISCUSSION OF POSSIBLE SOCIAL INTERACTION.
DO YOU OBJECT?
NOT PER SE, BUT--
WE ARE BOTH SHAPE-SHIFTERS, SO WE CAN EACH IMPLEMENT PREFERRED GENITALIA IN ORDER TO--
I AM GOING OUT THE DOOR NOW.
REALLY?
YES.
AS YOU WISH.
WARLOCK! HOW DID IT GO WITH--?
CYPHER
SHE WANTS TO HAVE SEXUAL INTERCOURSE. SELF IS GOING TO LEAVE THE EARTH NOW.
OOOKAY...

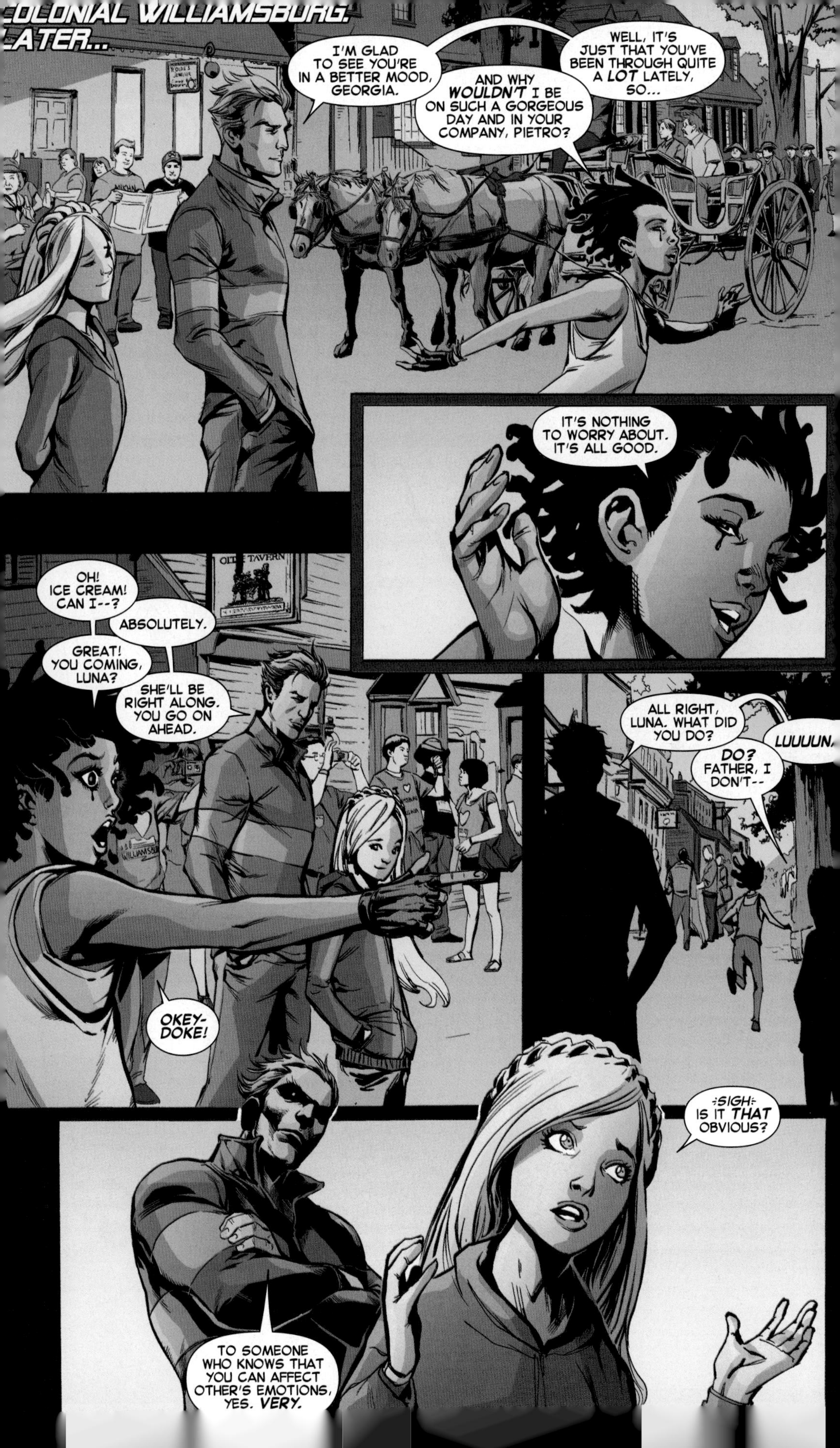
COLONIAL WILLIAMSBURG. LATER...
I'M GLAD TO SEE YOU'RE IN A BETTER MOOD, GEORGIA.
AND WHY WOULDN'T I BE ON SUCH A GORGEOUS DAY AND IN YOUR COMPANY, PIETRO?
WELL, IT'S JUST THAT YOU'VE BEEN THROUGH QUITE A LOT LATELY, SO...
IT'S NOTHING TO WORRY ABOUT. IT'S ALL GOOD.
OLDE TAVERN
OH! ICE CREAM! CAN I--?
ABSOLUTELY.
GREAT! YOU COMING, LUNA?
SHE'LL BE RIGHT ALONG. YOU GO ON AHEAD.
OKEY-DOKE!
ALL RIGHT, LUNA. WHAT DID YOU DO?
DO? FATHER, I DON'T--
LUUUUN
*SIGH* IS IT THAT OBVIOUS?
TO SOMEONE WHO KNOWS THAT YOU CAN AFFECT OTHER'S EMOTIONS, YES. VERY.

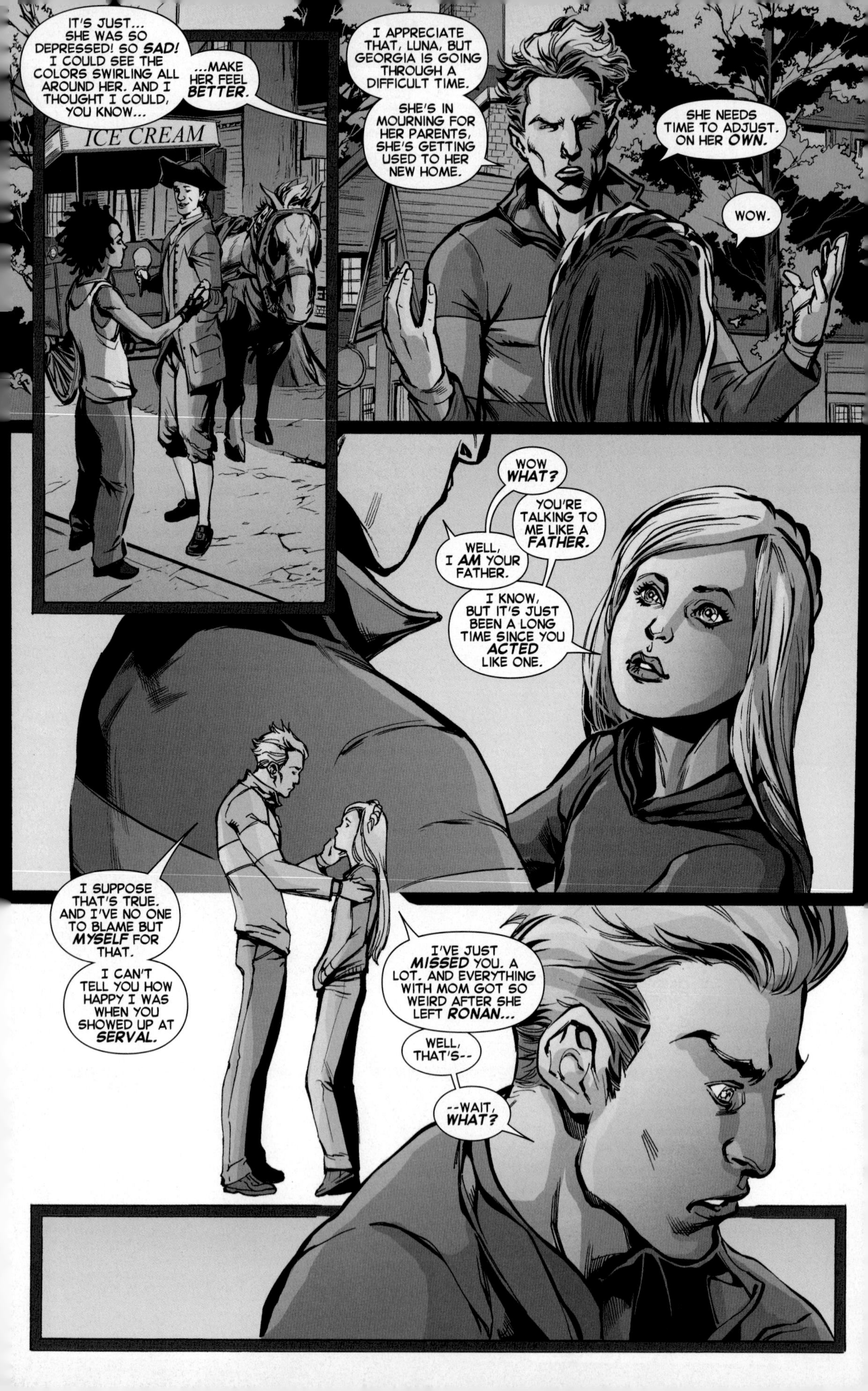

IT'S JUST... SHE WAS SO DEPRESSED! SO SAD! I COULD SEE THE COLORS SWIRLING ALL AROUND HER. AND I THOUGHT I COULD, YOU KNOW...
...MAKE HER FEEL BETTER.
ICE CREAM
I APPRECIATE THAT, LUNA, BUT GEORGIA IS GOING THROUGH A DIFFICULT TIME.
SHE'S IN MOURNING FOR HER PARENTS, SHE'S GETTING USED TO HER NEW HOME.
SHE NEEDS TIME TO ADJUST. ON HER OWN.
WOW.
WOW WHAT?
YOU'RE TALKING TO ME LIKE A FATHER.
WELL, I AM YOUR FATHER.
I KNOW, BUT IT'S JUST BEEN A LONG TIME SINCE YOU ACTED LIKE ONE.
I SUPPOSE THAT'S TRUE. AND I'VE NO ONE TO BLAME BUT MYSELF FOR THAT.
I CAN'T TELL YOU HOW HAPPY I WAS WHEN YOU SHOWED UP AT SERVAL.
I'VE JUST MISSED YOU. A LOT. AND EVERYTHING WITH MOM GOT SO WEIRD AFTER SHE LEFT RONAN...
WELL, THAT'S--
--WAIT, WHAT?

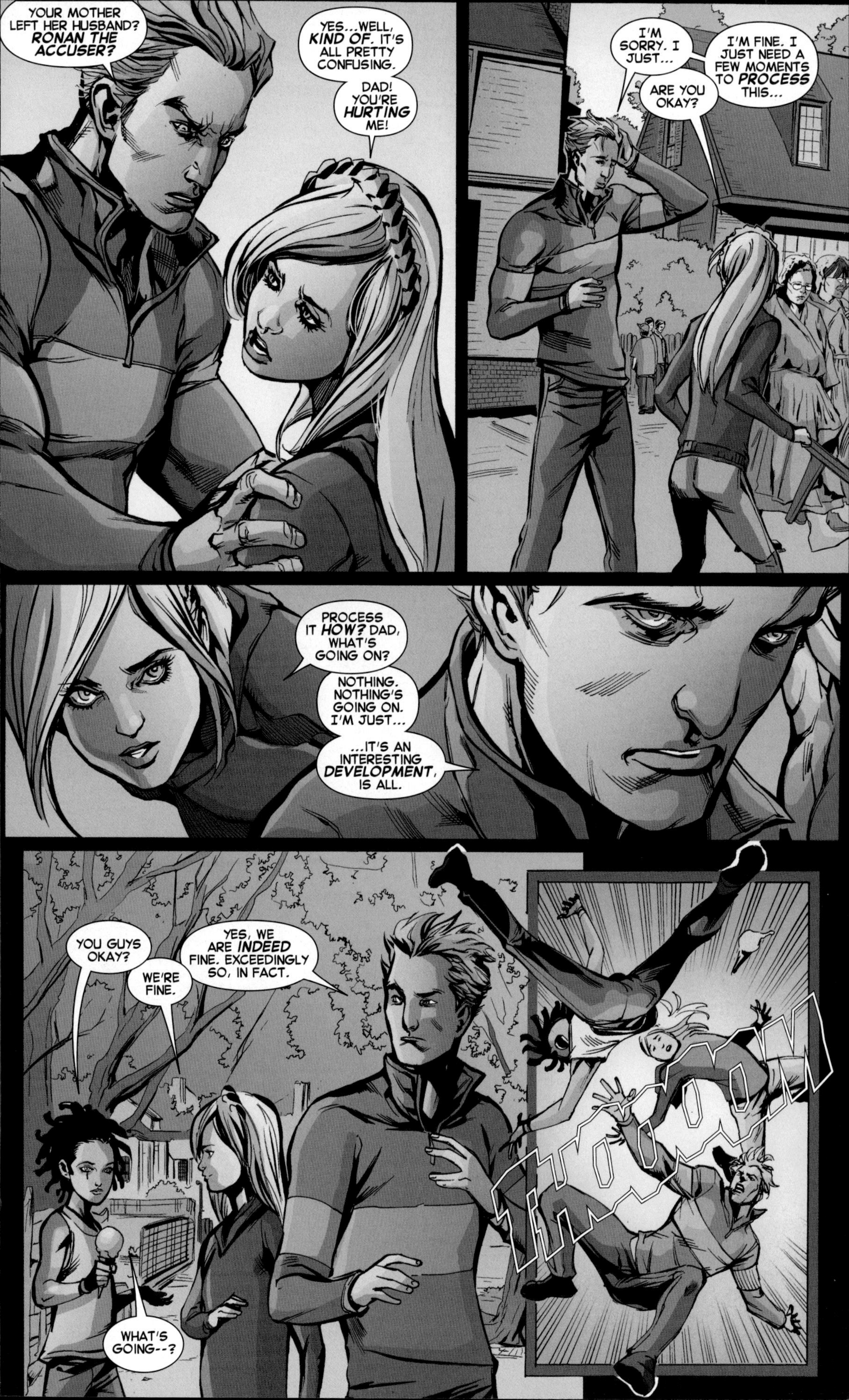

YOUR MOTHER LEFT HER HUSBAND? RONAN THE ACCUSER?
YES...WELL, KIND OF. IT'S ALL PRETTY CONFUSING.
DAD! YOU'RE HURTING ME!
I'M SORRY. I JUST...
ARE YOU OKAY?
I'M FINE. I JUST NEED A FEW MOMENTS TO PROCESS THIS...
PROCESS IT HOW? DAD, WHAT'S GOING ON?
NOTHING. NOTHING'S GOING ON. I'M JUST...
...IT'S AN INTERESTING DEVELOPMENT, IS ALL.
YOU GUYS OKAY?
WE'RE FINE.
YES, WE ARE INDEED FINE. EXCEEDINGLY SO, IN FACT.
WHAT'S GOING--?
THOOOOM

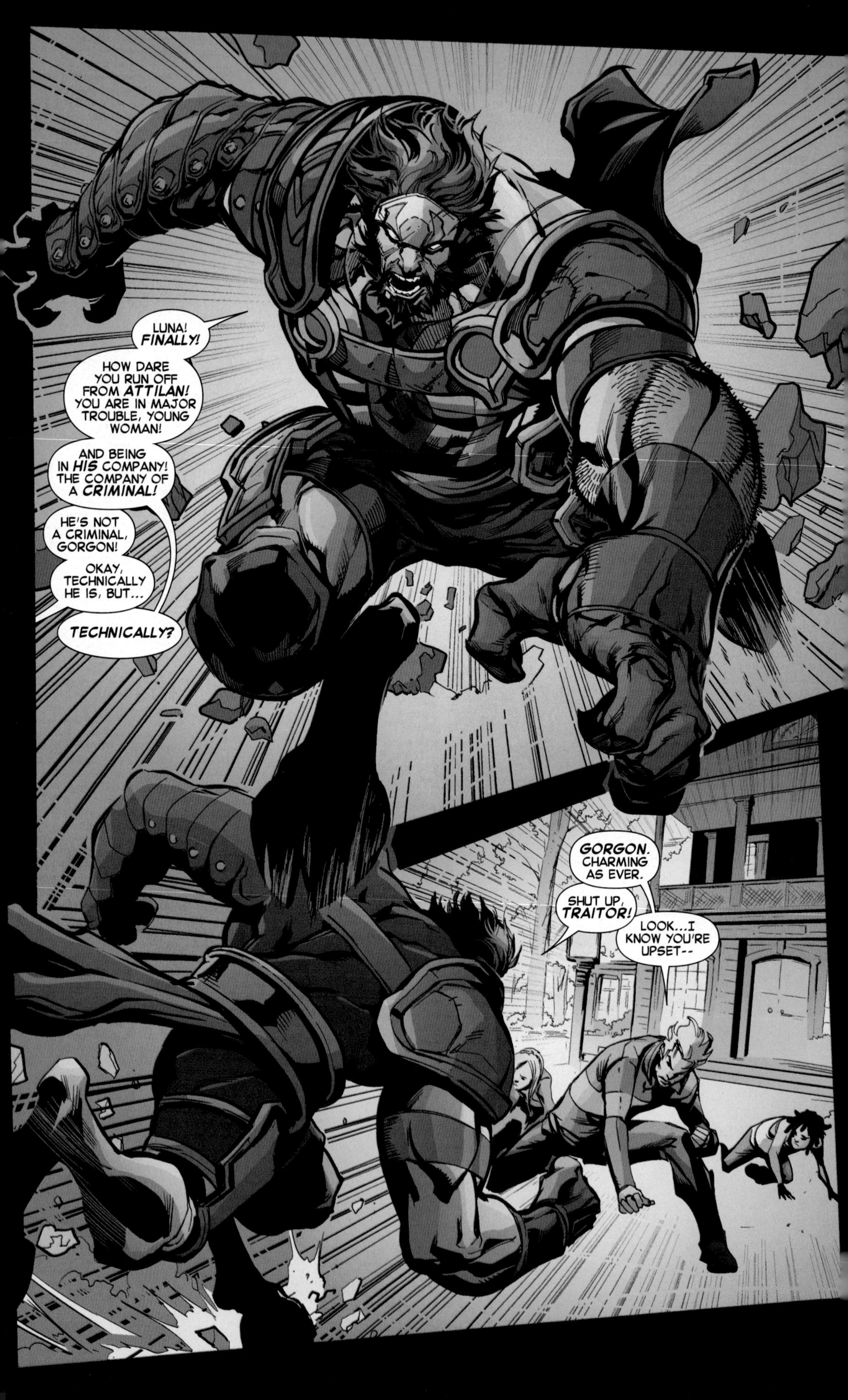

LUNA! FINALLY!
HOW DARE YOU RUN OFF FROM ATTILAN! YOU ARE IN MAJOR TROUBLE, YOUNG WOMAN!
AND BEING IN HIS COMPANY! THE COMPANY OF A CRIMINAL!
HE'S NOT A CRIMINAL, GORGON!
OKAY, TECHNICALLY HE IS, BUT...
TECHNICALLY?
GORGON. CHARMING AS EVER.
SHUT UP, TRAITOR!
LOOK...I KNOW YOU'RE UPSET--

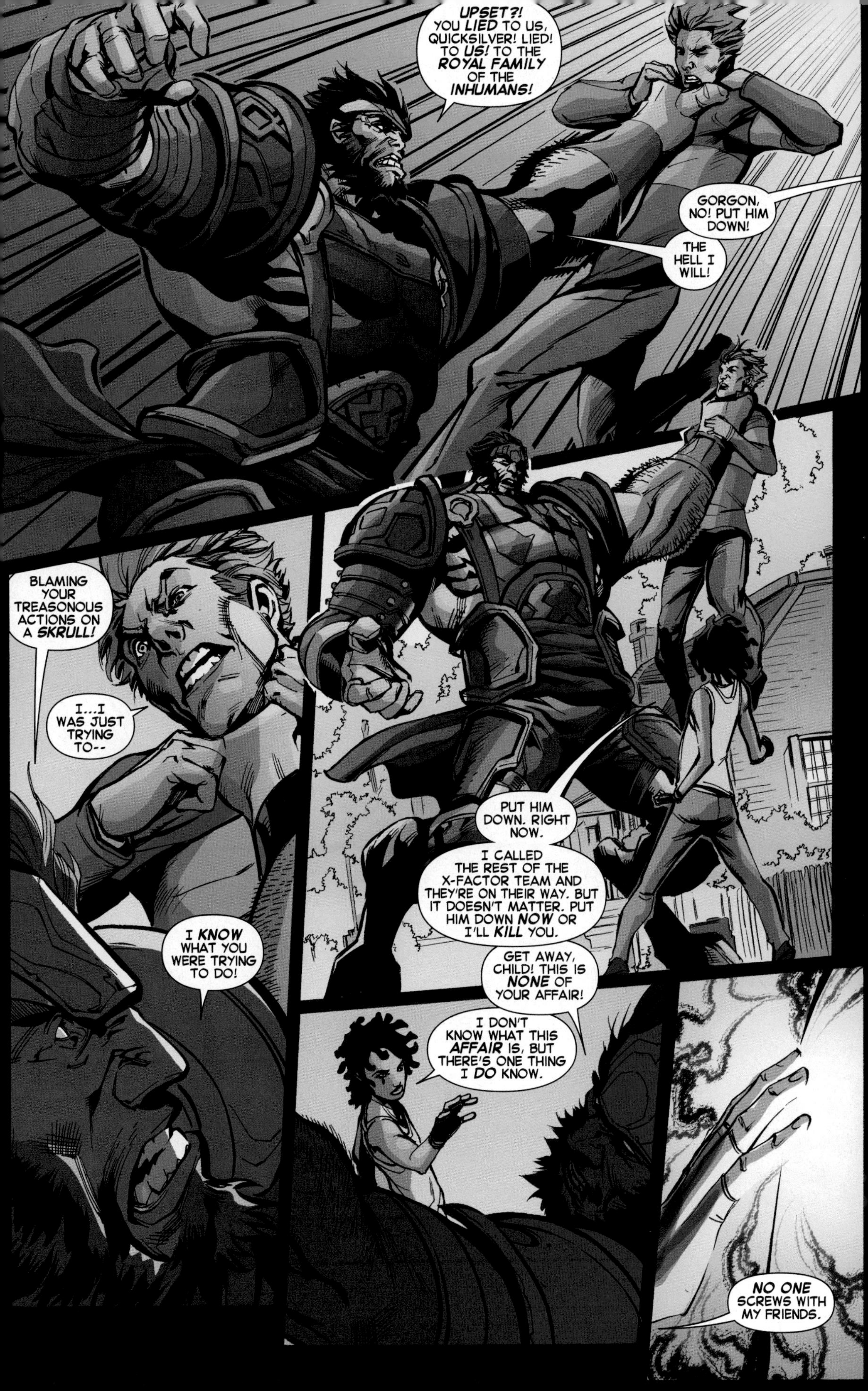
UPSET?! YOU LIED TO US, QUICKSILVER! LIED! TO US! TO THE ROYAL FAMILY OF THE INHUMANS!
GORGON, NO! PUT HIM DOWN!
THE HELL I WILL!
BLAMING YOUR TREASONOUS ACTIONS ON A SKRULL!
I...I WAS JUST TRYING TO--
I KNOW WHAT YOU WERE TRYING TO DO!
PUT HIM DOWN. RIGHT NOW.
I CALLED THE REST OF THE X-FACTOR TEAM AND THEY'RE ON THEIR WAY. BUT IT DOESN'T MATTER. PUT HIM DOWN NOW OR I'LL KILL YOU.
GET AWAY, CHILD! THIS IS NONE OF YOUR AFFAIR!
I DON'T KNOW WHAT THIS AFFAIR IS, BUT THERE'S ONE THING I DO KNOW.
NO ONE SCREWS WITH MY FRIENDS.

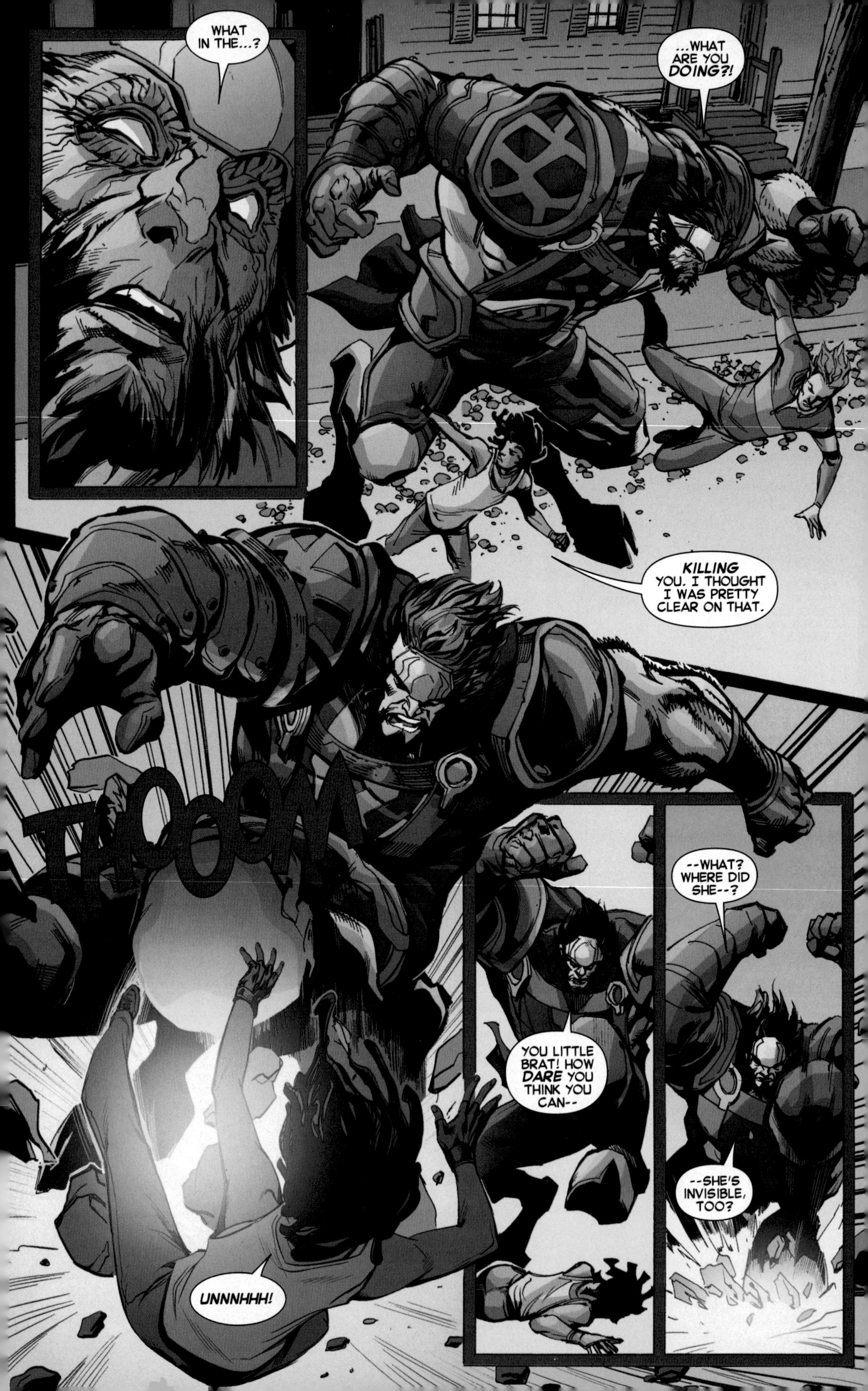
WHAT IN THE...?
...WHAT ARE YOU *DOING?!*
*KILLING* YOU. I THOUGHT I WAS PRETTY CLEAR ON THAT.
THOOOM
*UNNNHHH!*
YOU LITTLE BRAT! HOW *DARE* YOU THINK YOU CAN--
--WHAT? WHERE DID SHE--?
--SHE'S INVISIBLE, TOO?

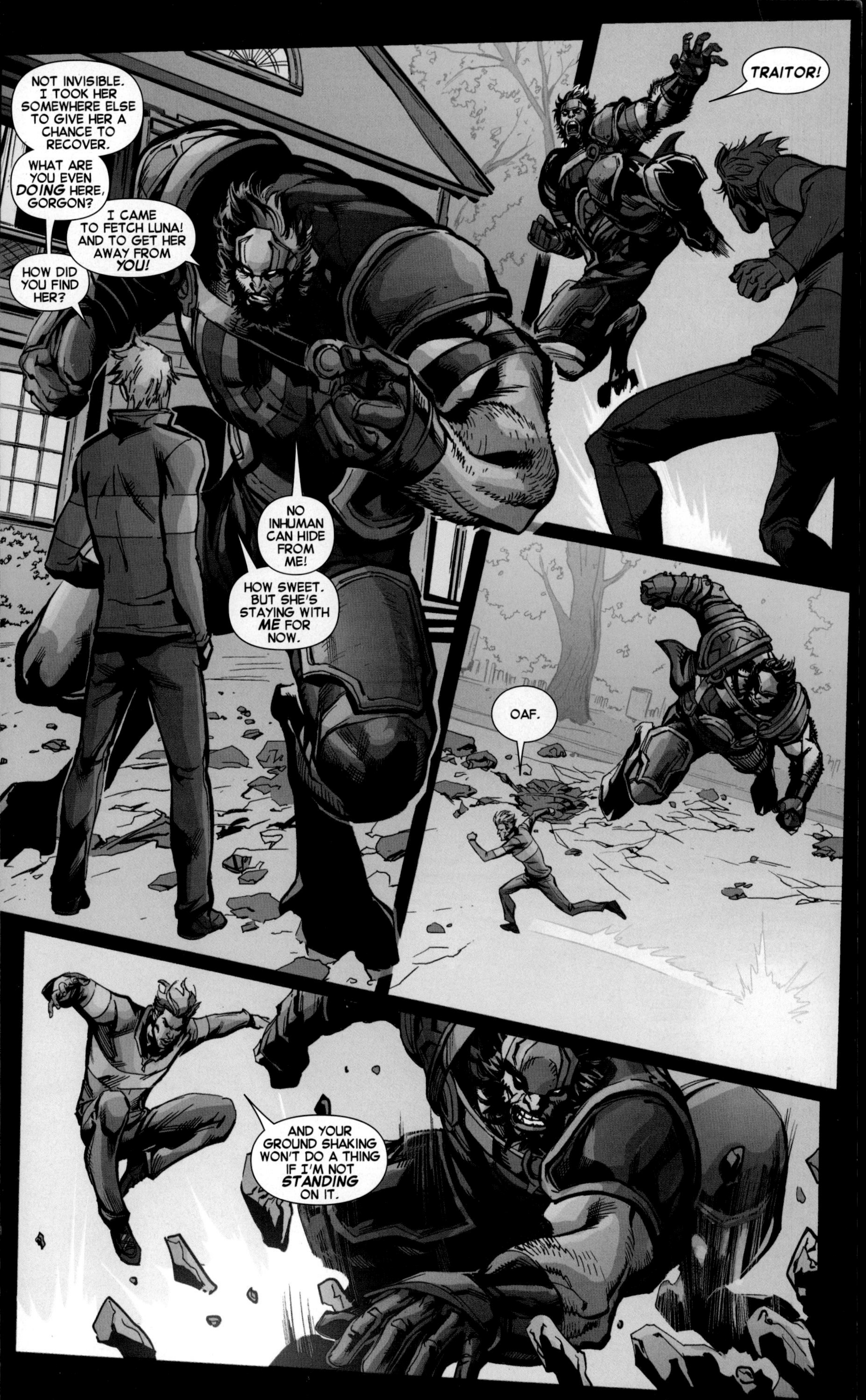
NOT INVISIBLE. I TOOK HER SOMEWHERE ELSE TO GIVE HER A CHANCE TO RECOVER.
WHAT ARE YOU EVEN DOING HERE, GORGON?
I CAME TO FETCH LUNA! AND TO GET HER AWAY FROM YOU!
HOW DID YOU FIND HER?
NO INHUMAN CAN HIDE FROM ME!
HOW SWEET. BUT SHE'S STAYING WITH ME FOR NOW.
TRAITOR!
OAF.
AND YOUR GROUND SHAKING WON'T DO A THING IF I'M NOT STANDING ON IT.

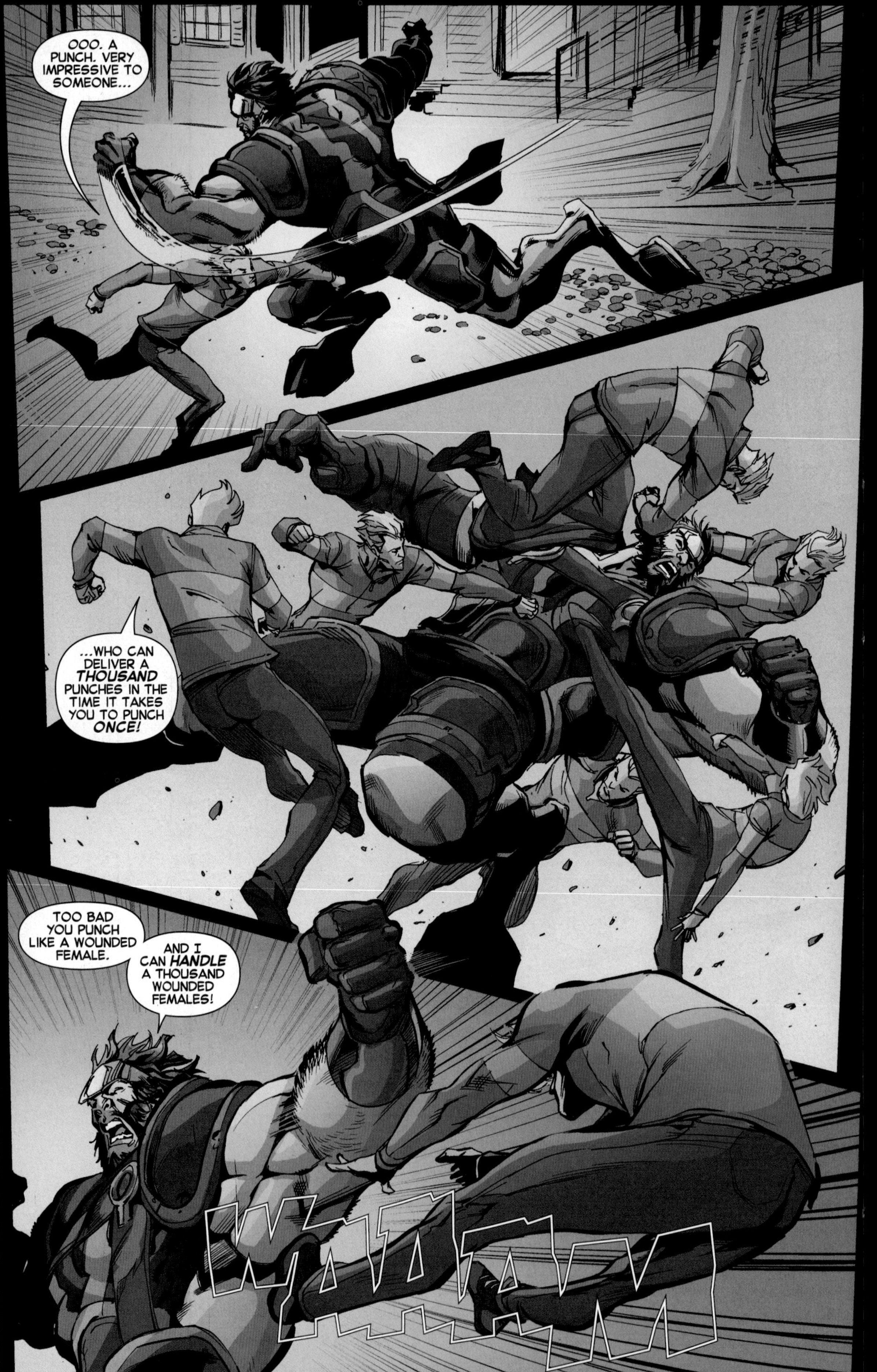
OOO. A PUNCH. VERY IMPRESSIVE TO SOMEONE...
...WHO CAN DELIVER A THOUSAND PUNCHES IN THE TIME IT TAKES YOU TO PUNCH ONCE!
TOO BAD YOU PUNCH LIKE A WOUNDED FEMALE.
AND I CAN HANDLE A THOUSAND WOUNDED FEMALES!
WHAM

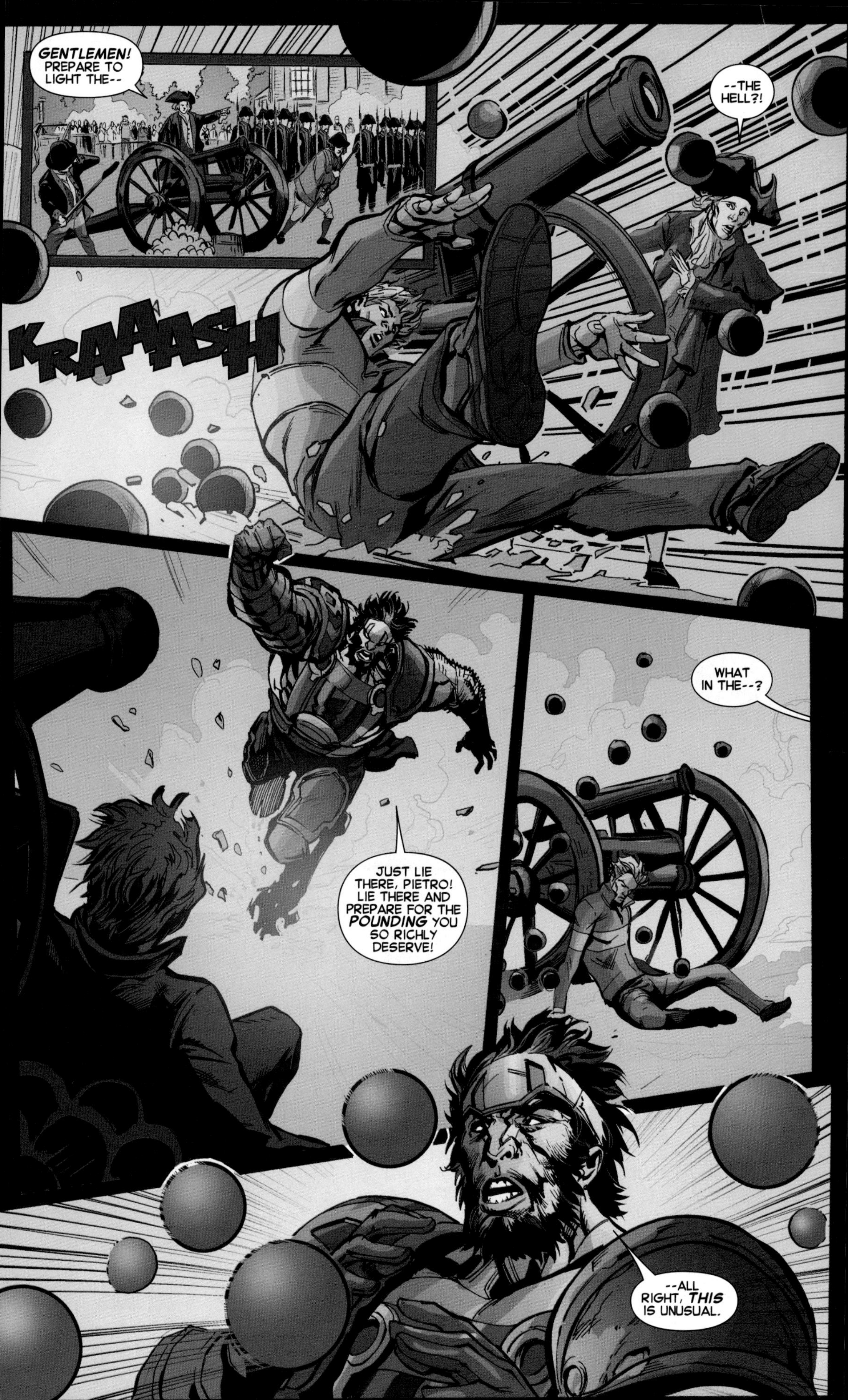
GENTLEMEN! PREPARE TO LIGHT THE--
--THE HELL?!
KRAAAASH
JUST LIE THERE, PIETRO! LIE THERE AND PREPARE FOR THE POUNDING YOU SO RICHLY DESERVE!
WHAT IN THE--?
--ALL RIGHT, THIS IS UNUSUAL.

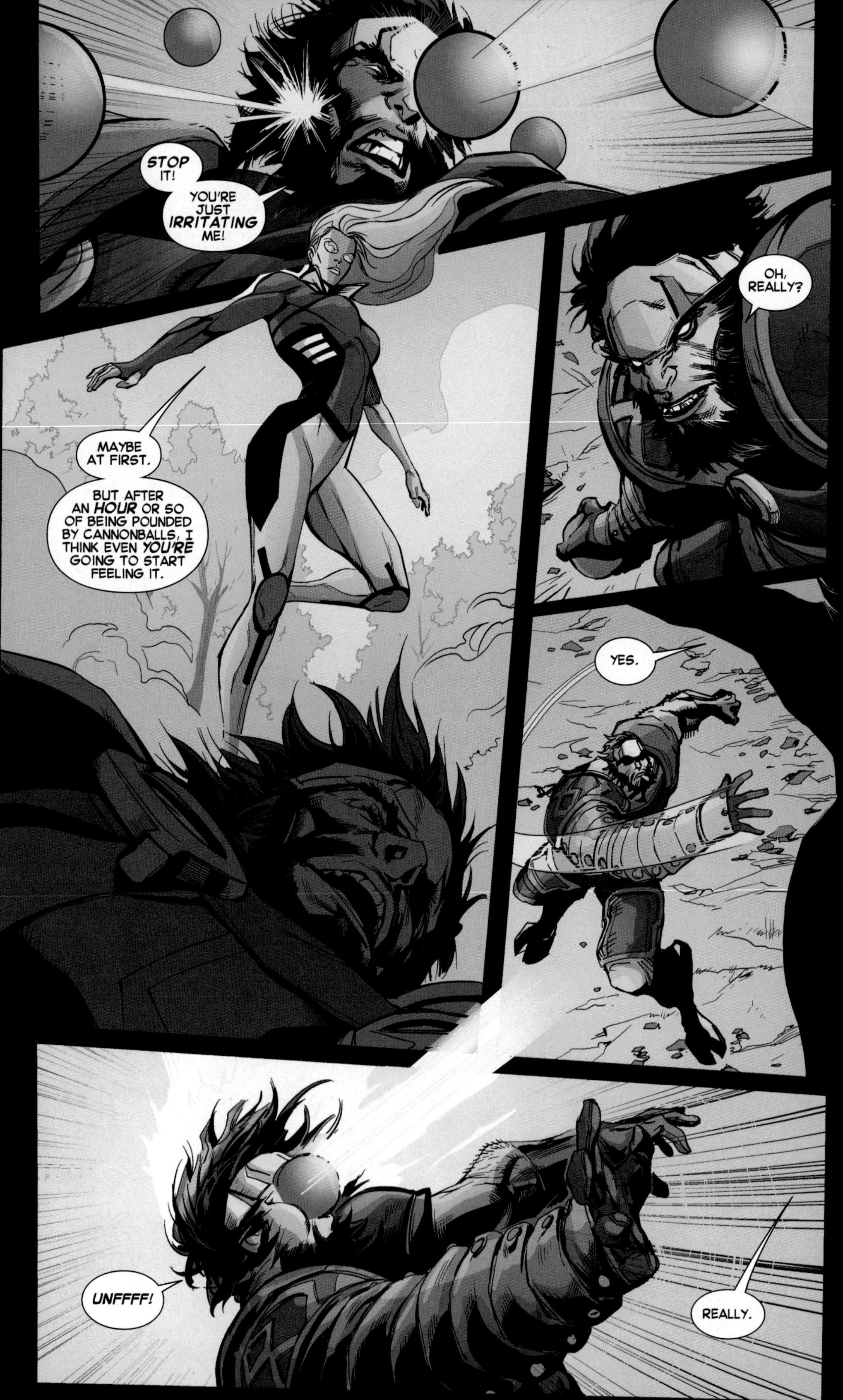

STOP IT!
YOU'RE JUST IRRITATING ME!
OH, REALLY?
MAYBE AT FIRST.
BUT AFTER AN HOUR OR SO OF BEING POUNDED BY CANNONBALLS, I THINK EVEN YOU'RE GOING TO START FEELING IT.
YES.
UNFFFF!
REALLY.

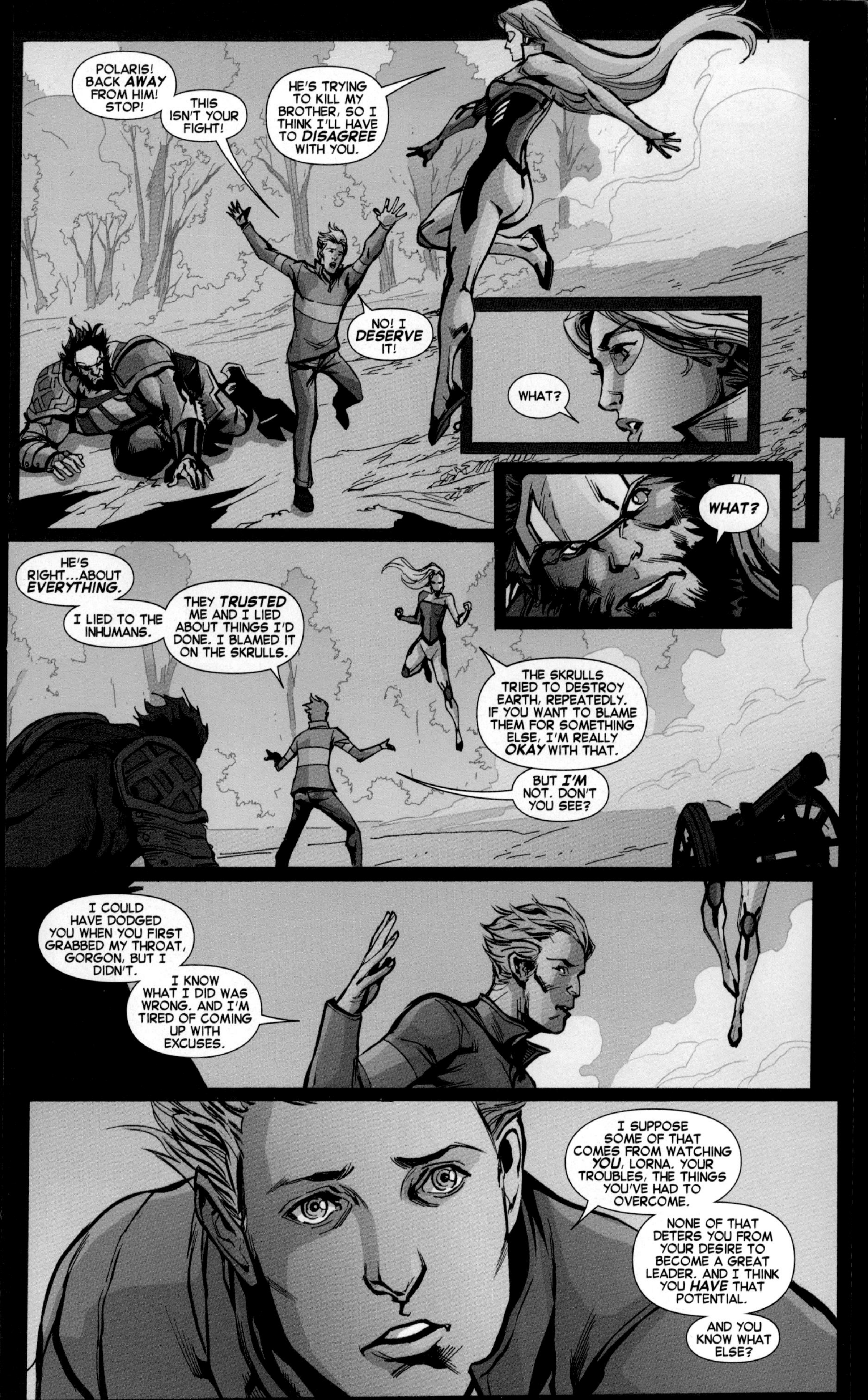
POLARIS! BACK AWAY FROM HIM! STOP!
THIS ISN'T YOUR FIGHT!
HE'S TRYING TO KILL MY BROTHER, SO I THINK I'LL HAVE TO DISAGREE WITH YOU.
NO! I DESERVE IT!
WHAT?
WHAT?
HE'S RIGHT...ABOUT EVERYTHING.
I LIED TO THE INHUMANS.
THEY TRUSTED ME AND I LIED ABOUT THINGS I'D DONE. I BLAMED IT ON THE SKRULLS.
THE SKRULLS TRIED TO DESTROY EARTH, REPEATEDLY. IF YOU WANT TO BLAME THEM FOR SOMETHING ELSE, I'M REALLY OKAY WITH THAT.
BUT I'M NOT. DON'T YOU SEE?
I COULD HAVE DODGED YOU WHEN YOU FIRST GRABBED MY THROAT, GORGON, BUT I DIDN'T.
I KNOW WHAT I DID WAS WRONG. AND I'M TIRED OF COMING UP WITH EXCUSES.
I SUPPOSE SOME OF THAT COMES FROM WATCHING YOU, LORNA. YOUR TROUBLES, THE THINGS YOU'VE HAD TO OVERCOME.
NONE OF THAT DETERS YOU FROM YOUR DESIRE TO BECOME A GREAT LEADER. AND I THINK YOU HAVE THAT POTENTIAL.
AND YOU KNOW WHAT ELSE?

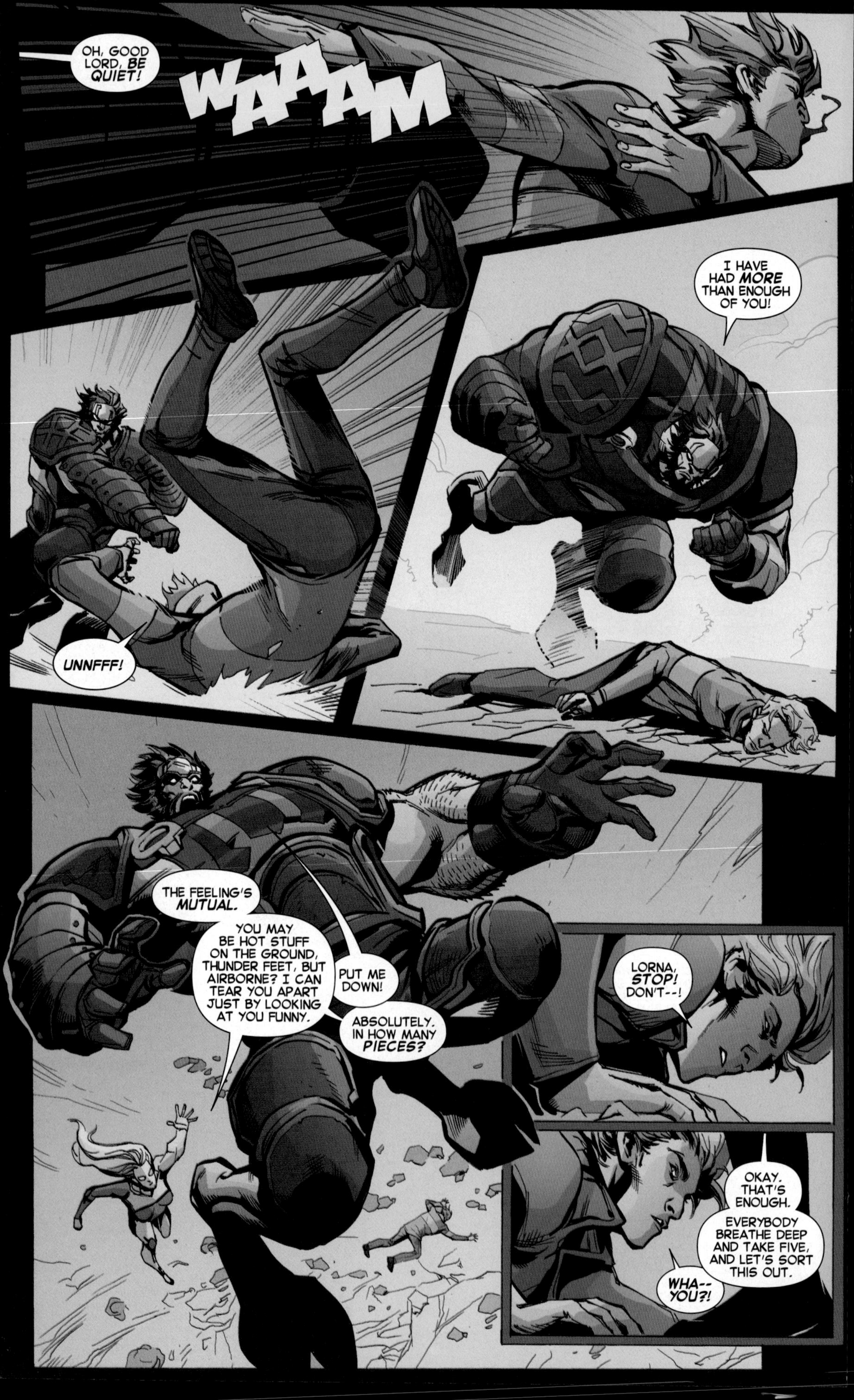
OH, GOOD LORD, BE QUIET!
WAAAAM
I HAVE HAD MORE THAN ENOUGH OF YOU!
UNNFFF!
THE FEELING'S MUTUAL.
YOU MAY BE HOT STUFF ON THE GROUND, THUNDER FEET, BUT AIRBORNE? I CAN TEAR YOU APART JUST BY LOOKING AT YOU FUNNY.
PUT ME DOWN!
ABSOLUTELY. IN HOW MANY PIECES?
LORNA, STOP! DON'T--!
OKAY. THAT'S ENOUGH.
EVERYBODY BREATHE DEEP AND TAKE FIVE, AND LET'S SORT THIS OUT.
WHA-- YOU?!

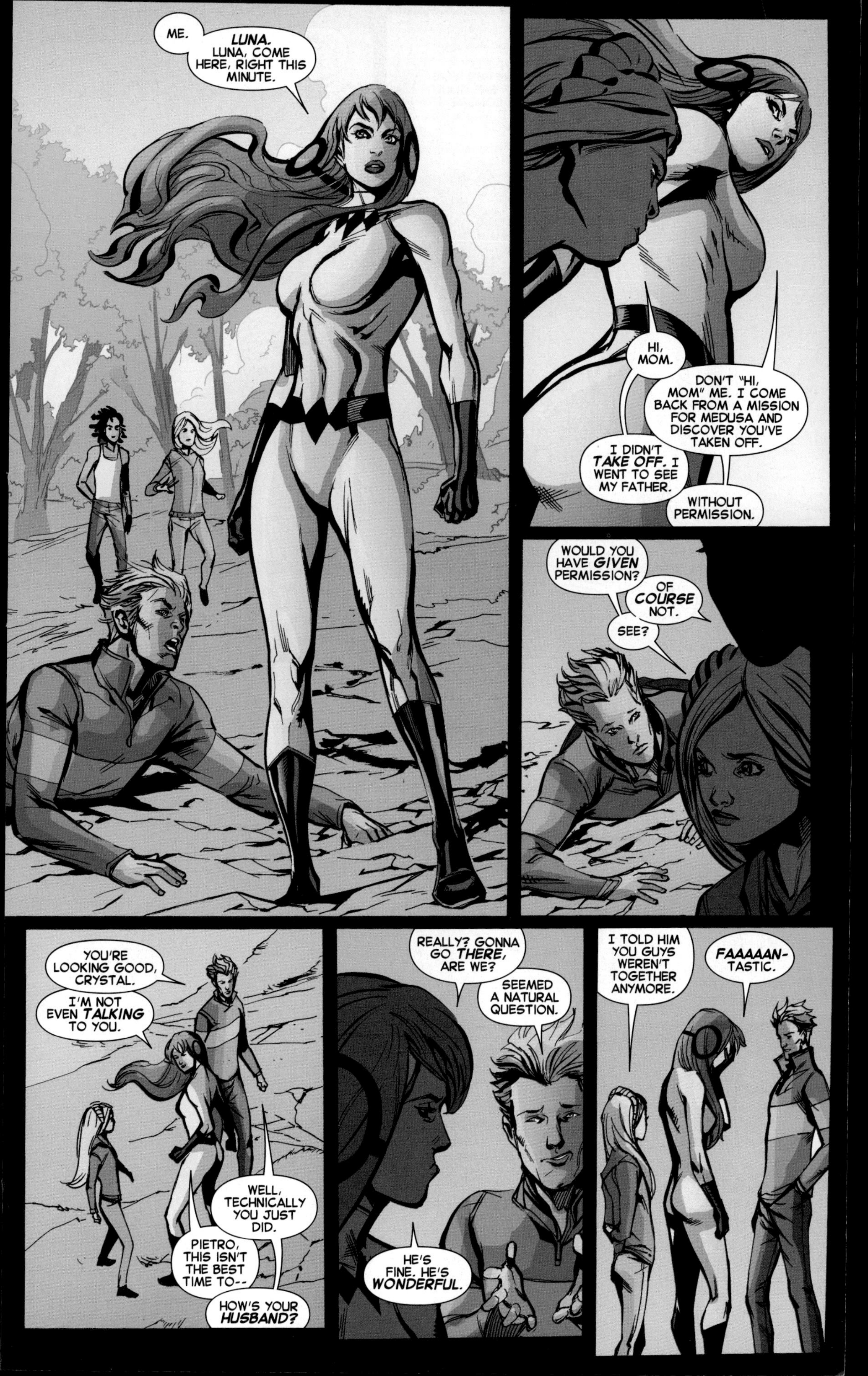
ME.
LUNA. LUNA, COME HERE, RIGHT THIS MINUTE.
HI, MOM.
DON'T "HI, MOM" ME. I COME BACK FROM A MISSION FOR MEDUSA AND DISCOVER YOU'VE TAKEN OFF.
I DIDN'T TAKE OFF. I WENT TO SEE MY FATHER.
WITHOUT PERMISSION.
WOULD YOU HAVE GIVEN PERMISSION?
OF COURSE NOT.
SEE?
YOU'RE LOOKING GOOD, CRYSTAL.
I'M NOT EVEN TALKING TO YOU.
WELL, TECHNICALLY YOU JUST DID.
PIETRO, THIS ISN'T THE BEST TIME TO--
HOW'S YOUR HUSBAND?
REALLY? GONNA GO THERE, ARE WE?
SEEMED A NATURAL QUESTION.
HE'S FINE. HE'S WONDERFUL.
I TOLD HIM YOU GUYS WEREN'T TOGETHER ANYMORE.
FAAAAAN-TASTIC.

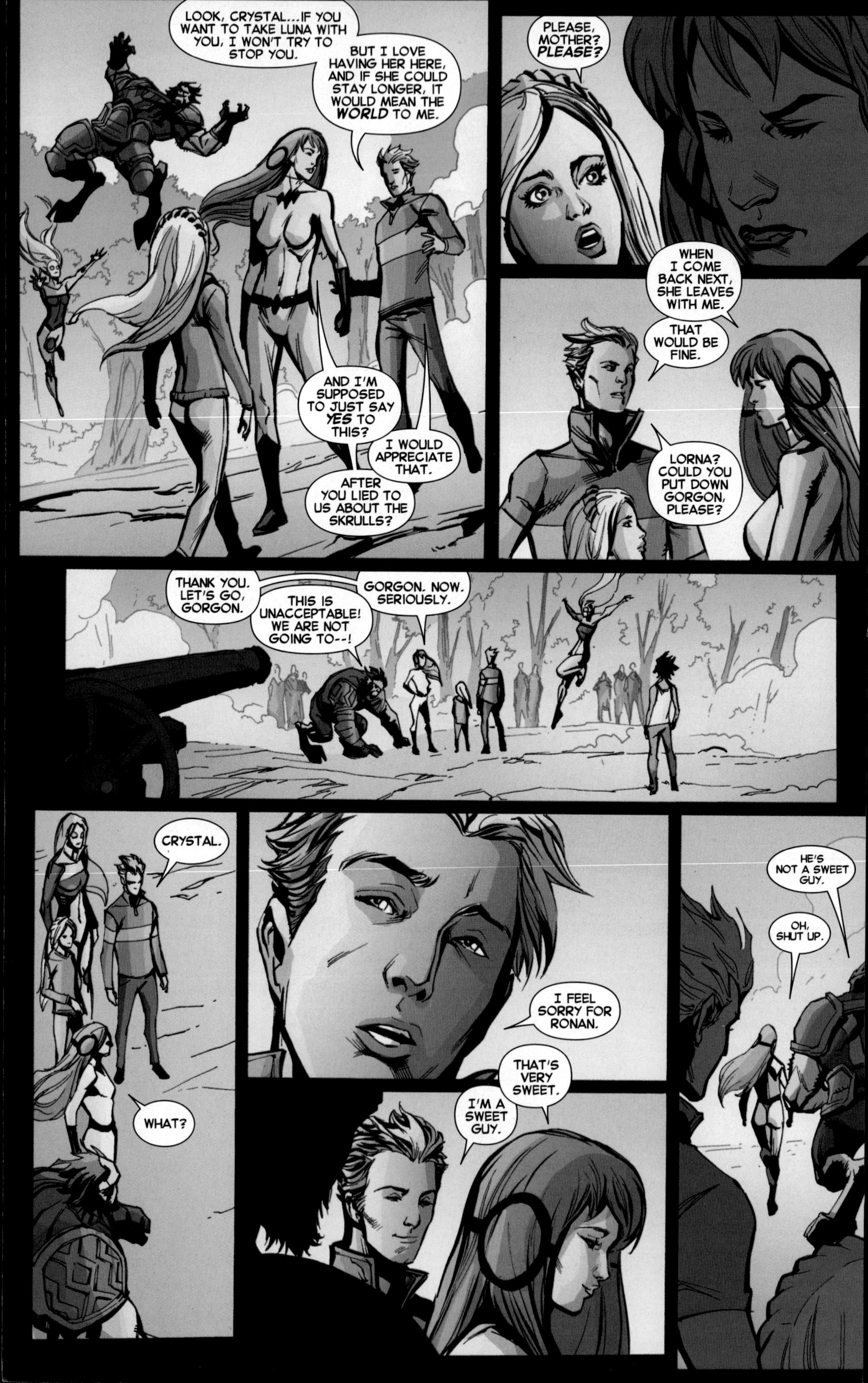
LOOK, CRYSTAL...IF YOU WANT TO TAKE LUNA WITH YOU, I WON'T TRY TO STOP YOU.
BUT I LOVE HAVING HER HERE, AND IF SHE COULD STAY LONGER, IT WOULD MEAN THE WORLD TO ME.
AND I'M SUPPOSED TO JUST SAY YES TO THIS?
I WOULD APPRECIATE THAT.
AFTER YOU LIED TO US ABOUT THE SKRULLS?
PLEASE, MOTHER? PLEASE?
WHEN I COME BACK NEXT, SHE LEAVES WITH ME.
THAT WOULD BE FINE.
LORNA? COULD YOU PUT DOWN GORGON, PLEASE?
THANK YOU. LET'S GO, GORGON.
THIS IS UNACCEPTABLE! WE ARE NOT GOING TO--!
GORGON. NOW. SERIOUSLY.
CRYSTAL.
WHAT?
I FEEL SORRY FOR RONAN.
THAT'S VERY SWEET.
I'M A SWEET GUY.
HE'S NOT A SWEET GUY.
OH, SHUT UP.

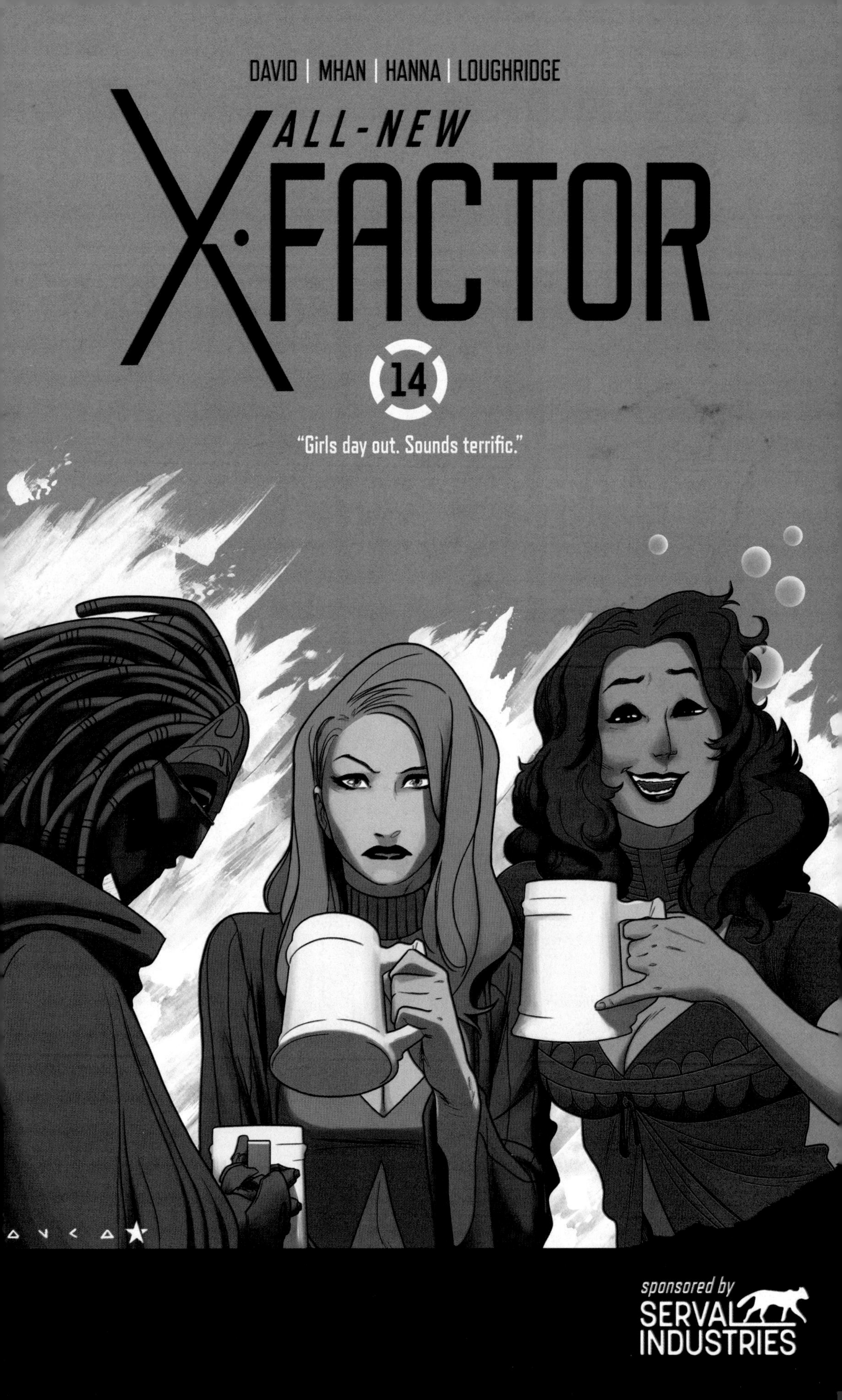
DAVID | MHAN | HANNA | LOUGHRIDGE
ALL-NEW
X-FACTOR
14
"Girls day out. Sounds terrific."
sponsored by
SERVAL
INDUSTRIES

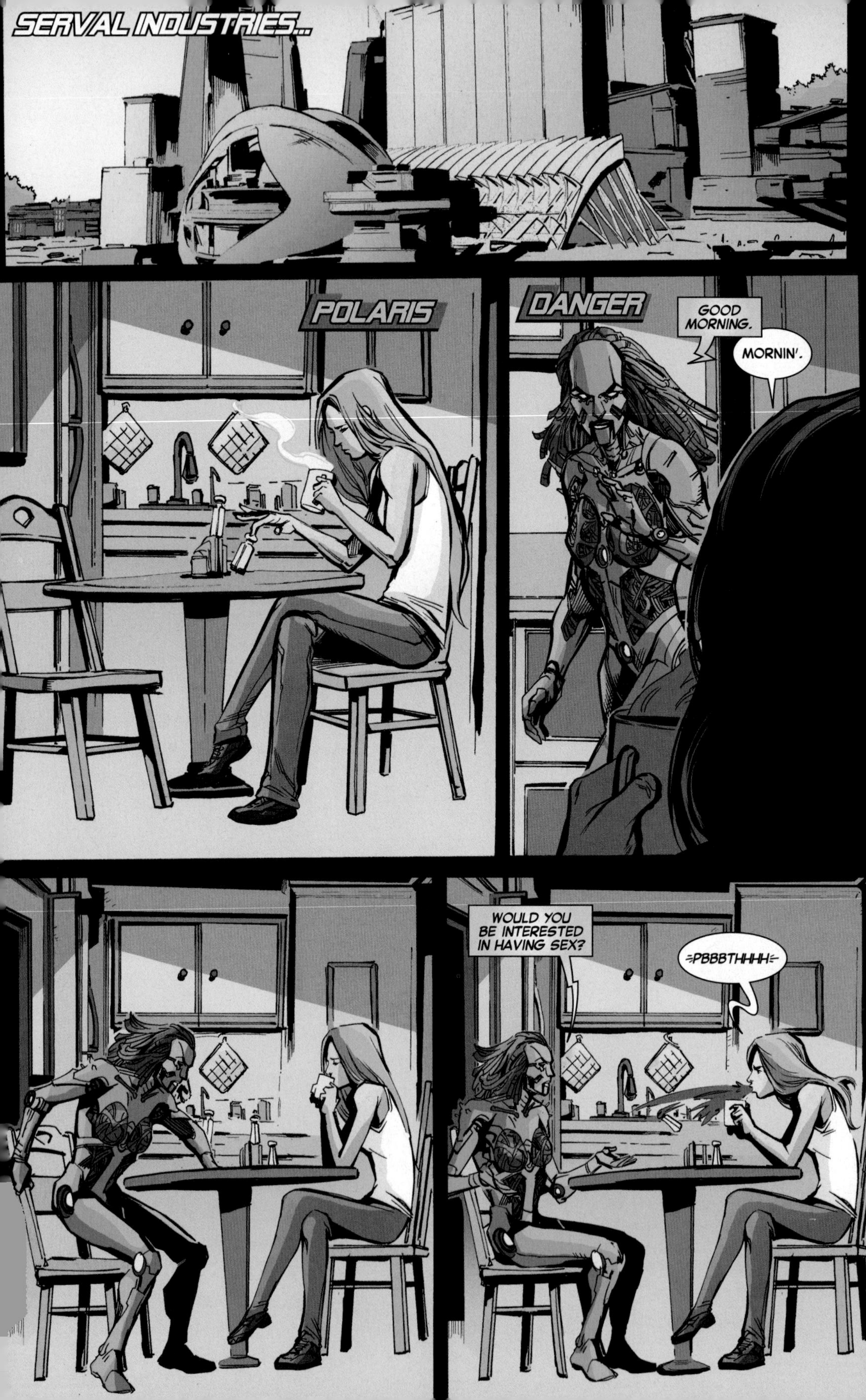
SERVAL INDUSTRIES...
POLARIS
DANGER
GOOD MORNING.
MORNIN'.
WOULD YOU BE INTERESTED IN HAVING SEX?
PBBBTHHHH

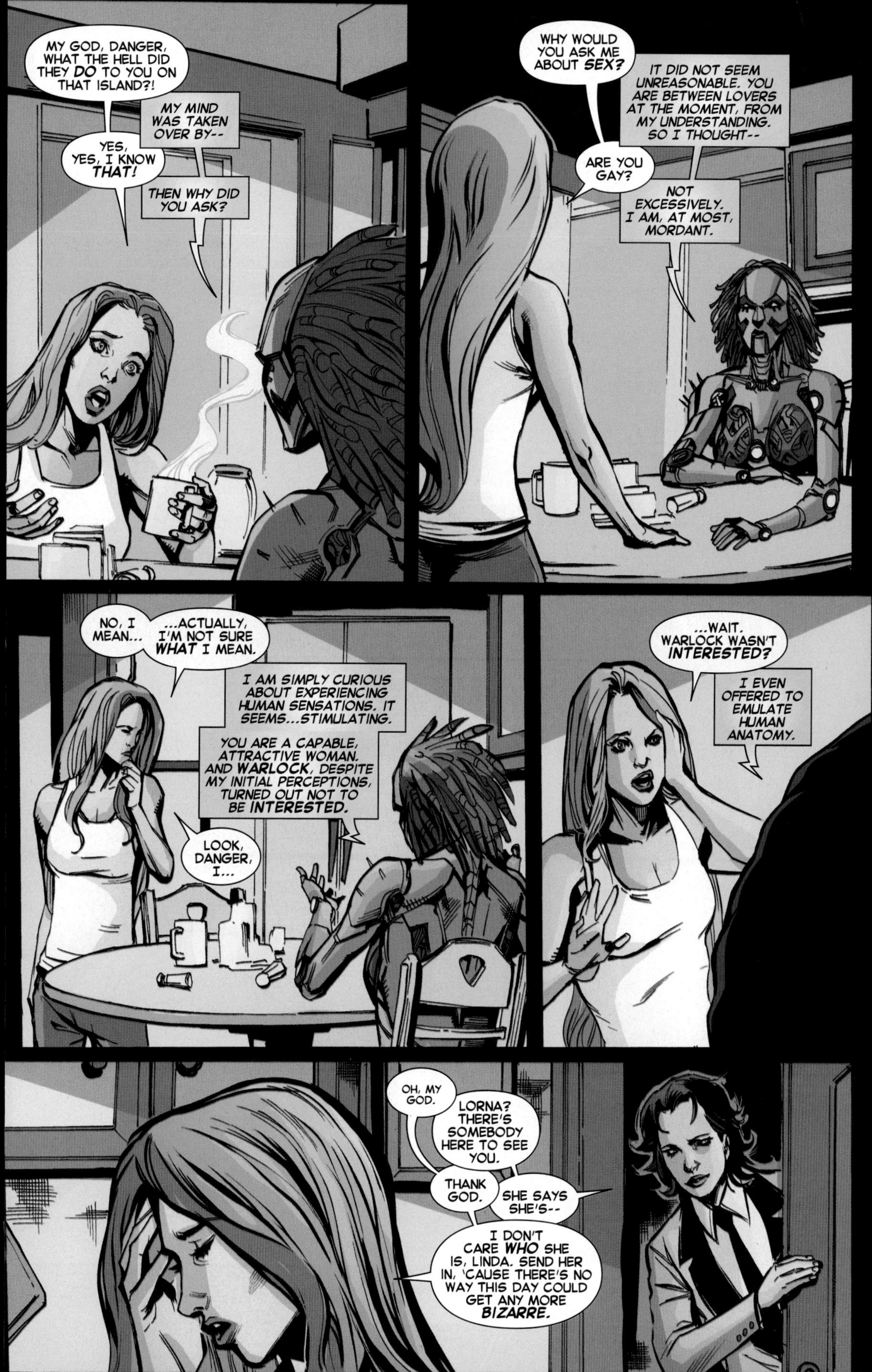
MY GOD, DANGER, WHAT THE HELL DID THEY DO TO YOU ON THAT ISLAND?!
MY MIND WAS TAKEN OVER BY--
YES, YES, I KNOW THAT!
THEN WHY DID YOU ASK?
WHY WOULD YOU ASK ME ABOUT SEX?
IT DID NOT SEEM UNREASONABLE. YOU ARE BETWEEN LOVERS AT THE MOMENT, FROM MY UNDERSTANDING. SO I THOUGHT--
ARE YOU GAY?
NOT EXCESSIVELY. I AM, AT MOST, MORDANT.
NO, I MEAN...
...ACTUALLY, I'M NOT SURE WHAT I MEAN.
I AM SIMPLY CURIOUS ABOUT EXPERIENCING HUMAN SENSATIONS. IT SEEMS...STIMULATING.
YOU ARE A CAPABLE, ATTRACTIVE WOMAN. AND WARLOCK, DESPITE MY INITIAL PERCEPTIONS, TURNED OUT NOT TO BE INTERESTED.
LOOK, DANGER, I...
...WAIT. WARLOCK WASN'T INTERESTED?
I EVEN OFFERED TO EMULATE HUMAN ANATOMY.
OH, MY GOD.
LORNA? THERE'S SOMEBODY HERE TO SEE YOU.
THANK GOD.
SHE SAYS SHE'S--
I DON'T CARE WHO SHE IS, LINDA. SEND HER IN, 'CAUSE THERE'S NO WAY THIS DAY COULD GET ANY MORE BIZARRE.

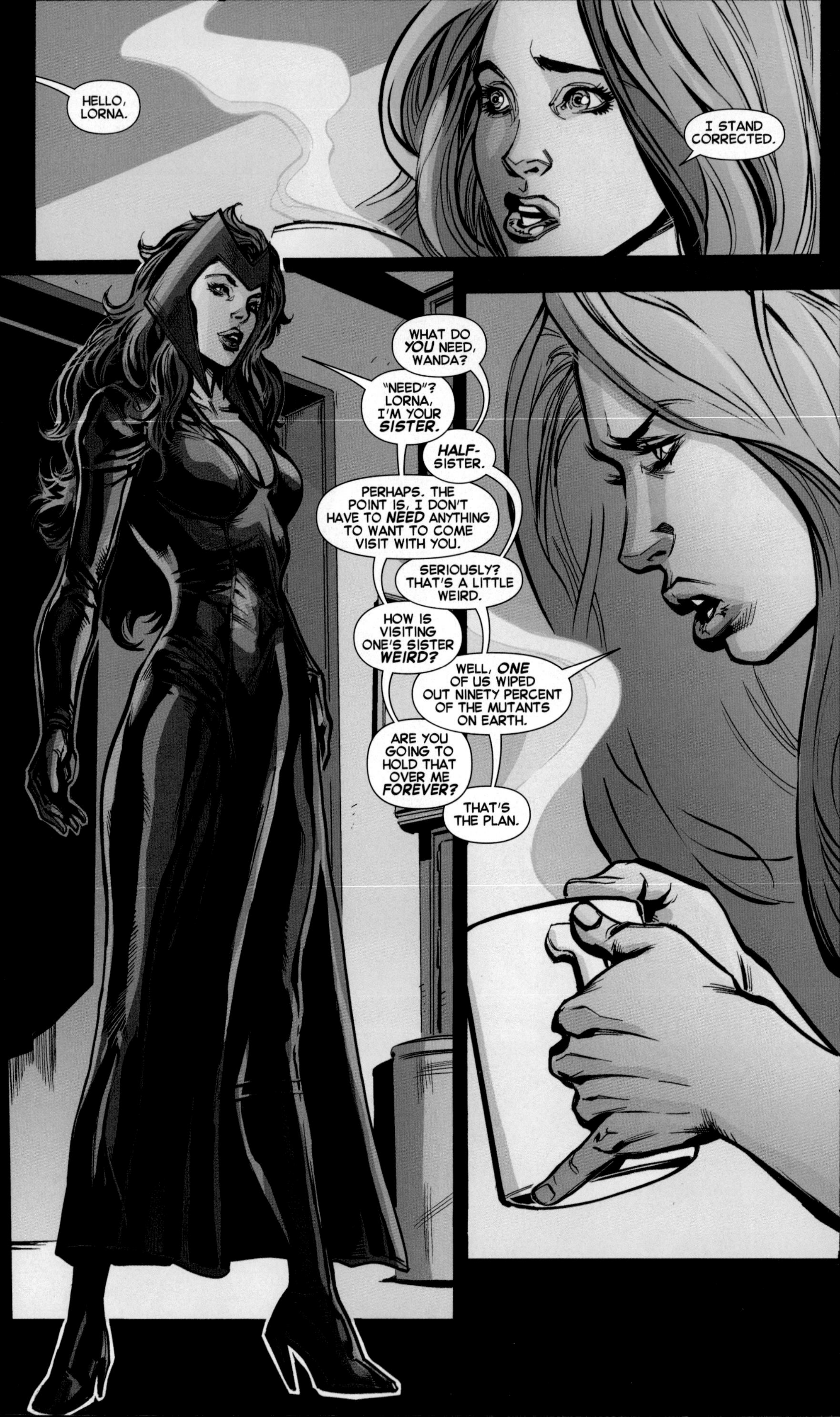
HELLO, LORNA.
I STAND CORRECTED.
WHAT DO YOU NEED, WANDA?
"NEED"? LORNA, I'M YOUR SISTER.
HALF-SISTER.
PERHAPS. THE POINT IS, I DON'T HAVE TO NEED ANYTHING TO WANT TO COME VISIT WITH YOU.
SERIOUSLY? THAT'S A LITTLE WEIRD.
HOW IS VISITING ONE'S SISTER WEIRD?
WELL, ONE OF US WIPED OUT NINETY PERCENT OF THE MUTANTS ON EARTH.
ARE YOU GOING TO HOLD THAT OVER ME FOREVER?
THAT'S THE PLAN.

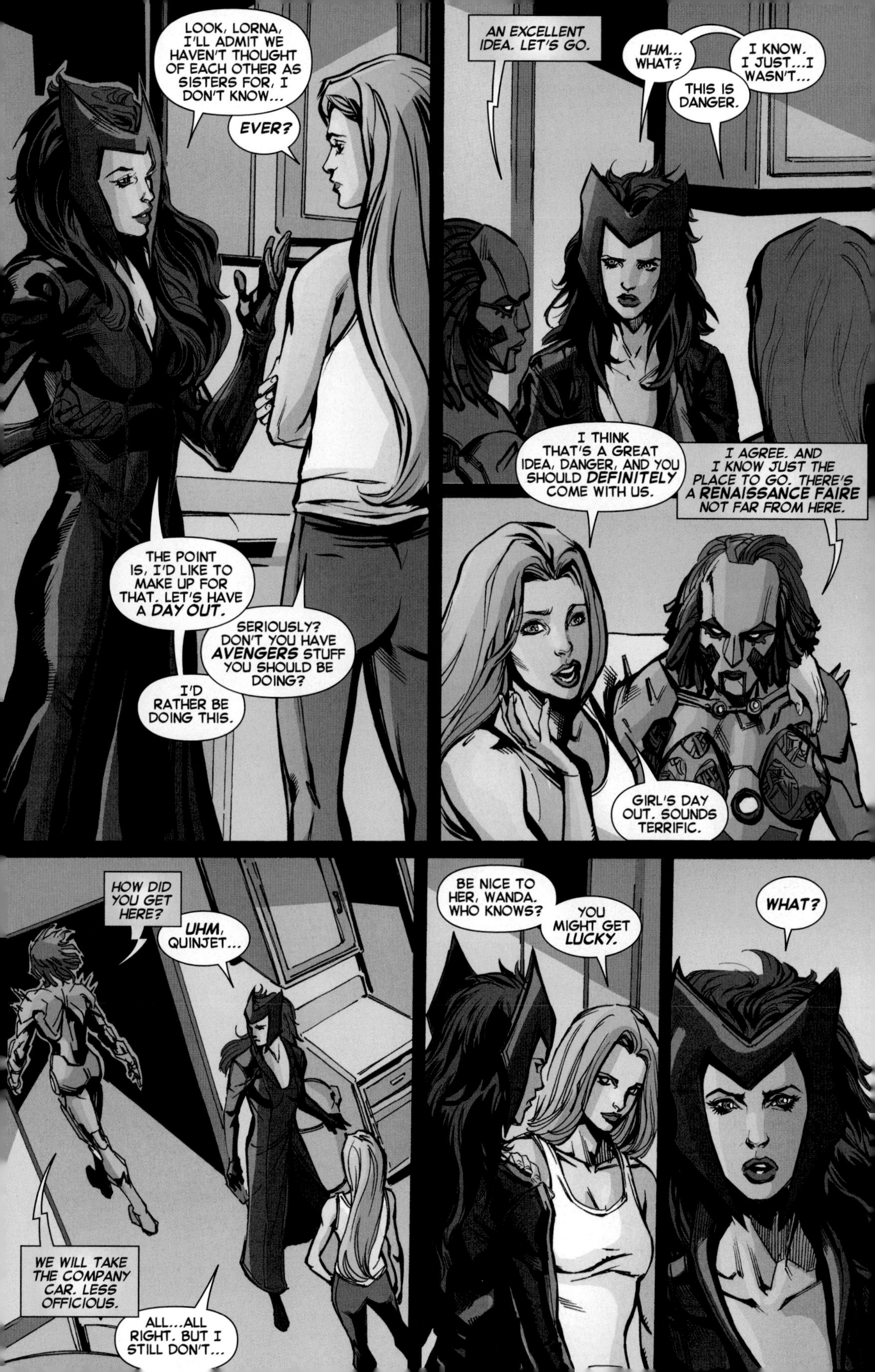
LOOK, LORNA, I'LL ADMIT WE HAVEN'T THOUGHT OF EACH OTHER AS SISTERS FOR, I DON'T KNOW...
EVER?
THE POINT IS, I'D LIKE TO MAKE UP FOR THAT. LET'S HAVE A DAY OUT.
SERIOUSLY? DON'T YOU HAVE AVENGERS STUFF YOU SHOULD BE DOING?
I'D RATHER BE DOING THIS.
AN EXCELLENT IDEA. LET'S GO.
UHM... WHAT?
THIS IS DANGER.
I KNOW. I JUST...I WASN'T...
I THINK THAT'S A GREAT IDEA, DANGER, AND YOU SHOULD DEFINITELY COME WITH US.
I AGREE. AND I KNOW JUST THE PLACE TO GO. THERE'S A RENAISSANCE FAIRE NOT FAR FROM HERE.
GIRL'S DAY OUT. SOUNDS TERRIFIC.
HOW DID YOU GET HERE?
UHM, QUINJET...
WE WILL TAKE THE COMPANY CAR. LESS OFFICIOUS.
ALL...ALL RIGHT. BUT I STILL DON'T...
BE NICE TO HER, WANDA. WHO KNOWS?
YOU MIGHT GET LUCKY.
WHAT?

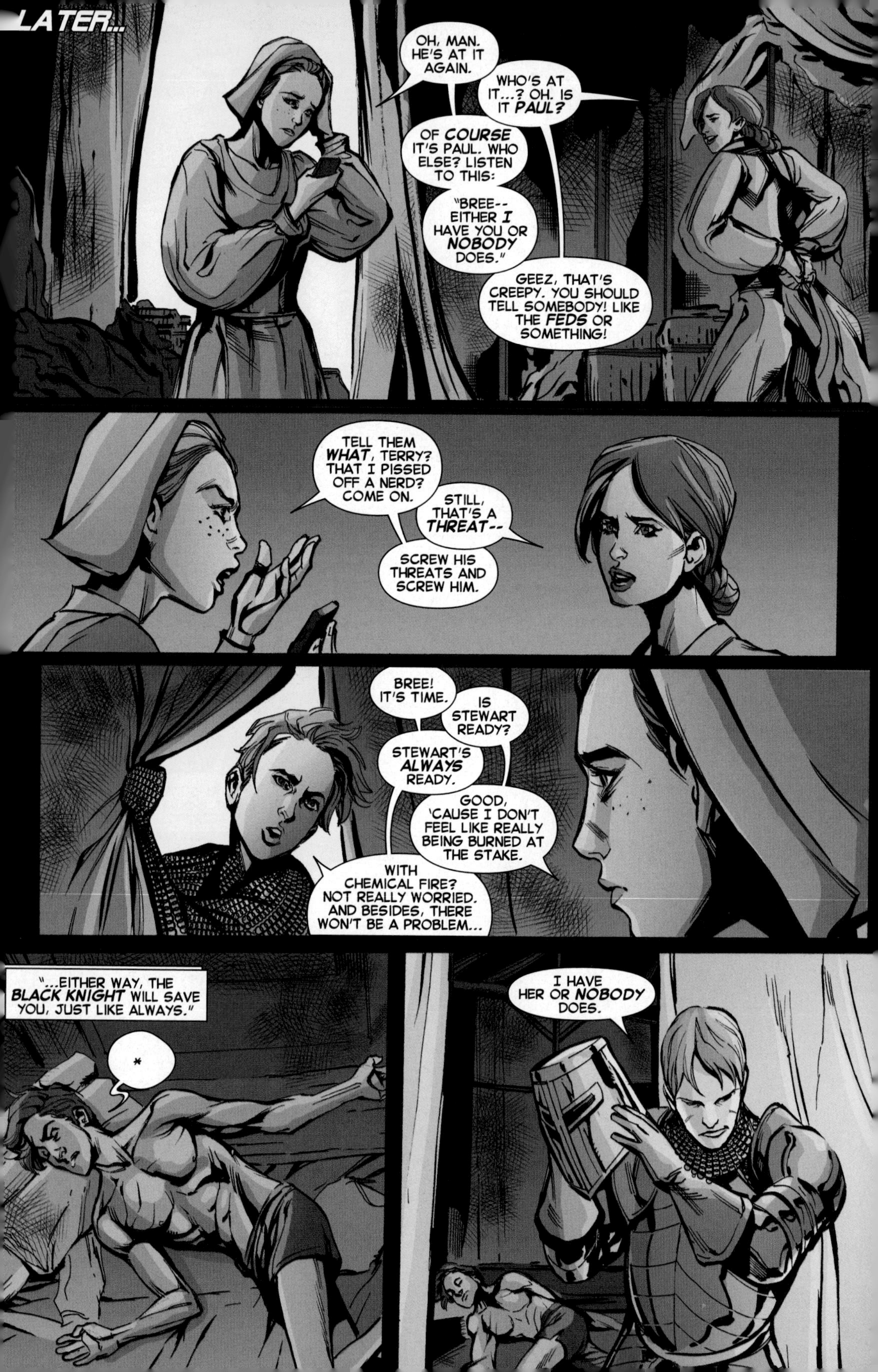
LATER...
OH, MAN. HE'S AT IT AGAIN.
WHO'S AT IT...? OH. IS IT PAUL?
OF COURSE IT'S PAUL. WHO ELSE? LISTEN TO THIS:
"BREE-- EITHER I HAVE YOU OR NOBODY DOES."
GEEZ, THAT'S CREEPY. YOU SHOULD TELL SOMEBODY! LIKE THE FEDS OR SOMETHING!
TELL THEM WHAT, TERRY? THAT I PISSED OFF A NERD? COME ON.
STILL, THAT'S A THREAT--
SCREW HIS THREATS AND SCREW HIM.
BREE! IT'S TIME.
IS STEWART READY?
STEWART'S ALWAYS READY.
GOOD, 'CAUSE I DON'T FEEL LIKE REALLY BEING BURNED AT THE STAKE.
WITH CHEMICAL FIRE? NOT REALLY WORRIED. AND BESIDES, THERE WON'T BE A PROBLEM...
"...EITHER WAY, THE BLACK KNIGHT WILL SAVE YOU, JUST LIKE ALWAYS."
*
I HAVE HER OR NOBODY DOES.

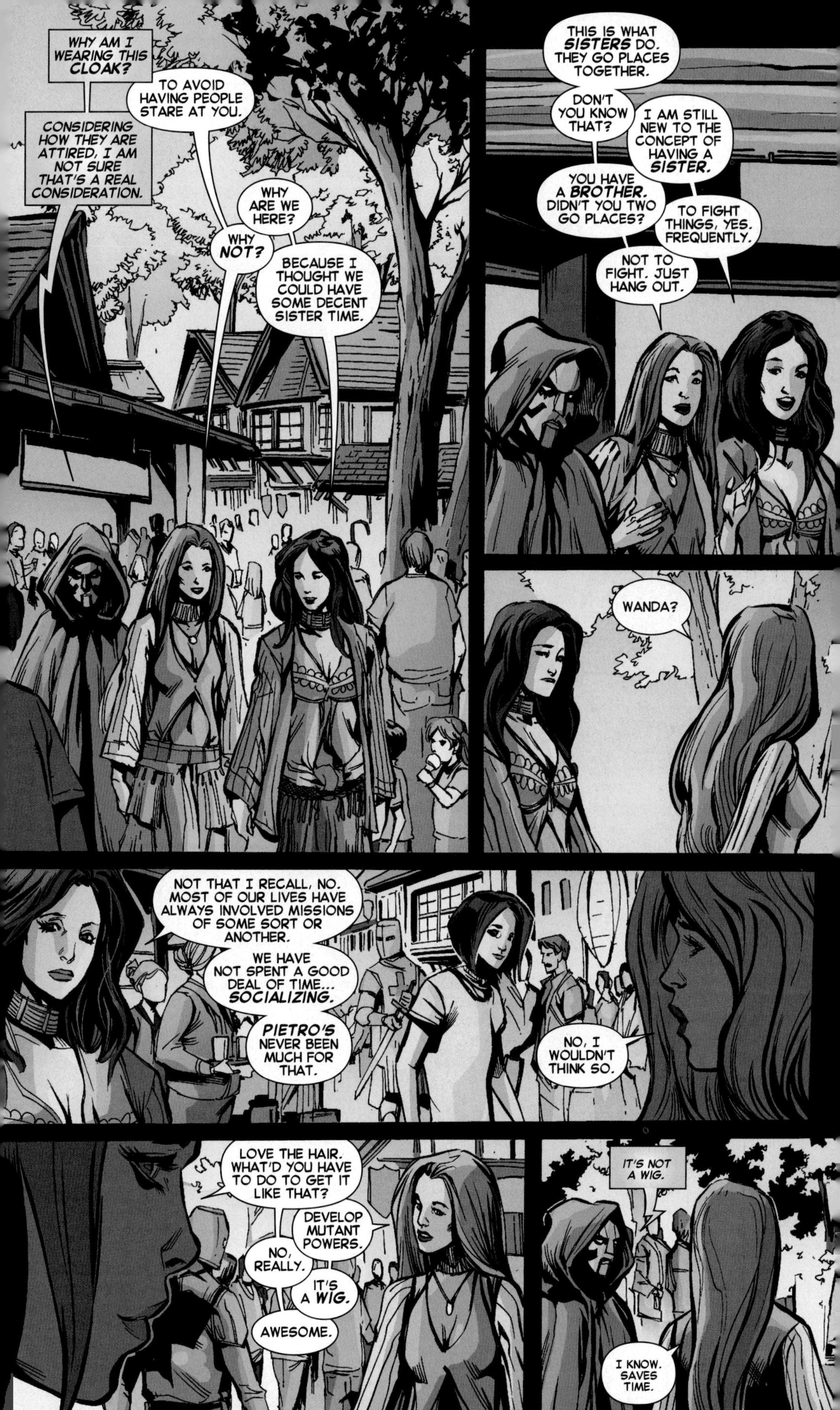
WHY AM I WEARING THIS CLOAK?
TO AVOID HAVING PEOPLE STARE AT YOU.
CONSIDERING HOW THEY ARE ATTIRED, I AM NOT SURE THAT'S A REAL CONSIDERATION.
WHY ARE WE HERE?
WHY NOT?
BECAUSE I THOUGHT WE COULD HAVE SOME DECENT SISTER TIME.
THIS IS WHAT SISTERS DO. THEY GO PLACES TOGETHER.
DON'T YOU KNOW THAT?
I AM STILL NEW TO THE CONCEPT OF HAVING A SISTER.
YOU HAVE A BROTHER. DIDN'T YOU TWO GO PLACES?
TO FIGHT THINGS, YES. FREQUENTLY.
NOT TO FIGHT. JUST HANG OUT.
WANDA?
NOT THAT I RECALL, NO. MOST OF OUR LIVES HAVE ALWAYS INVOLVED MISSIONS OF SOME SORT OR ANOTHER.
WE HAVE NOT SPENT A GOOD DEAL OF TIME... SOCIALIZING.
PIETRO'S NEVER BEEN MUCH FOR THAT.
NO, I WOULDN'T THINK SO.
LOVE THE HAIR. WHAT'D YOU HAVE TO DO TO GET IT LIKE THAT?
DEVELOP MUTANT POWERS.
NO, REALLY.
IT'S A WIG.
AWESOME.
IT'S NOT A WIG.
I KNOW. SAVES TIME.

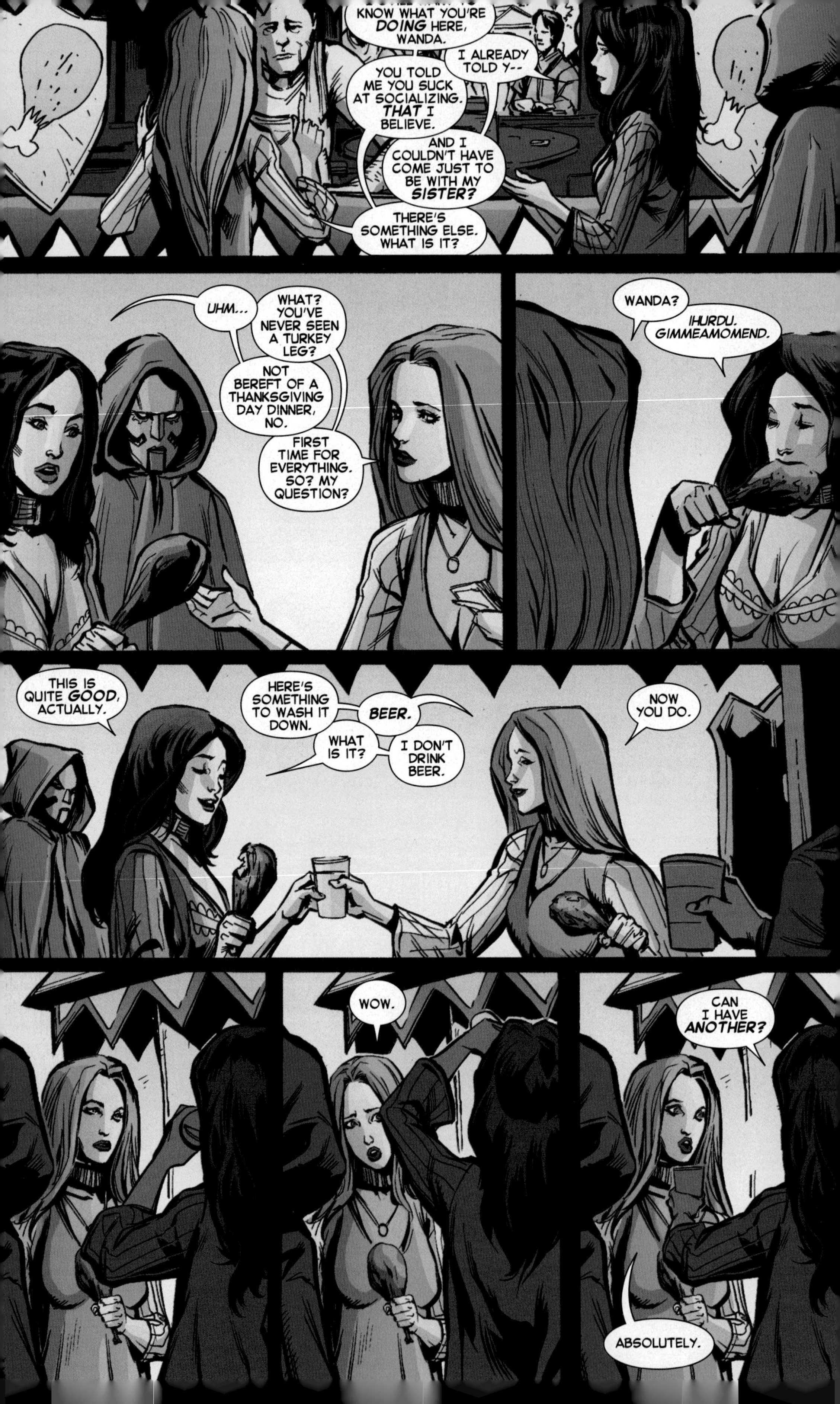
KNOW WHAT YOU'RE DOING HERE, WANDA.
I ALREADY TOLD Y--
YOU TOLD ME YOU SUCK AT SOCIALIZING. THAT I BELIEVE.
AND I COULDN'T HAVE COME JUST TO BE WITH MY SISTER?
THERE'S SOMETHING ELSE. WHAT IS IT?
UHM...
WHAT? YOU'VE NEVER SEEN A TURKEY LEG?
NOT BEREFT OF A THANKSGIVING DAY DINNER, NO.
FIRST TIME FOR EVERYTHING. SO? MY QUESTION?
WANDA?
IHURDU. GIMMEAMOMEND.
THIS IS QUITE GOOD, ACTUALLY.
HERE'S SOMETHING TO WASH IT DOWN.
BEER.
WHAT IS IT?
I DON'T DRINK BEER.
NOW YOU DO.
WOW.
CAN I HAVE ANOTHER?
ABSOLUTELY.

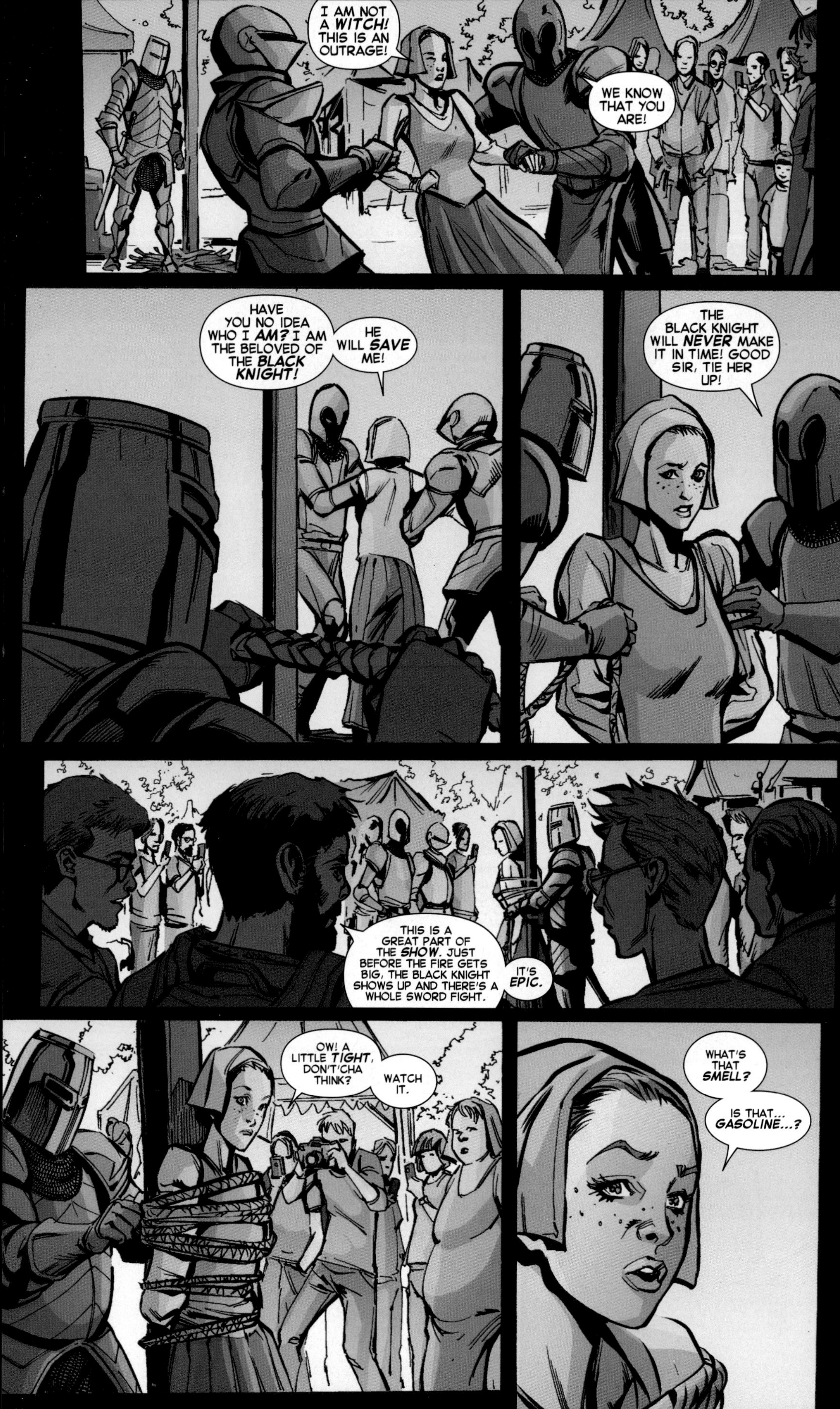
I AM NOT A WITCH! THIS IS AN OUTRAGE!
WE KNOW THAT YOU ARE!
HAVE YOU NO IDEA WHO I AM? I AM THE BELOVED OF THE BLACK KNIGHT!
HE WILL SAVE ME!
THE BLACK KNIGHT WILL NEVER MAKE IT IN TIME! GOOD SIR, TIE HER UP!
THIS IS A GREAT PART OF THE SHOW. JUST BEFORE THE FIRE GETS BIG, THE BLACK KNIGHT SHOWS UP AND THERE'S A WHOLE SWORD FIGHT.
IT'S EPIC.
OW! A LITTLE TIGHT, DON'T'CHA THINK?
WATCH IT.
WHAT'S THAT SMELL?
IS THAT... GASOLINE...?

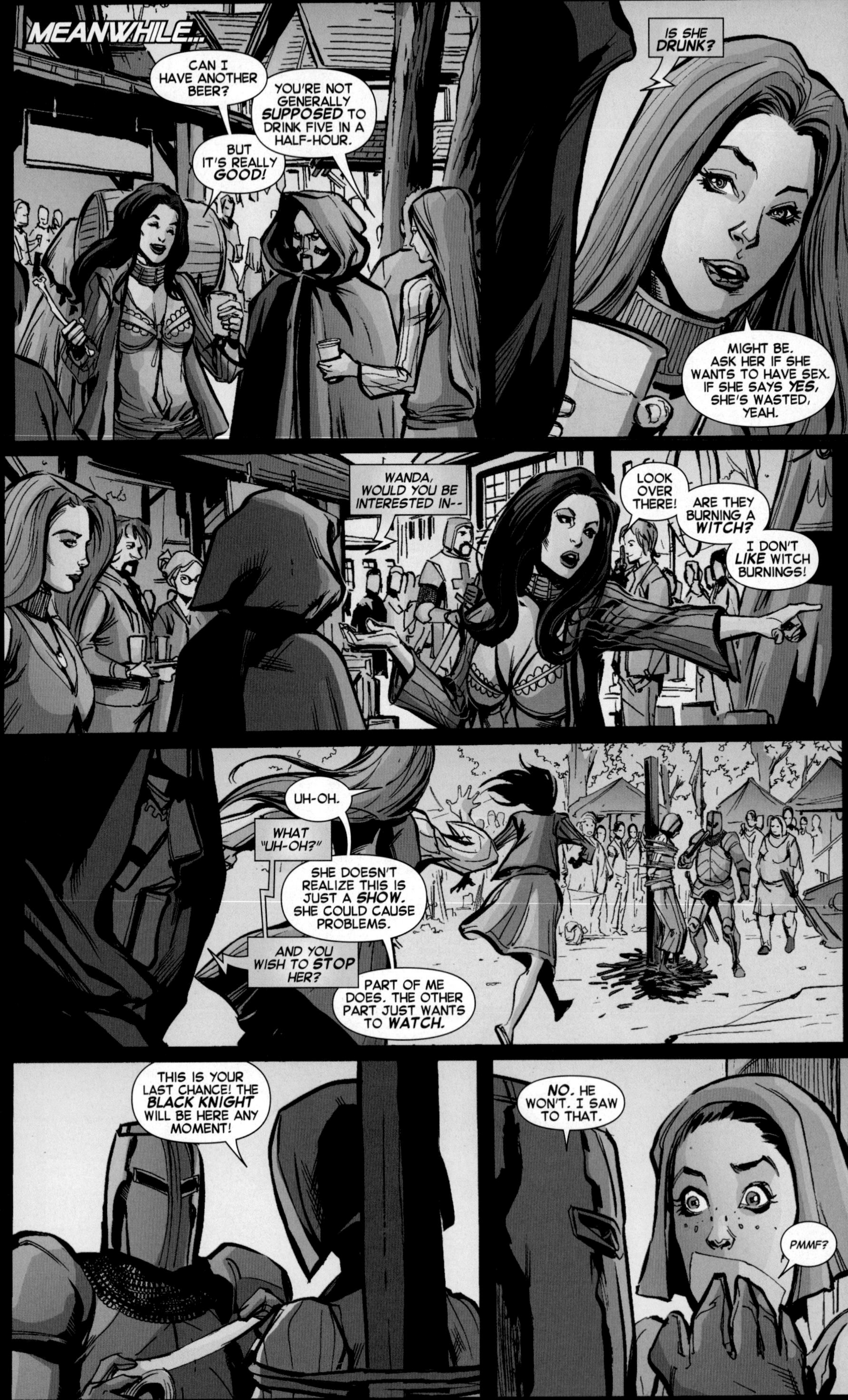
MEANWHILE...
CAN I HAVE ANOTHER BEER?
YOU'RE NOT GENERALLY SUPPOSED TO DRINK FIVE IN A HALF-HOUR.
BUT IT'S REALLY GOOD!
IS SHE DRUNK?
MIGHT BE. ASK HER IF SHE WANTS TO HAVE SEX. IF SHE SAYS YES, SHE'S WASTED, YEAH.
WANDA, WOULD YOU BE INTERESTED IN--
LOOK OVER THERE!
ARE THEY BURNING A WITCH?
I DON'T LIKE WITCH BURNINGS!
UH-OH.
WHAT "UH-OH?"
SHE DOESN'T REALIZE THIS IS JUST A SHOW. SHE COULD CAUSE PROBLEMS.
AND YOU WISH TO STOP HER?
PART OF ME DOES. THE OTHER PART JUST WANTS TO WATCH.
THIS IS YOUR LAST CHANCE! THE BLACK KNIGHT WILL BE HERE ANY MOMENT!
NO. HE WON'T. I SAW TO THAT.
PMMF?

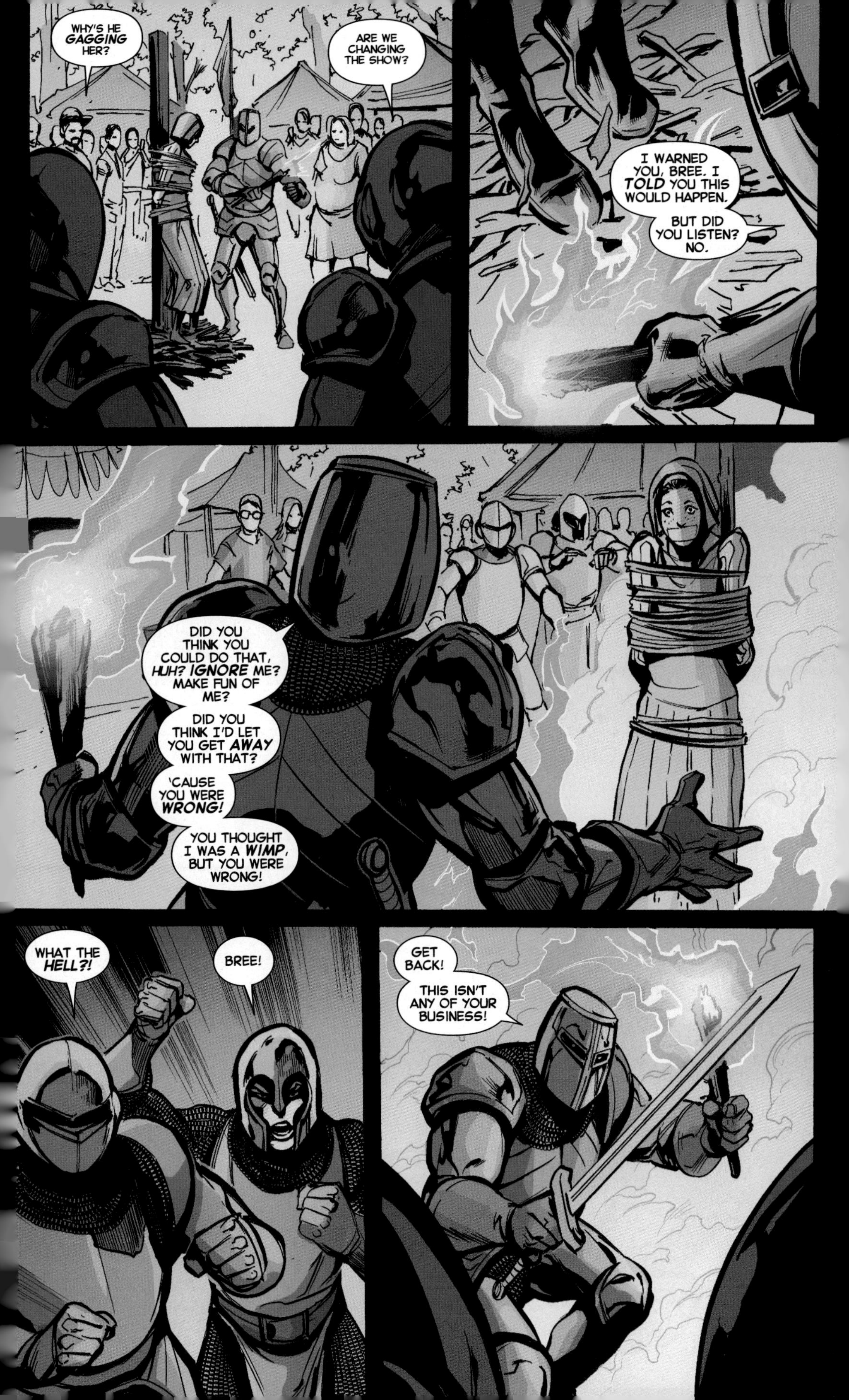
WHY'S HE GAGGING HER?
ARE WE CHANGING THE SHOW?
I WARNED YOU, BREE. I TOLD YOU THIS WOULD HAPPEN.
BUT DID YOU LISTEN? NO.
DID YOU THINK YOU COULD DO THAT, HUH? IGNORE ME? MAKE FUN OF ME?
DID YOU THINK I'D LET YOU GET AWAY WITH THAT?
'CAUSE YOU WERE WRONG!
YOU THOUGHT I WAS A WIMP, BUT YOU WERE WRONG!
WHAT THE HELL?!
BREE!
GET BACK!
THIS ISN'T ANY OF YOUR BUSINESS!

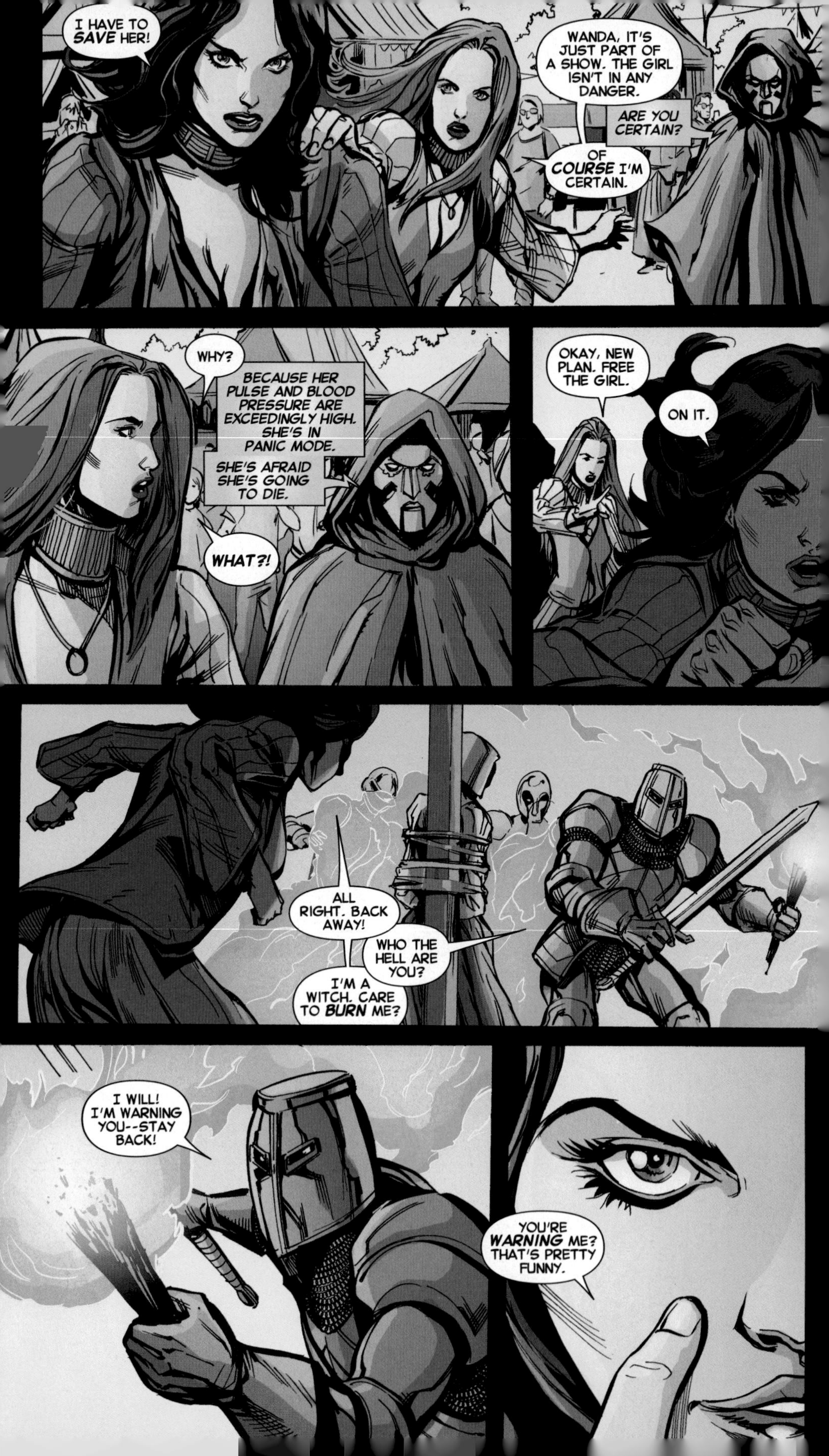
I HAVE TO SAVE HER!
WANDA, IT'S JUST PART OF A SHOW. THE GIRL ISN'T IN ANY DANGER.
ARE YOU CERTAIN?
OF COURSE I'M CERTAIN.
WHY?
BECAUSE HER PULSE AND BLOOD PRESSURE ARE EXCEEDINGLY HIGH. SHE'S IN PANIC MODE.
SHE'S AFRAID SHE'S GOING TO DIE.
WHAT?!
OKAY, NEW PLAN. FREE THE GIRL.
ON IT.
ALL RIGHT. BACK AWAY!
WHO THE HELL ARE YOU?
I'M A WITCH. CARE TO BURN ME?
I WILL! I'M WARNING YOU--STAY BACK!
YOU'RE WARNING ME? THAT'S PRETTY FUNNY.

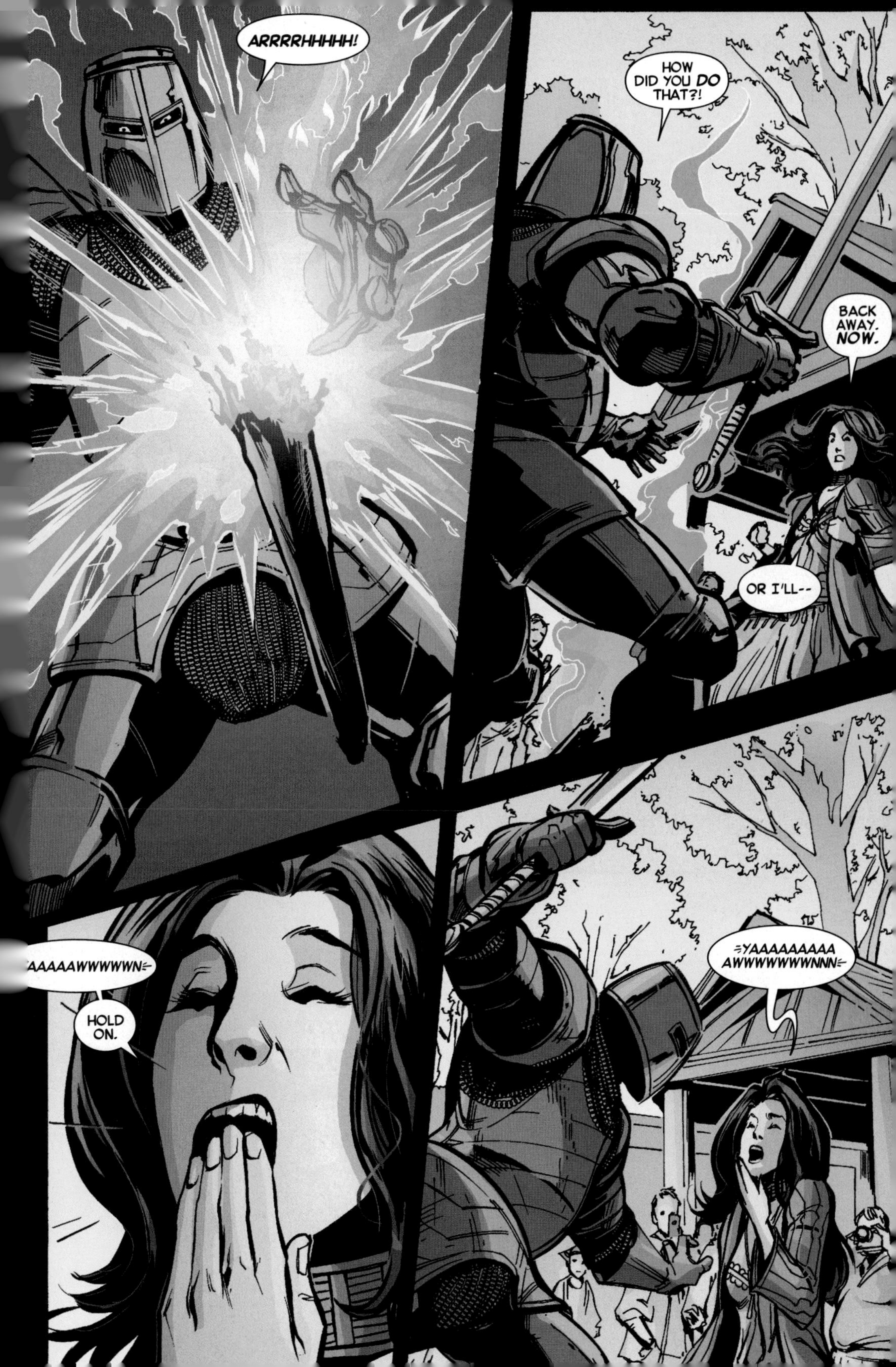

ARRRRHHHHH!
HOW DID YOU DO THAT?!
BACK AWAY. NOW.
OR I'LL--
=YAAAAAAAAA AWWWWWWWNNN=
AAAAAAWWWWWN=
HOLD ON.

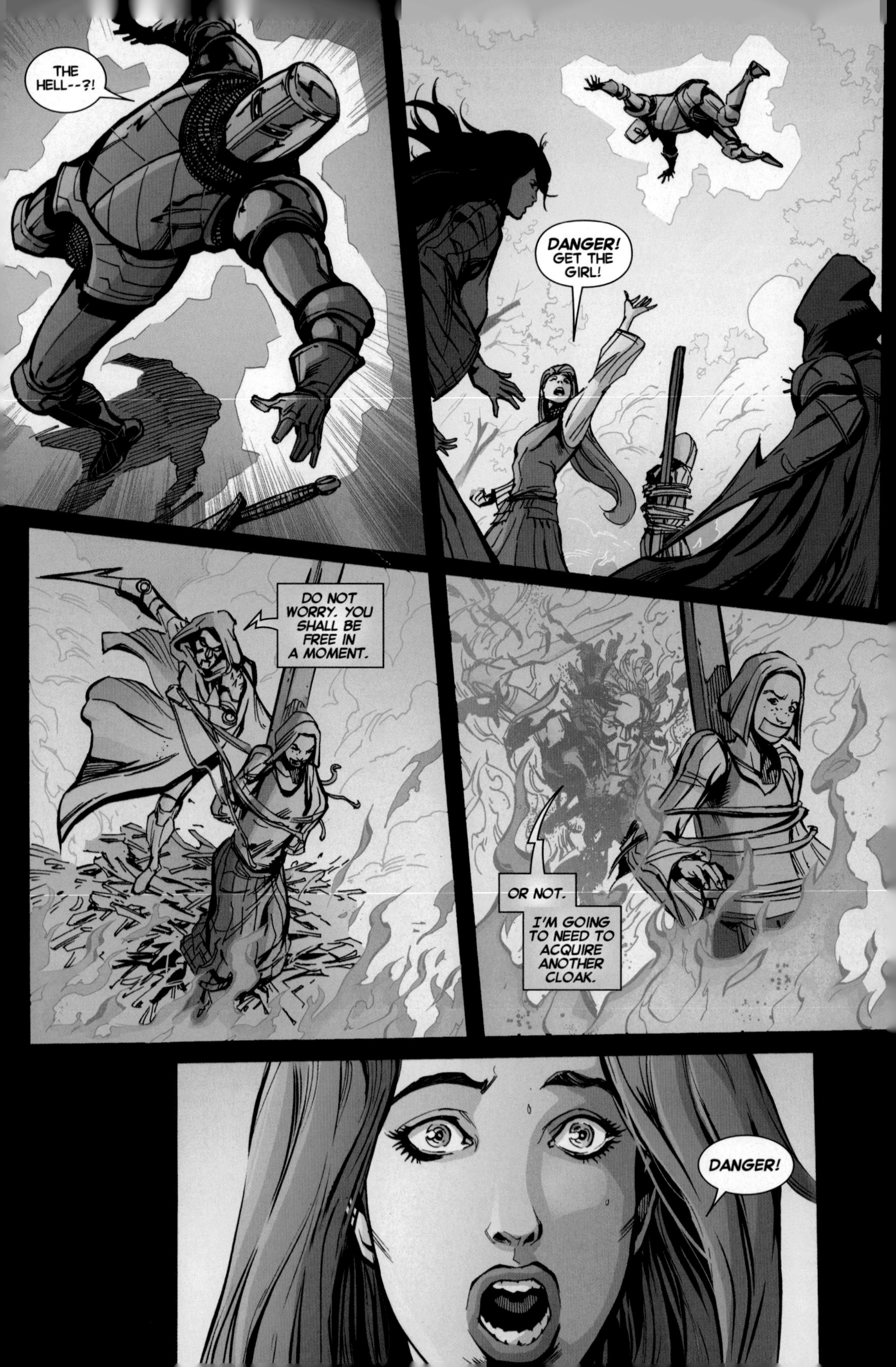
THE HELL--?!
DANGER! GET THE GIRL!
DO NOT WORRY. YOU SHALL BE FREE IN A MOMENT.
OR NOT.
I'M GOING TO NEED TO ACQUIRE ANOTHER CLOAK.
DANGER!

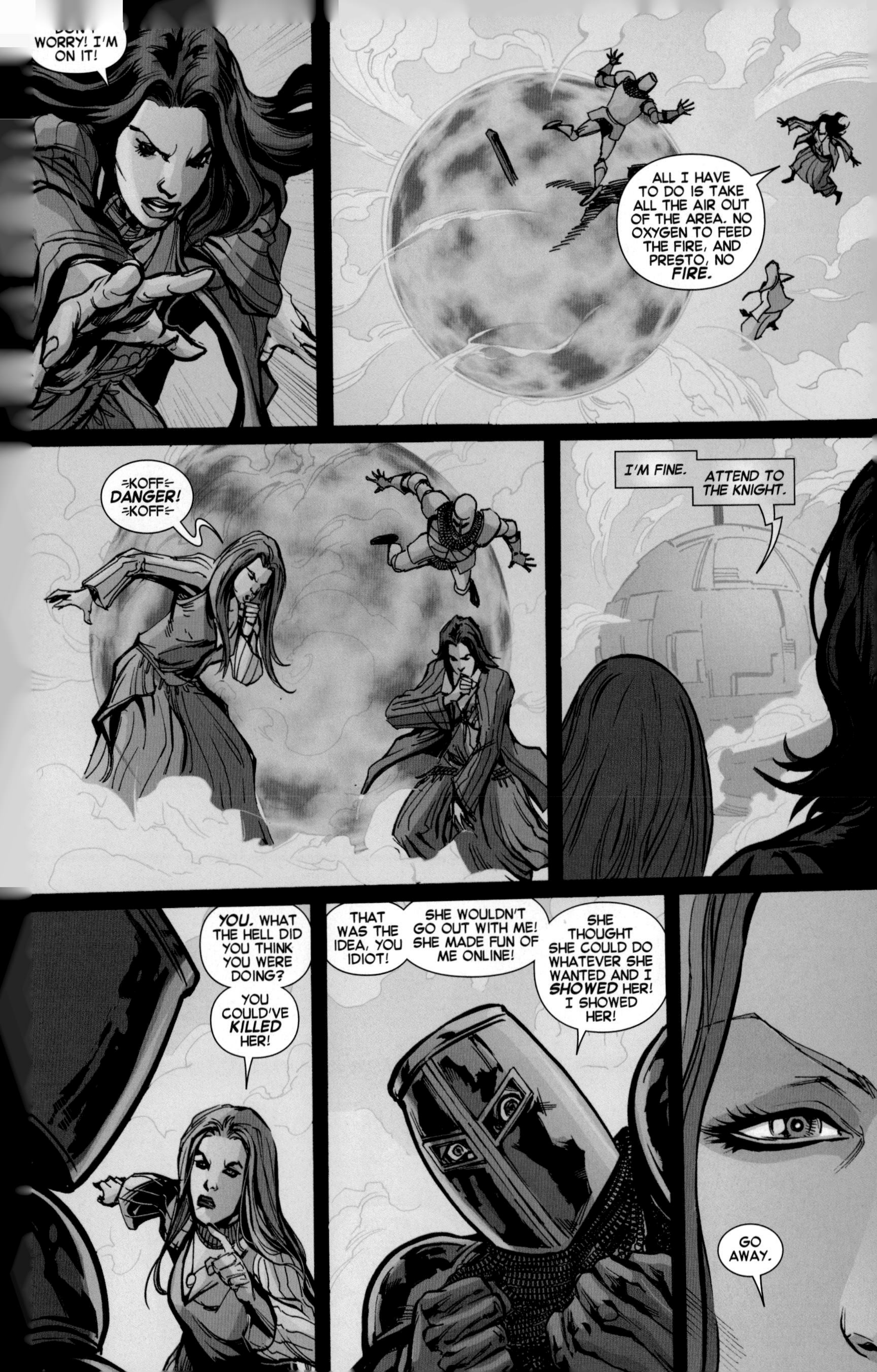
WORRY! I'M ON IT!
ALL I HAVE TO DO IS TAKE ALL THE AIR OUT OF THE AREA. NO OXYGEN TO FEED THE FIRE, AND PRESTO, NO FIRE.
=KOFF= DANGER! =KOFF=
I'M FINE.
ATTEND TO THE KNIGHT.
YOU. WHAT THE HELL DID YOU THINK YOU WERE DOING?
YOU COULD'VE KILLED HER!
THAT WAS THE IDEA, YOU IDIOT!
SHE WOULDN'T GO OUT WITH ME! SHE MADE FUN OF ME ONLINE!
SHE THOUGHT SHE COULD DO WHATEVER SHE WANTED AND I SHOWED HER! I SHOWED HER!
GO AWAY.

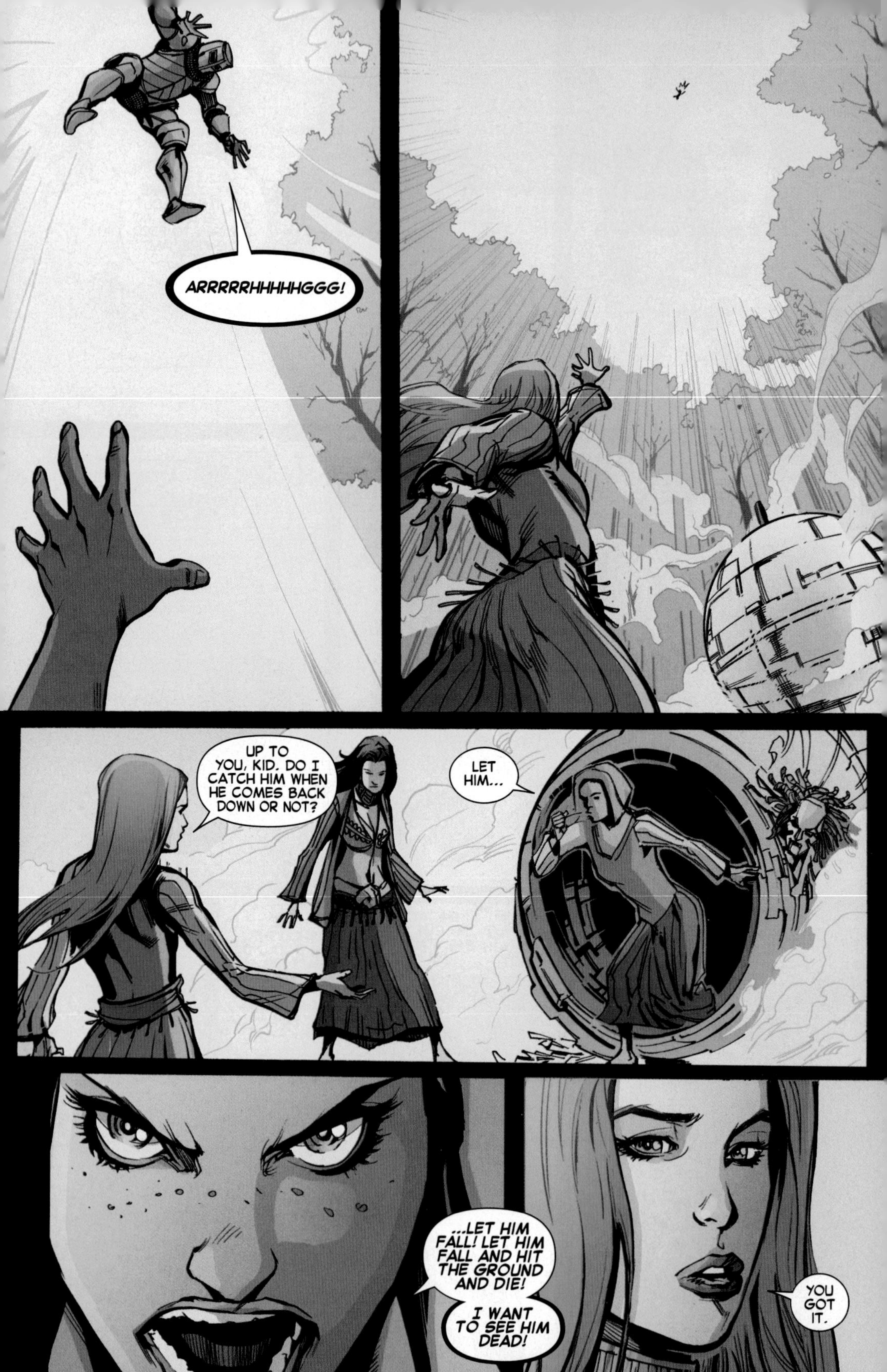
ARRRRRHHHHHGGG!
UP TO YOU, KID. DO I CATCH HIM WHEN HE COMES BACK DOWN OR NOT?
LET HIM...
...LET HIM FALL! LET HIM FALL AND HIT THE GROUND AND DIE!
I WANT TO SEE HIM DEAD!
YOU GOT IT.

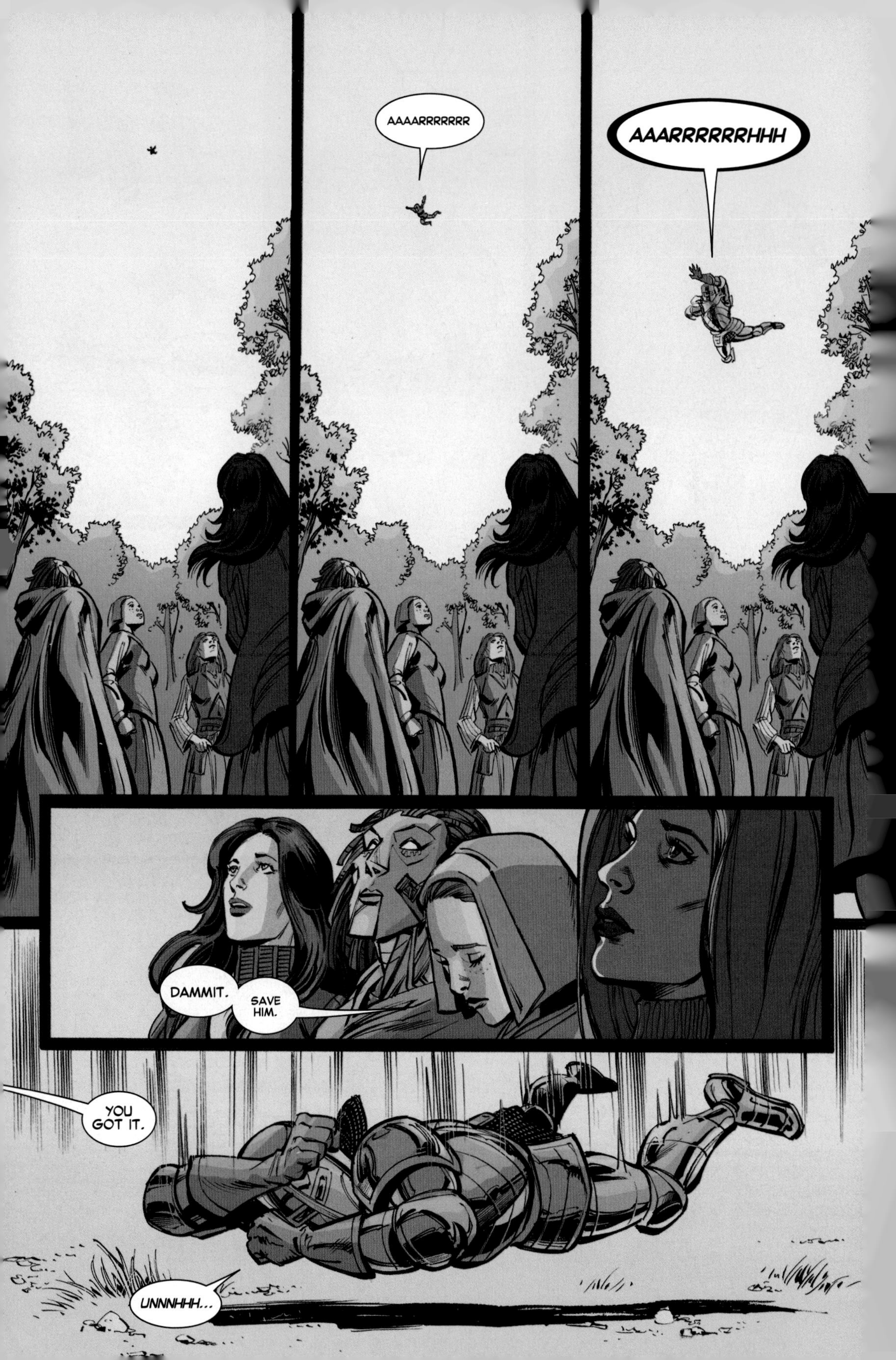
AAAARRRRRRR
AAARRRRRRHHH
DAMMIT.
SAVE HIM.
YOU GOT IT.
UNNNHHH...

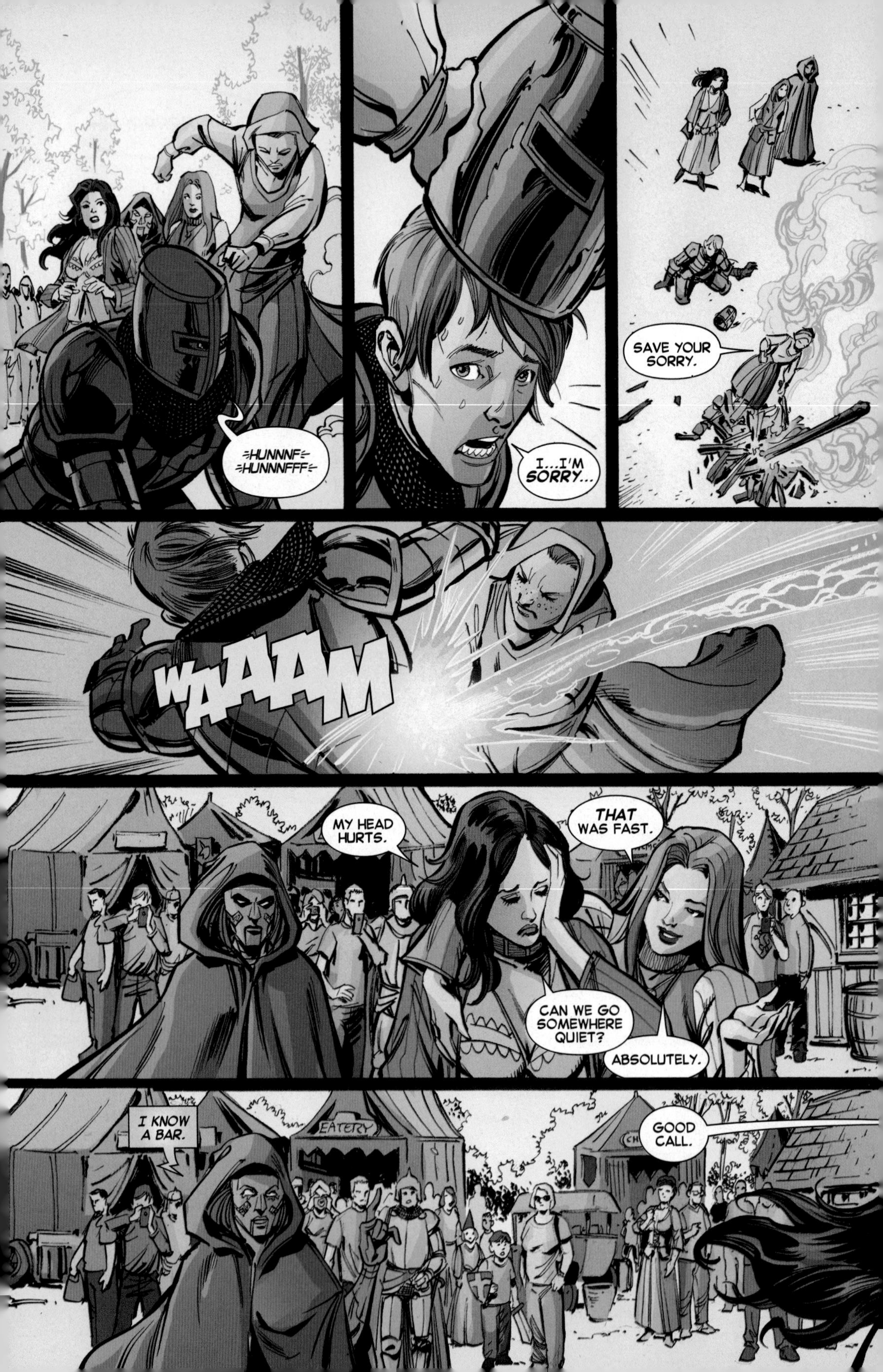

HUNNNF
HUNNNFFF
I...I'M SORRY...
SAVE YOUR SORRY.
WAAAM
MY HEAD HURTS.
THAT WAS FAST.
CAN WE GO SOMEWHERE QUIET?
ABSOLUTELY.
EATERY
I KNOW A BAR.
GOOD CALL.

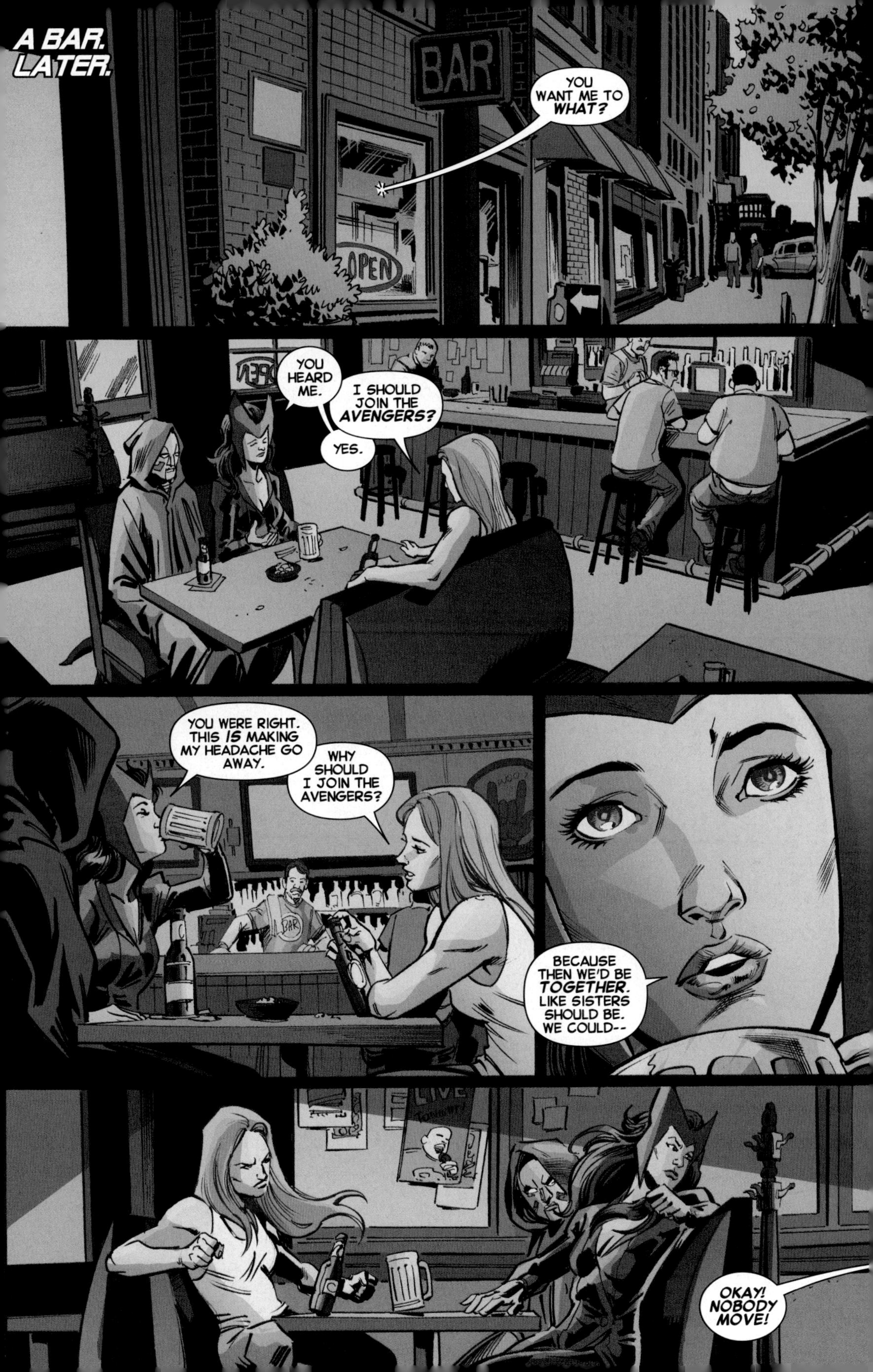
A BAR. LATER.
BAR
OPEN
YOU WANT ME TO WHAT?
YOU HEARD ME.
I SHOULD JOIN THE AVENGERS?
YES.
YOU WERE RIGHT. THIS IS MAKING MY HEADACHE GO AWAY.
WHY SHOULD I JOIN THE AVENGERS?
BECAUSE THEN WE'D BE TOGETHER. LIKE SISTERS SHOULD BE. WE COULD--
OKAY! NOBODY MOVE!

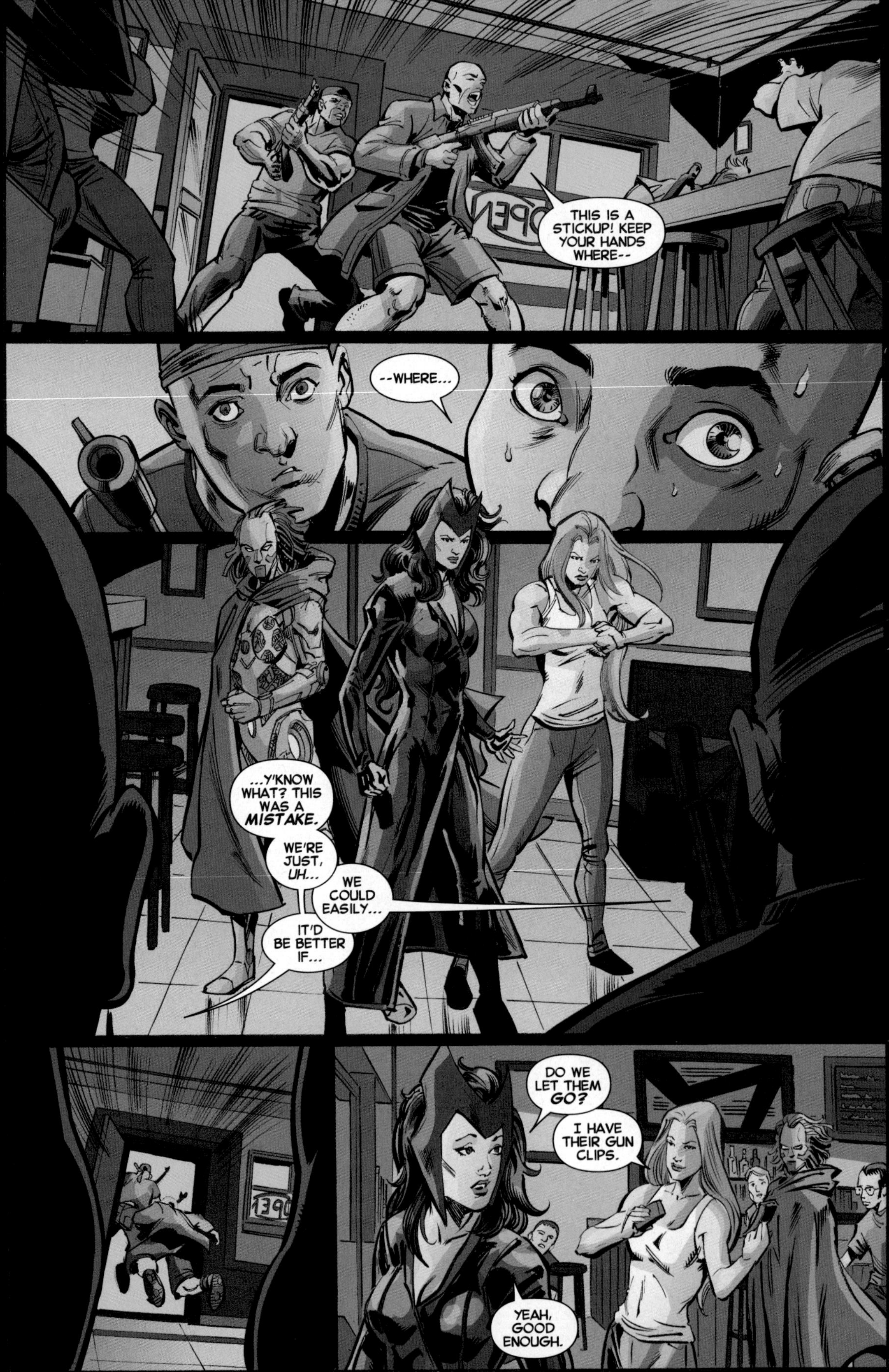
THIS IS A STICKUP! KEEP YOUR HANDS WHERE--
--WHERE...
...Y'KNOW WHAT? THIS WAS A MISTAKE.
WE'RE JUST, UH...
WE COULD EASILY...
IT'D BE BETTER IF...
DO WE LET THEM GO?
I HAVE THEIR GUN CLIPS.
YEAH, GOOD ENOUGH.

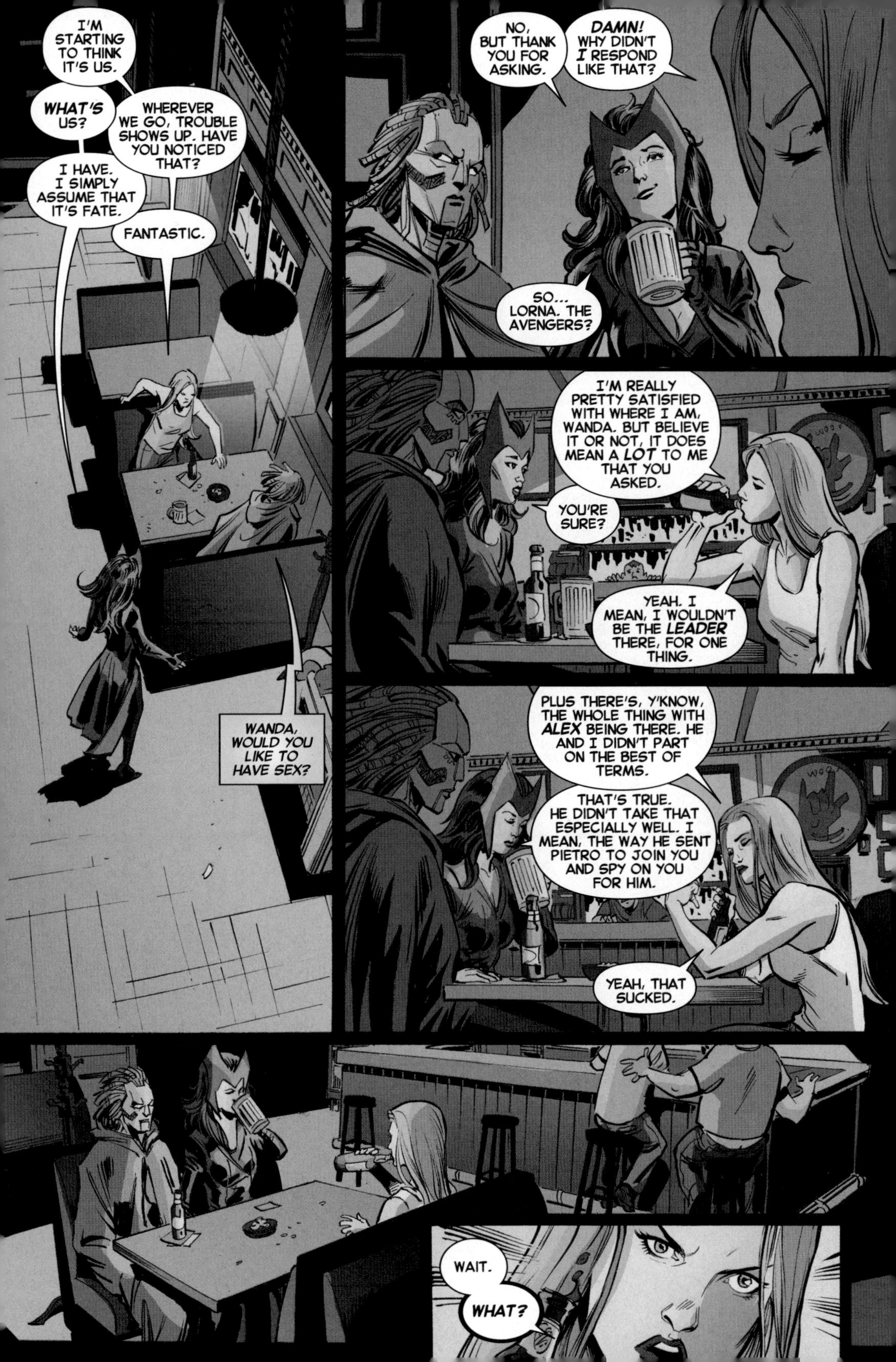
I'M STARTING TO THINK IT'S US.
WHAT'S US?
WHEREVER WE GO, TROUBLE SHOWS UP. HAVE YOU NOTICED THAT?
I HAVE. I SIMPLY ASSUME THAT IT'S FATE.
FANTASTIC.
WANDA, WOULD YOU LIKE TO HAVE SEX?
NO, BUT THANK YOU FOR ASKING.
DAMN! WHY DIDN'T I RESPOND LIKE THAT?
SO... LORNA. THE AVENGERS?
I'M REALLY PRETTY SATISFIED WITH WHERE I AM, WANDA. BUT BELIEVE IT OR NOT, IT DOES MEAN A LOT TO ME THAT YOU ASKED.
YOU'RE SURE?
YEAH. I MEAN, I WOULDN'T BE THE LEADER THERE, FOR ONE THING.
PLUS THERE'S, Y'KNOW, THE WHOLE THING WITH ALEX BEING THERE. HE AND I DIDN'T PART ON THE BEST OF TERMS.
THAT'S TRUE. HE DIDN'T TAKE THAT ESPECIALLY WELL. I MEAN, THE WAY HE SENT PIETRO TO JOIN YOU AND SPY ON YOU FOR HIM.
YEAH, THAT SUCKED.
WAIT.
WHAT?

#20 variant by
ALEX GARNER

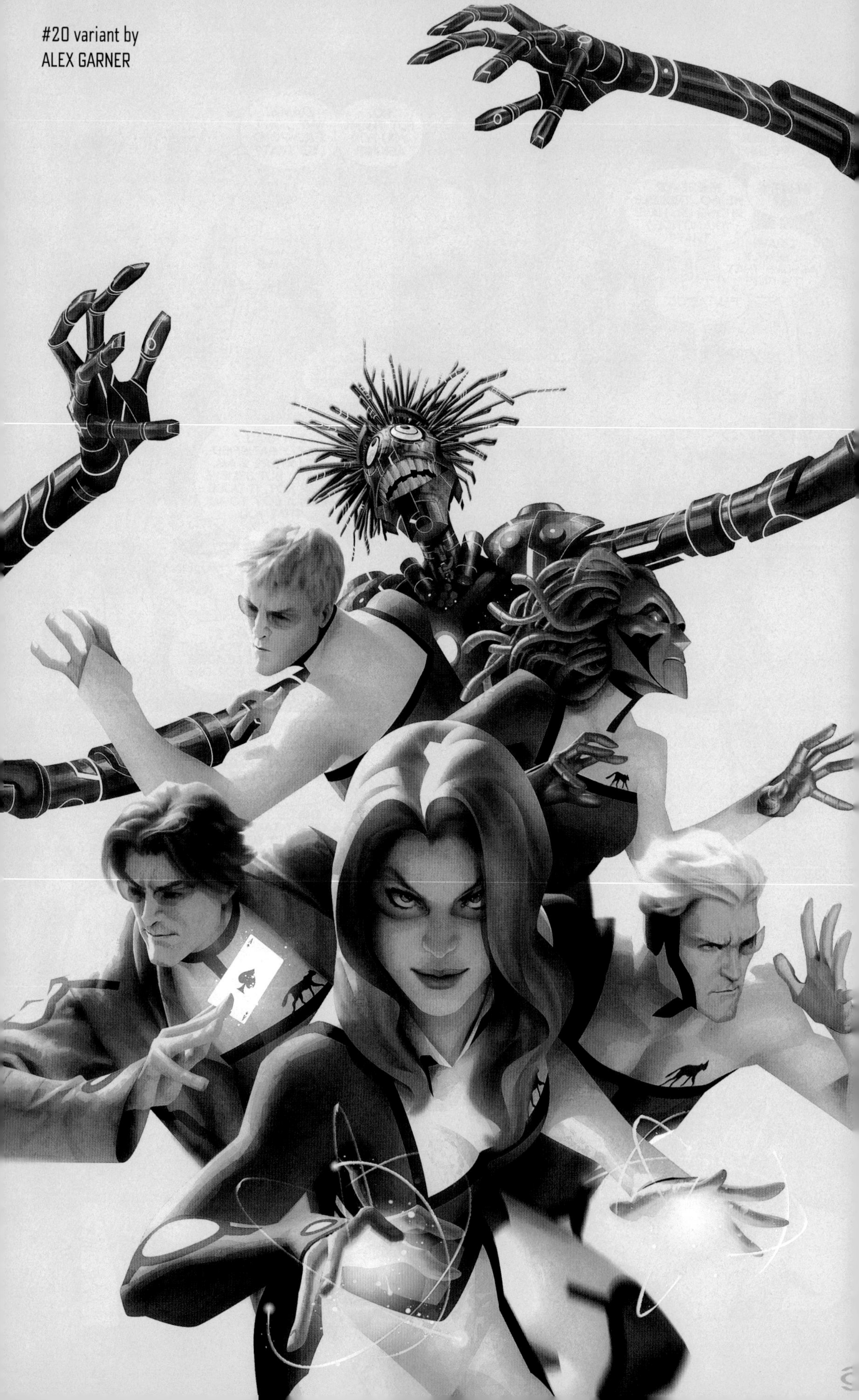

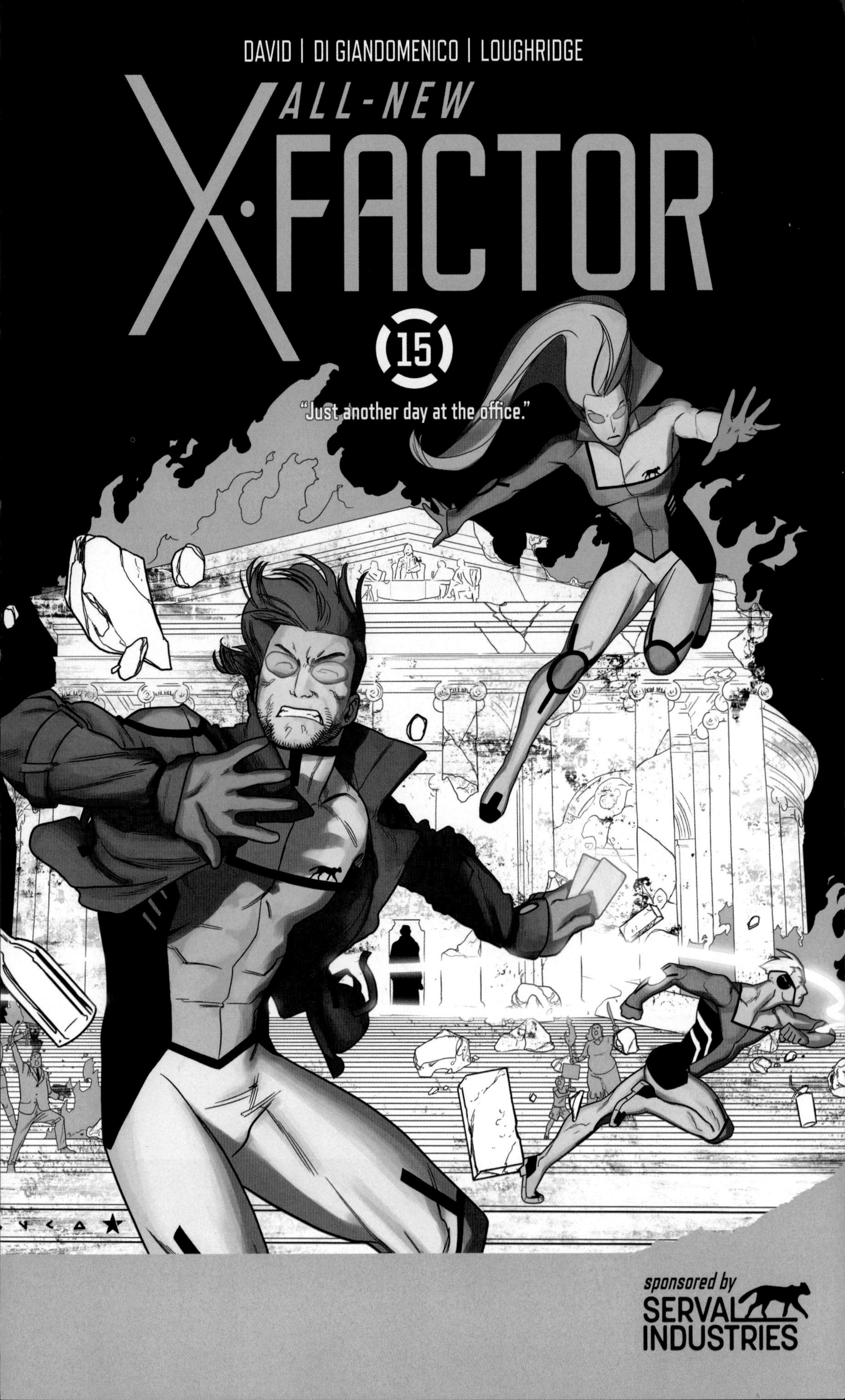
DAVID | DI GIANDOMENICO | LOUGHRIDGE
ALL-NEW
X-FACTOR
15
"Just another day at the office."
sponsored by
SERVAL
INDUSTRIES

# PREVIOUSLY IN *AXIS*

Things are not looking good for the world at large. The Red Skull, using power taken from the late Charles Xavier, is influencing the minds of heroes throughout the world, twisting them toward evil. But it's not just heroes...it's everyone, and at the moment, Washington, D.C., is filled with rioting and flames. One of the few groups spared from the transformation is X-Factor (for reasons that will become clear), and they are endeavoring to keep their neighborhood sane in any way that they can.

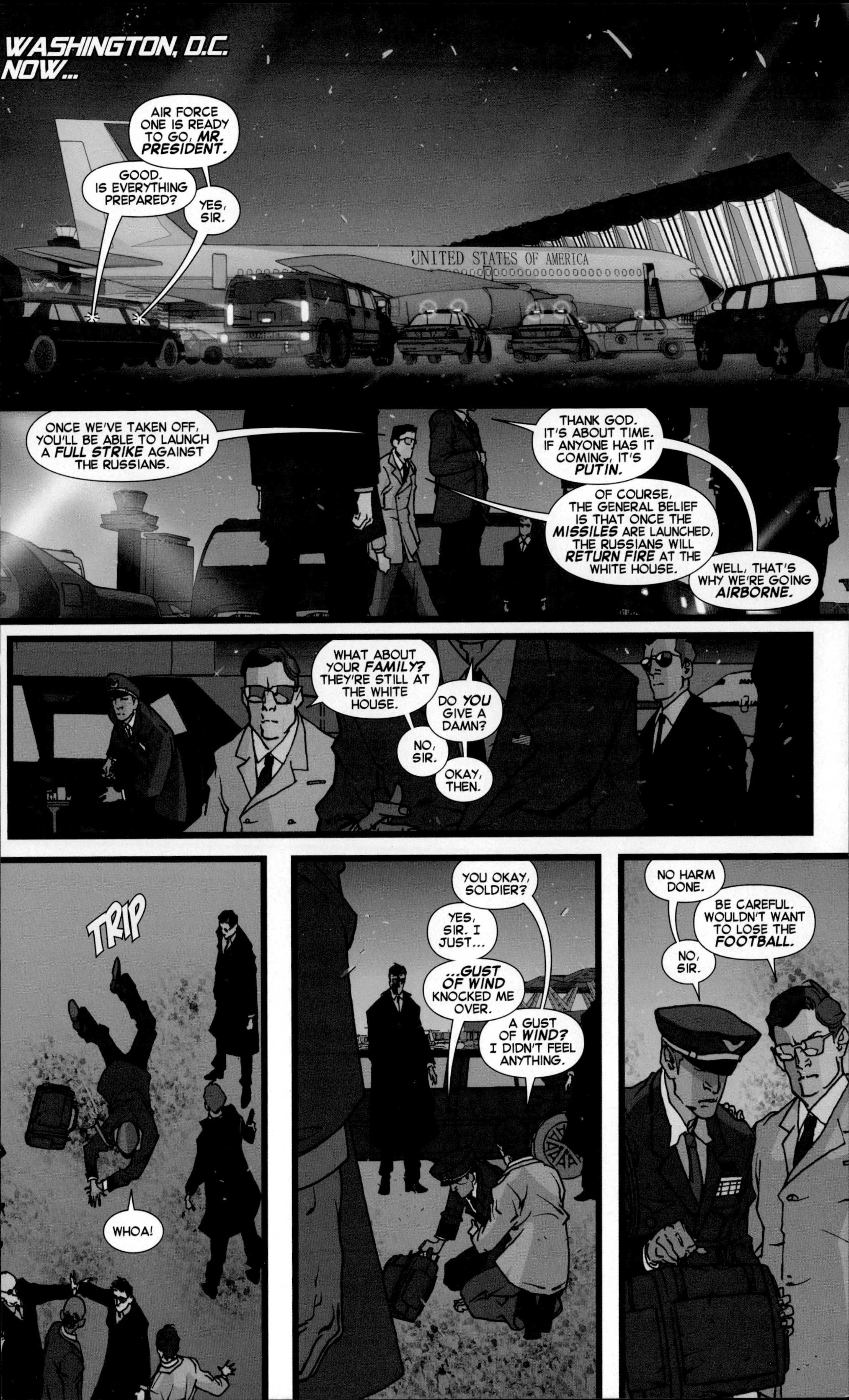
WASHINGTON, D.C. NOW...
AIR FORCE ONE IS READY TO GO, MR. PRESIDENT.
GOOD. IS EVERYTHING PREPARED?
YES, SIR.
UNITED STATES OF AMERICA
ONCE WE'VE TAKEN OFF, YOU'LL BE ABLE TO LAUNCH A FULL STRIKE AGAINST THE RUSSIANS.
THANK GOD. IT'S ABOUT TIME. IF ANYONE HAS IT COMING, IT'S PUTIN.
OF COURSE, THE GENERAL BELIEF IS THAT ONCE THE MISSILES ARE LAUNCHED, THE RUSSIANS WILL RETURN FIRE AT THE WHITE HOUSE.
WELL, THAT'S WHY WE'RE GOING AIRBORNE.
WHAT ABOUT YOUR FAMILY? THEY'RE STILL AT THE WHITE HOUSE.
DO YOU GIVE A DAMN?
NO, SIR.
OKAY, THEN.
TRIP
WHOA!
YOU OKAY, SOLDIER?
YES, SIR. I JUST...
...GUST OF WIND KNOCKED ME OVER.
A GUST OF WIND? I DIDN'T FEEL ANYTHING.
NO HARM DONE.
BE CAREFUL. WOULDN'T WANT TO LOSE THE FOOTBALL.
NO, SIR.

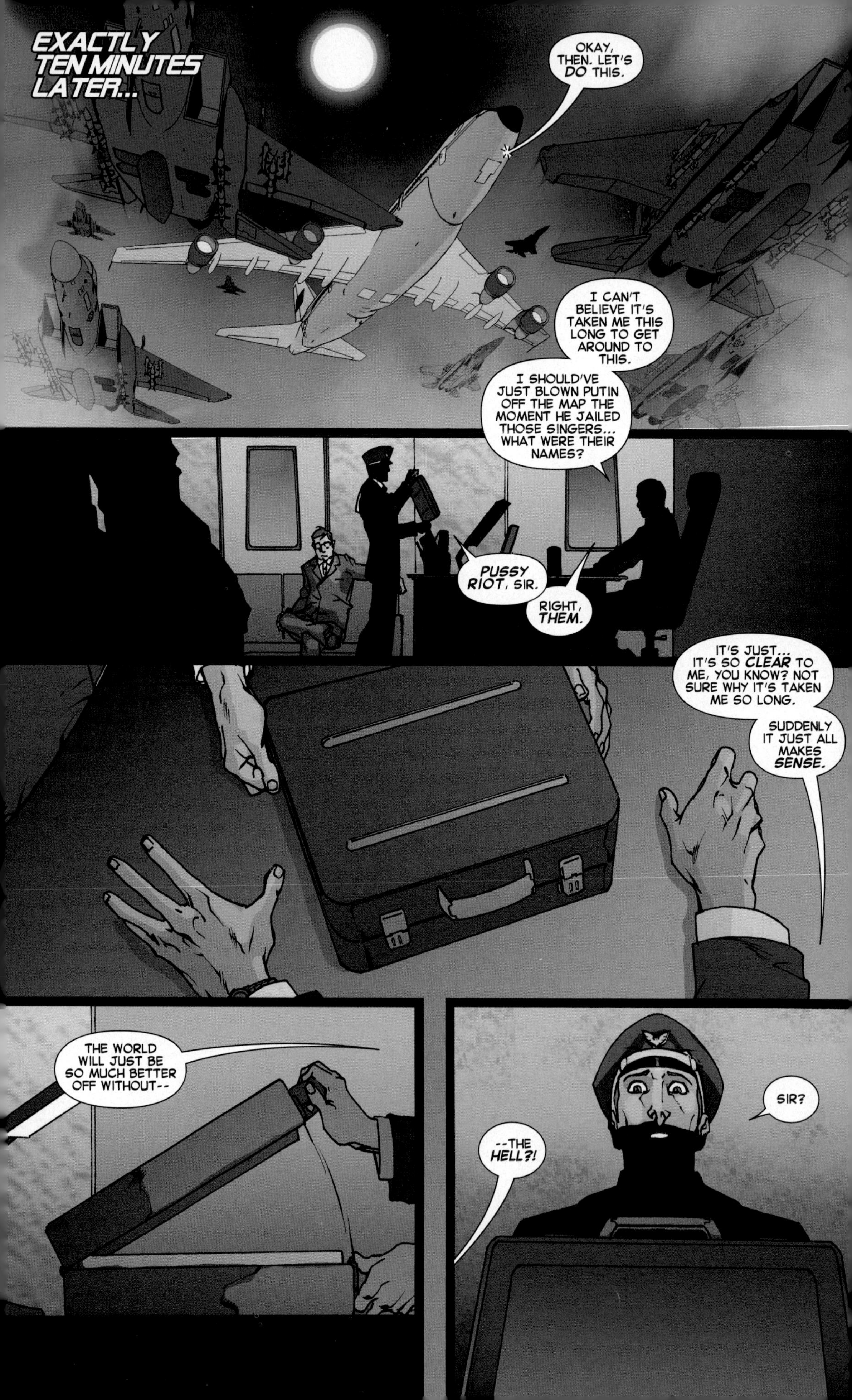
EXACTLY TEN MINUTES LATER...
OKAY, THEN. LET'S DO THIS.
I CAN'T BELIEVE IT'S TAKEN ME THIS LONG TO GET AROUND TO THIS.
I SHOULD'VE JUST BLOWN PUTIN OFF THE MAP THE MOMENT HE JAILED THOSE SINGERS... WHAT WERE THEIR NAMES?
PUSSY RIOT, SIR.
RIGHT, THEM.
IT'S JUST... IT'S SO CLEAR TO ME, YOU KNOW? NOT SURE WHY IT'S TAKEN ME SO LONG.
SUDDENLY IT JUST ALL MAKES SENSE.
THE WORLD WILL JUST BE SO MUCH BETTER OFF WITHOUT--
SIR?
--THE HELL?!

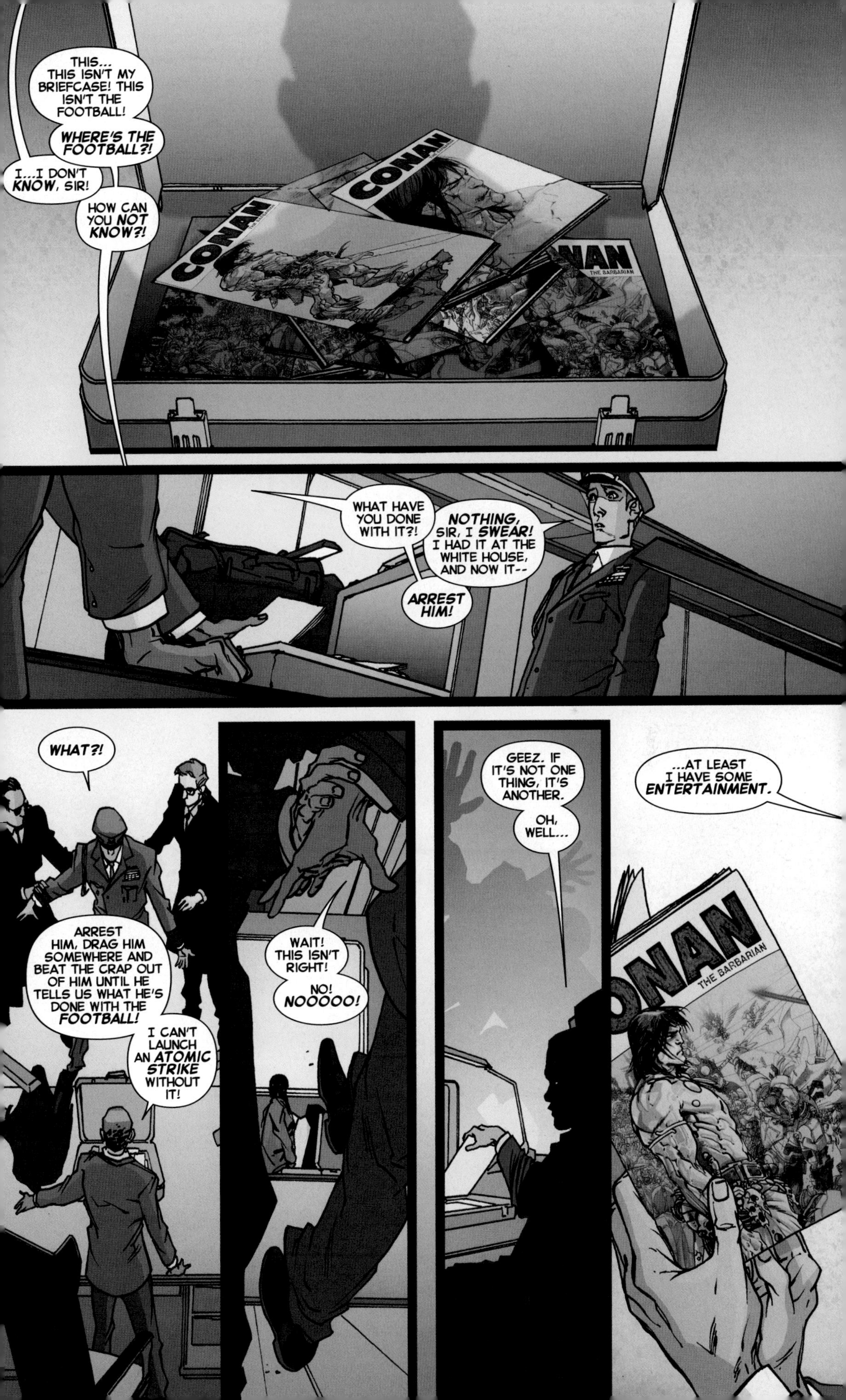
THIS... THIS ISN'T MY BRIEFCASE! THIS ISN'T THE FOOTBALL!
WHERE'S THE FOOTBALL?!
I...I DON'T KNOW, SIR!
HOW CAN YOU NOT KNOW?!
CONAN
NAN THE BARBARIAN
WHAT HAVE YOU DONE WITH IT?!
NOTHING, SIR, I SWEAR! I HAD IT AT THE WHITE HOUSE, AND NOW IT--
ARREST HIM!
WHAT?!
ARREST HIM, DRAG HIM SOMEWHERE AND BEAT THE CRAP OUT OF HIM UNTIL HE TELLS US WHAT HE'S DONE WITH THE FOOTBALL!
I CAN'T LAUNCH AN ATOMIC STRIKE WITHOUT IT!
WAIT! THIS ISN'T RIGHT!
NO! NOOOOO!
GEEZ. IF IT'S NOT ONE THING, IT'S ANOTHER.
OH, WELL...
...AT LEAST I HAVE SOME ENTERTAINMENT.
ONAN THE BARBARIAN

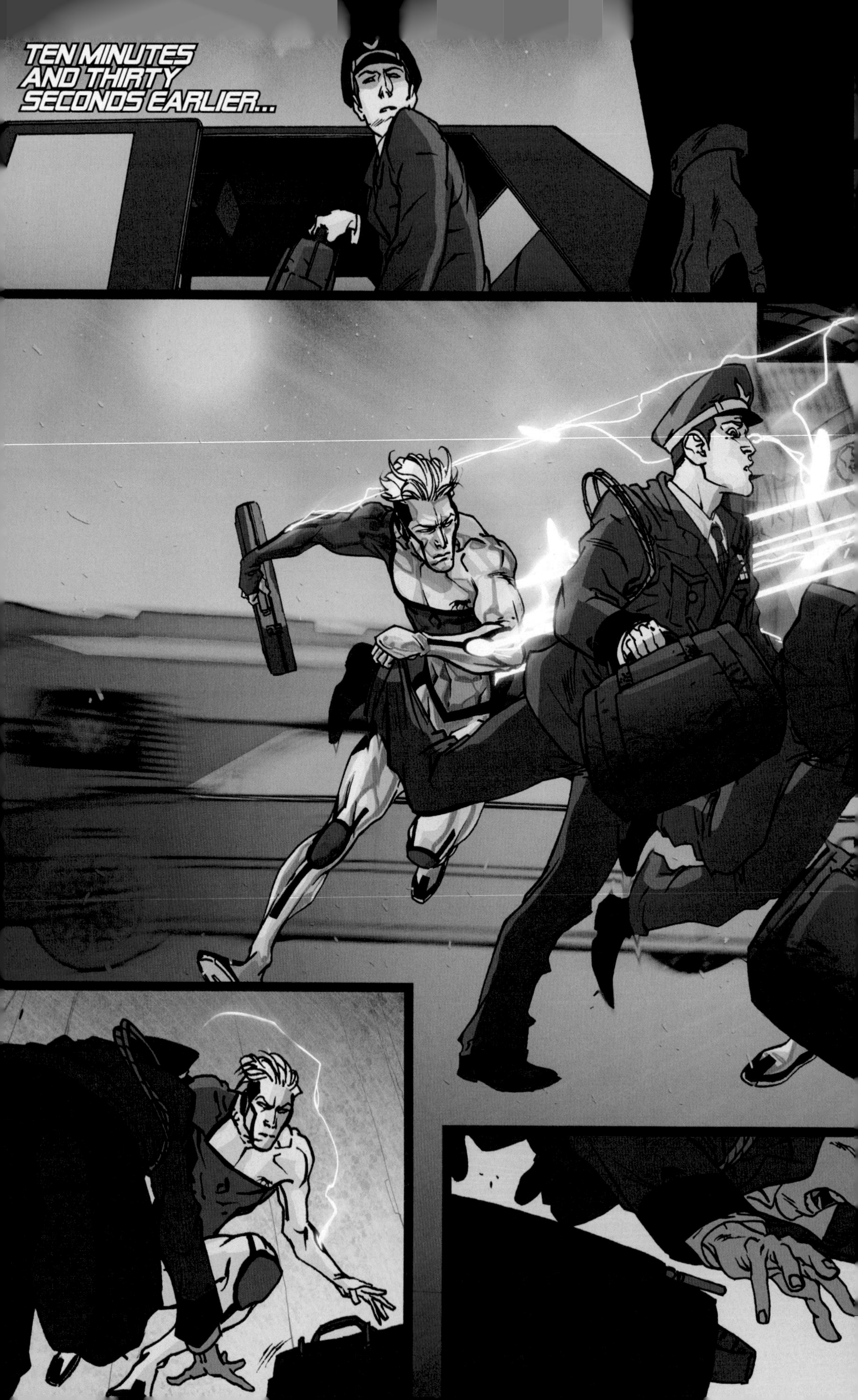
TEN MINUTES AND THIRTY SECONDS EARLIER...

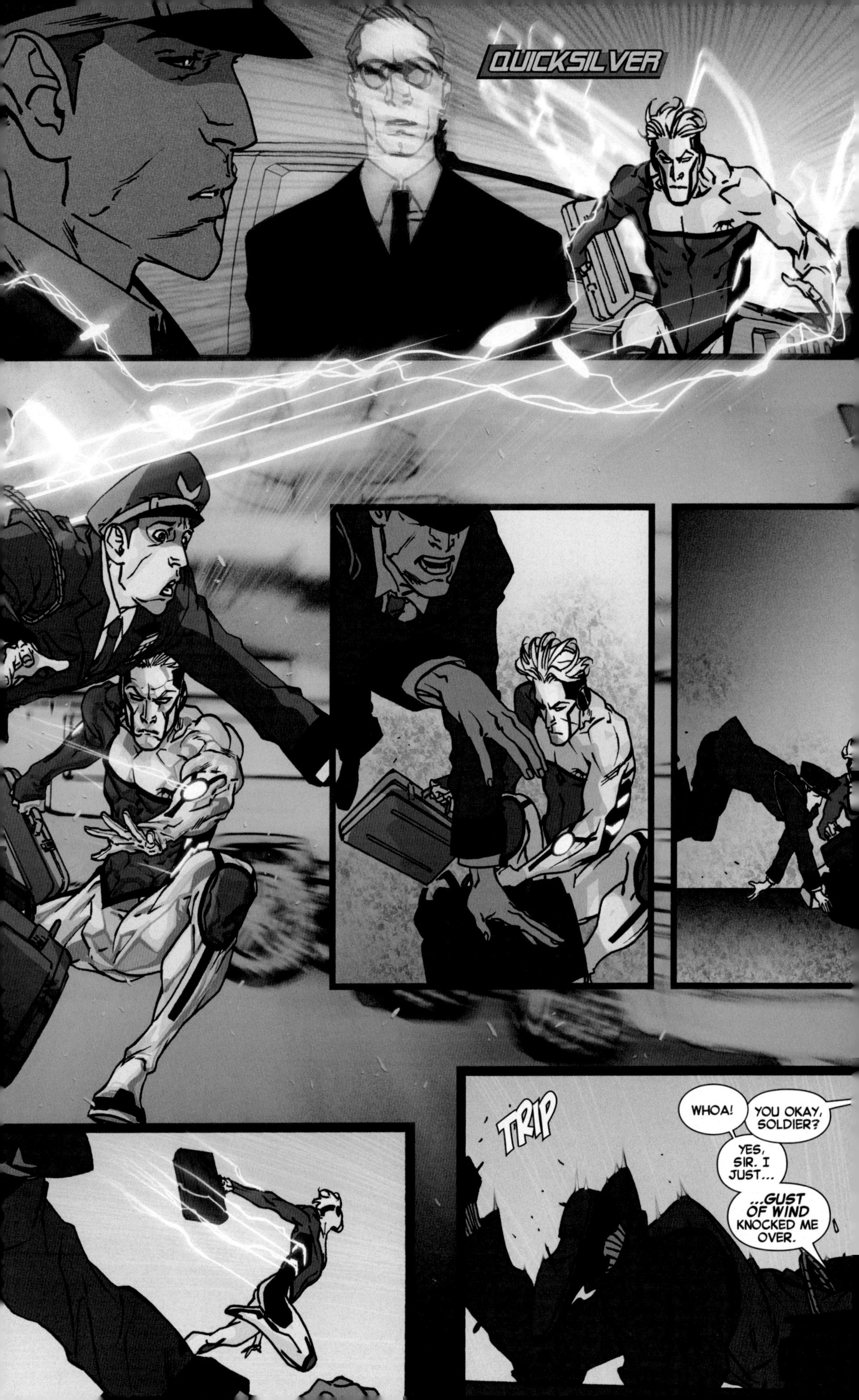
QUICKSILVER
TRIP
WHOA!
YOU OKAY, SOLDIER?
YES, SIR. I JUST...
...GUST OF WIND KNOCKED ME OVER.

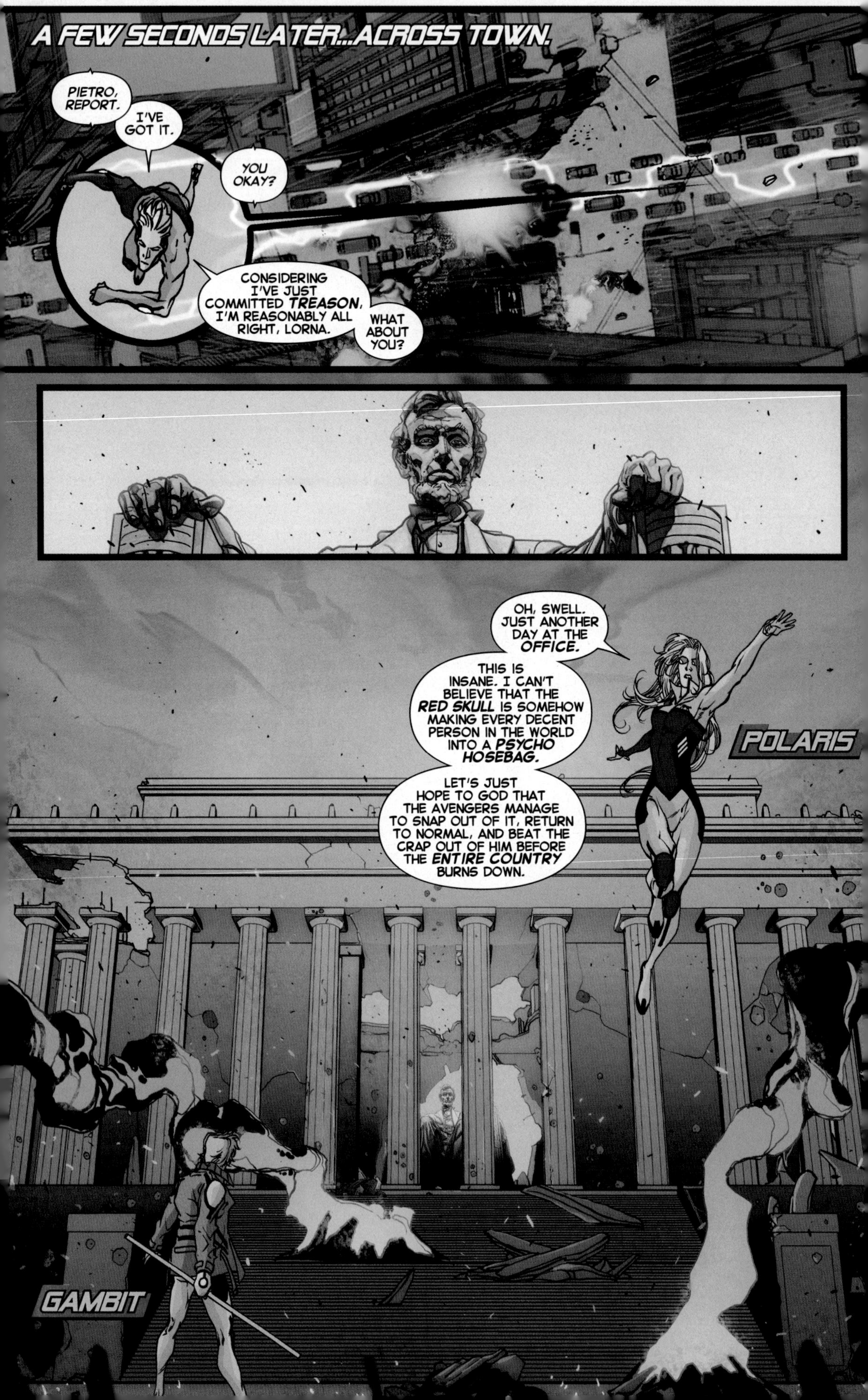
A FEW SECONDS LATER...ACROSS TOWN.
PIETRO, REPORT.
I'VE GOT IT.
YOU OKAY?
CONSIDERING I'VE JUST COMMITTED TREASON, I'M REASONABLY ALL RIGHT, LORNA.
WHAT ABOUT YOU?
OH, SWELL. JUST ANOTHER DAY AT THE OFFICE.
THIS IS INSANE. I CAN'T BELIEVE THAT THE RED SKULL IS SOMEHOW MAKING EVERY DECENT PERSON IN THE WORLD INTO A PSYCHO HOSEBAG.
LET'S JUST HOPE TO GOD THAT THE AVENGERS MANAGE TO SNAP OUT OF IT, RETURN TO NORMAL, AND BEAT THE CRAP OUT OF HIM BEFORE THE ENTIRE COUNTRY BURNS DOWN.
POLARIS
GAMBIT

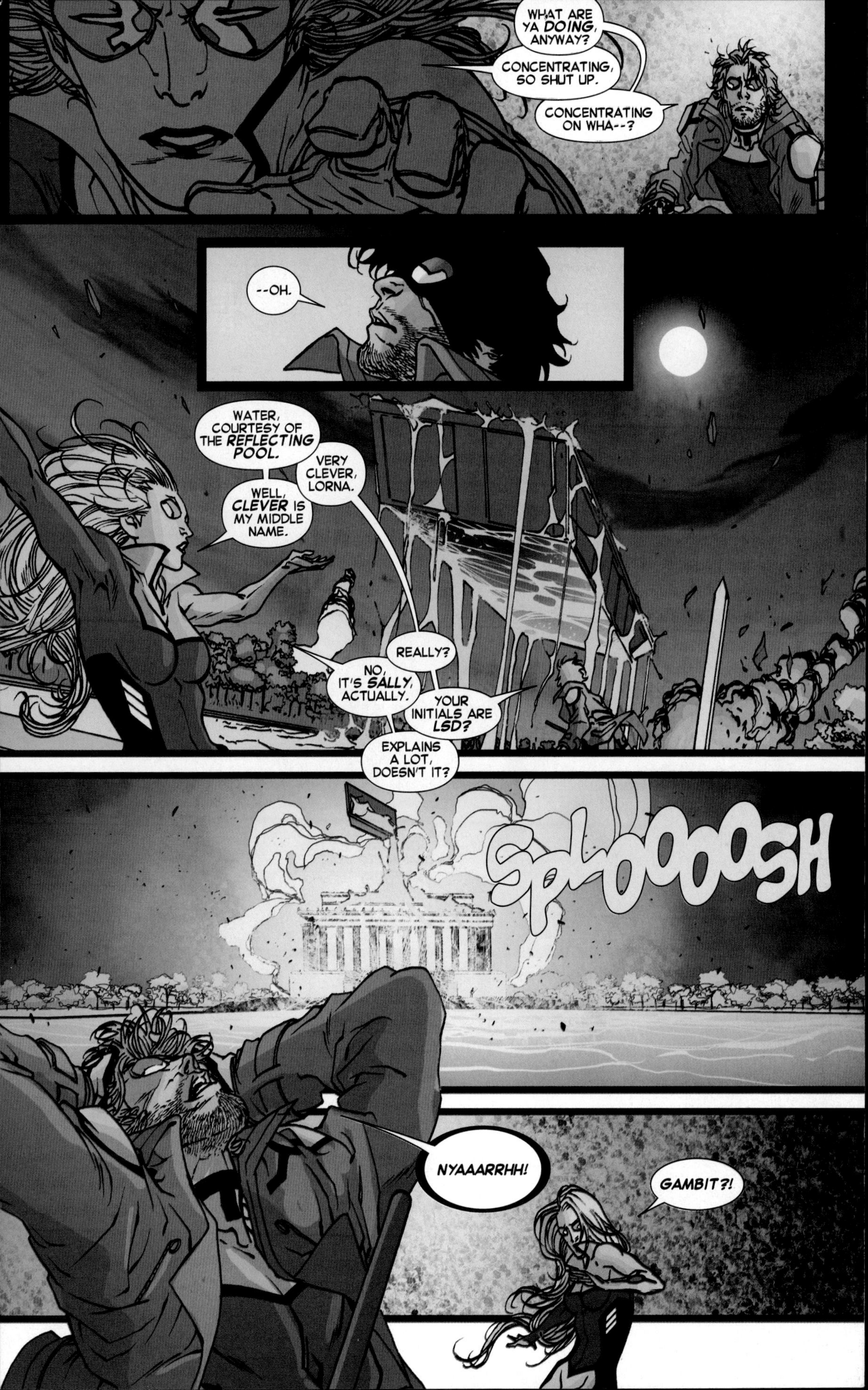
WHAT ARE YA DOING, ANYWAY?
CONCENTRATING, SO SHUT UP.
CONCENTRATING ON WHA--?
--OH.
WATER, COURTESY OF THE REFLECTING POOL.
VERY CLEVER, LORNA.
WELL, CLEVER IS MY MIDDLE NAME.
REALLY?
NO, IT'S SALLY, ACTUALLY.
YOUR INITIALS ARE LSD?
EXPLAINS A LOT, DOESN'T IT?
SPLOOOOOSH
NYAAARRHH!
GAMBIT?!

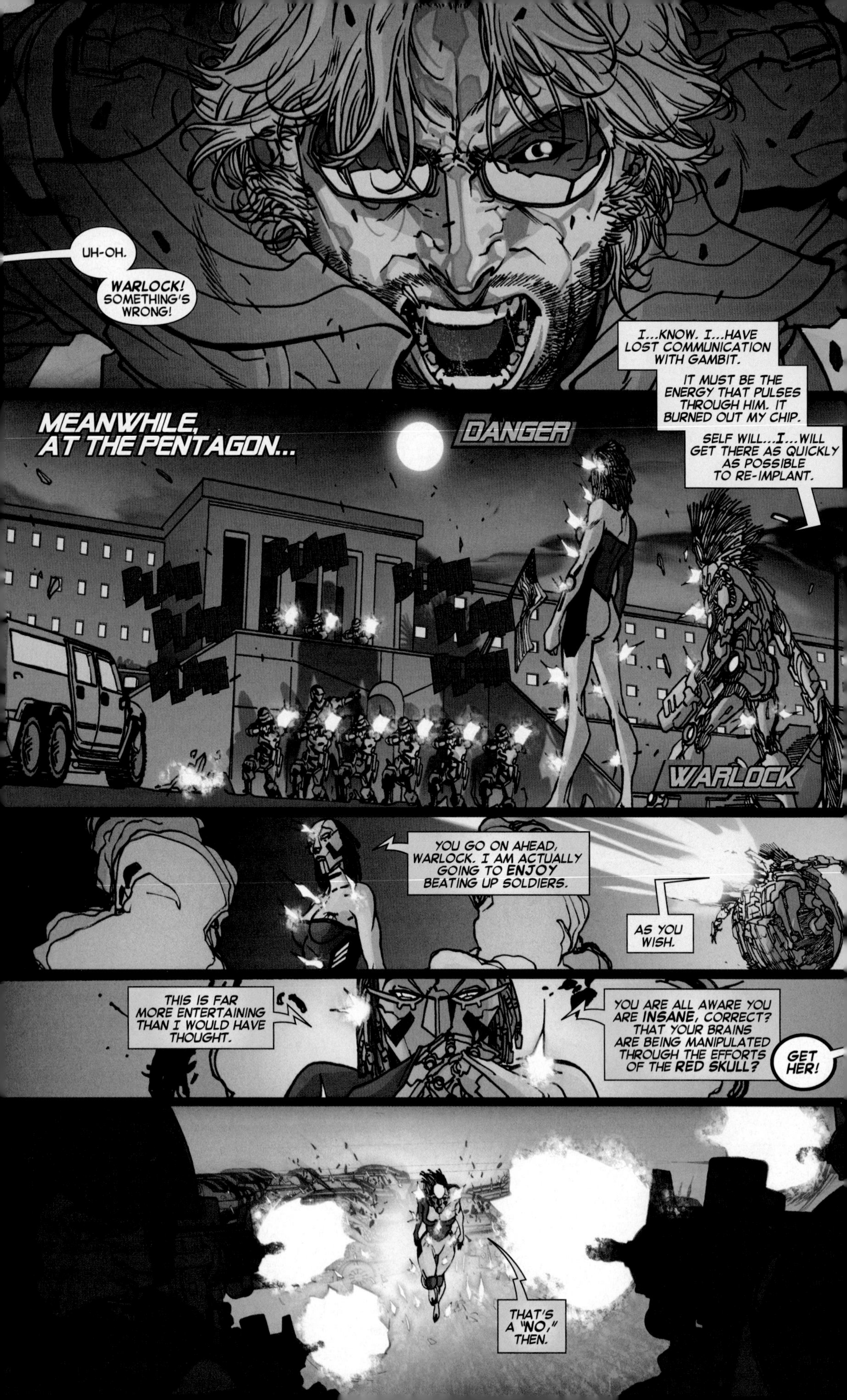
UH-OH.
WARLOCK! SOMETHING'S WRONG!
I...KNOW. I...HAVE LOST COMMUNICATION WITH GAMBIT.
IT MUST BE THE ENERGY THAT PULSES THROUGH HIM. IT BURNED OUT MY CHIP.
SELF WILL...I...WILL GET THERE AS QUICKLY AS POSSIBLE TO RE-IMPLANT.
MEANWHILE, AT THE PENTAGON...
DANGER
WARLOCK
YOU GO ON AHEAD, WARLOCK. I AM ACTUALLY GOING TO ENJOY BEATING UP SOLDIERS.
AS YOU WISH.
THIS IS FAR MORE ENTERTAINING THAN I WOULD HAVE THOUGHT.
YOU ARE ALL AWARE YOU ARE INSANE, CORRECT? THAT YOUR BRAINS ARE BEING MANIPULATED THROUGH THE EFFORTS OF THE RED SKULL?
GET HER!
THAT'S A "NO," THEN.

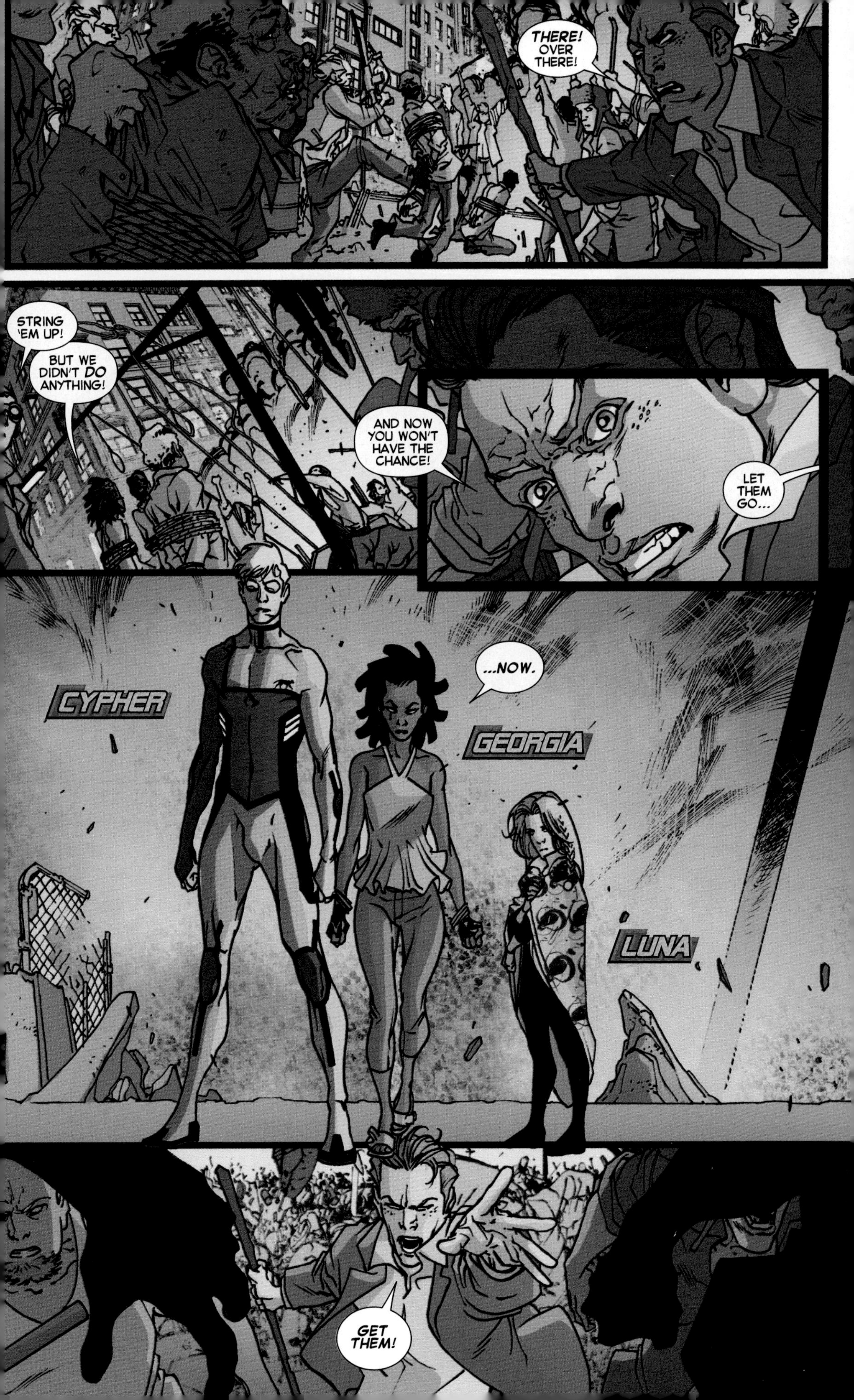
THERE! OVER THERE!
STRING 'EM UP!
BUT WE DIDN'T DO ANYTHING!
AND NOW YOU WON'T HAVE THE CHANCE!
LET THEM GO...
...NOW.
CYPHER
GEORGIA
LUNA
GET THEM!

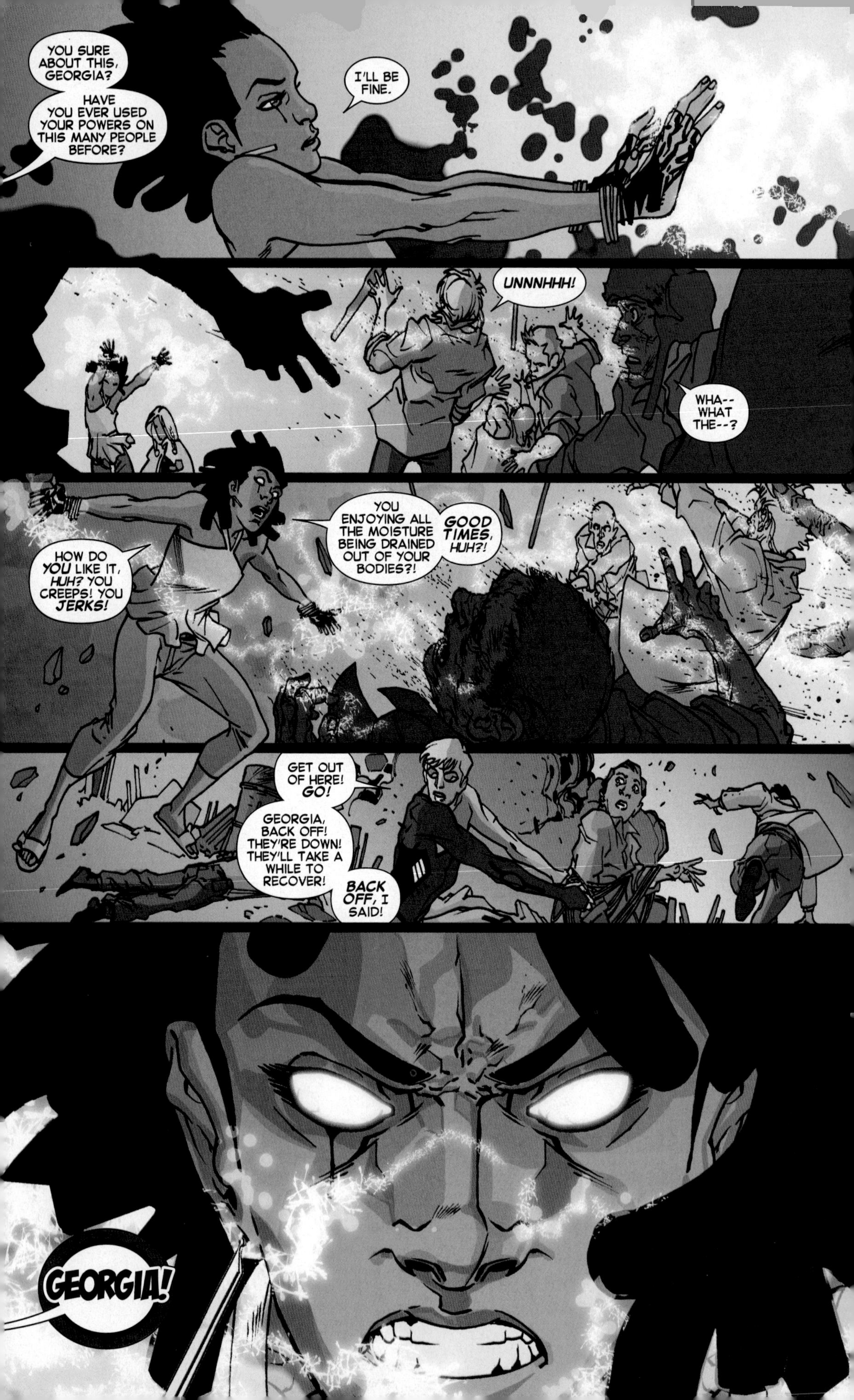
YOU SURE ABOUT THIS, GEORGIA?
HAVE YOU EVER USED YOUR POWERS ON THIS MANY PEOPLE BEFORE?
I'LL BE FINE.
UNNNHHH!
WHA-- WHAT THE--?
YOU ENJOYING ALL THE MOISTURE BEING DRAINED OUT OF YOUR BODIES?!
GOOD TIMES, HUH?!
HOW DO YOU LIKE IT, HUH? YOU CREEPS! YOU JERKS!
GET OUT OF HERE! GO!
GEORGIA, BACK OFF! THEY'RE DOWN! THEY'LL TAKE A WHILE TO RECOVER!
BACK OFF, I SAID!
GEORGIA!

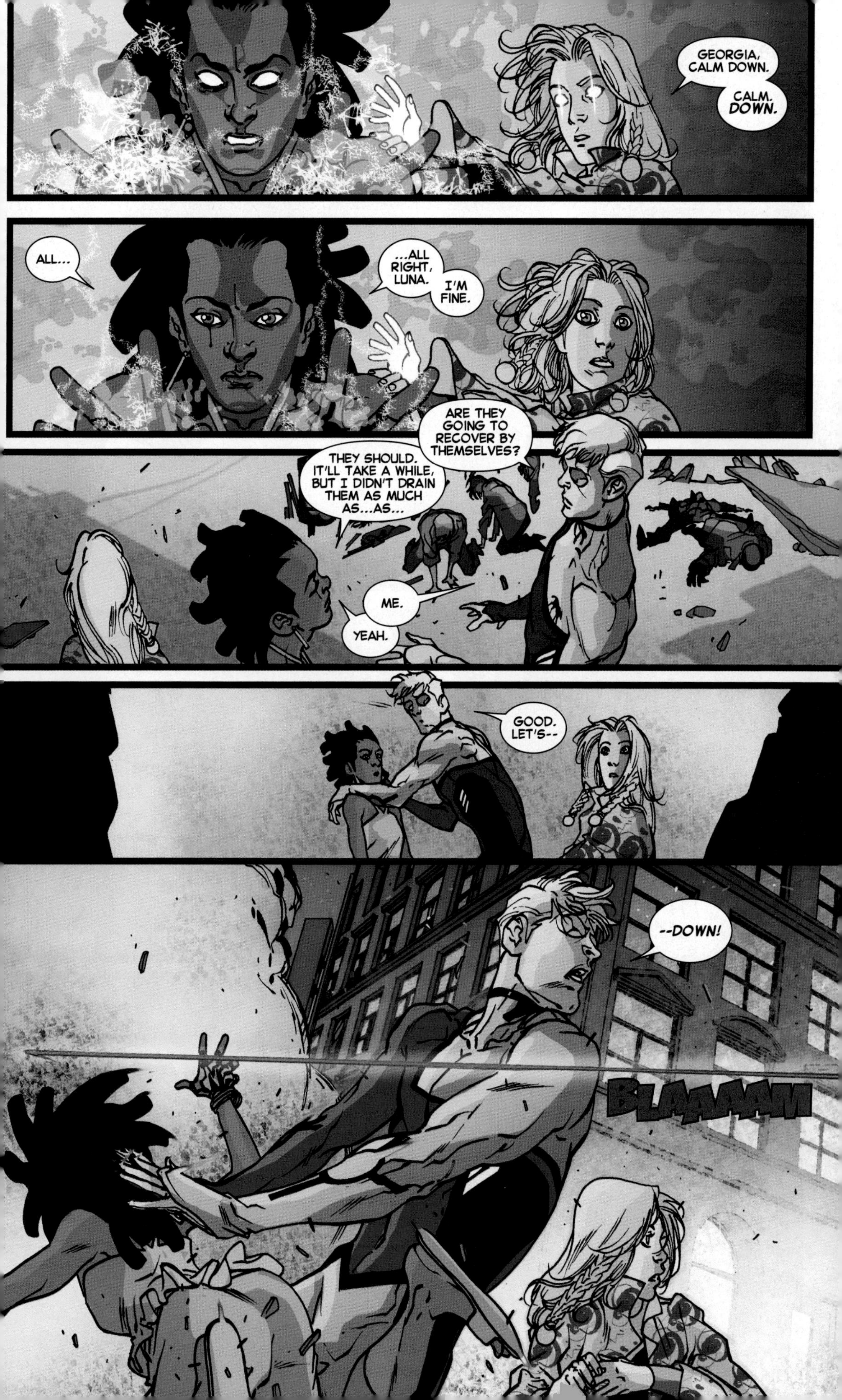

GEORGIA, CALM DOWN.
CALM. DOWN.
ALL...
...ALL RIGHT, LUNA.
I'M FINE.
ARE THEY GOING TO RECOVER BY THEMSELVES?
THEY SHOULD. IT'LL TAKE A WHILE, BUT I DIDN'T DRAIN THEM AS MUCH AS...AS...
ME.
YEAH.
GOOD. LET'S--
--DOWN!
BLAAAAM

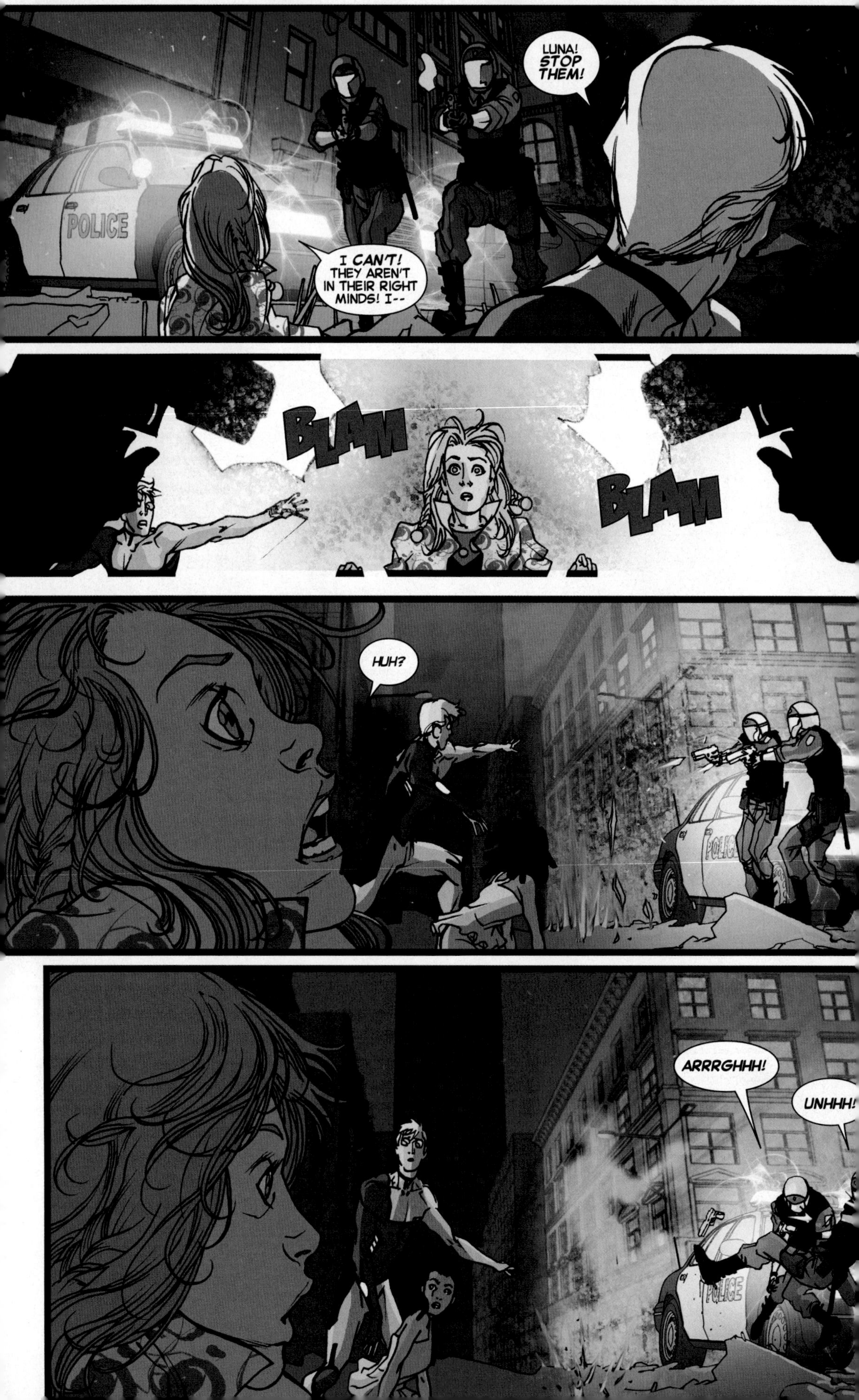
LUNA! STOP THEM!
I CAN'T! THEY AREN'T IN THEIR RIGHT MINDS! I--
POLICE
BLAM
BLAM
HUH?
ARRRGHHH!
UNHHH!

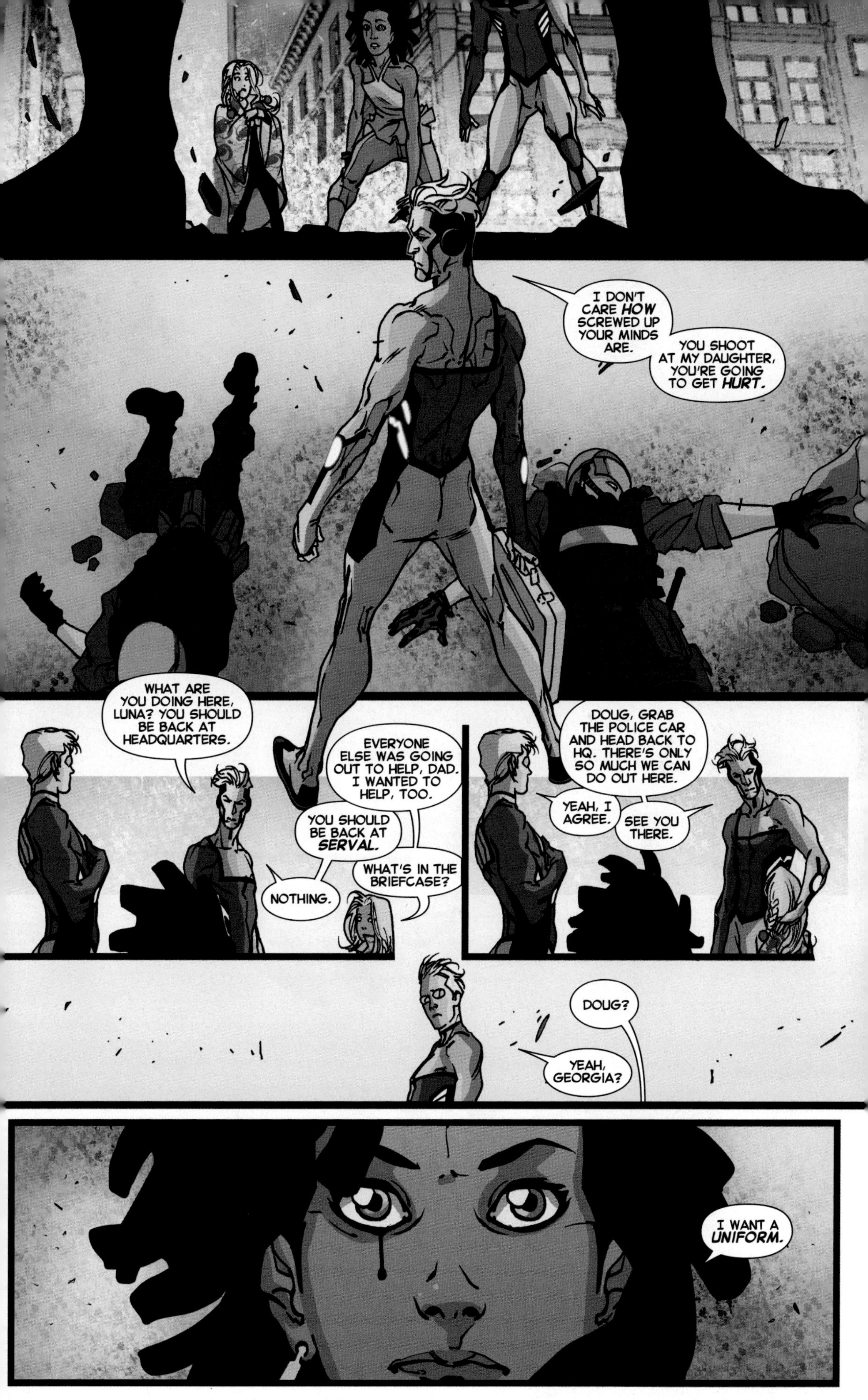
I DON'T CARE HOW SCREWED UP YOUR MINDS ARE.
YOU SHOOT AT MY DAUGHTER, YOU'RE GOING TO GET HURT.
WHAT ARE YOU DOING HERE, LUNA? YOU SHOULD BE BACK AT HEADQUARTERS.
EVERYONE ELSE WAS GOING OUT TO HELP, DAD. I WANTED TO HELP, TOO.
YOU SHOULD BE BACK AT SERVAL.
WHAT'S IN THE BRIEFCASE?
NOTHING.
DOUG, GRAB THE POLICE CAR AND HEAD BACK TO HQ. THERE'S ONLY SO MUCH WE CAN DO OUT HERE.
YEAH, I AGREE.
SEE YOU THERE.
DOUG?
YEAH, GEORGIA?
I WANT A UNIFORM.

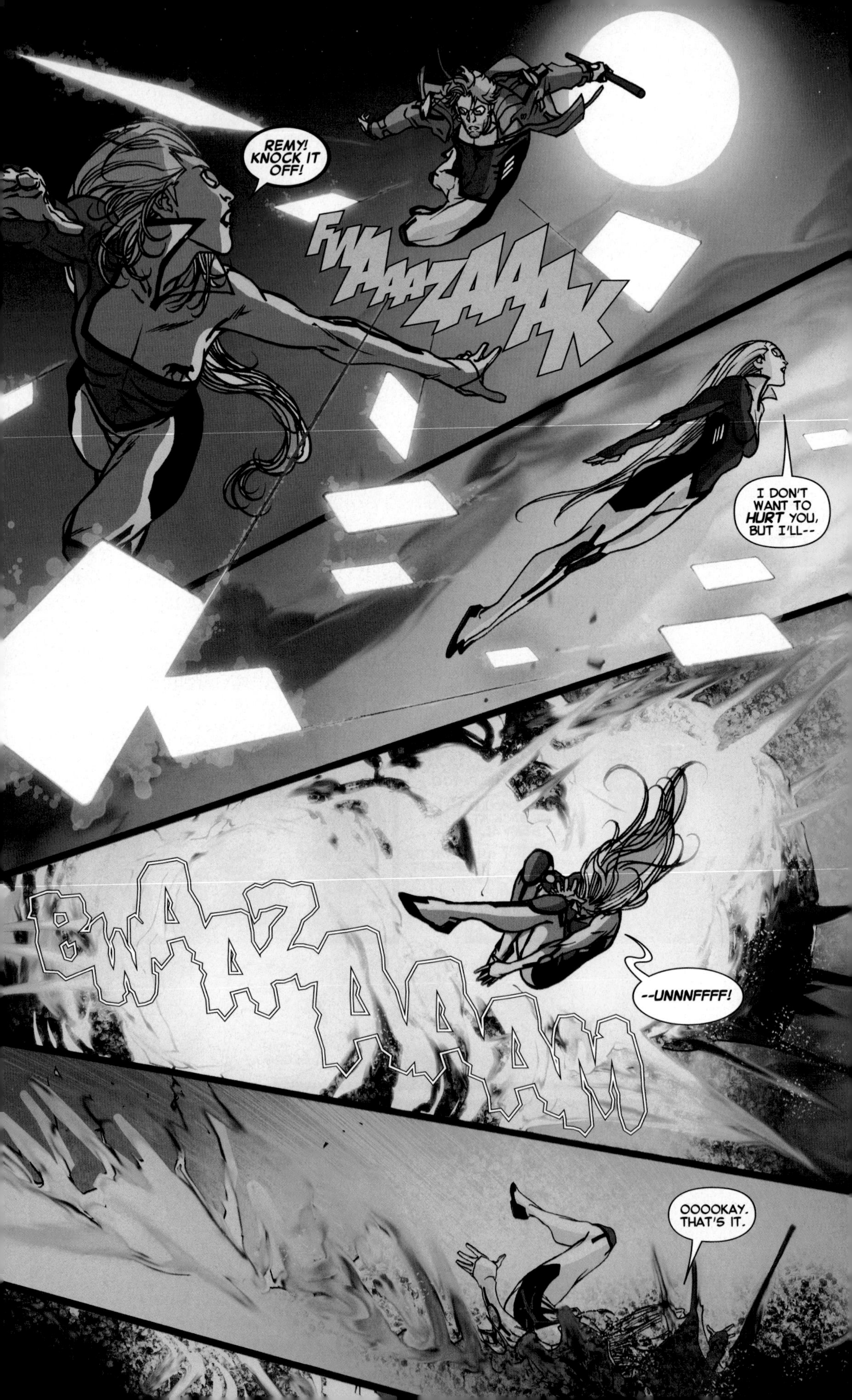
REMY! KNOCK IT OFF!
FWAAAZAAAK
I DON'T WANT TO **HURT** YOU, BUT I'LL--
BWAZAAAM
--UNNNFFFF!
OOOOKAY. THAT'S IT.

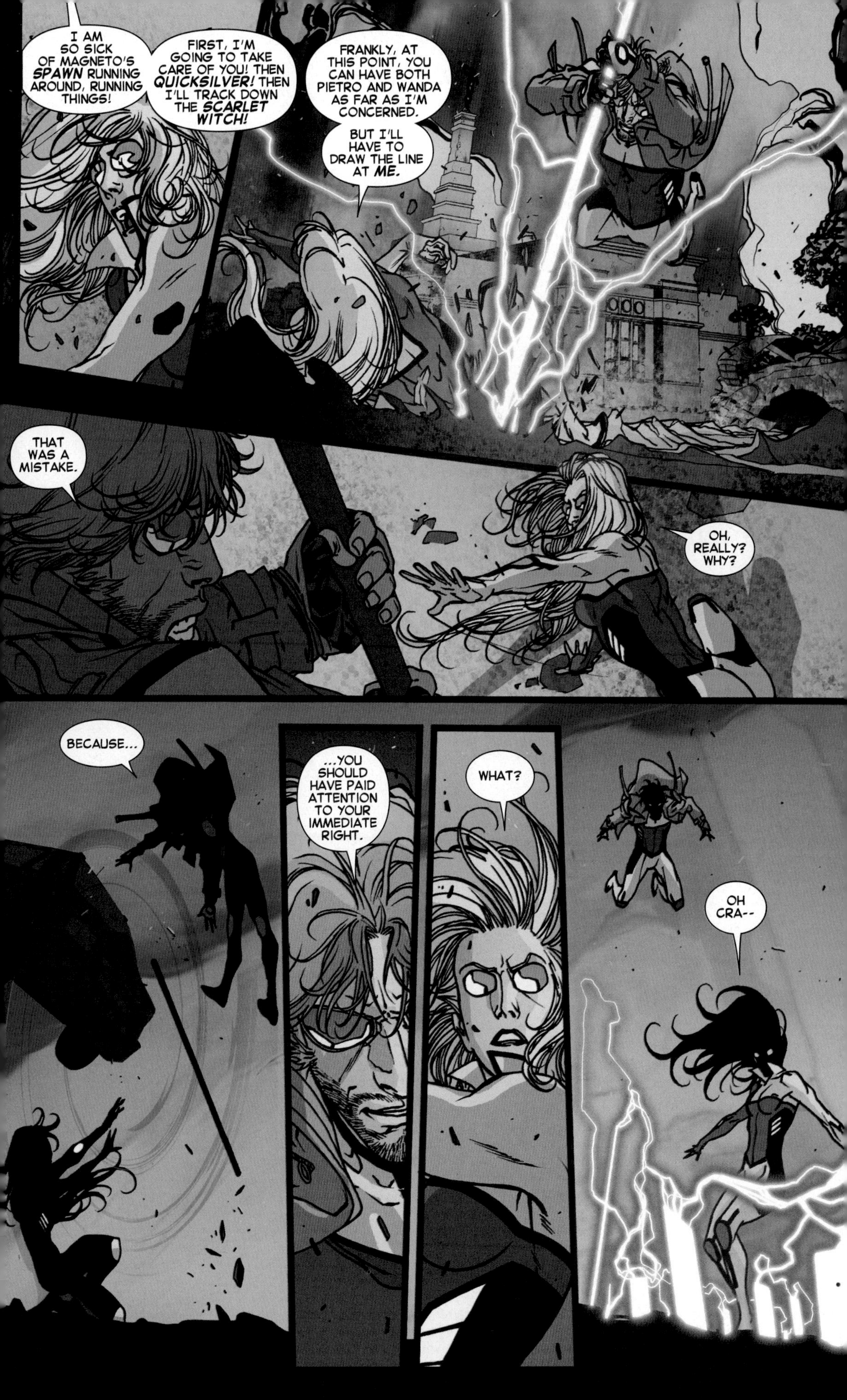

I AM SO SICK OF MAGNETO'S SPAWN RUNNING AROUND, RUNNING THINGS!
FIRST, I'M GOING TO TAKE CARE OF YOU! THEN QUICKSILVER! THEN I'LL TRACK DOWN THE SCARLET WITCH!
FRANKLY, AT THIS POINT, YOU CAN HAVE BOTH PIETRO AND WANDA AS FAR AS I'M CONCERNED.
BUT I'LL HAVE TO DRAW THE LINE AT ME.
THAT WAS A MISTAKE.
OH, REALLY? WHY?
BECAUSE...
...YOU SHOULD HAVE PAID ATTENTION TO YOUR IMMEDIATE RIGHT.
WHAT?
OH CRA--

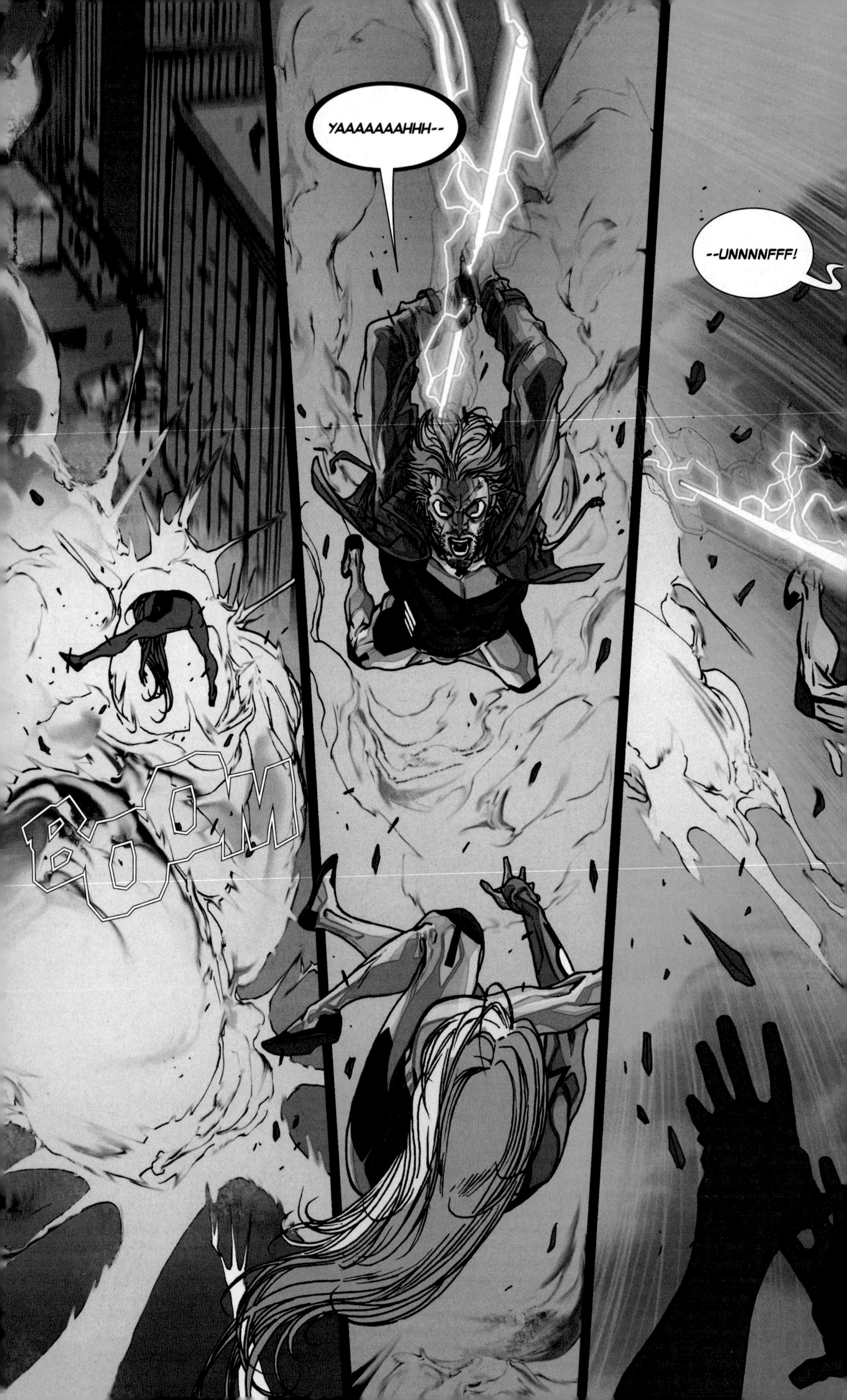
BOOM
YAAAAAAAAHHH--
--UNNNNFFF!

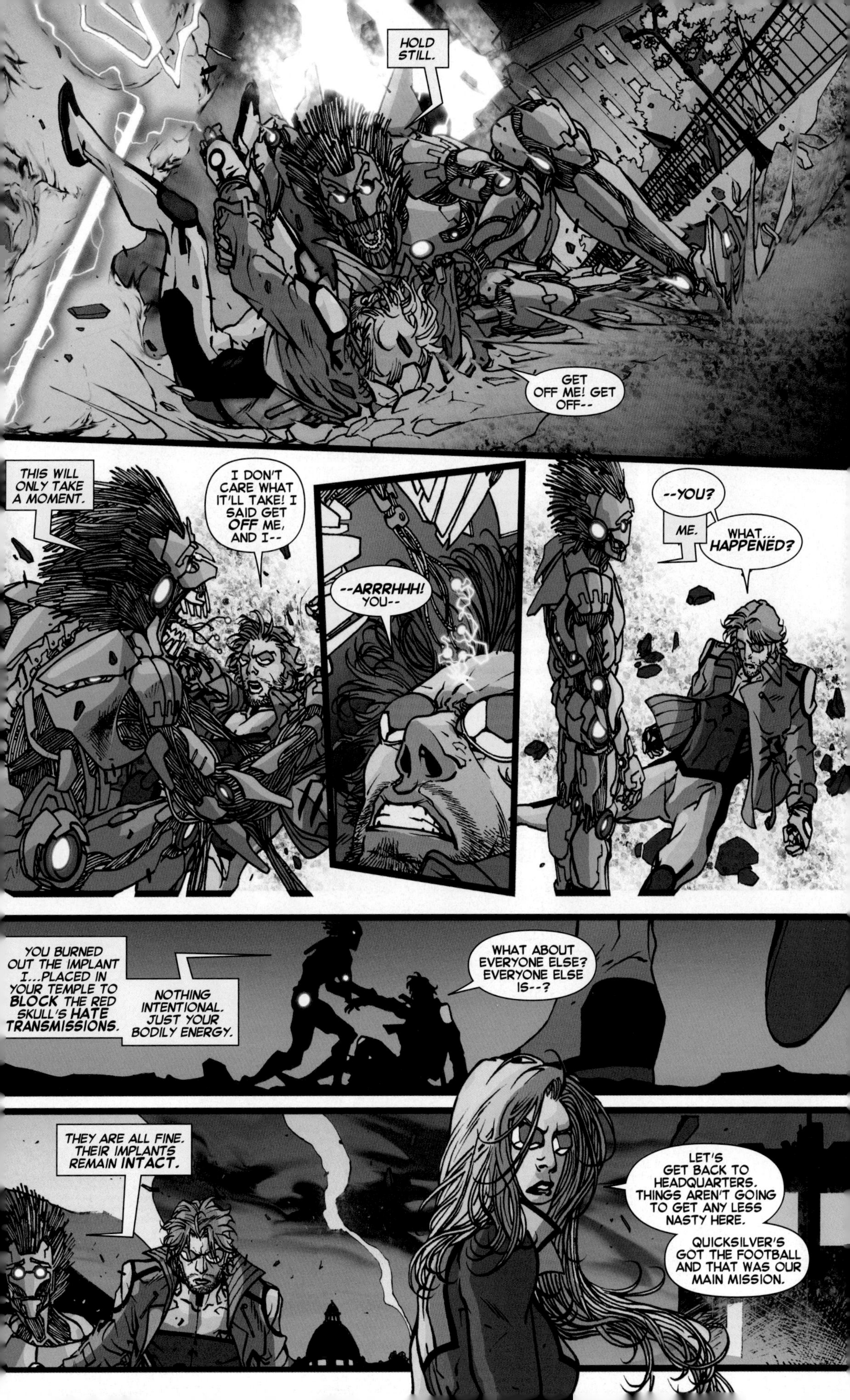
HOLD STILL.
GET OFF ME! GET OFF--
THIS WILL ONLY TAKE A MOMENT.
I DON'T CARE WHAT IT'LL TAKE! I SAID GET OFF ME, AND I--
--ARRRHHH! YOU--
--YOU?
ME.
WHAT... HAPPENED?
YOU BURNED OUT THE IMPLANT I...PLACED IN YOUR TEMPLE TO BLOCK THE RED SKULL'S HATE TRANSMISSIONS.
NOTHING INTENTIONAL. JUST YOUR BODILY ENERGY.
WHAT ABOUT EVERYONE ELSE? EVERYONE ELSE IS--?
THEY ARE ALL FINE. THEIR IMPLANTS REMAIN INTACT.
LET'S GET BACK TO HEADQUARTERS. THINGS AREN'T GOING TO GET ANY LESS NASTY HERE.
QUICKSILVER'S GOT THE FOOTBALL AND THAT WAS OUR MAIN MISSION.

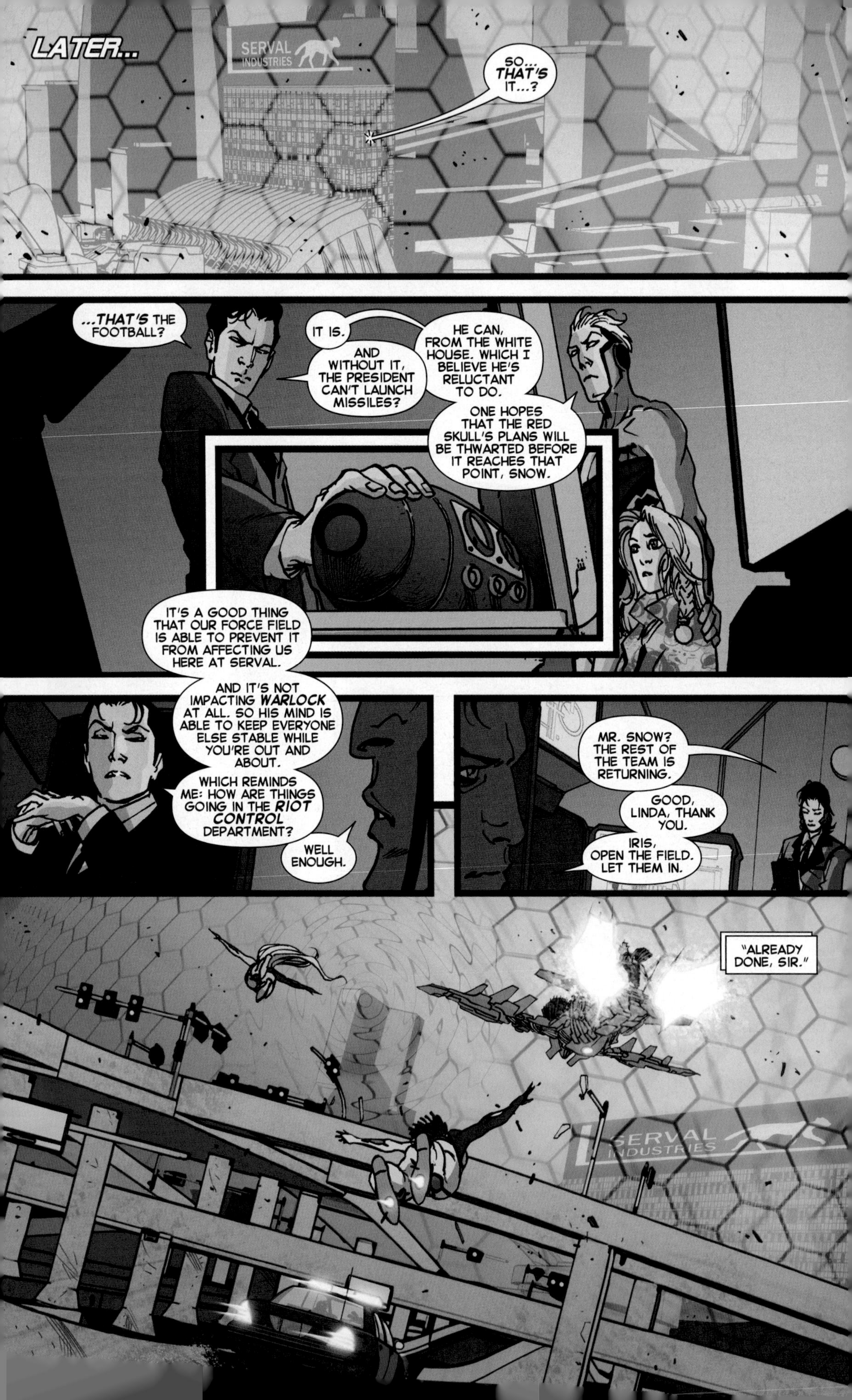
LATER...
SERVAL INDUSTRIES
SO... THAT'S IT...?
...THAT'S THE FOOTBALL?
IT IS.
AND WITHOUT IT, THE PRESIDENT CAN'T LAUNCH MISSILES?
HE CAN, FROM THE WHITE HOUSE. WHICH I BELIEVE HE'S RELUCTANT TO DO.
ONE HOPES THAT THE RED SKULL'S PLANS WILL BE THWARTED BEFORE IT REACHES THAT POINT, SNOW.
IT'S A GOOD THING THAT OUR FORCE FIELD IS ABLE TO PREVENT IT FROM AFFECTING US HERE AT SERVAL.
AND IT'S NOT IMPACTING WARLOCK AT ALL. SO HIS MIND IS ABLE TO KEEP EVERYONE ELSE STABLE WHILE YOU'RE OUT AND ABOUT.
WHICH REMINDS ME: HOW ARE THINGS GOING IN THE RIOT CONTROL DEPARTMENT?
WELL ENOUGH.
MR. SNOW? THE REST OF THE TEAM IS RETURNING.
GOOD, LINDA, THANK YOU.
IRIS, OPEN THE FIELD. LET THEM IN.
"ALREADY DONE, SIR."
SERVAL INDUSTRIES

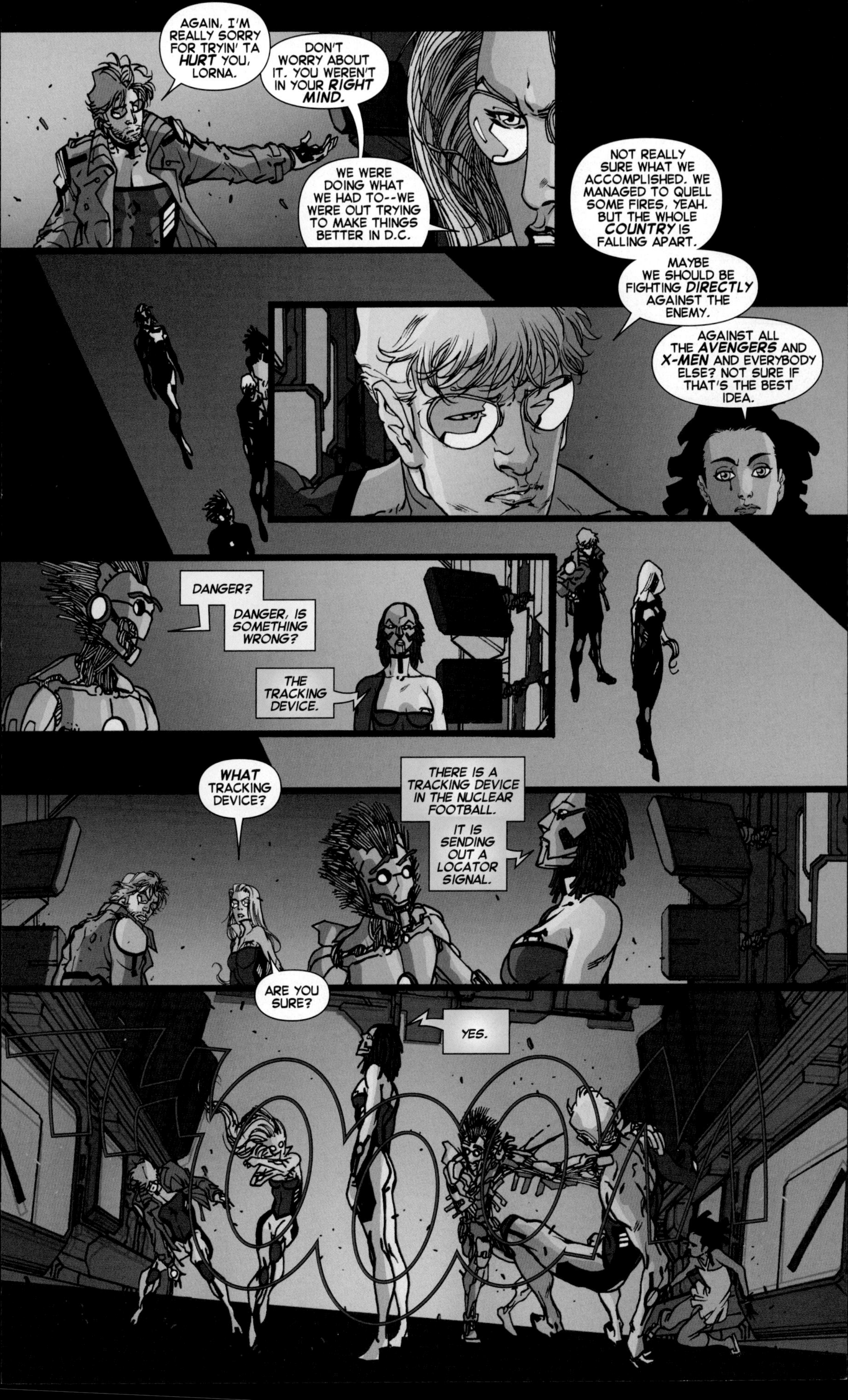
AGAIN, I'M REALLY SORRY FOR TRYIN' TA HURT YOU, LORNA.
DON'T WORRY ABOUT IT. YOU WEREN'T IN YOUR RIGHT MIND.
WE WERE DOING WHAT WE HAD TO--WE WERE OUT TRYING TO MAKE THINGS BETTER IN D.C.
NOT REALLY SURE WHAT WE ACCOMPLISHED. WE MANAGED TO QUELL SOME FIRES, YEAH. BUT THE WHOLE COUNTRY IS FALLING APART.
MAYBE WE SHOULD BE FIGHTING DIRECTLY AGAINST THE ENEMY.
AGAINST ALL THE AVENGERS AND X-MEN AND EVERYBODY ELSE? NOT SURE IF THAT'S THE BEST IDEA.
DANGER?
DANGER, IS SOMETHING WRONG?
THE TRACKING DEVICE.
WHAT TRACKING DEVICE?
THERE IS A TRACKING DEVICE IN THE NUCLEAR FOOTBALL.
IT IS SENDING OUT A LOCATOR SIGNAL.
ARE YOU SURE?
YES.

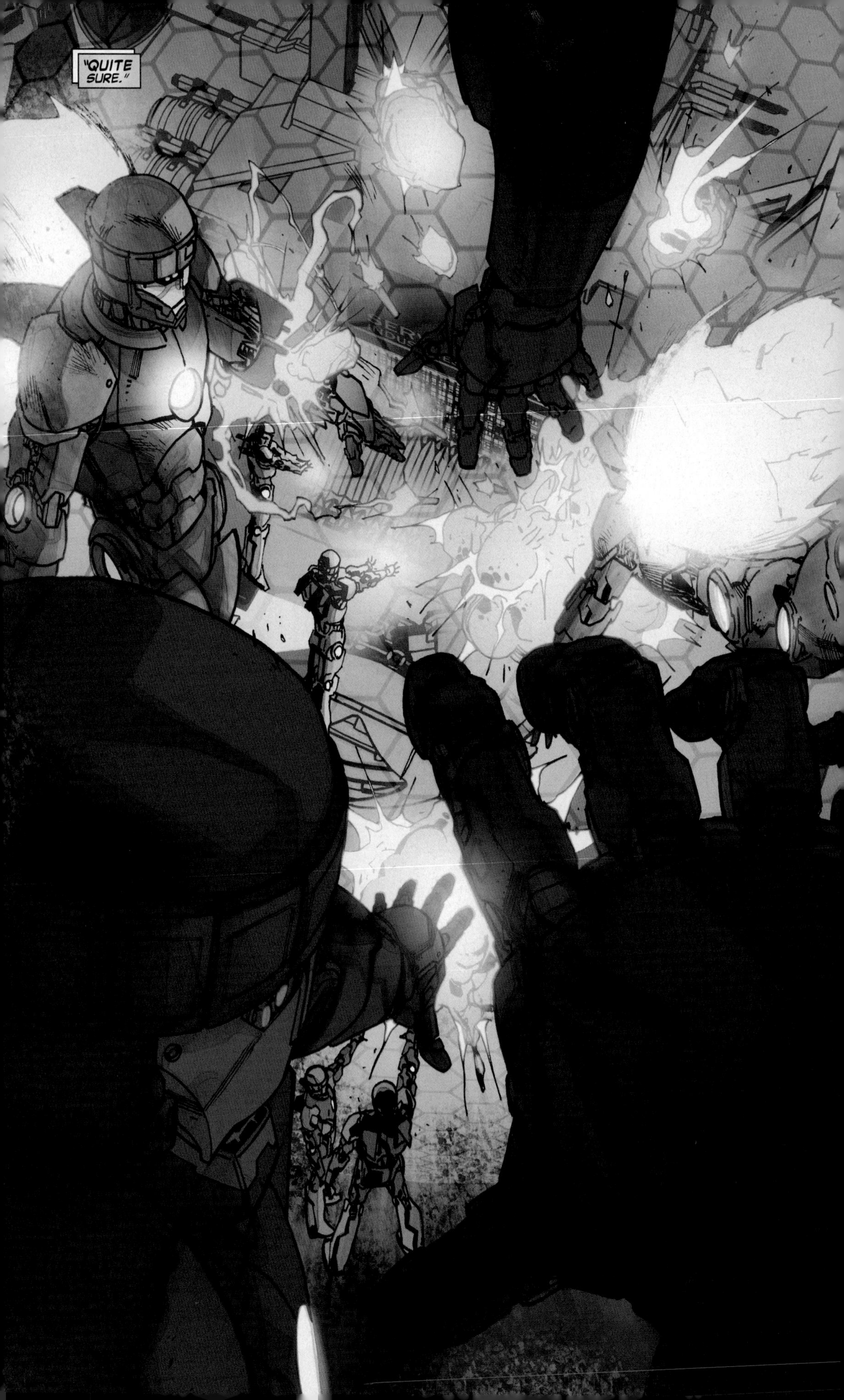
"QUITE SURE."

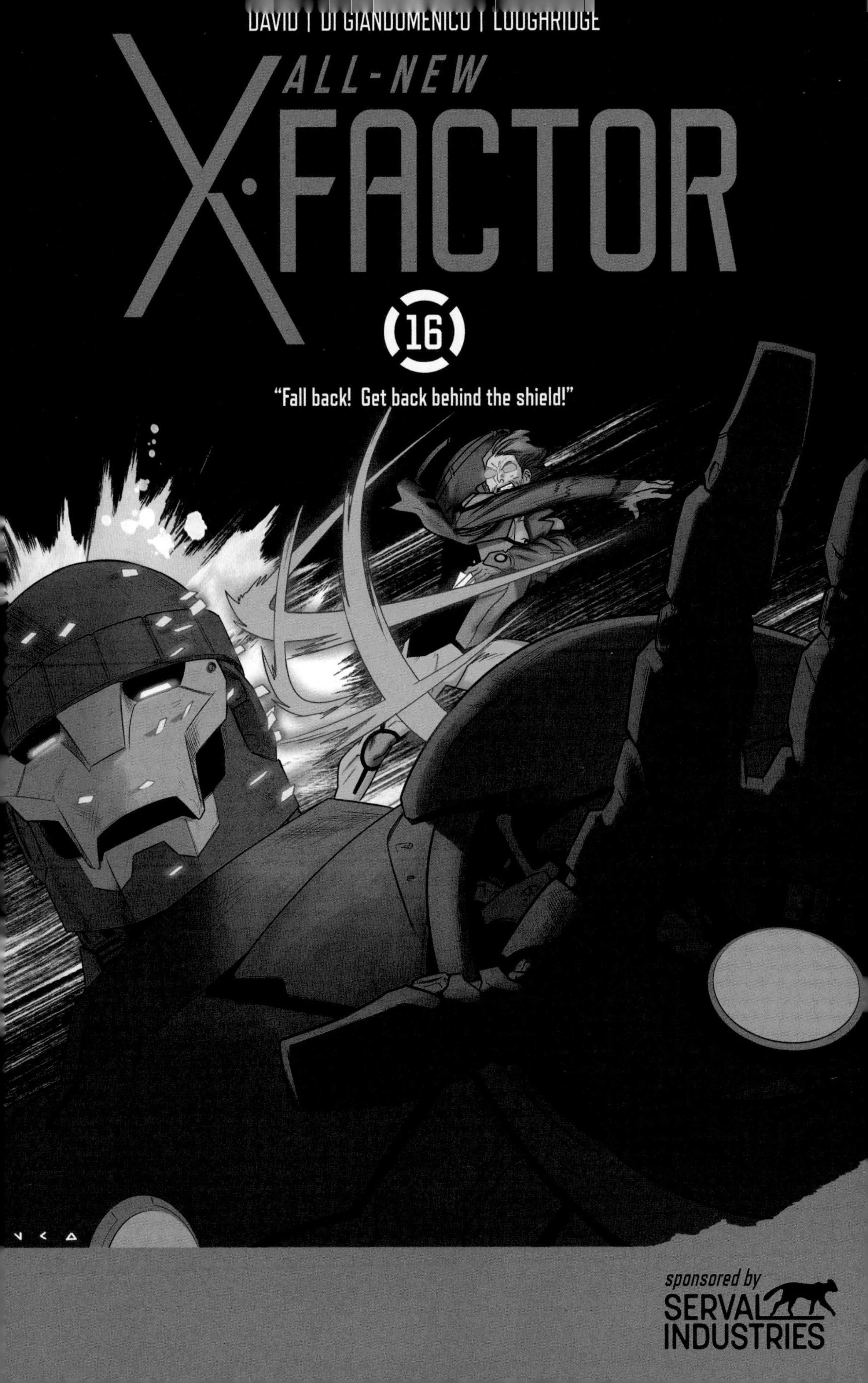
DAVID | DI GIANDOMENICO | LOUGHRIDGE
ALL-NEW
X-FACTOR
16
"Fall back! Get back behind the shield!"
sponsored by
SERVAL
INDUSTRIES

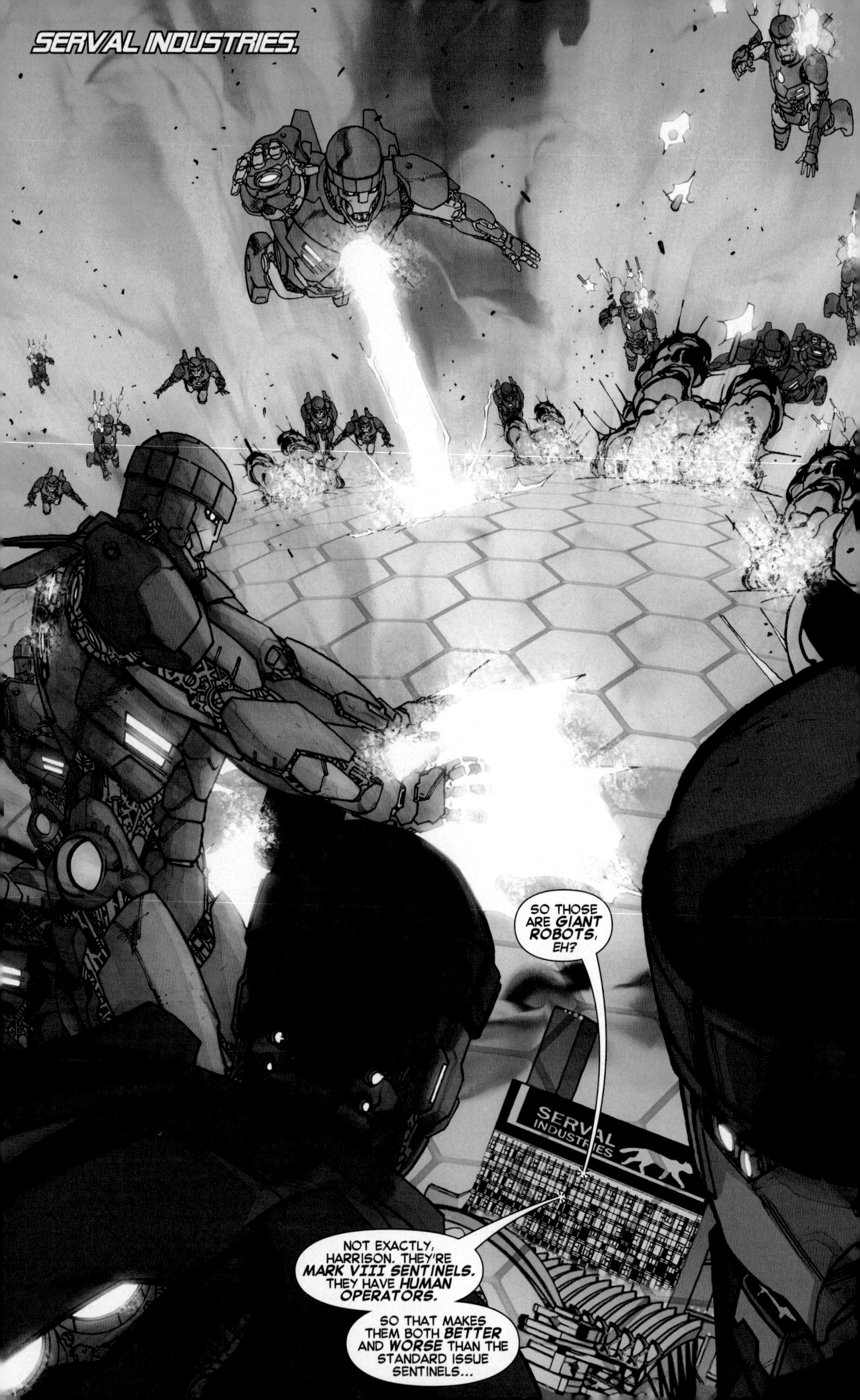
SERVAL INDUSTRIES.
SO THOSE ARE GIANT ROBOTS, EH?
NOT EXACTLY, HARRISON. THEY'RE MARK VIII SENTINELS. THEY HAVE HUMAN OPERATORS.
SO THAT MAKES THEM BOTH BETTER AND WORSE THAN THE STANDARD ISSUE SENTINELS...
SERVAL INDUSTRIES

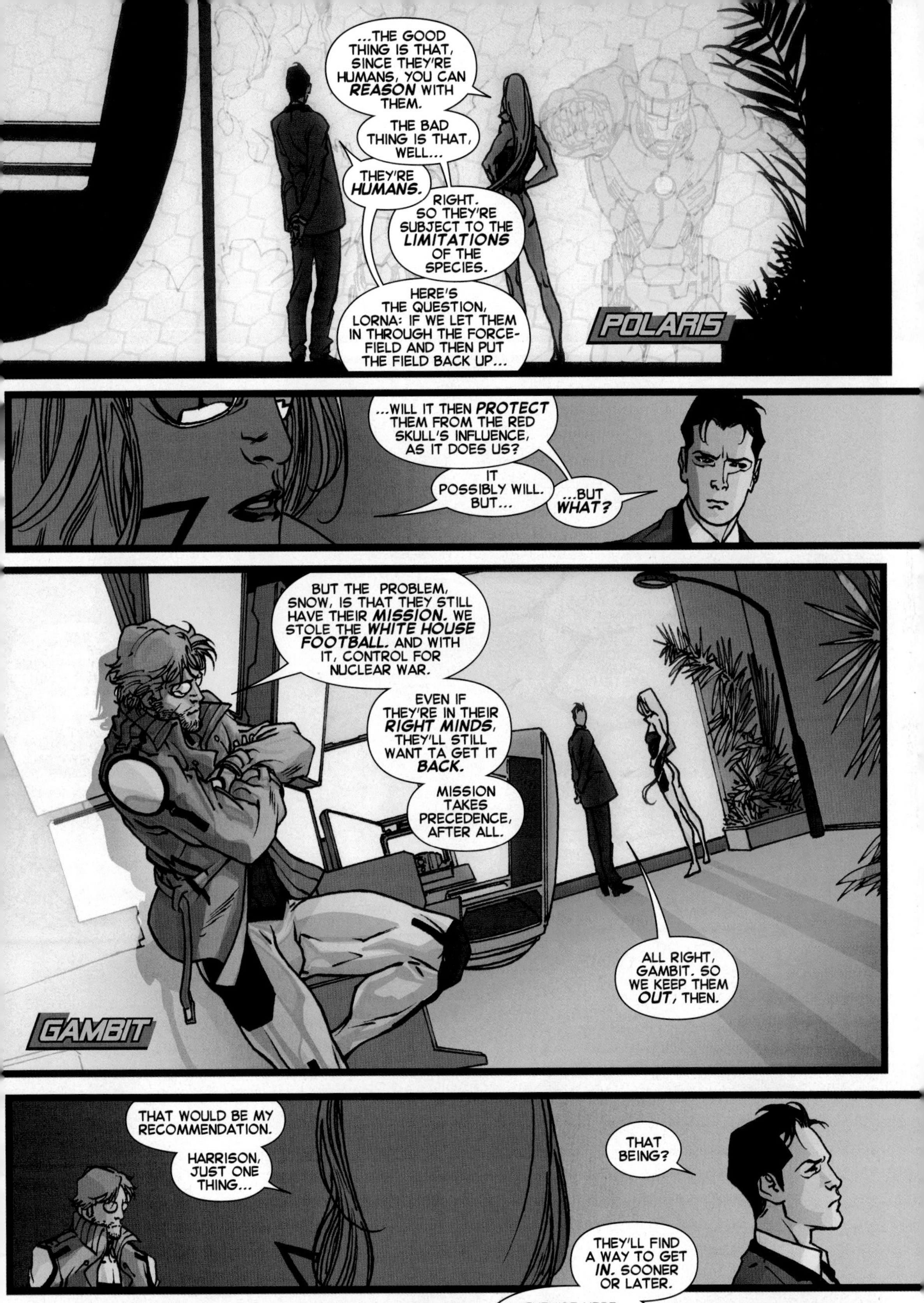
...THE GOOD THING IS THAT, SINCE THEY'RE HUMANS, YOU CAN REASON WITH THEM.
THE BAD THING IS THAT, WELL...
THEY'RE HUMANS.
RIGHT. SO THEY'RE SUBJECT TO THE LIMITATIONS OF THE SPECIES.
HERE'S THE QUESTION, LORNA: IF WE LET THEM IN THROUGH THE FORCE-FIELD AND THEN PUT THE FIELD BACK UP...
POLARIS
...WILL IT THEN PROTECT THEM FROM THE RED SKULL'S INFLUENCE, AS IT DOES US?
IT POSSIBLY WILL. BUT...
...BUT WHAT?
BUT THE PROBLEM, SNOW, IS THAT THEY STILL HAVE THEIR MISSION. WE STOLE THE WHITE HOUSE FOOTBALL. AND WITH IT, CONTROL FOR NUCLEAR WAR.
EVEN IF THEY'RE IN THEIR RIGHT MINDS, THEY'LL STILL WANT TA GET IT BACK.
MISSION TAKES PRECEDENCE, AFTER ALL.
ALL RIGHT, GAMBIT. SO WE KEEP THEM OUT, THEN.
GAMBIT
THAT WOULD BE MY RECOMMENDATION.
HARRISON, JUST ONE THING...
THAT BEING?
THEY'LL FIND A WAY TO GET IN. SOONER OR LATER.

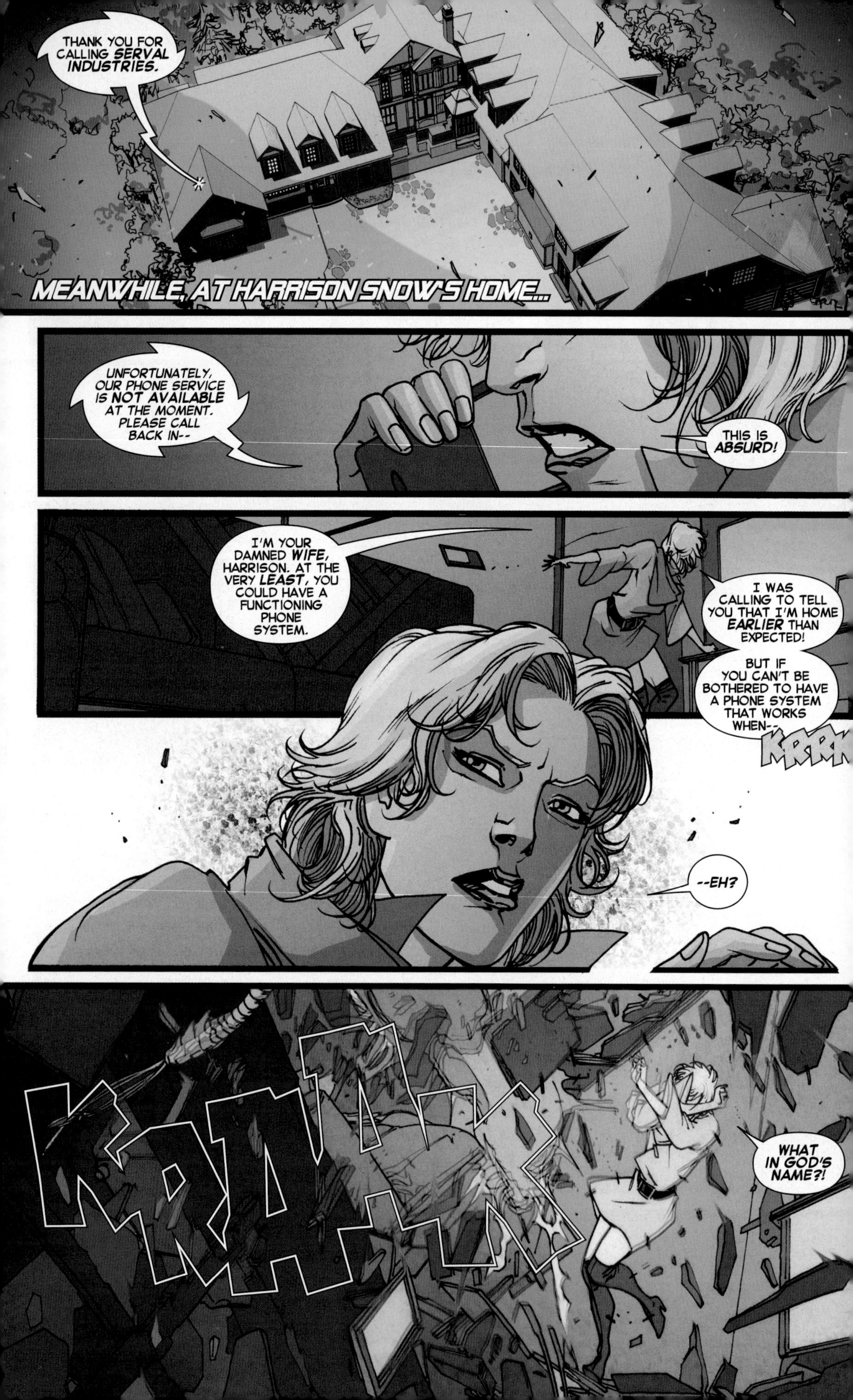
THANK YOU FOR CALLING SERVAL INDUSTRIES.
MEANWHILE, AT HARRISON SNOW'S HOME...
UNFORTUNATELY, OUR PHONE SERVICE IS NOT AVAILABLE AT THE MOMENT. PLEASE CALL BACK IN--
THIS IS ABSURD!
I'M YOUR DAMNED WIFE, HARRISON. AT THE VERY LEAST, YOU COULD HAVE A FUNCTIONING PHONE SYSTEM.
I WAS CALLING TO TELL YOU THAT I'M HOME EARLIER THAN EXPECTED!
BUT IF YOU CAN'T BE BOTHERED TO HAVE A PHONE SYSTEM THAT WORKS WHEN--
KRRK
--EH?
WHAT IN GOD'S NAME?!

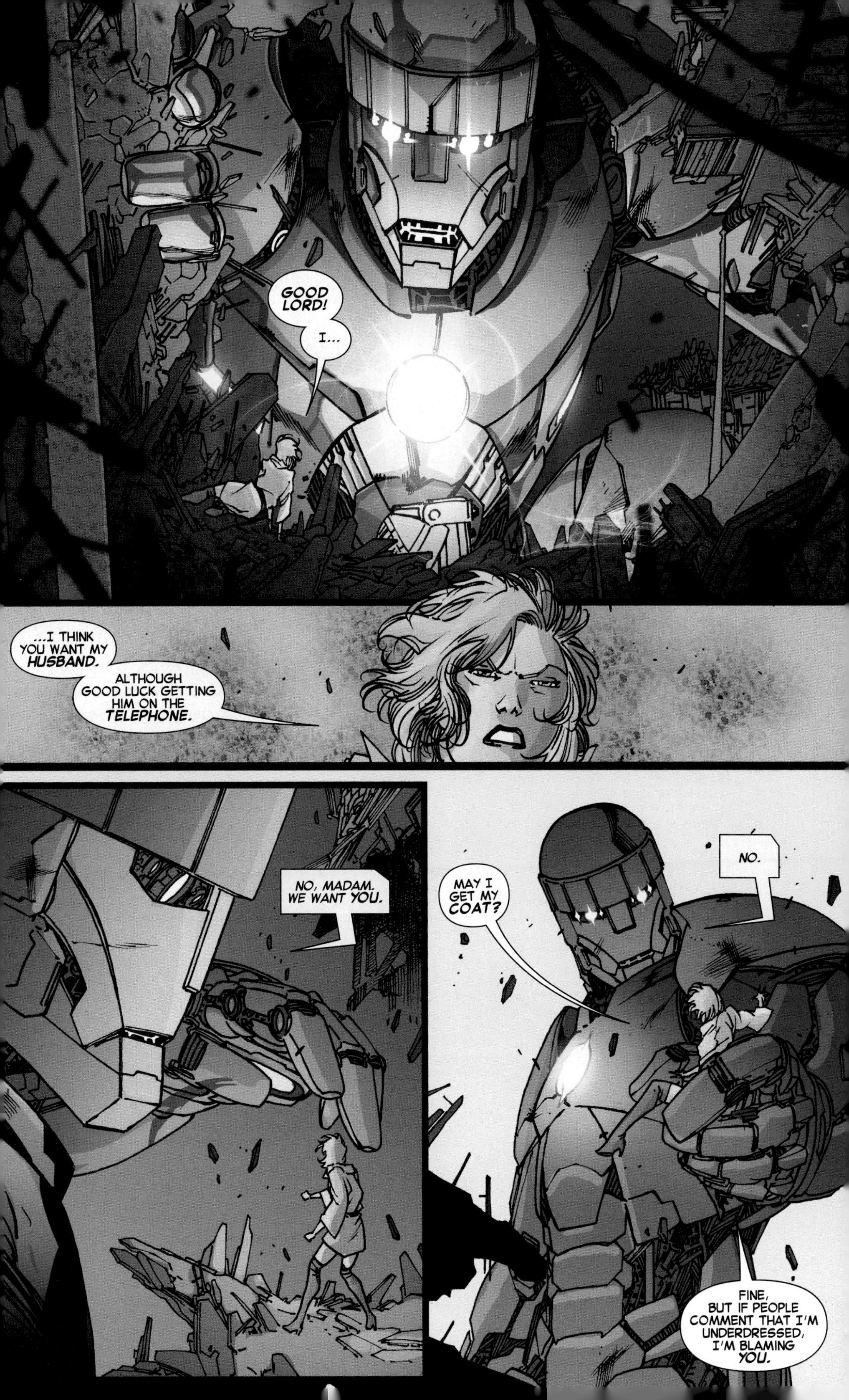
GOOD LORD!
I...
...I THINK YOU WANT MY HUSBAND.
ALTHOUGH GOOD LUCK GETTING HIM ON THE TELEPHONE.
NO, MADAM. WE WANT YOU.
MAY I GET MY COAT?
NO.
FINE, BUT IF PEOPLE COMMENT THAT I'M UNDERDRESSED, I'M BLAMING YOU.

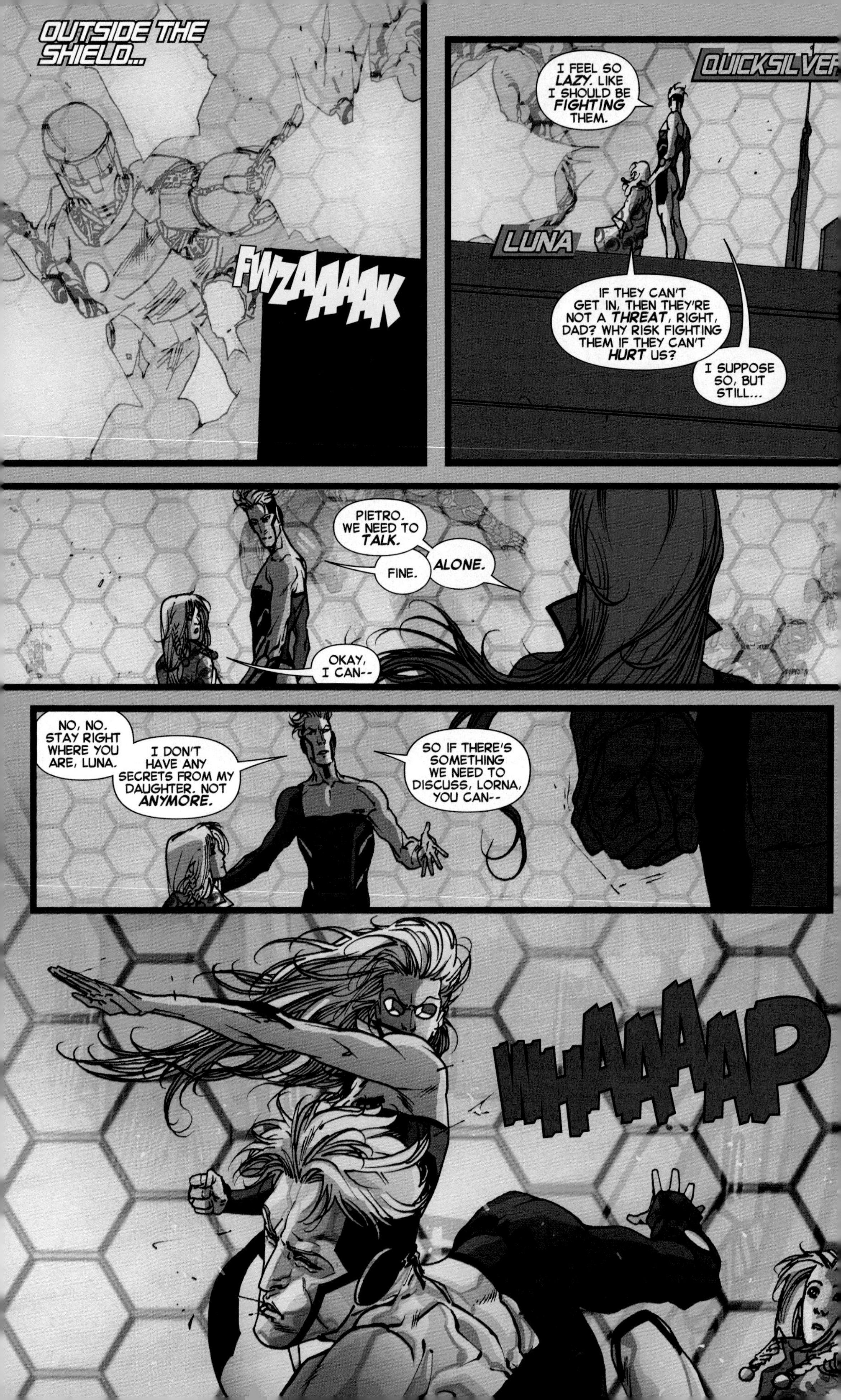

OUTSIDE THE SHIELD...
FWZAAAAK
QUICKSILVER
I FEEL SO LAZY. LIKE I SHOULD BE FIGHTING THEM.
LUNA
IF THEY CAN'T GET IN, THEN THEY'RE NOT A THREAT, RIGHT, DAD? WHY RISK FIGHTING THEM IF THEY CAN'T HURT US?
I SUPPOSE SO, BUT STILL...
PIETRO. WE NEED TO TALK.
FINE.
ALONE.
OKAY, I CAN--
NO, NO. STAY RIGHT WHERE YOU ARE, LUNA.
I DON'T HAVE ANY SECRETS FROM MY DAUGHTER. NOT ANYMORE.
SO IF THERE'S SOMETHING WE NEED TO DISCUSS, LORNA, YOU CAN--
WHAAAAAP

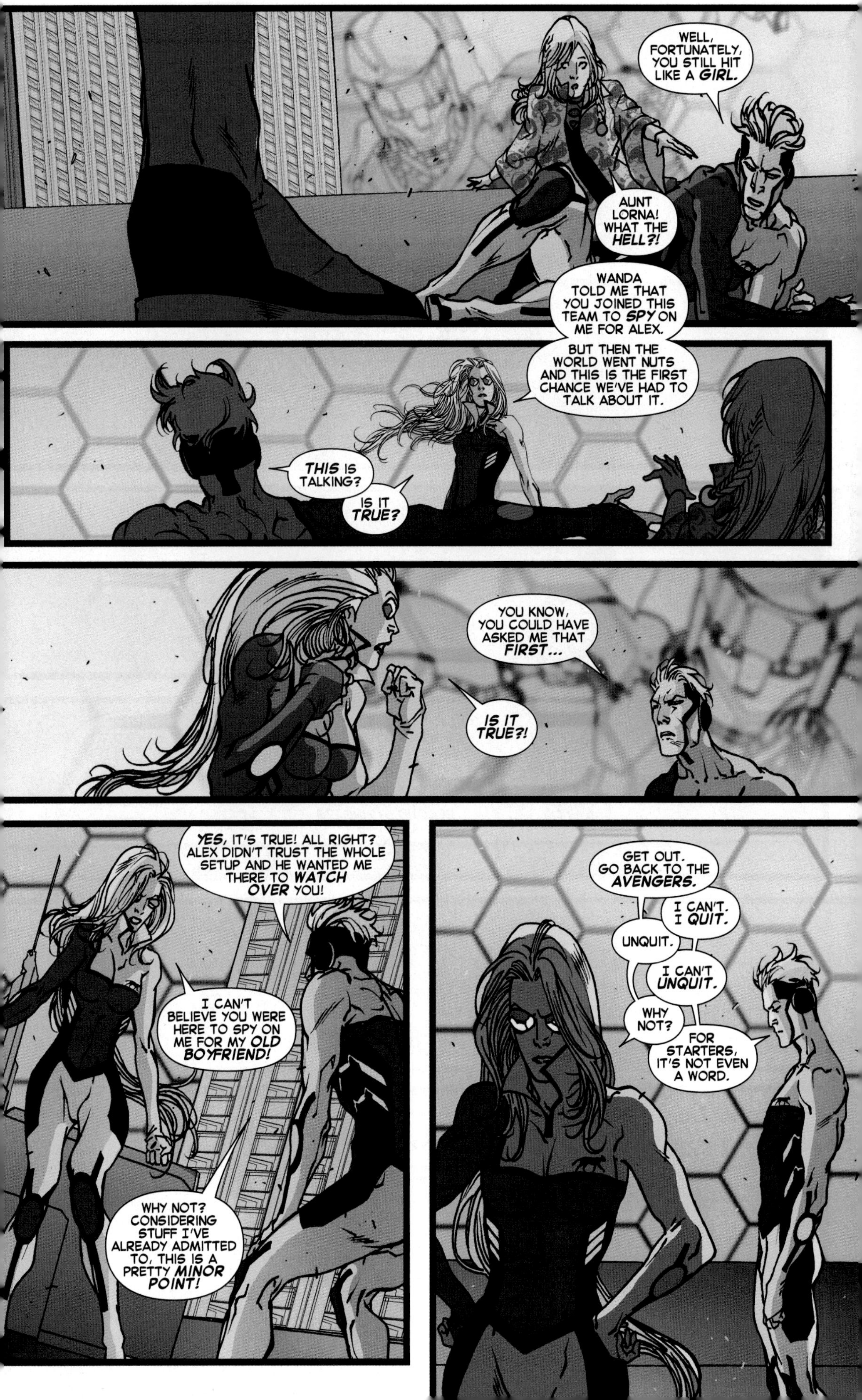
WELL, FORTUNATELY, YOU STILL HIT LIKE A GIRL.
AUNT LORNA! WHAT THE HELL?!
WANDA TOLD ME THAT YOU JOINED THIS TEAM TO SPY ON ME FOR ALEX.
BUT THEN THE WORLD WENT NUTS AND THIS IS THE FIRST CHANCE WE'VE HAD TO TALK ABOUT IT.
THIS IS TALKING?
IS IT TRUE?
YOU KNOW, YOU COULD HAVE ASKED ME THAT FIRST...
IS IT TRUE?!
YES, IT'S TRUE! ALL RIGHT? ALEX DIDN'T TRUST THE WHOLE SETUP AND HE WANTED ME THERE TO WATCH OVER YOU!
I CAN'T BELIEVE YOU WERE HERE TO SPY ON ME FOR MY OLD BOYFRIEND!
WHY NOT? CONSIDERING STUFF I'VE ALREADY ADMITTED TO, THIS IS A PRETTY MINOR POINT!
GET OUT. GO BACK TO THE AVENGERS.
I CAN'T. I QUIT.
UNQUIT.
I CAN'T UNQUIT.
WHY NOT?
FOR STARTERS, IT'S NOT EVEN A WORD.

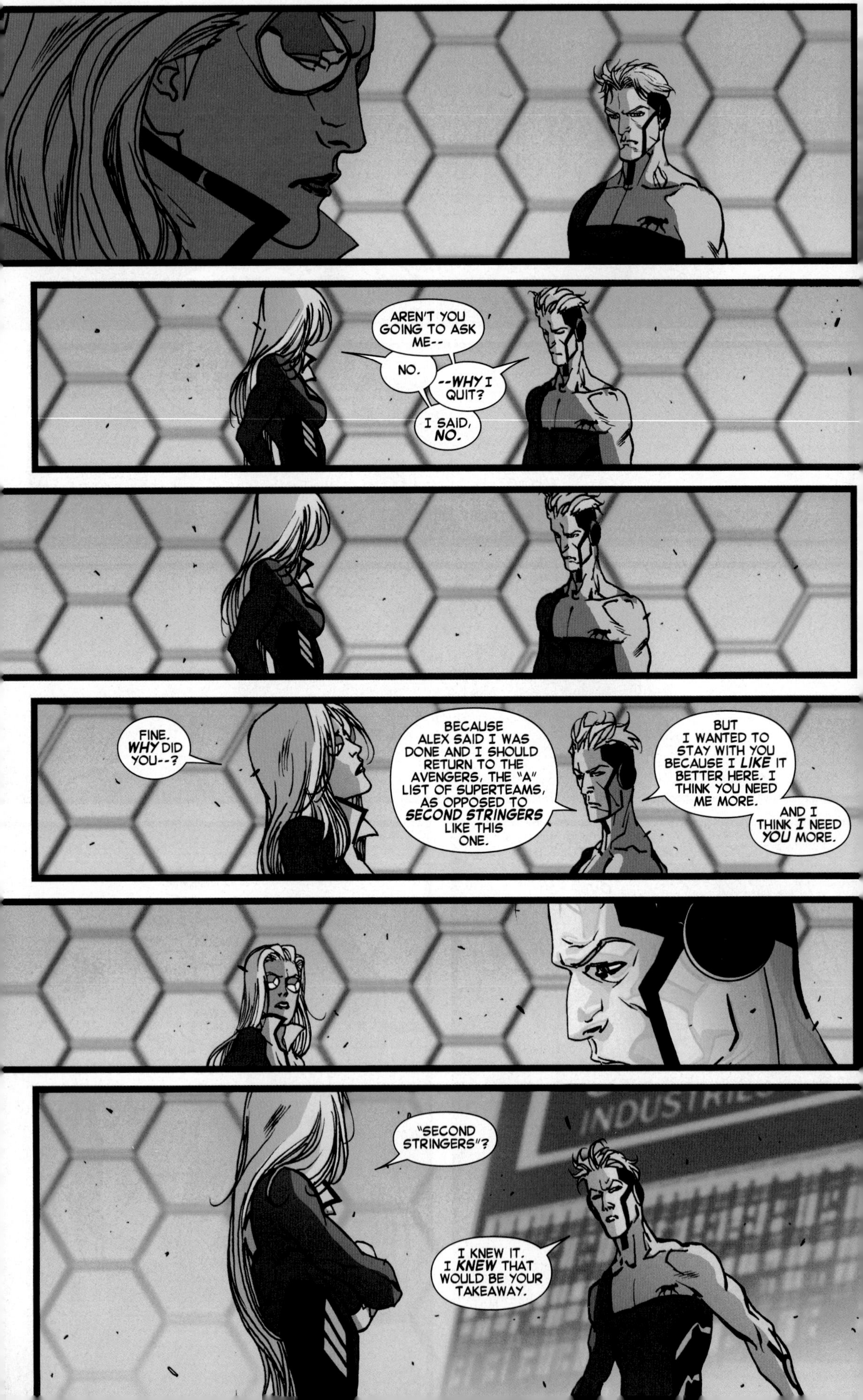

AREN'T YOU GOING TO ASK ME--
NO.
--WHY I QUIT?
I SAID, NO.
FINE. WHY DID YOU--?
BECAUSE ALEX SAID I WAS DONE AND I SHOULD RETURN TO THE AVENGERS, THE "A" LIST OF SUPERTEAMS, AS OPPOSED TO SECOND STRINGERS LIKE THIS ONE.
BUT I WANTED TO STAY WITH YOU BECAUSE I LIKE IT BETTER HERE. I THINK YOU NEED ME MORE.
AND I THINK I NEED YOU MORE.
INDUSTRIES
"SECOND STRINGERS"?
I KNEW IT. I KNEW THAT WOULD BE YOUR TAKEAWAY.

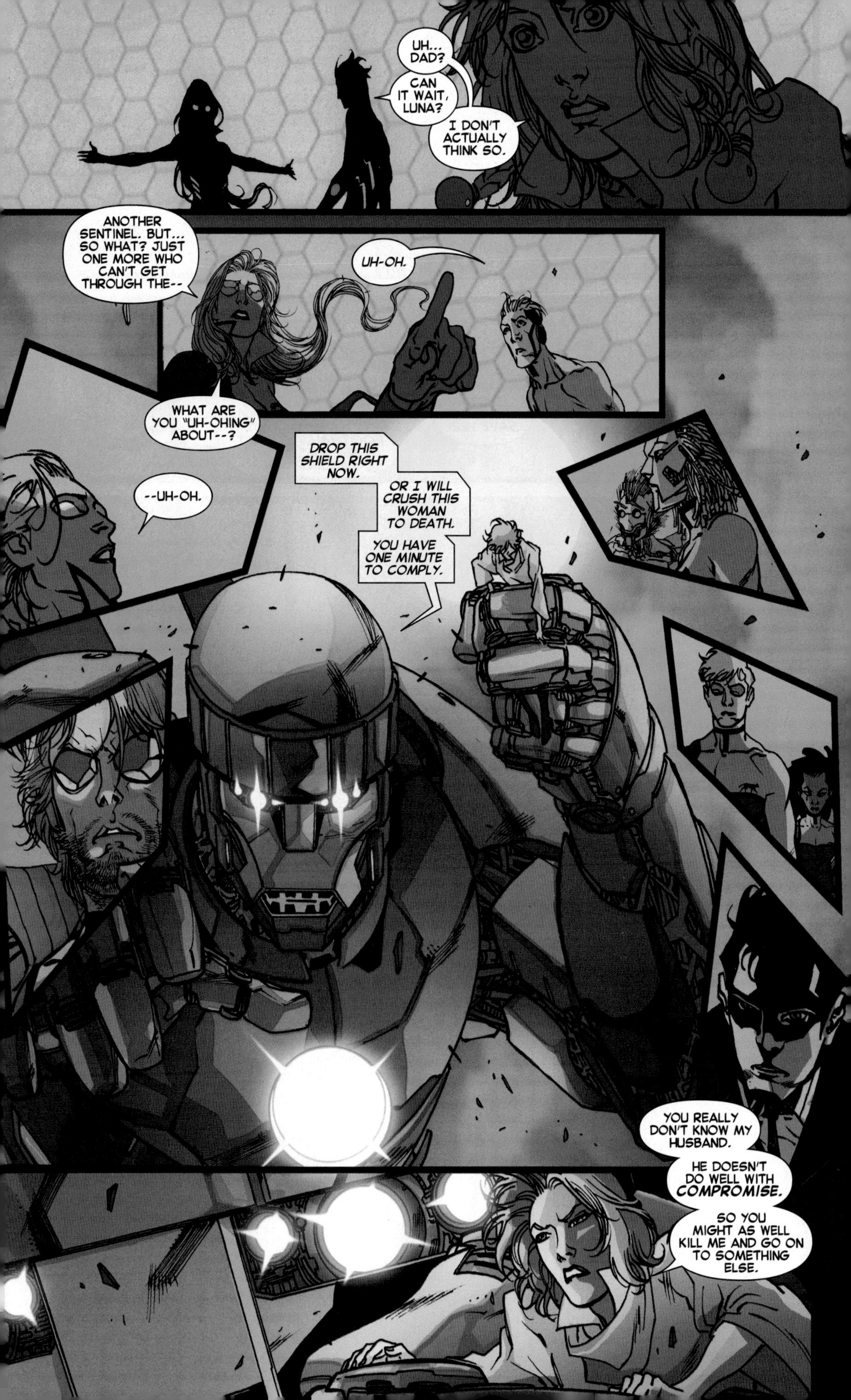
UH... DAD?
CAN IT WAIT, LUNA?
I DON'T ACTUALLY THINK SO.
ANOTHER SENTINEL. BUT... SO WHAT? JUST ONE MORE WHO CAN'T GET THROUGH THE--
UH-OH.
WHAT ARE YOU "UH-OHING" ABOUT--?
--UH-OH.
DROP THIS SHIELD RIGHT NOW.
OR I WILL CRUSH THIS WOMAN TO DEATH.
YOU HAVE ONE MINUTE TO COMPLY.
YOU REALLY DON'T KNOW MY HUSBAND.
HE DOESN'T DO WELL WITH COMPROMISE.
SO YOU MIGHT AS WELL KILL ME AND GO ON TO SOMETHING ELSE.

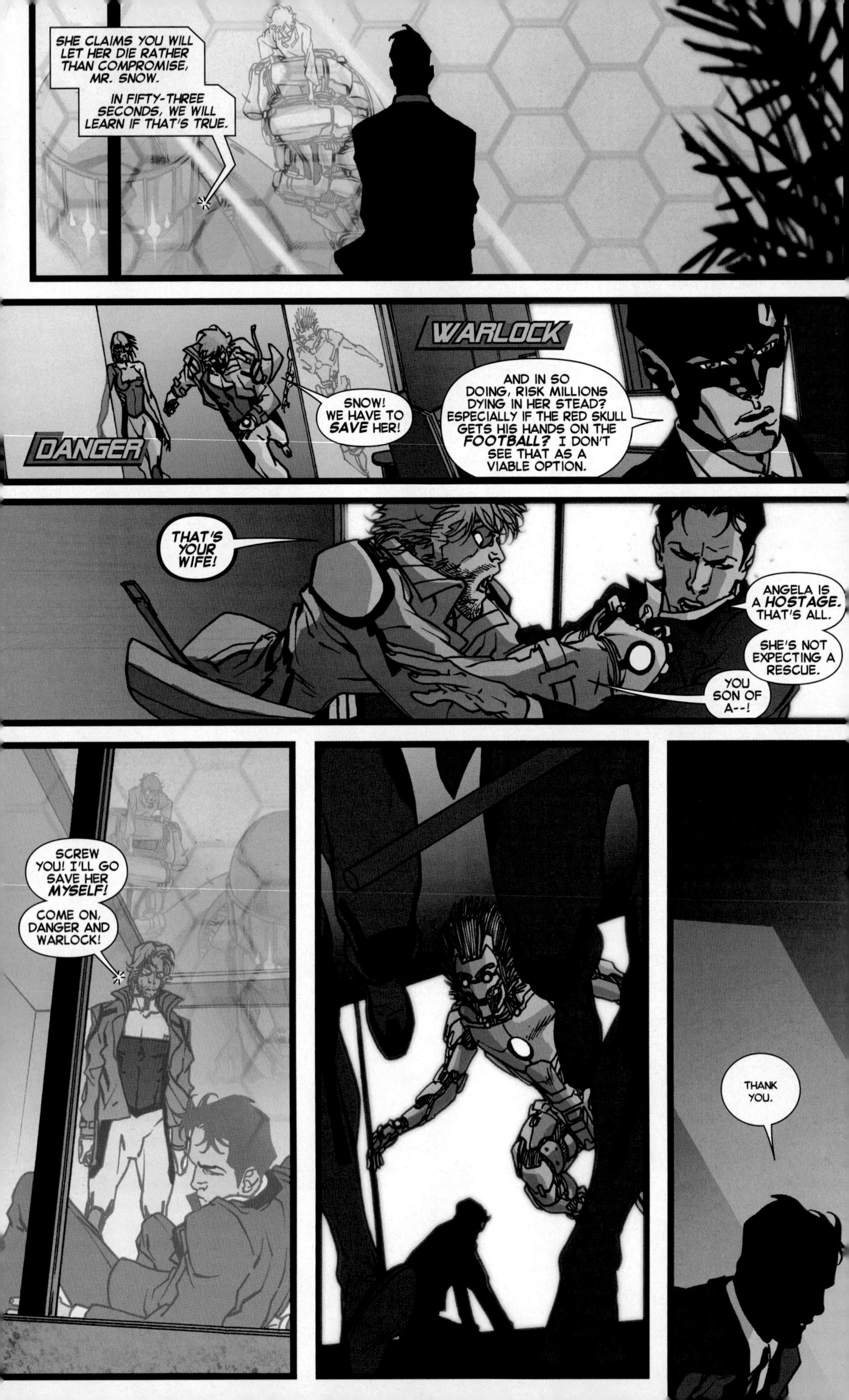
SHE CLAIMS YOU WILL LET HER DIE RATHER THAN COMPROMISE, MR. SNOW.
IN FIFTY-THREE SECONDS, WE WILL LEARN IF THAT'S TRUE.
WARLOCK
DANGER
SNOW! WE HAVE TO SAVE HER!
AND IN SO DOING, RISK MILLIONS DYING IN HER STEAD? ESPECIALLY IF THE RED SKULL GETS HIS HANDS ON THE FOOTBALL? I DON'T SEE THAT AS A VIABLE OPTION.
THAT'S YOUR WIFE!
ANGELA IS A HOSTAGE. THAT'S ALL.
SHE'S NOT EXPECTING A RESCUE.
YOU SON OF A--!
SCREW YOU! I'LL GO SAVE HER MYSELF!
COME ON, DANGER AND WARLOCK!
THANK YOU.

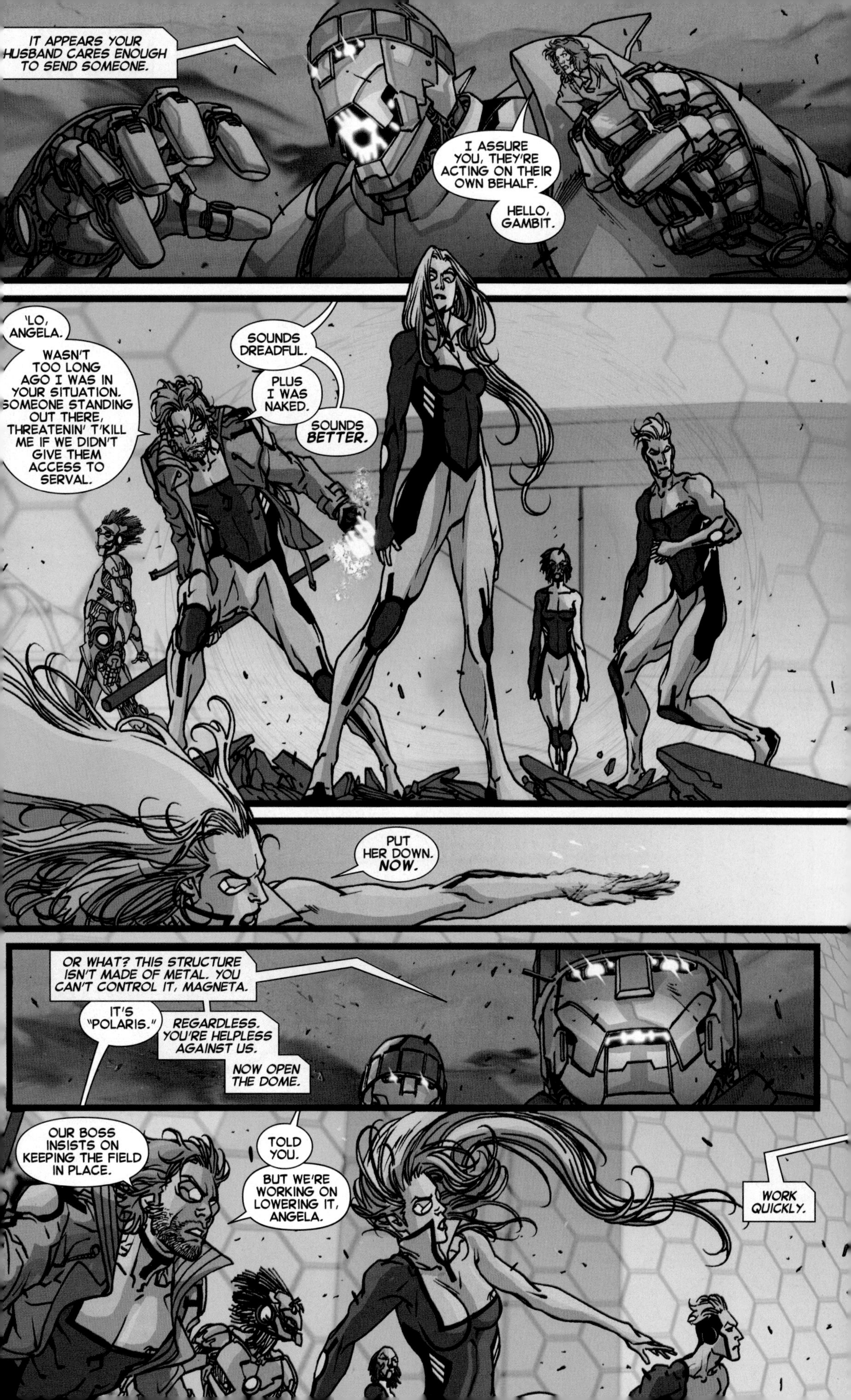
IT APPEARS YOUR HUSBAND CARES ENOUGH TO SEND SOMEONE.
I ASSURE YOU, THEY'RE ACTING ON THEIR OWN BEHALF.
HELLO, GAMBIT.
'LO, ANGELA.
WASN'T TOO LONG AGO I WAS IN YOUR SITUATION. SOMEONE STANDING OUT THERE, THREATENIN' T'KILL ME IF WE DIDN'T GIVE THEM ACCESS TO SERVAL.
SOUNDS DREADFUL.
PLUS I WAS NAKED.
SOUNDS BETTER.
PUT HER DOWN. NOW.
OR WHAT? THIS STRUCTURE ISN'T MADE OF METAL. YOU CAN'T CONTROL IT, MAGNETA.
IT'S "POLARIS."
REGARDLESS. YOU'RE HELPLESS AGAINST US.
NOW OPEN THE DOME.
OUR BOSS INSISTS ON KEEPING THE FIELD IN PLACE.
TOLD YOU.
BUT WE'RE WORKING ON LOWERING IT, ANGELA.
WORK QUICKLY.

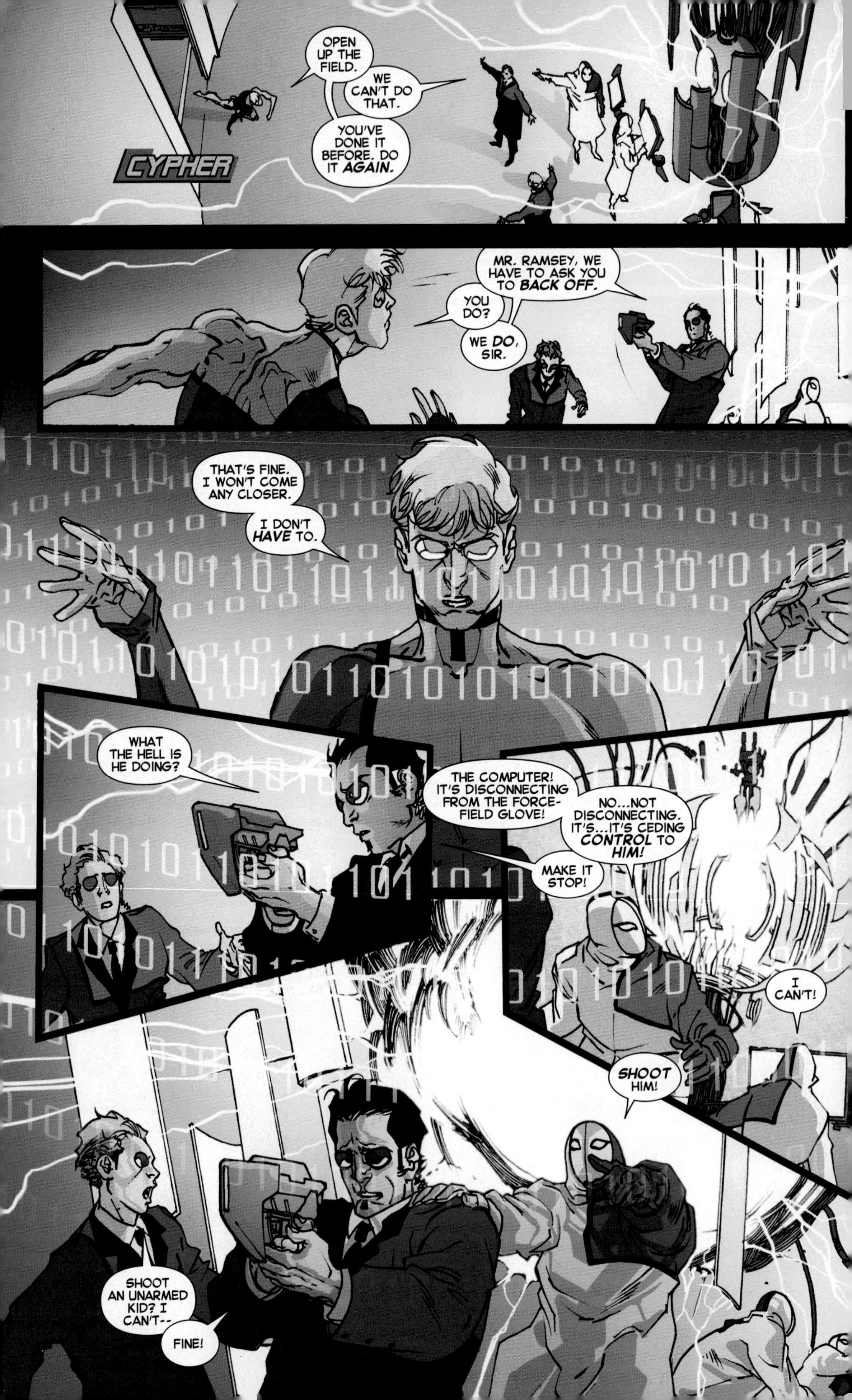
CYPHER
OPEN UP THE FIELD.
WE CAN'T DO THAT.
YOU'VE DONE IT BEFORE. DO IT AGAIN.
MR. RAMSEY, WE HAVE TO ASK YOU TO BACK OFF.
YOU DO?
WE DO, SIR.
THAT'S FINE. I WON'T COME ANY CLOSER.
I DON'T HAVE TO.
WHAT THE HELL IS HE DOING?
THE COMPUTER! IT'S DISCONNECTING FROM THE FORCE-FIELD GLOVE!
NO...NOT DISCONNECTING. IT'S...IT'S CEDING CONTROL TO HIM!
MAKE IT STOP!
I CAN'T!
SHOOT HIM!
SHOOT AN UNARMED KID? I CAN'T--
FINE!

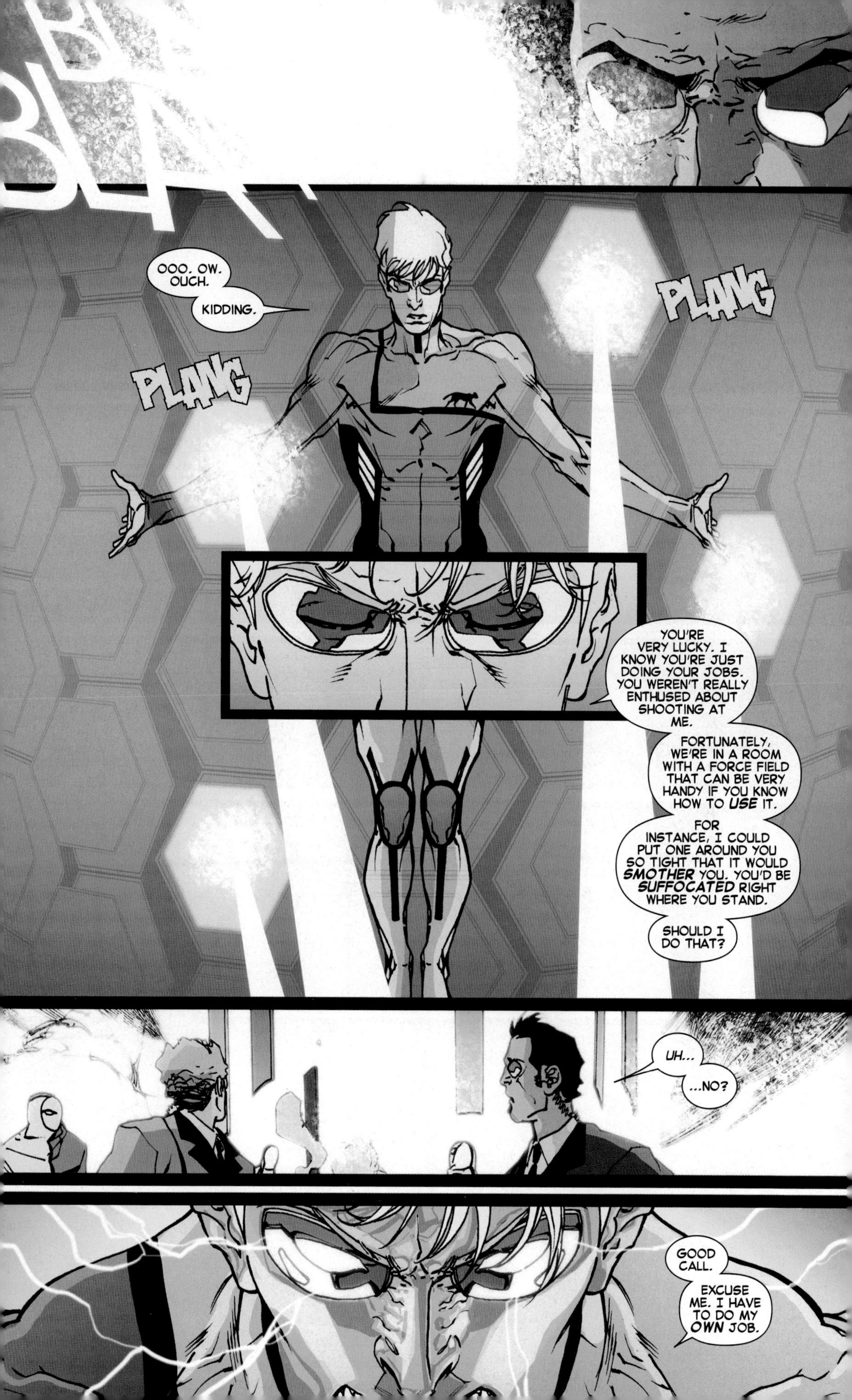
OOO. OW. OUCH.
KIDDING.
PLANG
PLANG
YOU'RE VERY LUCKY. I KNOW YOU'RE JUST DOING YOUR JOBS. YOU WEREN'T REALLY ENTHUSED ABOUT SHOOTING AT ME.
FORTUNATELY, WE'RE IN A ROOM WITH A FORCE FIELD THAT CAN BE VERY HANDY IF YOU KNOW HOW TO USE IT.
FOR INSTANCE, I COULD PUT ONE AROUND YOU SO TIGHT THAT IT WOULD SMOTHER YOU. YOU'D BE SUFFOCATED RIGHT WHERE YOU STAND.
SHOULD I DO THAT?
UH...
...NO?
GOOD CALL.
EXCUSE ME. I HAVE TO DO MY OWN JOB.

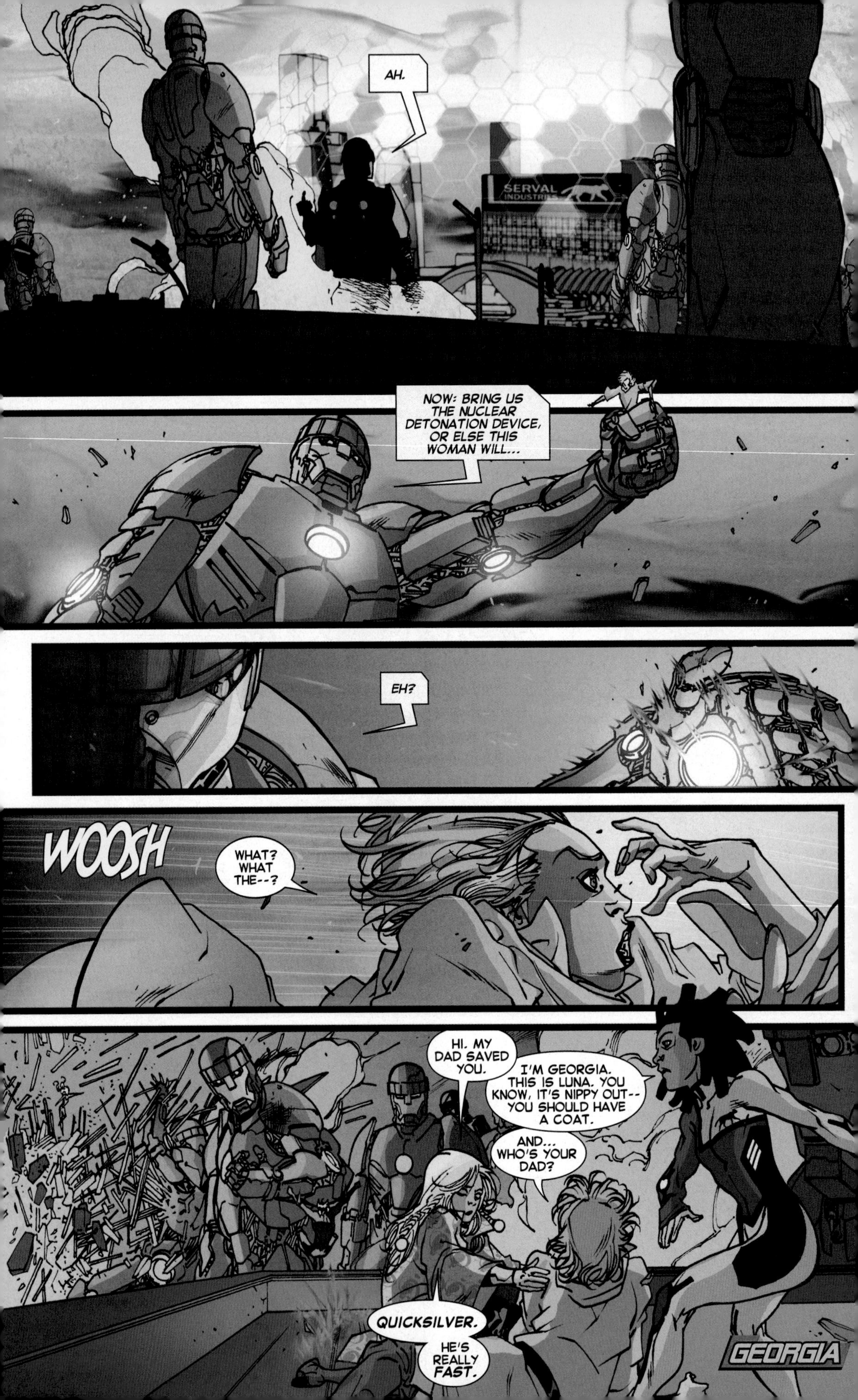
AH.
SERVAL INDUSTRIES
NOW: BRING US THE NUCLEAR DETONATION DEVICE, OR ELSE THIS WOMAN WILL...
EH?
WOOSH
WHAT? WHAT THE--?
HI. MY DAD SAVED YOU.
I'M GEORGIA. THIS IS LUNA. YOU KNOW, IT'S NIPPY OUT--YOU SHOULD HAVE A COAT.
AND... WHO'S YOUR DAD?
QUICKSILVER.
HE'S REALLY FAST.
GEORGIA

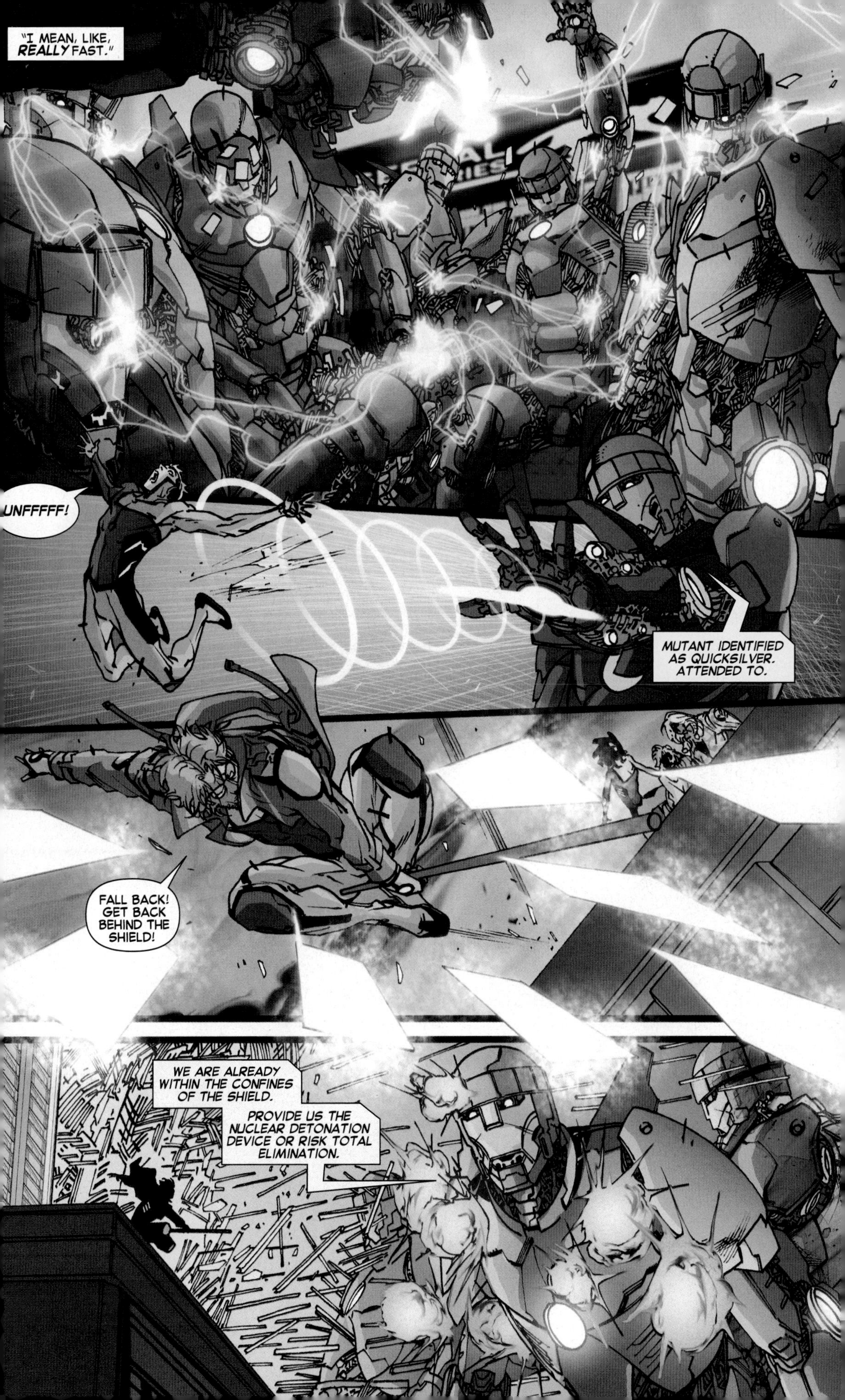
"I MEAN, LIKE, REALLY FAST."
UNFFFFF!
MUTANT IDENTIFIED AS QUICKSILVER. ATTENDED TO.
FALL BACK! GET BACK BEHIND THE SHIELD!
WE ARE ALREADY WITHIN THE CONFINES OF THE SHIELD.
PROVIDE US THE NUCLEAR DETONATION DEVICE OR RISK TOTAL ELIMINATION.

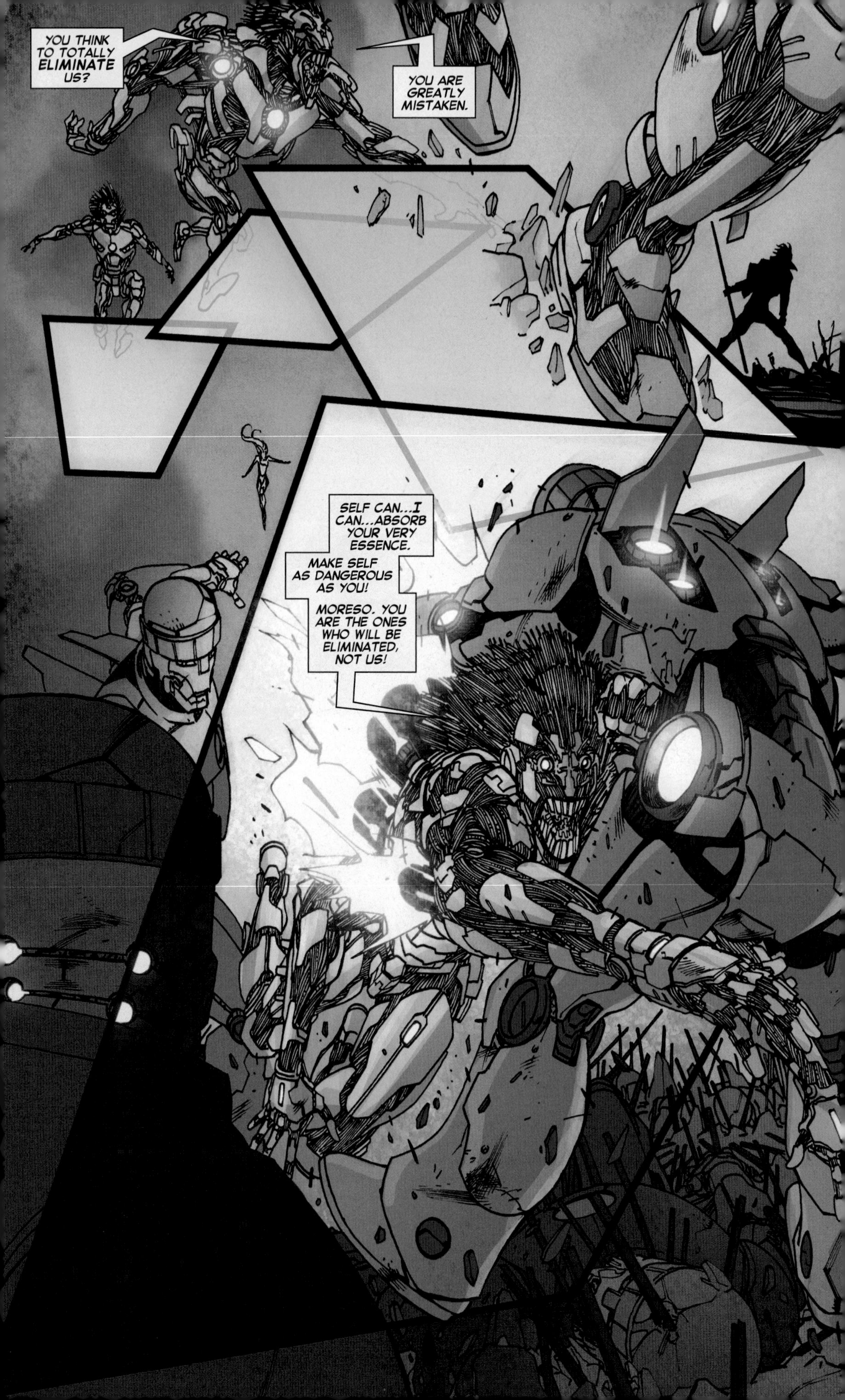

YOU THINK TO TOTALLY ELIMINATE US?
YOU ARE GREATLY MISTAKEN.
SELF CAN...I CAN...ABSORB YOUR VERY ESSENCE.
MAKE SELF AS DANGEROUS AS YOU!
MORESO. YOU ARE THE ONES WHO WILL BE ELIMINATED, NOT US!

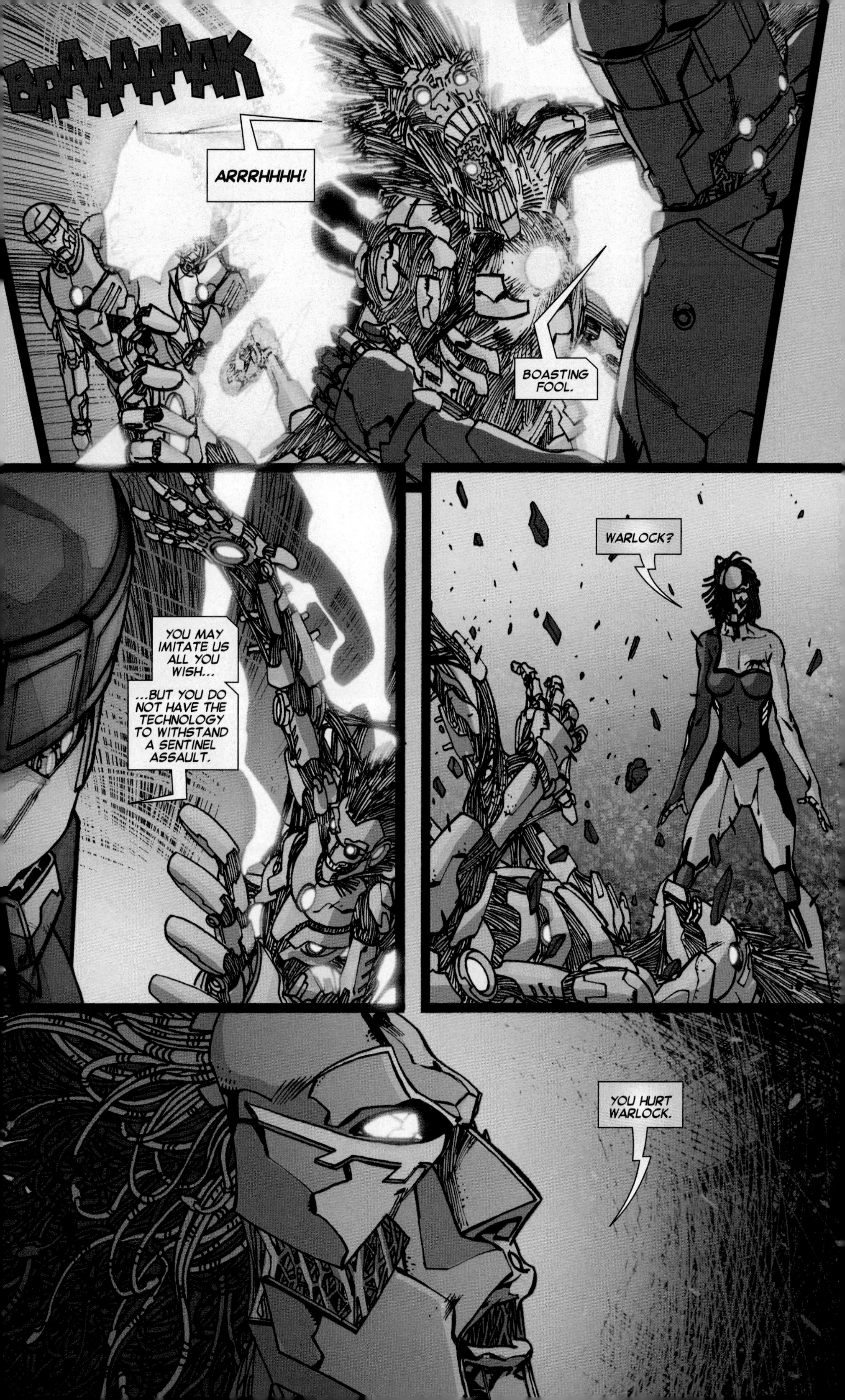
BRAAAAAK
ARRRHHHH!
BOASTING FOOL.
YOU MAY IMITATE US ALL YOU WISH...
...BUT YOU DO NOT HAVE THE TECHNOLOGY TO WITHSTAND A SENTINEL ASSAULT.
WARLOCK?
YOU HURT WARLOCK.

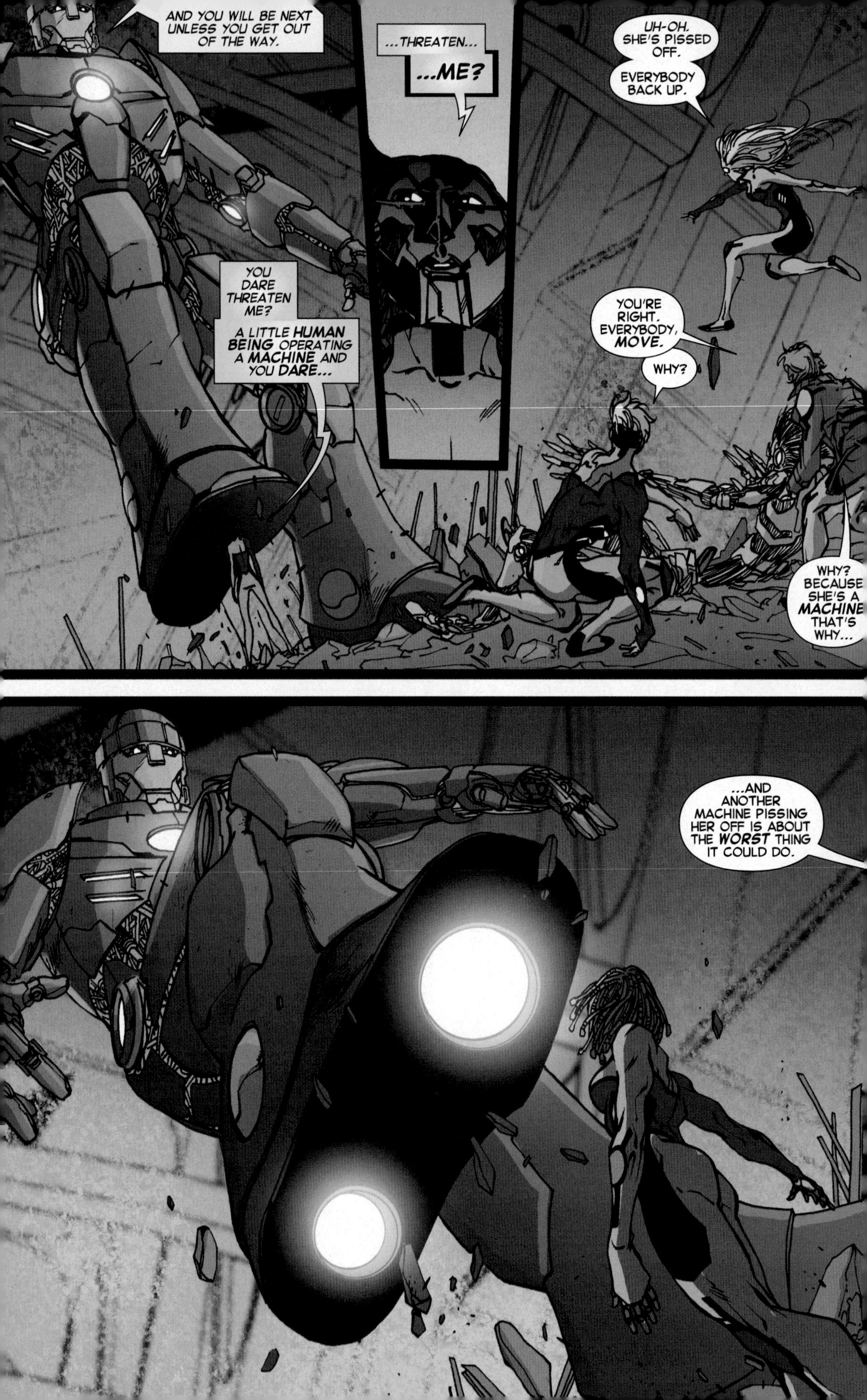
AND YOU WILL BE NEXT UNLESS YOU GET OUT OF THE WAY.
...THREATEN...
...ME?
UH-OH. SHE'S PISSED OFF.
EVERYBODY BACK UP.
YOU DARE THREATEN ME?
A LITTLE HUMAN BEING OPERATING A MACHINE AND YOU DARE...
YOU'RE RIGHT. EVERYBODY, MOVE.
WHY?
WHY? BECAUSE SHE'S A MACHINE THAT'S WHY...
...AND ANOTHER MACHINE PISSING HER OFF IS ABOUT THE WORST THING IT COULD DO.

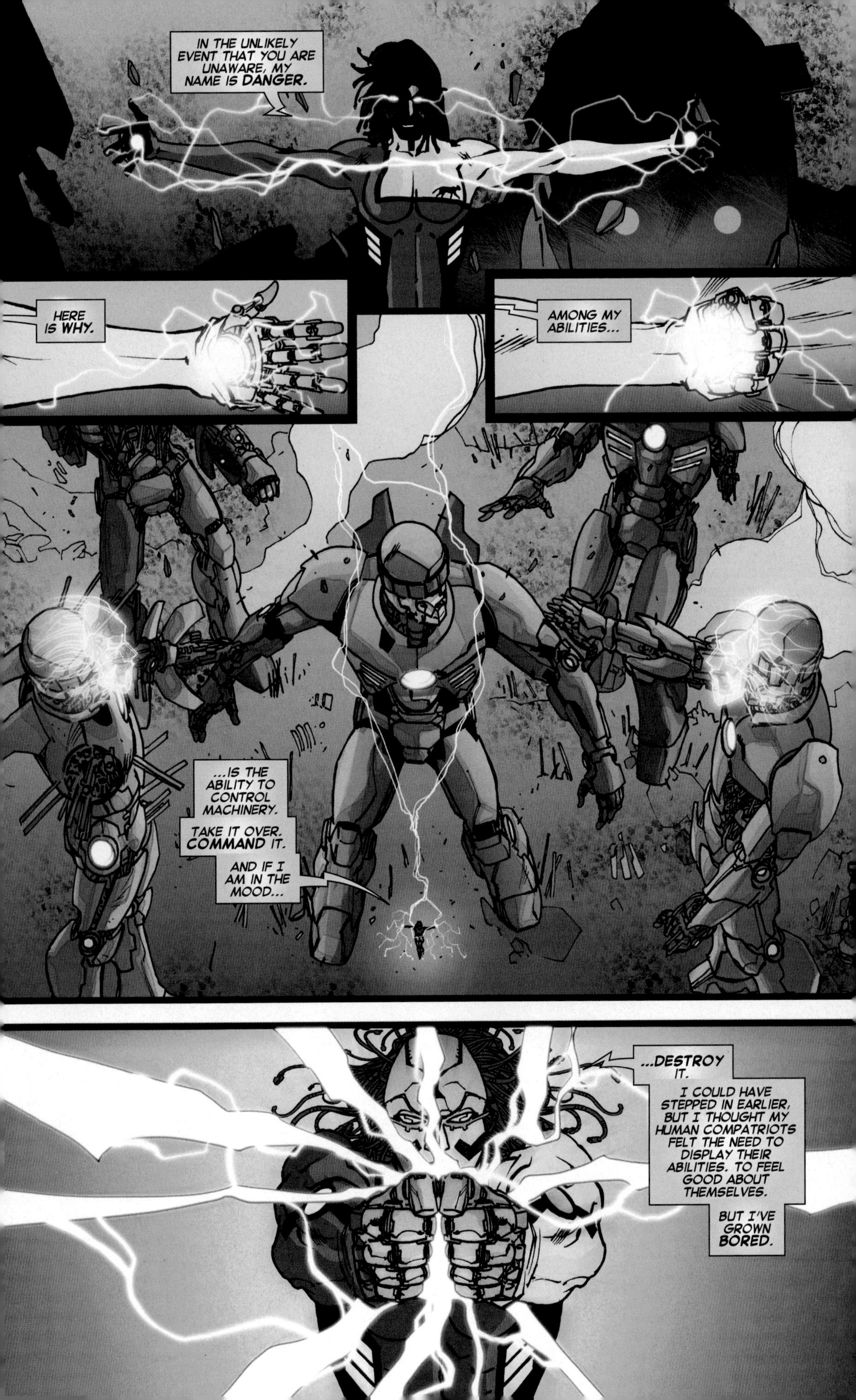
IN THE UNLIKELY EVENT THAT YOU ARE UNAWARE, MY NAME IS DANGER.
HERE IS WHY.
AMONG MY ABILITIES...
...IS THE ABILITY TO CONTROL MACHINERY.
TAKE IT OVER. COMMAND IT.
AND IF I AM IN THE MOOD...
...DESTROY IT.
I COULD HAVE STEPPED IN EARLIER, BUT I THOUGHT MY HUMAN COMPATRIOTS FELT THE NEED TO DISPLAY THEIR ABILITIES. TO FEEL GOOD ABOUT THEMSELVES.
BUT I'VE GROWN BORED.

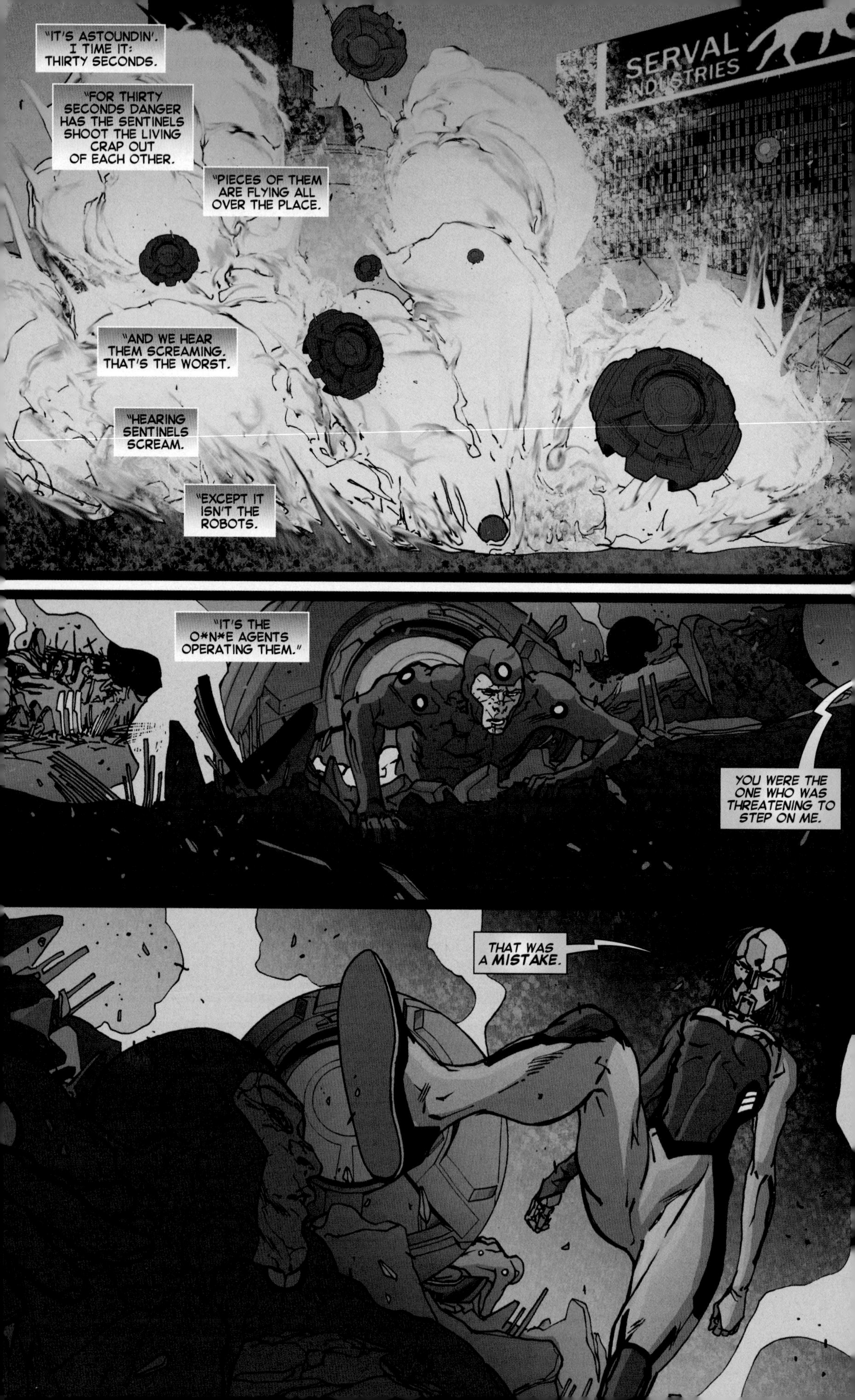

"IT'S ASTOUNDIN'. I TIME IT: THIRTY SECONDS.
"FOR THIRTY SECONDS DANGER HAS THE SENTINELS SHOOT THE LIVING CRAP OUT OF EACH OTHER.
"PIECES OF THEM ARE FLYING ALL OVER THE PLACE.
SERVAL INDUSTRIES
"AND WE HEAR THEM SCREAMING. THAT'S THE WORST.
"HEARING SENTINELS SCREAM.
"EXCEPT IT ISN'T THE ROBOTS.
"IT'S THE O*N*E AGENTS OPERATING THEM."
YOU WERE THE ONE WHO WAS THREATENING TO STEP ON ME.
THAT WAS A *MISTAKE*.

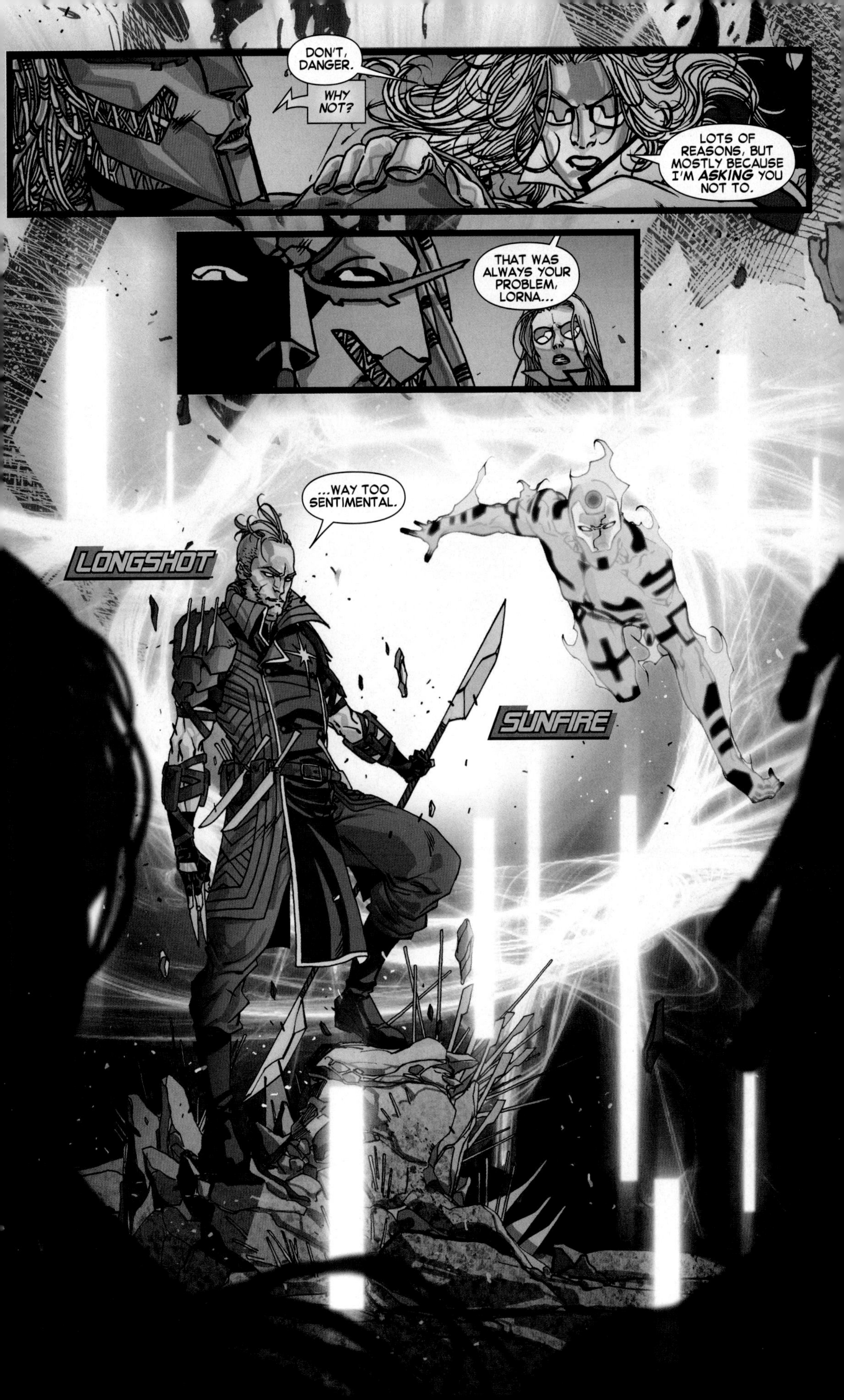
DON'T, DANGER.
WHY NOT?
LOTS OF REASONS, BUT MOSTLY BECAUSE I'M ASKING YOU NOT TO.
THAT WAS ALWAYS YOUR PROBLEM, LORNA...
...WAY TOO SENTIMENTAL.
LONGSHOT
SUNFIRE

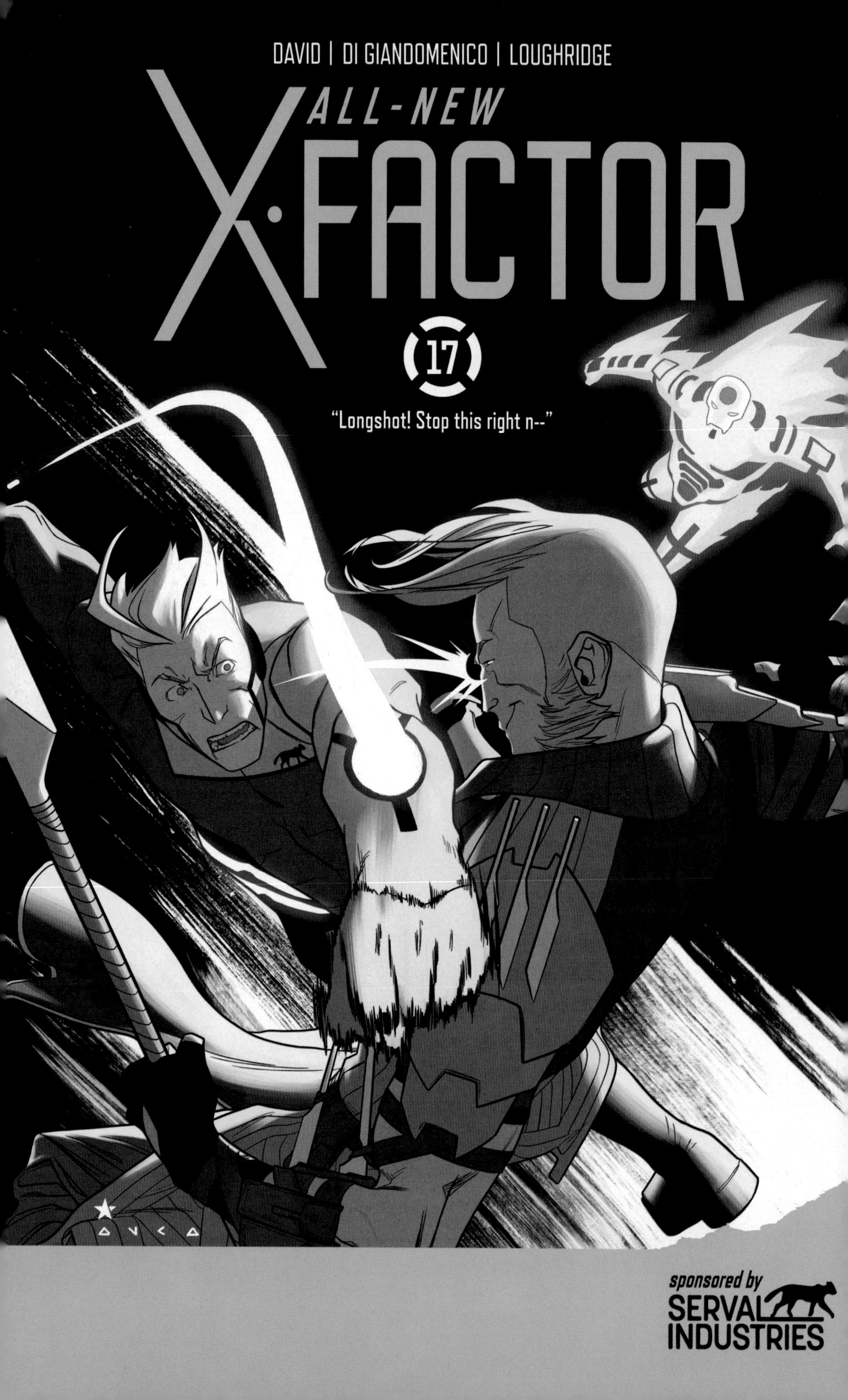
DAVID | DI GIANDOMENICO | LOUGHRIDGE
ALL-NEW
X-FACTOR
17
"Longshot! Stop this right n--"
sponsored by
SERVAL
INDUSTRIES

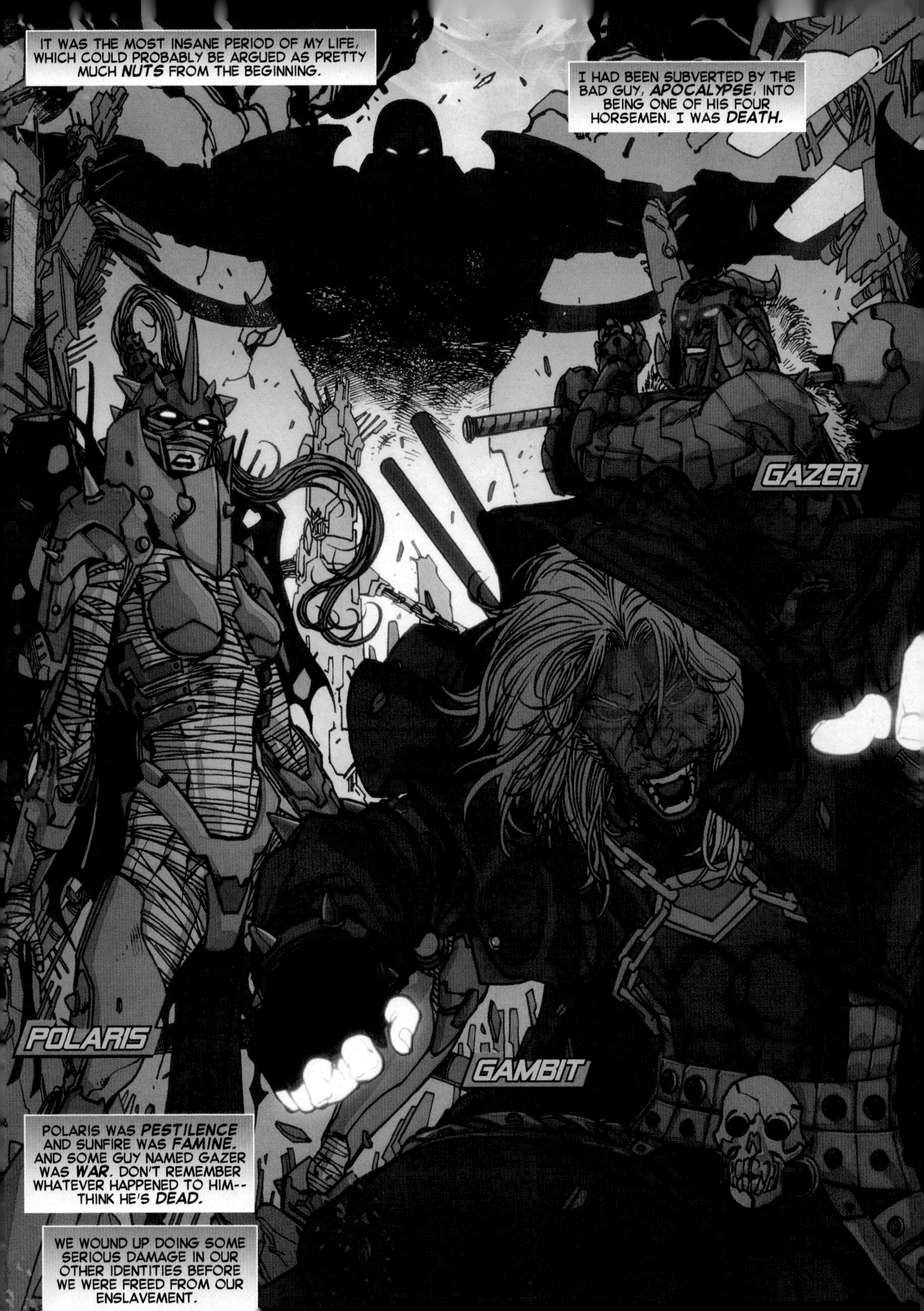
IT WAS THE MOST INSANE PERIOD OF MY LIFE, WHICH COULD PROBABLY BE ARGUED AS PRETTY MUCH NUTS FROM THE BEGINNING.
I HAD BEEN SUBVERTED BY THE BAD GUY, APOCALYPSE, INTO BEING ONE OF HIS FOUR HORSEMEN. I WAS DEATH.
GAZER
POLARIS
GAMBIT
POLARIS WAS PESTILENCE AND SUNFIRE WAS FAMINE. AND SOME GUY NAMED GAZER WAS WAR. DON'T REMEMBER WHATEVER HAPPENED TO HIM-- THINK HE'S DEAD.
WE WOUND UP DOING SOME SERIOUS DAMAGE IN OUR OTHER IDENTITIES BEFORE WE WERE FREED FROM OUR ENSLAVEMENT.

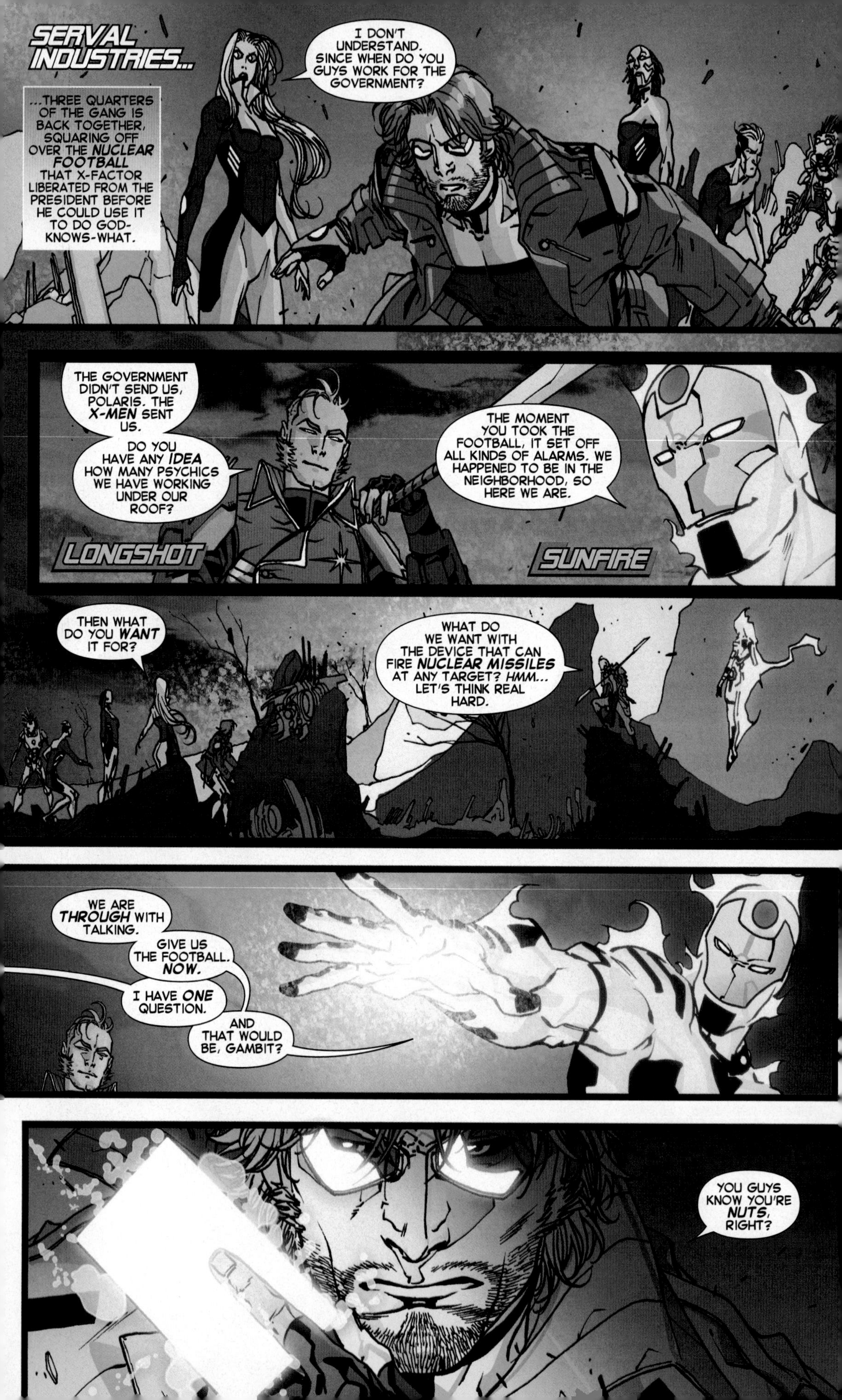
SERVAL INDUSTRIES...
...THREE QUARTERS OF THE GANG IS BACK TOGETHER, SQUARING OFF OVER THE NUCLEAR FOOTBALL THAT X-FACTOR LIBERATED FROM THE PRESIDENT BEFORE HE COULD USE IT TO DO GOD-KNOWS-WHAT.
I DON'T UNDERSTAND. SINCE WHEN DO YOU GUYS WORK FOR THE GOVERNMENT?
THE GOVERNMENT DIDN'T SEND US, POLARIS. THE X-MEN SENT US.
DO YOU HAVE ANY IDEA HOW MANY PSYCHICS WE HAVE WORKING UNDER OUR ROOF?
LONGSHOT
THE MOMENT YOU TOOK THE FOOTBALL, IT SET OFF ALL KINDS OF ALARMS. WE HAPPENED TO BE IN THE NEIGHBORHOOD, SO HERE WE ARE.
SUNFIRE
THEN WHAT DO YOU WANT IT FOR?
WHAT DO WE WANT WITH THE DEVICE THAT CAN FIRE NUCLEAR MISSILES AT ANY TARGET? HMM... LET'S THINK REAL HARD.
WE ARE THROUGH WITH TALKING.
GIVE US THE FOOTBALL. NOW.
I HAVE ONE QUESTION.
AND THAT WOULD BE, GAMBIT?
YOU GUYS KNOW YOU'RE NUTS, RIGHT?

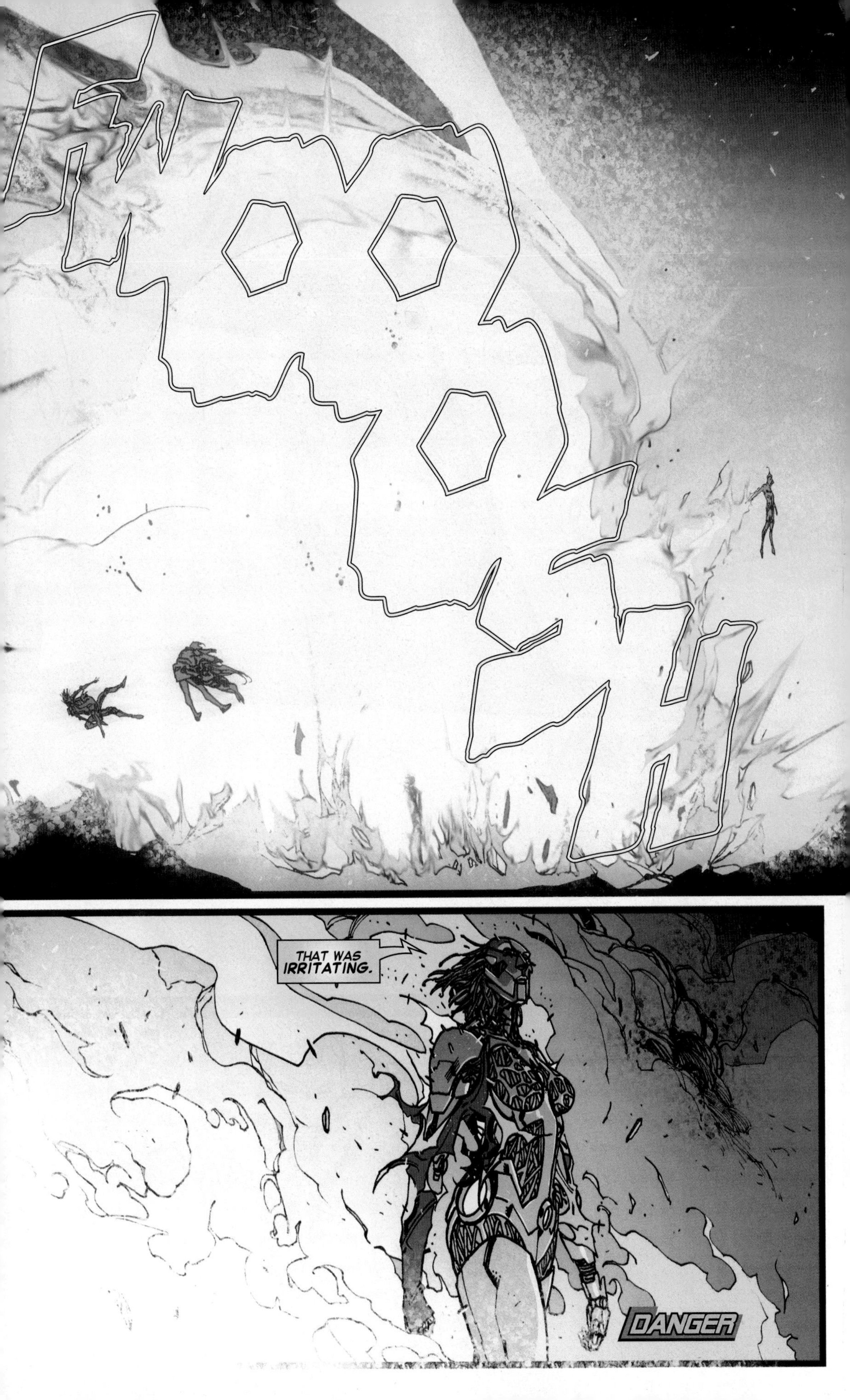
THAT WAS IRRITATING.
DANGER

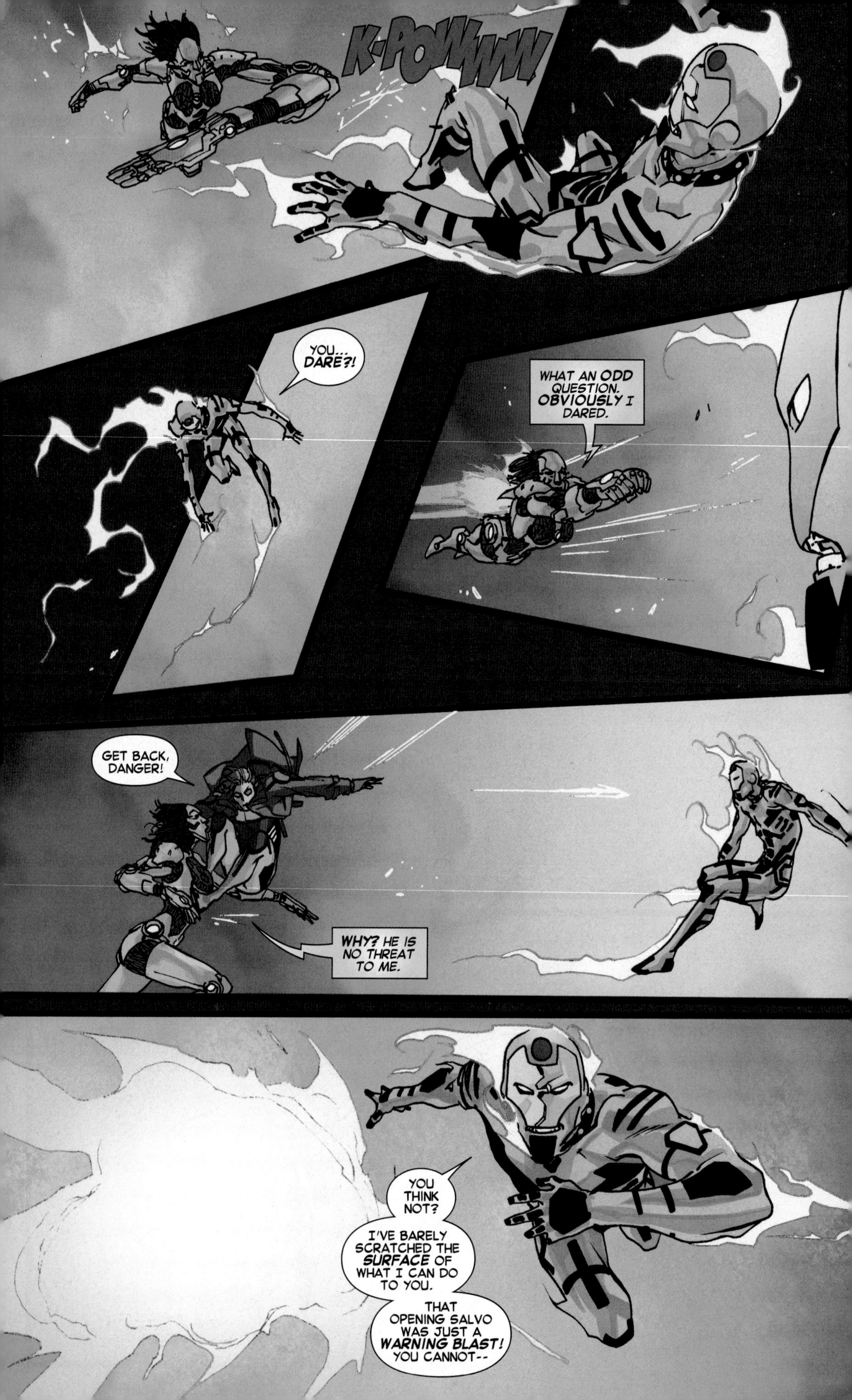
K-POWWW
YOU... DARE?!
WHAT AN ODD QUESTION. OBVIOUSLY I DARED.
GET BACK, DANGER!
WHY? HE IS NO THREAT TO ME.
YOU THINK NOT?
I'VE BARELY SCRATCHED THE SURFACE OF WHAT I CAN DO TO YOU.
THAT OPENING SALVO WAS JUST A WARNING BLAST! YOU CANNOT--

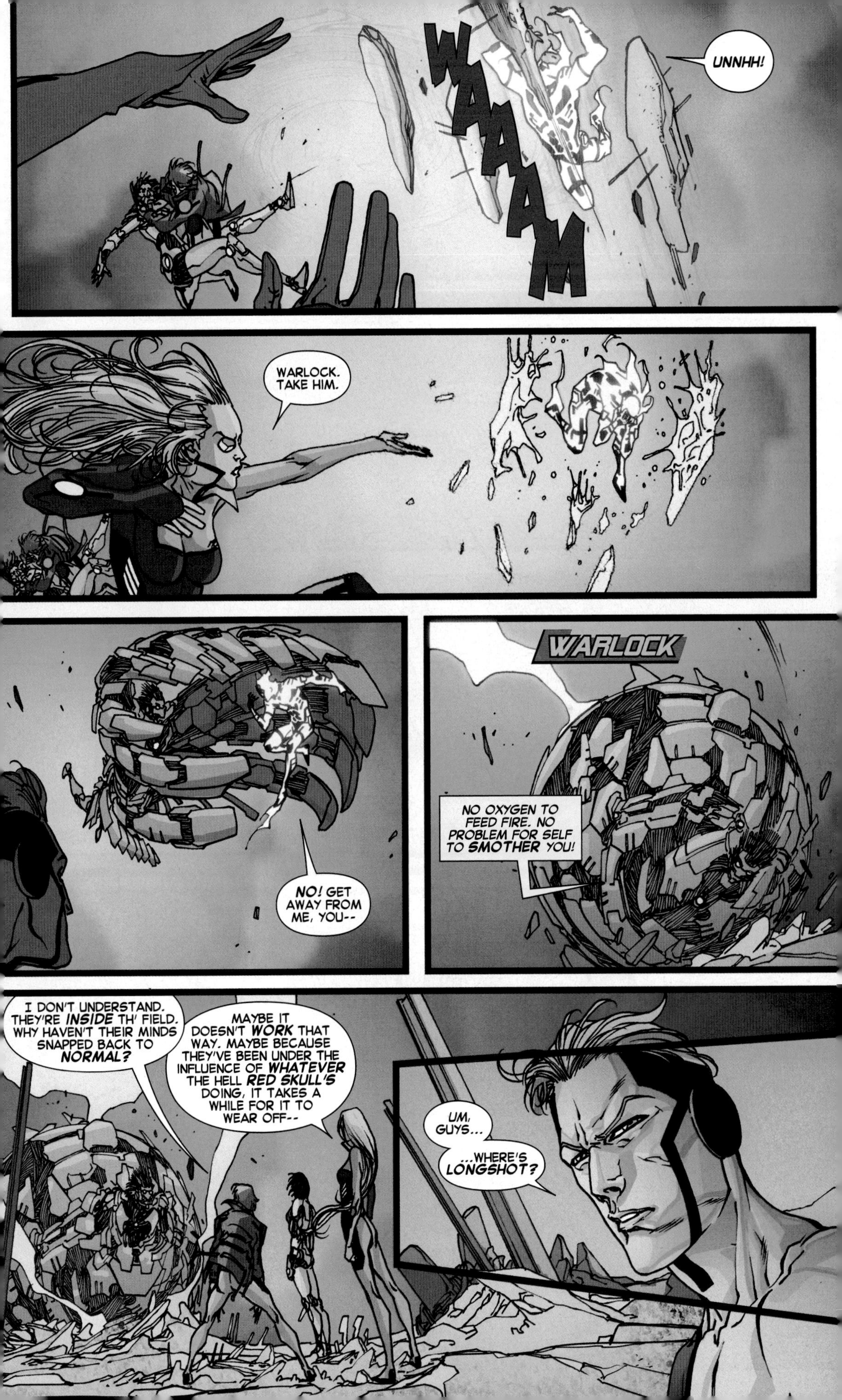
WAAAAM
UNNHH!
WARLOCK. TAKE HIM.
NO! GET AWAY FROM ME, YOU--
WARLOCK
NO OXYGEN TO FEED FIRE. NO PROBLEM FOR SELF TO SMOTHER YOU!
I DON'T UNDERSTAND. THEY'RE INSIDE TH' FIELD. WHY HAVEN'T THEIR MINDS SNAPPED BACK TO NORMAL?
MAYBE IT DOESN'T WORK THAT WAY. MAYBE BECAUSE THEY'VE BEEN UNDER THE INFLUENCE OF WHATEVER THE HELL RED SKULL'S DOING, IT TAKES A WHILE FOR IT TO WEAR OFF--
UM, GUYS...
...WHERE'S LONGSHOT?

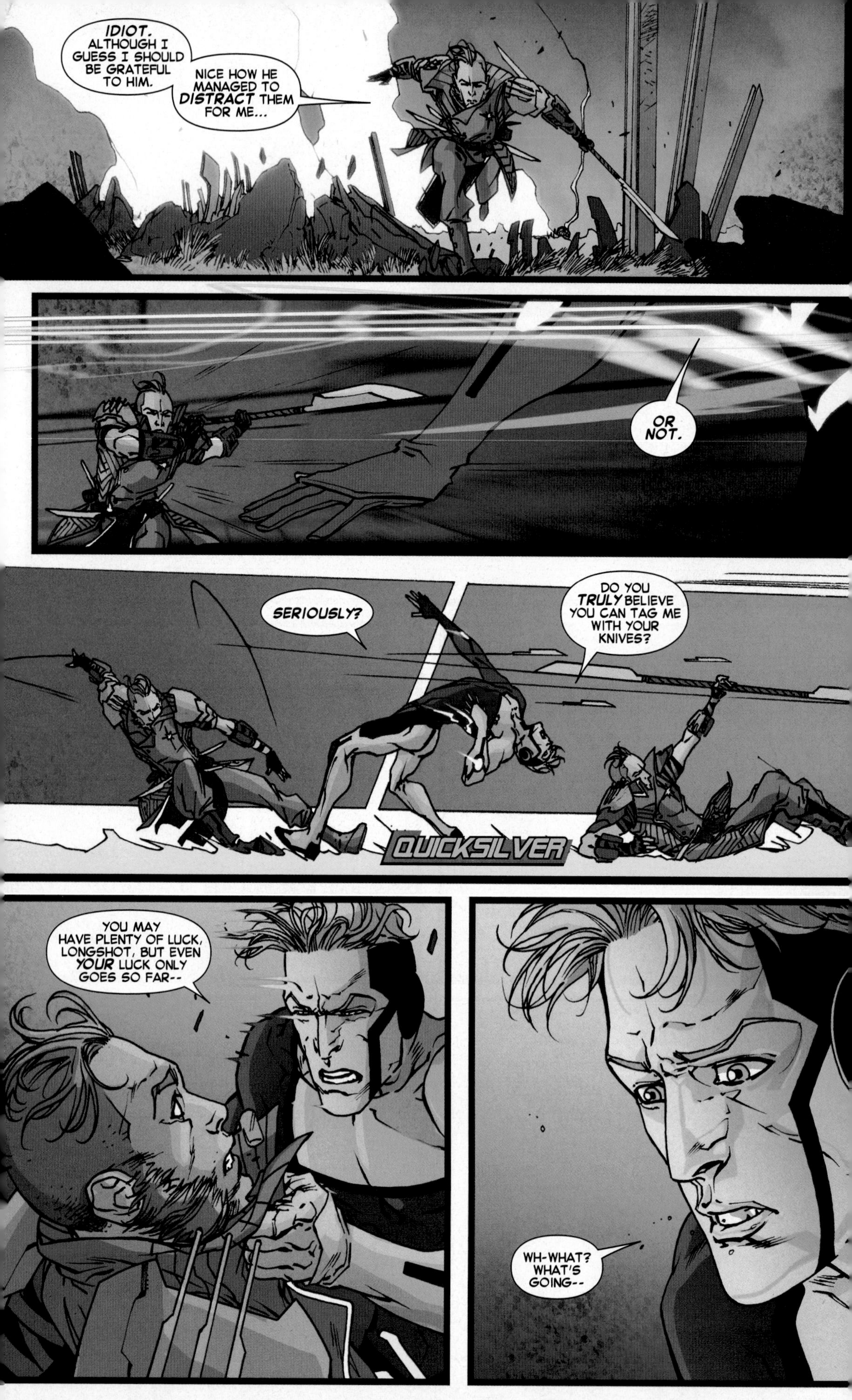
IDIOT. ALTHOUGH I GUESS I SHOULD BE GRATEFUL TO HIM.
NICE HOW HE MANAGED TO DISTRACT THEM FOR ME...
OR NOT.
SERIOUSLY?
DO YOU TRULY BELIEVE YOU CAN TAG ME WITH YOUR KNIVES?
QUICKSILVER
YOU MAY HAVE PLENTY OF LUCK, LONGSHOT, BUT EVEN YOUR LUCK ONLY GOES SO FAR--
WH-WHAT? WHAT'S GOING--

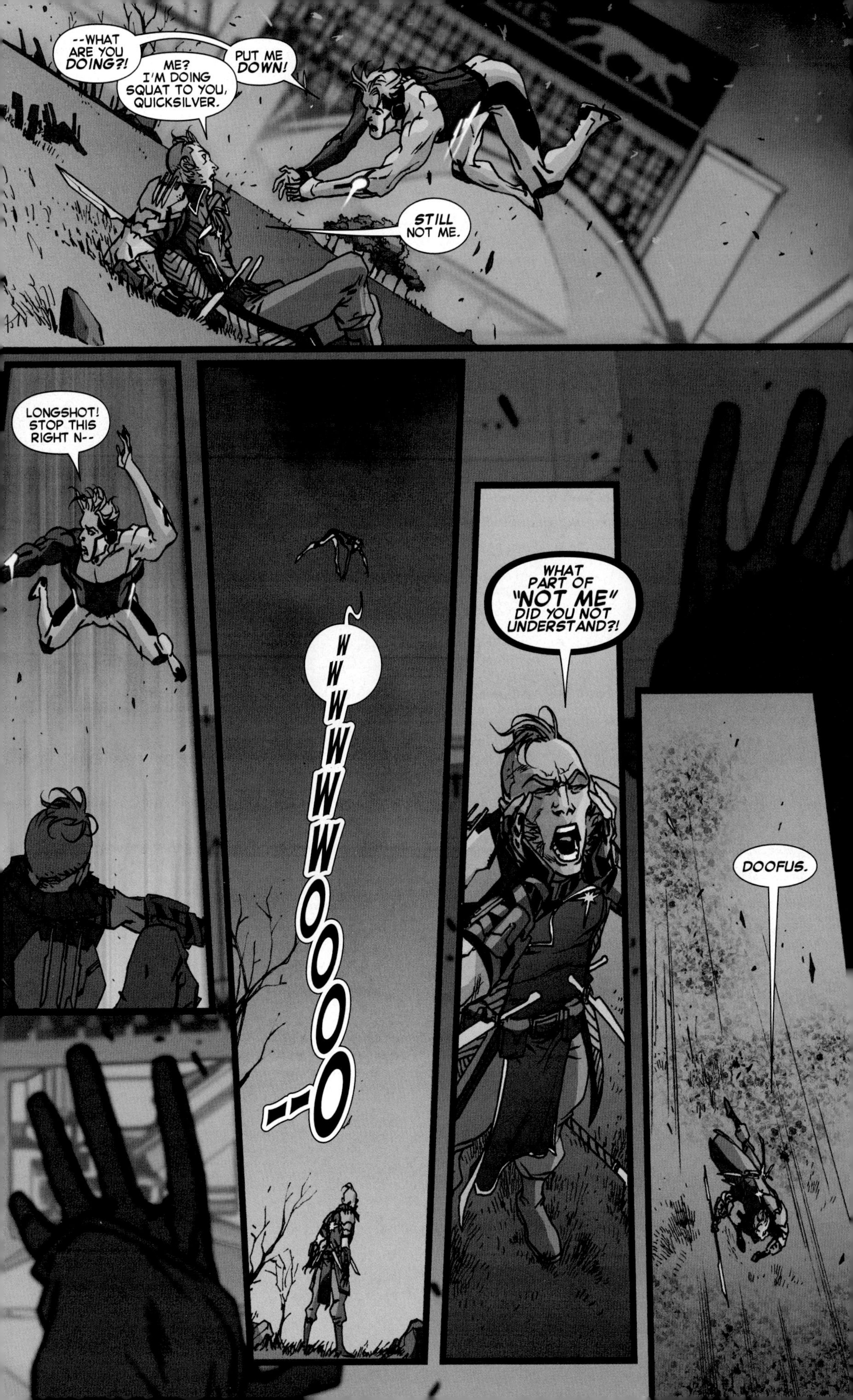
--WHAT ARE YOU DOING?!
PUT ME DOWN!
ME? I'M DOING SQUAT TO YOU, QUICKSILVER.
STILL NOT ME.
LONGSHOT! STOP THIS RIGHT N--
WWWWWWOOOOO!
WHAT PART OF "NOT ME" DID YOU NOT UNDERSTAND?!
DOOFUS.

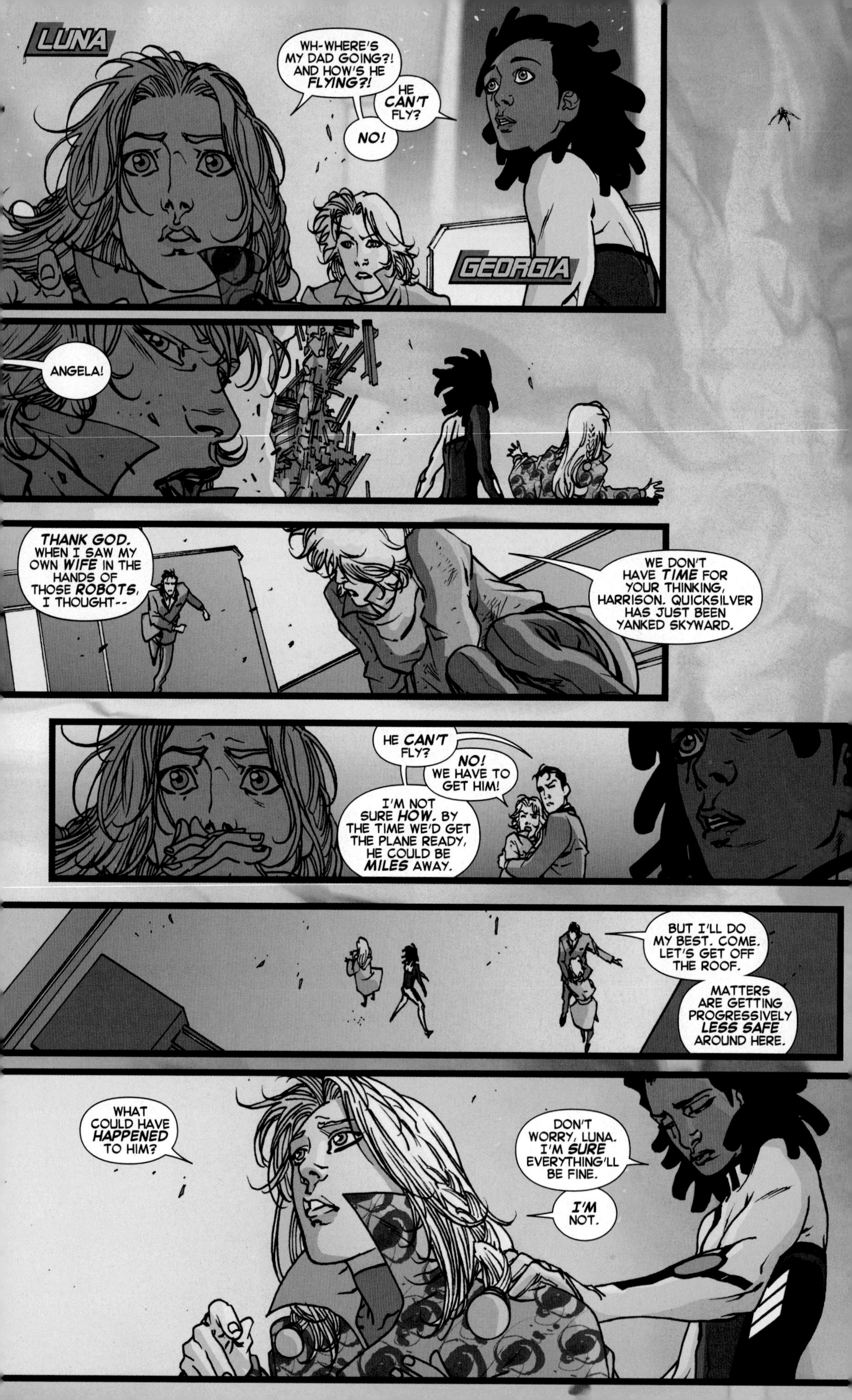
LUNA
WH-WHERE'S MY DAD GOING?! AND HOW'S HE FLYING?!
HE CAN'T FLY?
NO!
GEORGIA
ANGELA!
THANK GOD. WHEN I SAW MY OWN WIFE IN THE HANDS OF THOSE ROBOTS, I THOUGHT--
WE DON'T HAVE TIME FOR YOUR THINKING, HARRISON. QUICKSILVER HAS JUST BEEN YANKED SKYWARD.
HE CAN'T FLY?
NO! WE HAVE TO GET HIM!
I'M NOT SURE HOW. BY THE TIME WE'D GET THE PLANE READY, HE COULD BE MILES AWAY.
BUT I'LL DO MY BEST. COME. LET'S GET OFF THE ROOF.
MATTERS ARE GETTING PROGRESSIVELY LESS SAFE AROUND HERE.
WHAT COULD HAVE HAPPENED TO HIM?
DON'T WORRY, LUNA. I'M SURE EVERYTHING'LL BE FINE.
I'M NOT.

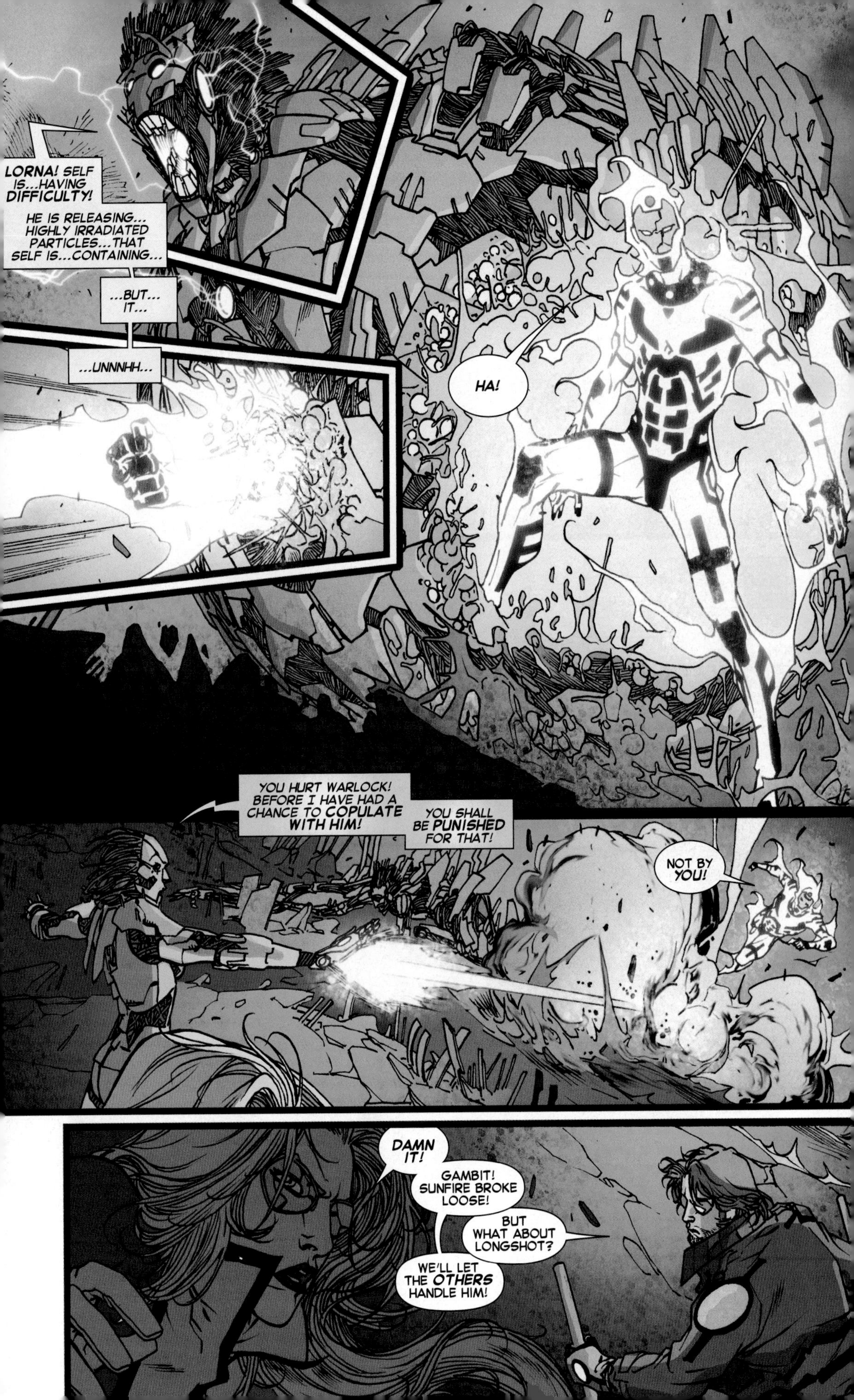

LORNA! SELF IS...HAVING DIFFICULTY!
HE IS RELEASING... HIGHLY IRRADIATED PARTICLES...THAT SELF IS...CONTAINING...
...BUT... IT...
...UNNNHH...
HA!
YOU HURT WARLOCK! BEFORE I HAVE HAD A CHANCE TO COPULATE WITH HIM!
YOU SHALL BE PUNISHED FOR THAT!
NOT BY YOU!
DAMN IT!
GAMBIT! SUNFIRE BROKE LOOSE!
BUT WHAT ABOUT LONGSHOT?
WE'LL LET THE OTHERS HANDLE HIM!

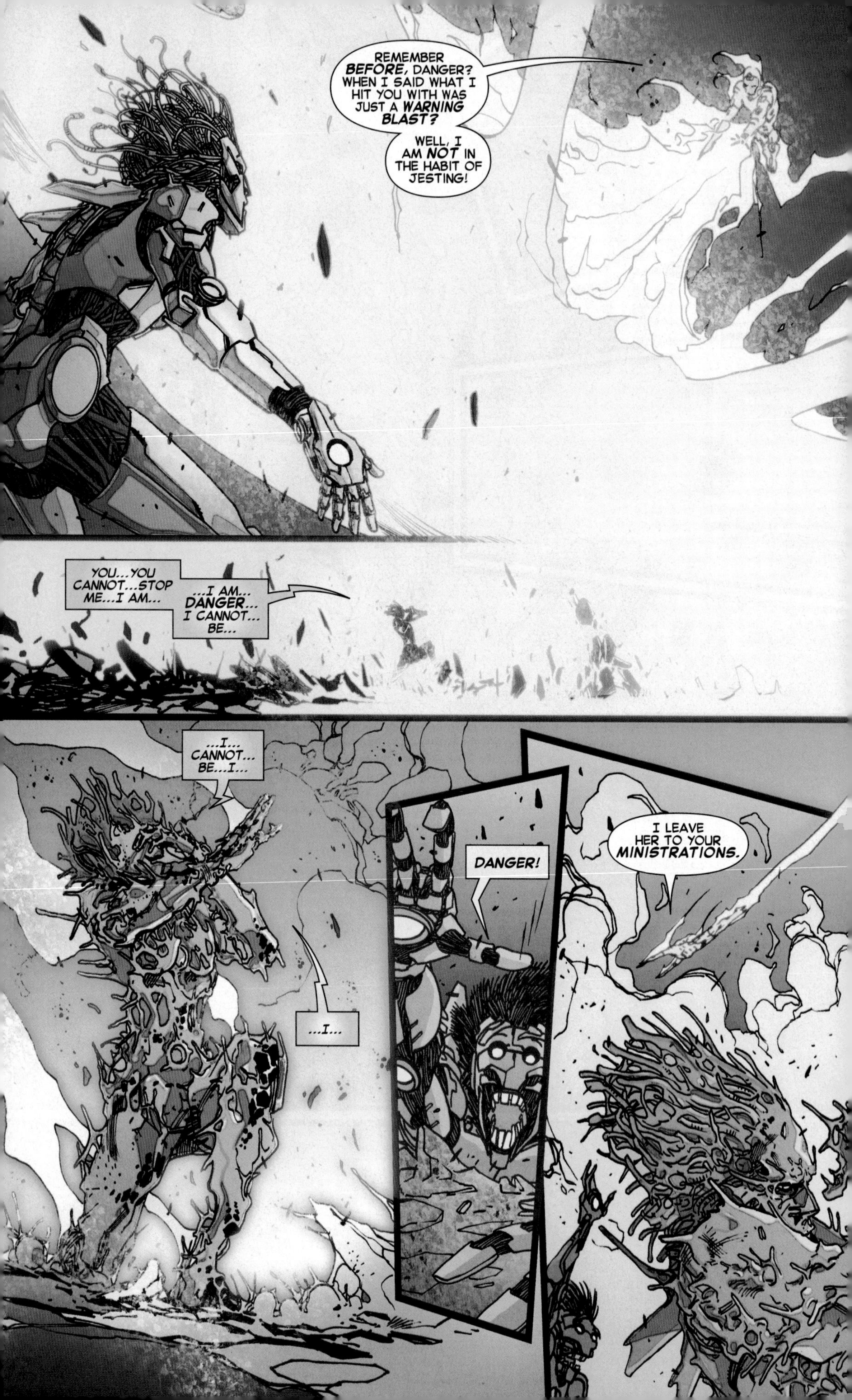
REMEMBER BEFORE, DANGER? WHEN I SAID WHAT I HIT YOU WITH WAS JUST A WARNING BLAST?
WELL, I AM NOT IN THE HABIT OF JESTING!
YOU...YOU CANNOT...STOP ME...I AM...
...I AM... DANGER... I CANNOT... BE...
...I... CANNOT... BE...I...
...I...
DANGER!
I LEAVE HER TO YOUR MINISTRATIONS.

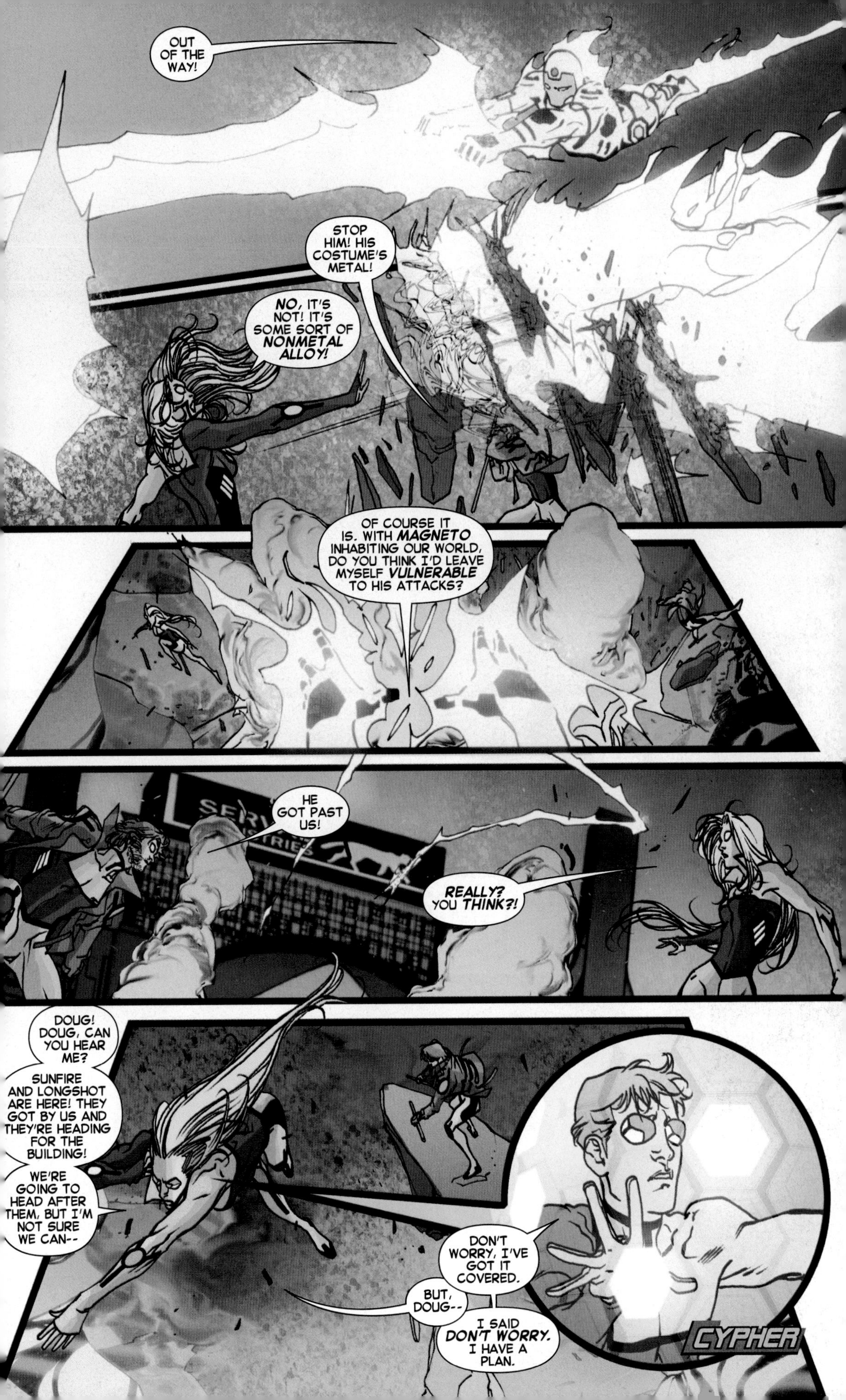
OUT OF THE WAY!
STOP HIM! HIS COSTUME'S METAL!
NO, IT'S NOT! IT'S SOME SORT OF NONMETAL ALLOY!
OF COURSE IT IS. WITH MAGNETO INHABITING OUR WORLD, DO YOU THINK I'D LEAVE MYSELF VULNERABLE TO HIS ATTACKS?
HE GOT PAST US!
REALLY? YOU THINK?!
DOUG! DOUG, CAN YOU HEAR ME?
SUNFIRE AND LONGSHOT ARE HERE! THEY GOT BY US AND THEY'RE HEADING FOR THE BUILDING!
WE'RE GOING TO HEAD AFTER THEM, BUT I'M NOT SURE WE CAN--
DON'T WORRY, I'VE GOT IT COVERED.
BUT, DOUG--
I SAID DON'T WORRY. I HAVE A PLAN.
CYPHER

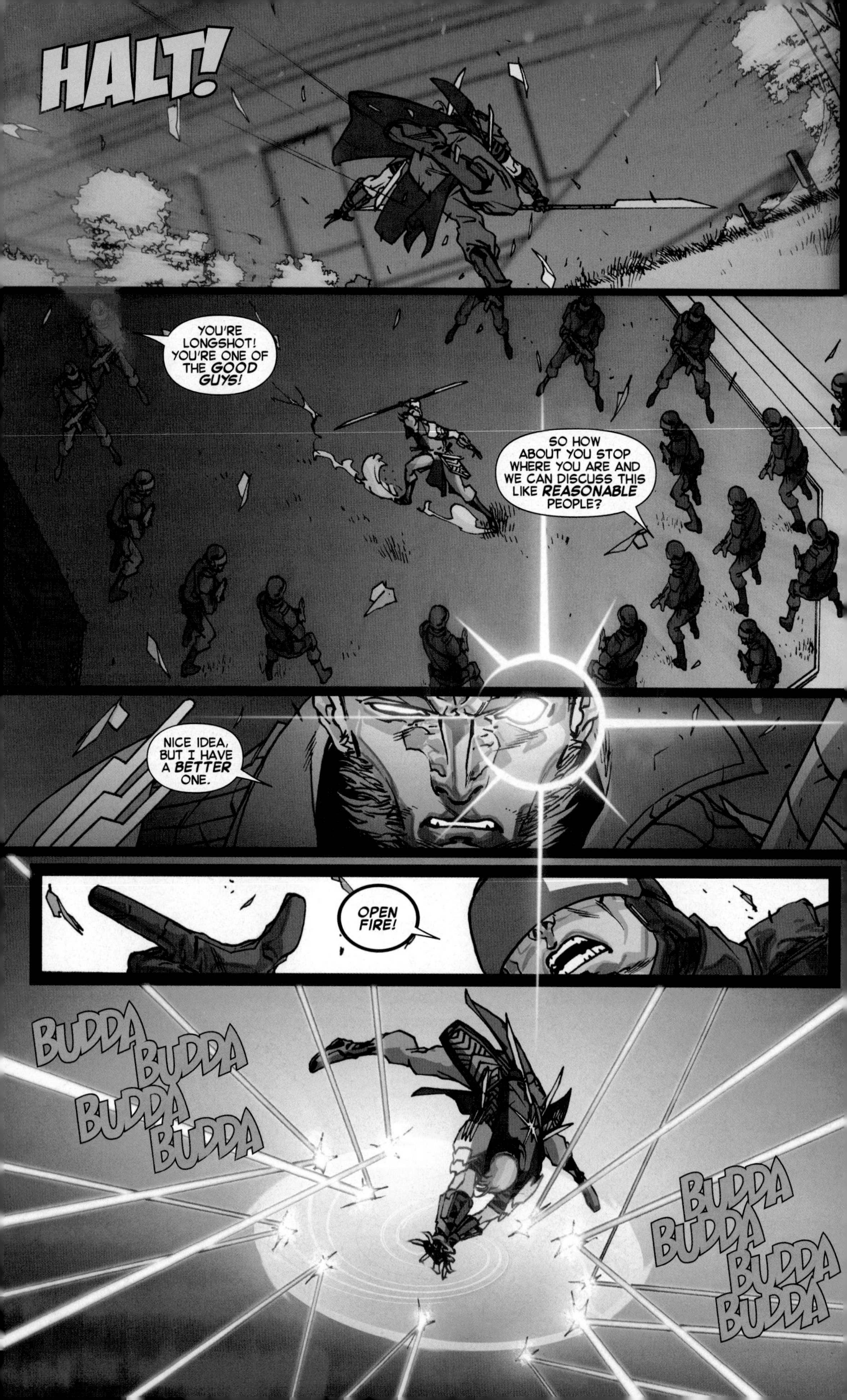
HALT!
YOU'RE LONGSHOT! YOU'RE ONE OF THE GOOD GUYS!
SO HOW ABOUT YOU STOP WHERE YOU ARE AND WE CAN DISCUSS THIS LIKE REASONABLE PEOPLE?
NICE IDEA, BUT I HAVE A BETTER ONE.
OPEN FIRE!
BUDDA BUDDA BUDDA BUDDA
BUDDA BUDDA BUDDA BUDDA

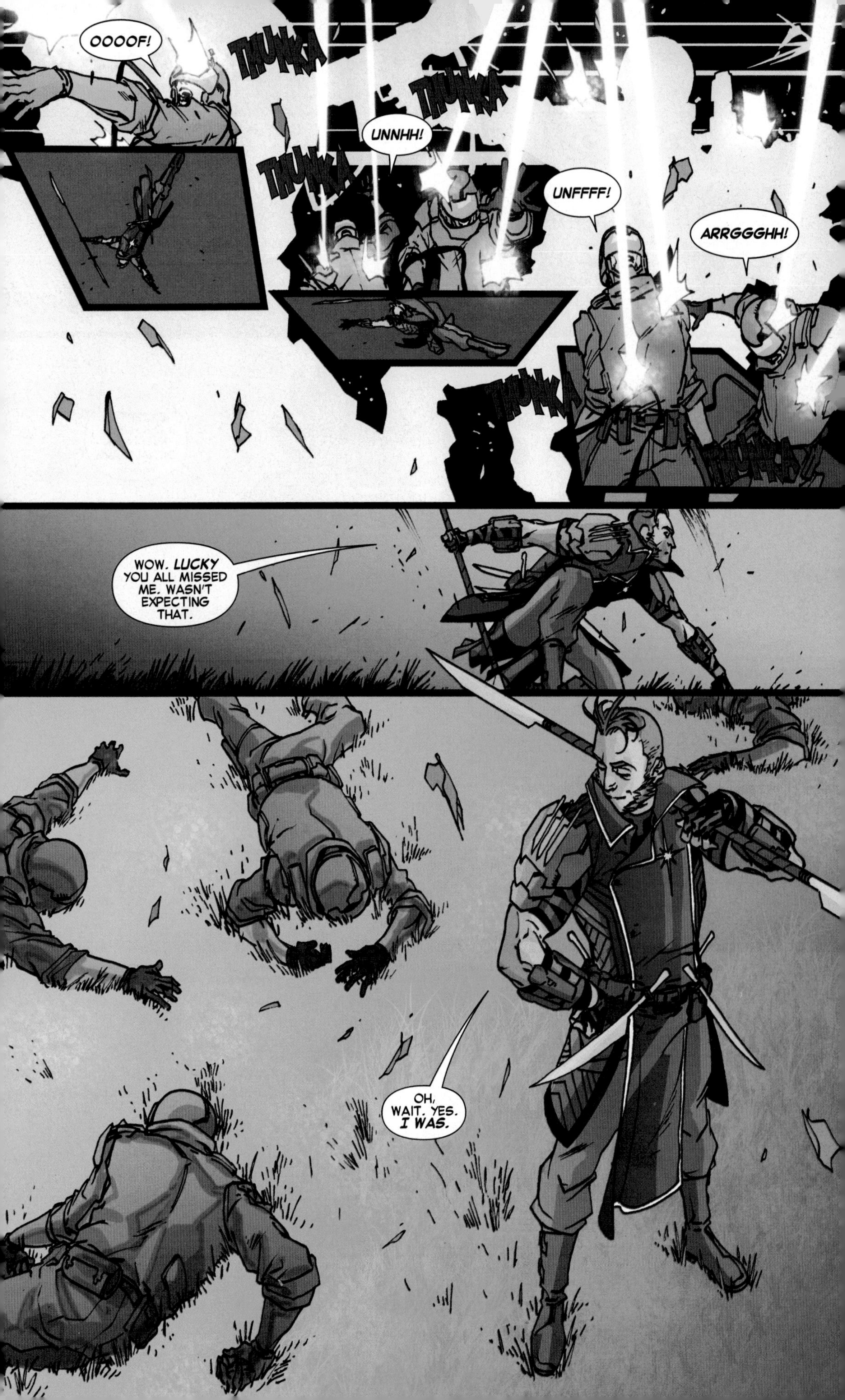
OOOOF!
THUNKA
THUNKA
UNNHH!
THUNKA
UNFFFF!
ARRGGGHH!
THUNKA
THUNKA
WOW. LUCKY YOU ALL MISSED ME. WASN'T EXPECTING THAT.
OH, WAIT. YES. I WAS.

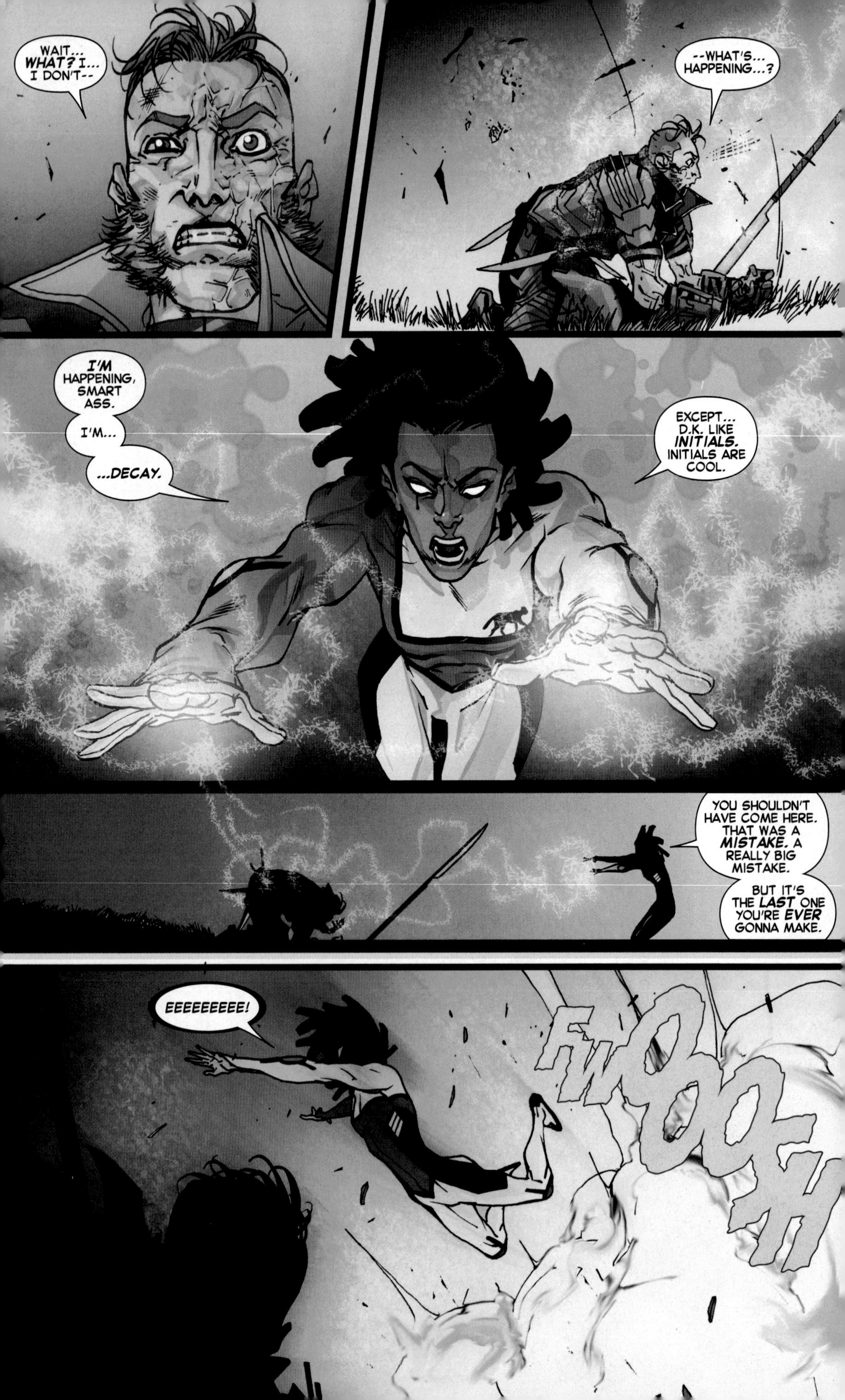
WAIT... WHAT? I... I DON'T--
--WHAT'S... HAPPENING...?
I'M HAPPENING, SMART ASS.
I'M...
...DECAY.
EXCEPT... D.K. LIKE INITIALS. INITIALS ARE COOL.
YOU SHOULDN'T HAVE COME HERE. THAT WAS A MISTAKE. A REALLY BIG MISTAKE.
BUT IT'S THE LAST ONE YOU'RE EVER GONNA MAKE.
EEEEEEEEE!
FWOOOOH

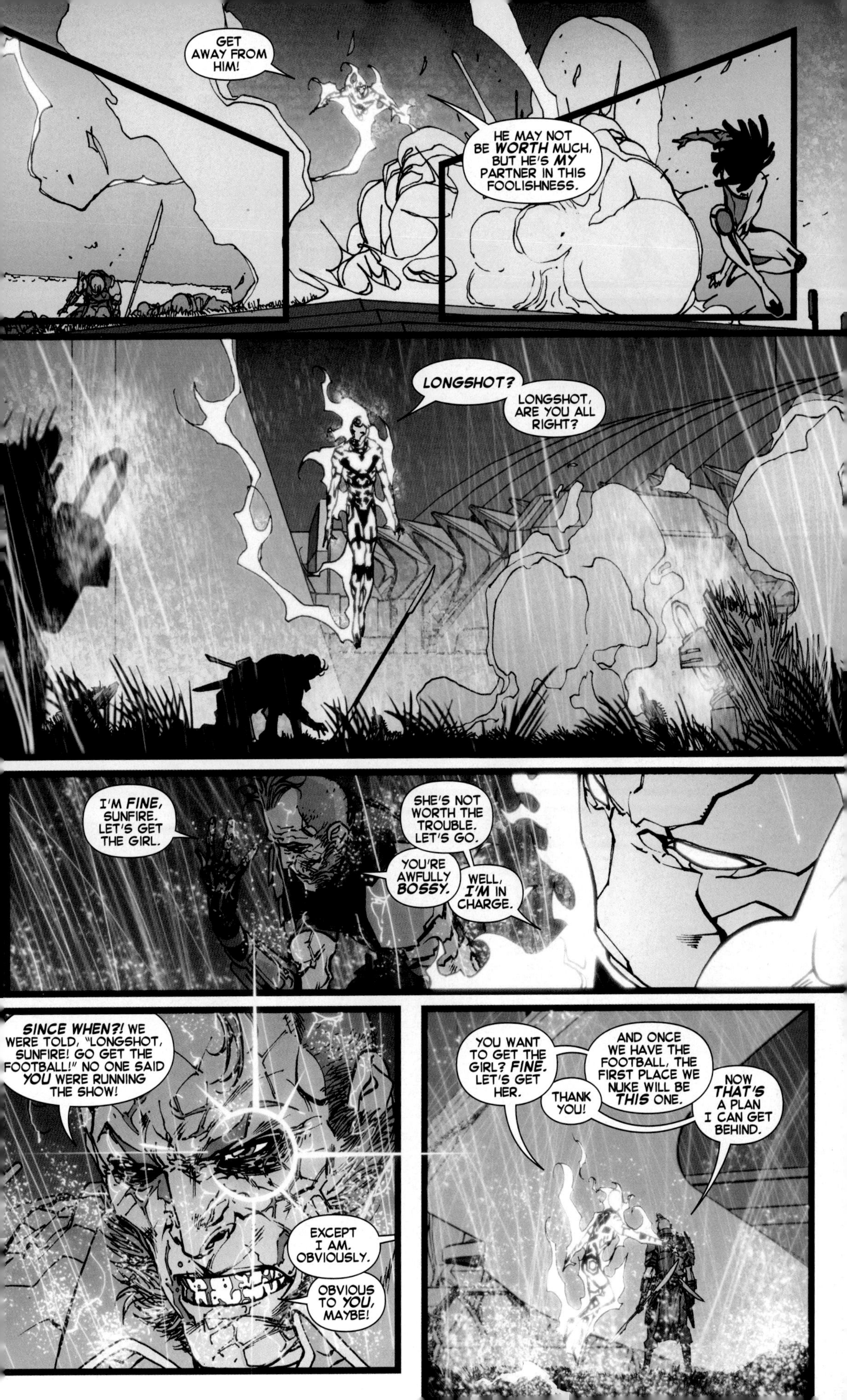

GET AWAY FROM HIM!
HE MAY NOT BE WORTH MUCH, BUT HE'S MY PARTNER IN THIS FOOLISHNESS.
LONGSHOT?
LONGSHOT, ARE YOU ALL RIGHT?
I'M FINE, SUNFIRE. LET'S GET THE GIRL.
SHE'S NOT WORTH THE TROUBLE. LET'S GO.
YOU'RE AWFULLY BOSSY.
WELL, I'M IN CHARGE.
SINCE WHEN?! WE WERE TOLD, "LONGSHOT, SUNFIRE! GO GET THE FOOTBALL!" NO ONE SAID YOU WERE RUNNING THE SHOW!
EXCEPT I AM. OBVIOUSLY.
OBVIOUS TO YOU, MAYBE!
YOU WANT TO GET THE GIRL? FINE. LET'S GET HER.
THANK YOU!
AND ONCE WE HAVE THE FOOTBALL, THE FIRST PLACE WE NUKE WILL BE THIS ONE.
NOW THAT'S A PLAN I CAN GET BEHIND.

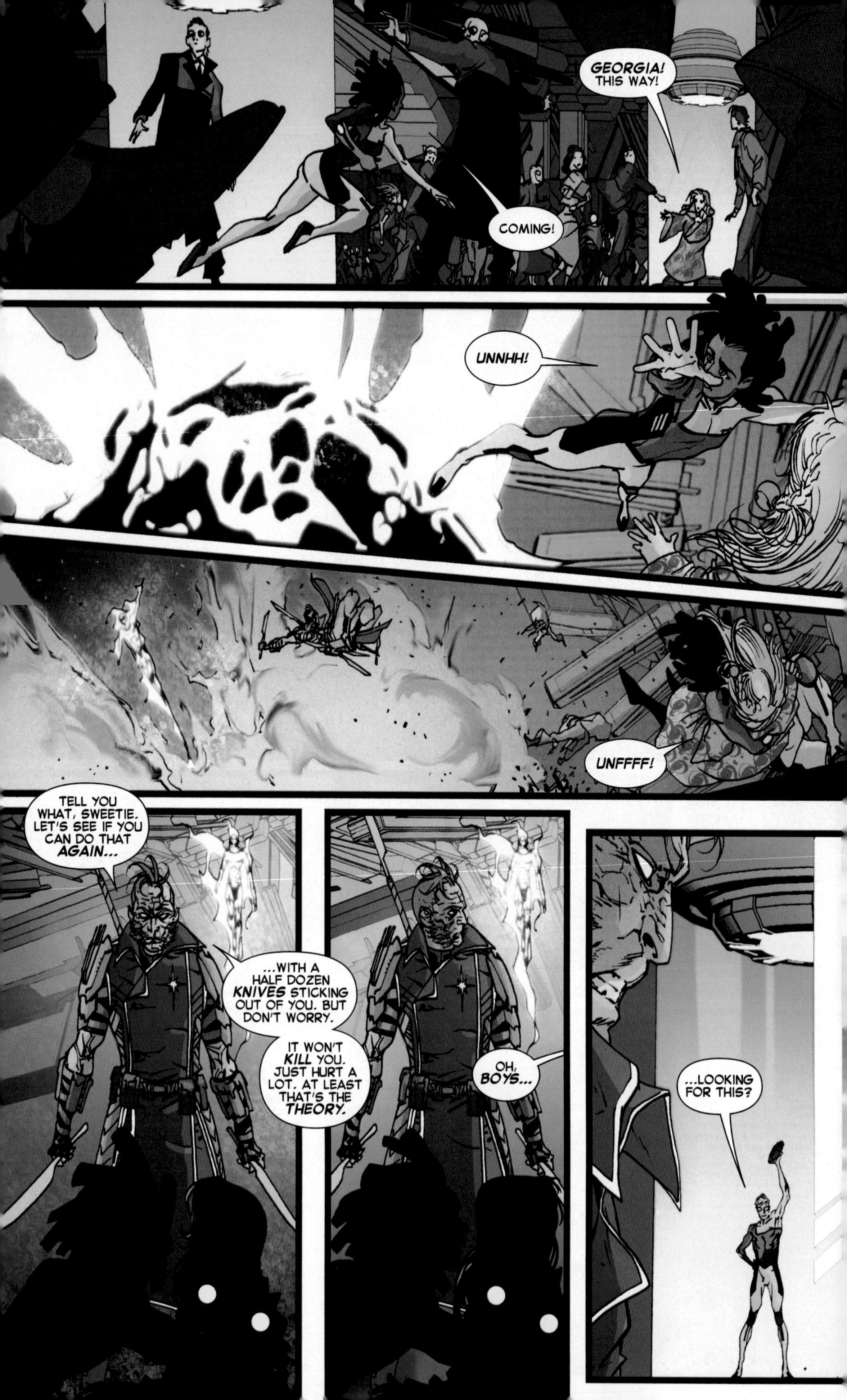
GEORGIA! THIS WAY!
COMING!
UNNHH!
UNFFFF!
TELL YOU WHAT, SWEETIE. LET'S SEE IF YOU CAN DO THAT AGAIN...
...WITH A HALF DOZEN KNIVES STICKING OUT OF YOU. BUT DON'T WORRY.
IT WON'T KILL YOU. JUST HURT A LOT. AT LEAST THAT'S THE THEORY.
OH, BOYS...
...LOOKING FOR THIS?

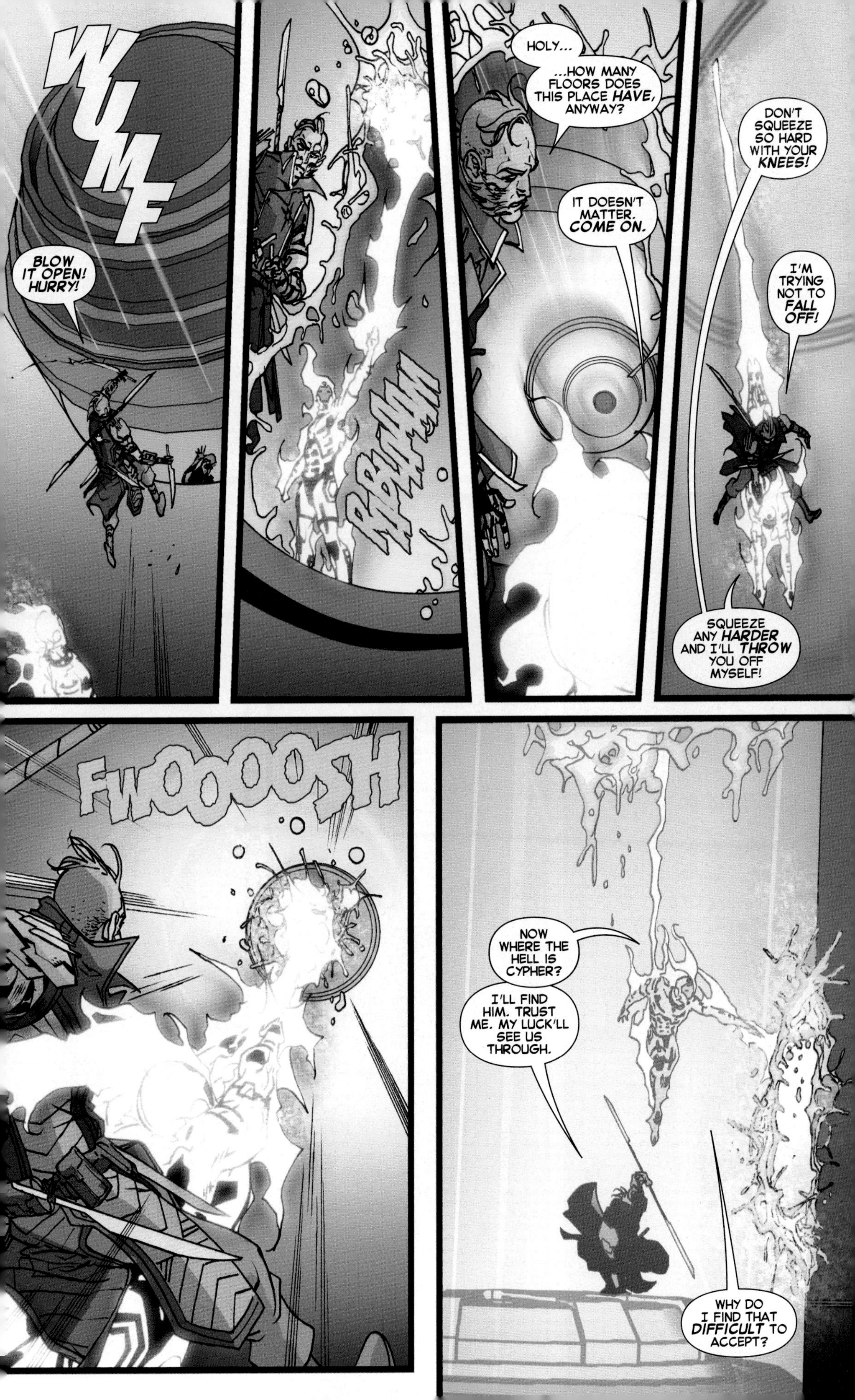

WUMF
BLOW IT OPEN! HURRY!
BRRRAMM
HOLY...
...HOW MANY FLOORS DOES THIS PLACE HAVE, ANYWAY?
IT DOESN'T MATTER. COME ON.
DON'T SQUEEZE SO HARD WITH YOUR KNEES!
I'M TRYING NOT TO FALL OFF!
SQUEEZE ANY HARDER AND I'LL THROW YOU OFF MYSELF!
FWOOOOSH
NOW WHERE THE HELL IS CYPHER?
I'LL FIND HIM. TRUST ME. MY LUCK'LL SEE US THROUGH.
WHY DO I FIND THAT DIFFICULT TO ACCEPT?

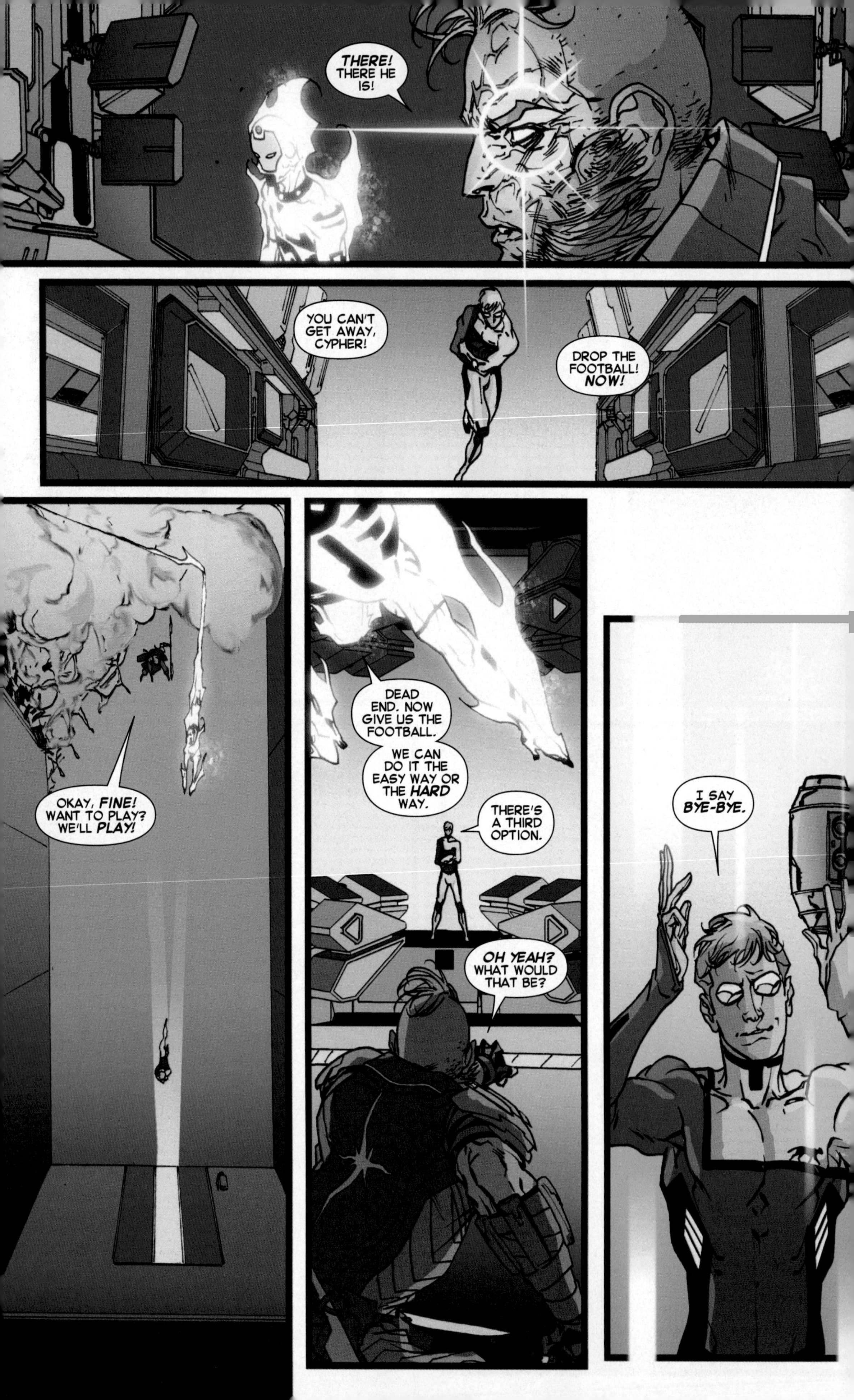
THERE! THERE HE IS!
YOU CAN'T GET AWAY, CYPHER!
DROP THE FOOTBALL! NOW!
OKAY, FINE! WANT TO PLAY? WE'LL PLAY!
DEAD END. NOW GIVE US THE FOOTBALL.
WE CAN DO IT THE EASY WAY OR THE HARD WAY.
THERE'S A THIRD OPTION.
OH YEAH? WHAT WOULD THAT BE?
I SAY BYE-BYE.

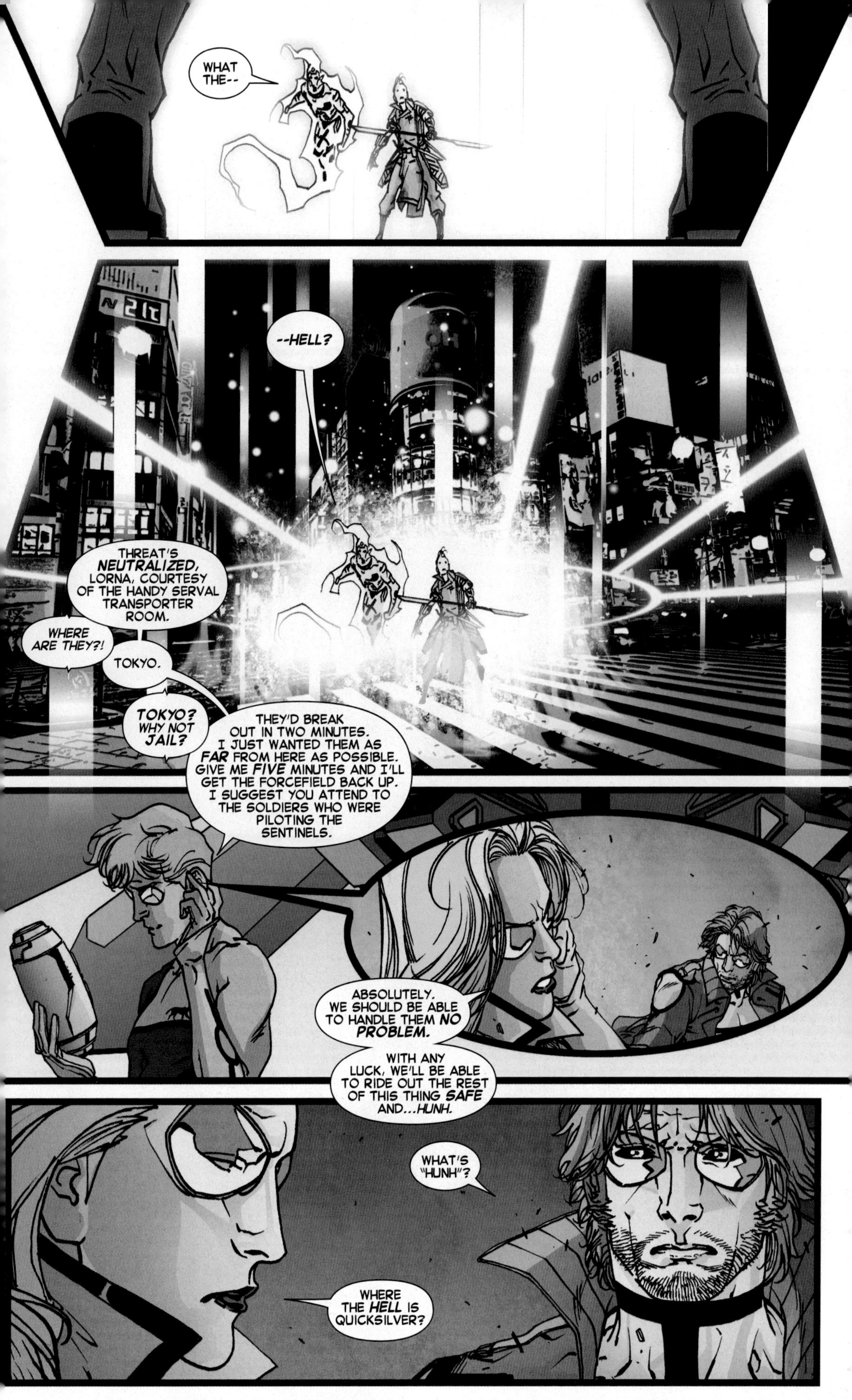
WHAT THE--
--HELL?
THREAT'S NEUTRALIZED, LORNA, COURTESY OF THE HANDY SERVAL TRANSPORTER ROOM.
WHERE ARE THEY?!
TOKYO.
TOKYO? WHY NOT JAIL?
THEY'D BREAK OUT IN TWO MINUTES. I JUST WANTED THEM AS FAR FROM HERE AS POSSIBLE. GIVE ME FIVE MINUTES AND I'LL GET THE FORCEFIELD BACK UP. I SUGGEST YOU ATTEND TO THE SOLDIERS WHO WERE PILOTING THE SENTINELS.
ABSOLUTELY. WE SHOULD BE ABLE TO HANDLE THEM NO PROBLEM.
WITH ANY LUCK, WE'LL BE ABLE TO RIDE OUT THE REST OF THIS THING SAFE AND...HUNH.
WHAT'S "HUNH"?
WHERE THE HELL IS QUICKSILVER?

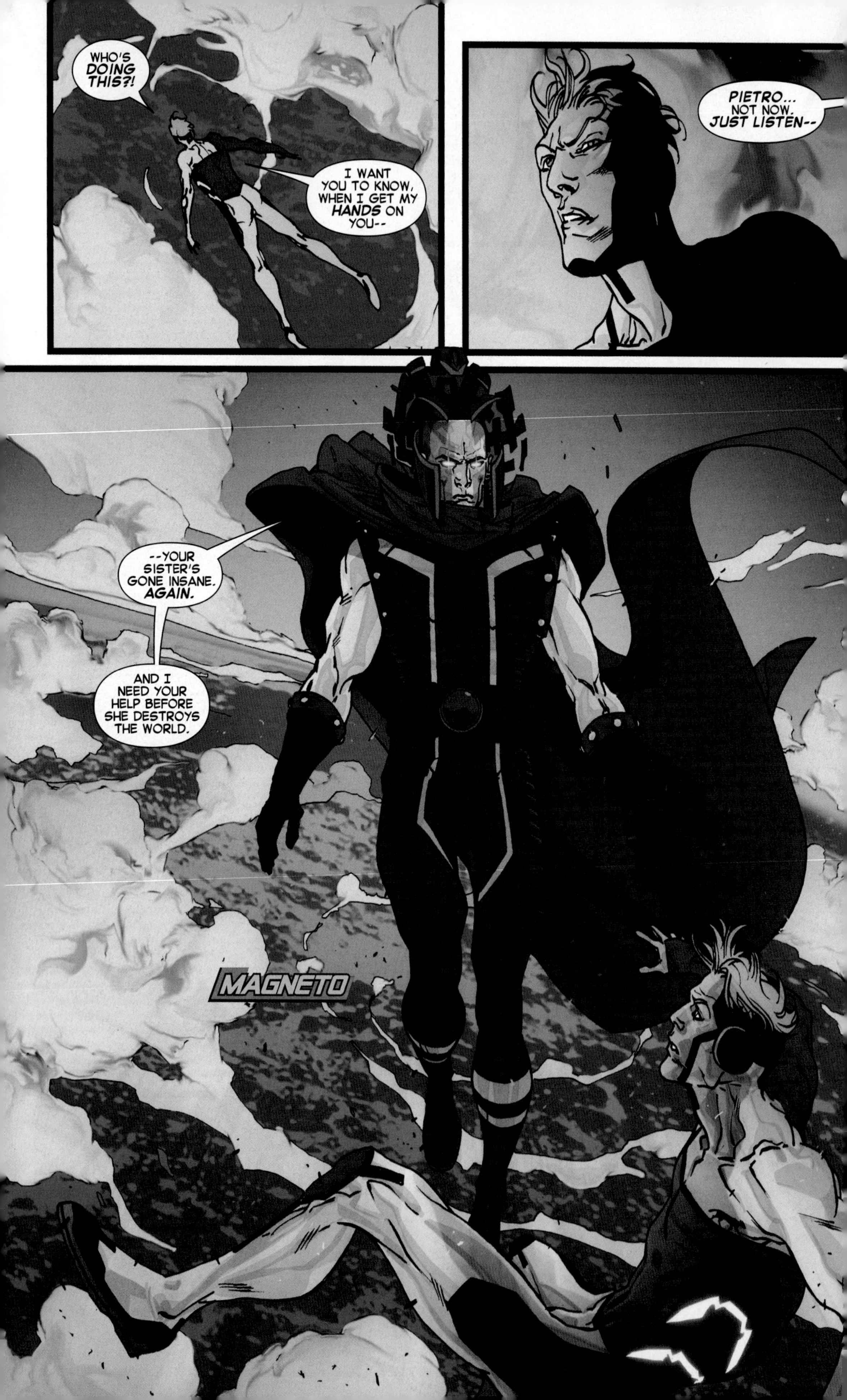
WHO'S DOING THIS?!
I WANT YOU TO KNOW, WHEN I GET MY HANDS ON YOU--
PIETRO... NOT NOW. JUST LISTEN--
--YOUR SISTER'S GONE INSANE. AGAIN.
AND I NEED YOUR HELP BEFORE SHE DESTROYS THE WORLD.
MAGNETO

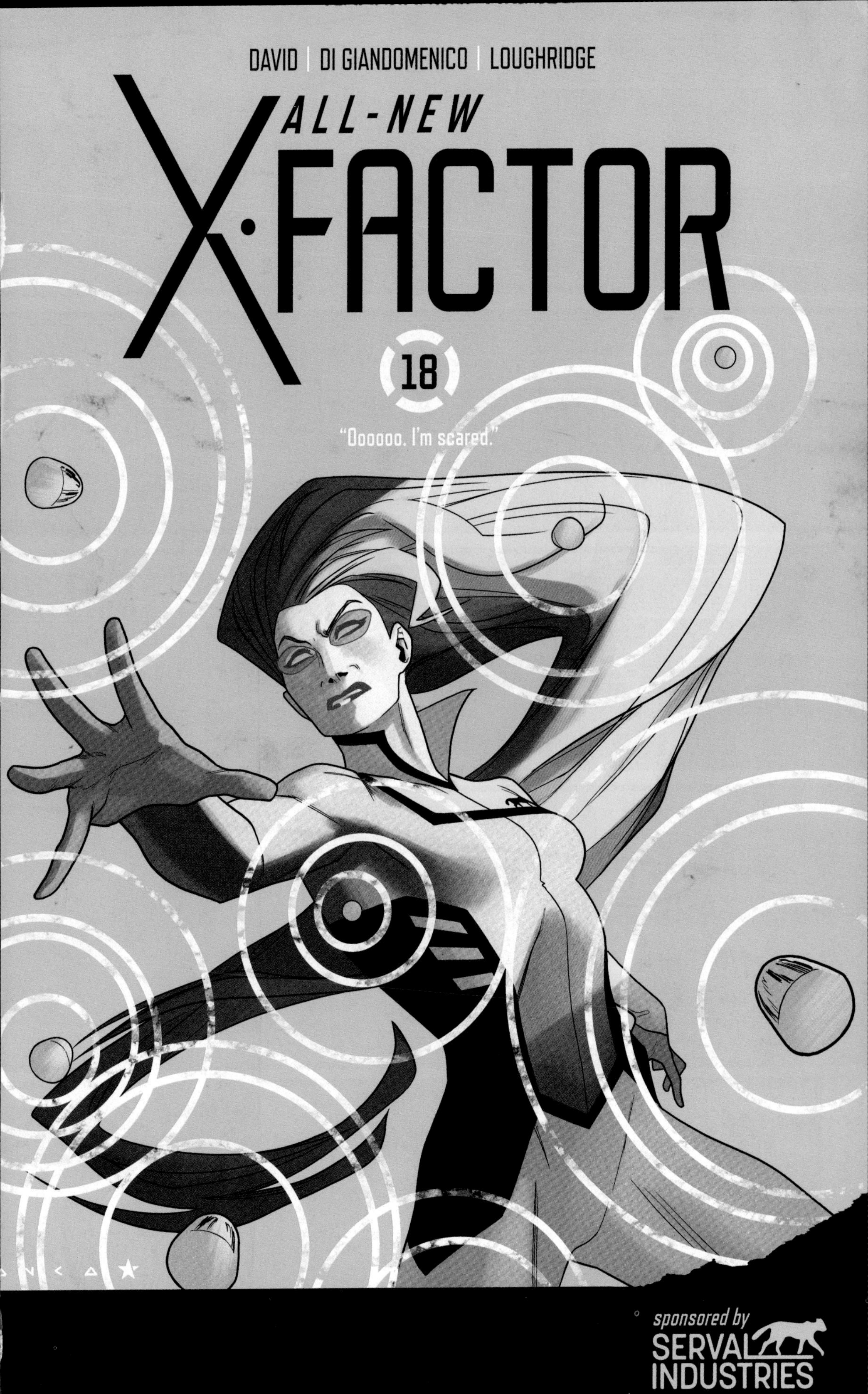
DAVID | DI GIANDOMENICO | LOUGHRIDGE
ALL-NEW
X-FACTOR
18
"Oooooo. I'm scared."
sponsored by
SERVAL
INDUSTRIES

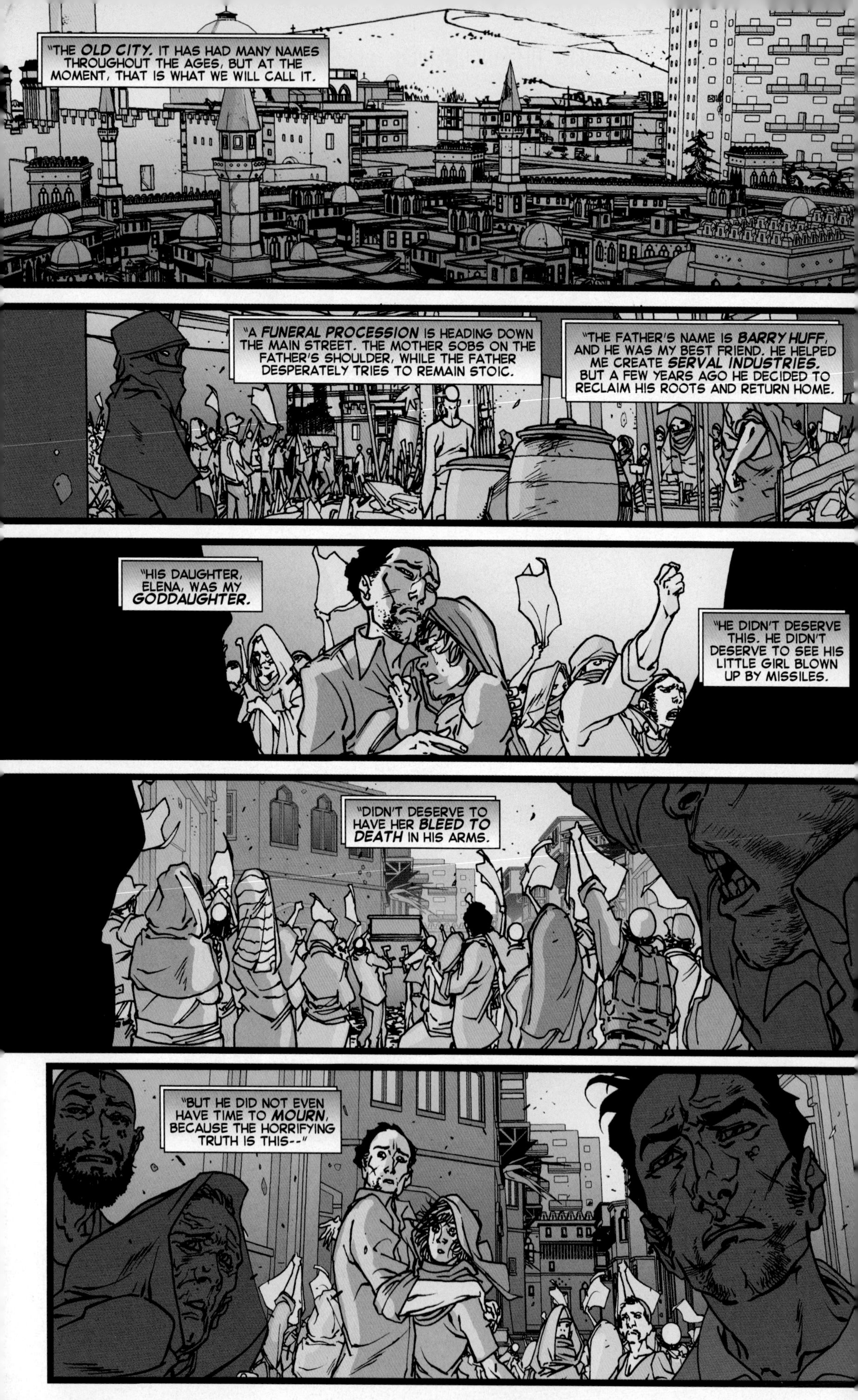
"THE OLD CITY. IT HAS HAD MANY NAMES THROUGHOUT THE AGES, BUT AT THE MOMENT, THAT IS WHAT WE WILL CALL IT.
"A FUNERAL PROCESSION IS HEADING DOWN THE MAIN STREET. THE MOTHER SOBS ON THE FATHER'S SHOULDER, WHILE THE FATHER DESPERATELY TRIES TO REMAIN STOIC.
"THE FATHER'S NAME IS BARRY HUFF, AND HE WAS MY BEST FRIEND. HE HELPED ME CREATE SERVAL INDUSTRIES. BUT A FEW YEARS AGO HE DECIDED TO RECLAIM HIS ROOTS AND RETURN HOME.
"HIS DAUGHTER, ELENA, WAS MY GODDAUGHTER.
"HE DIDN'T DESERVE THIS. HE DIDN'T DESERVE TO SEE HIS LITTLE GIRL BLOWN UP BY MISSILES.
"DIDN'T DESERVE TO HAVE HER BLEED TO DEATH IN HIS ARMS.
"BUT HE DID NOT EVEN HAVE TIME TO MOURN, BECAUSE THE HORRIFYING TRUTH IS THIS--"

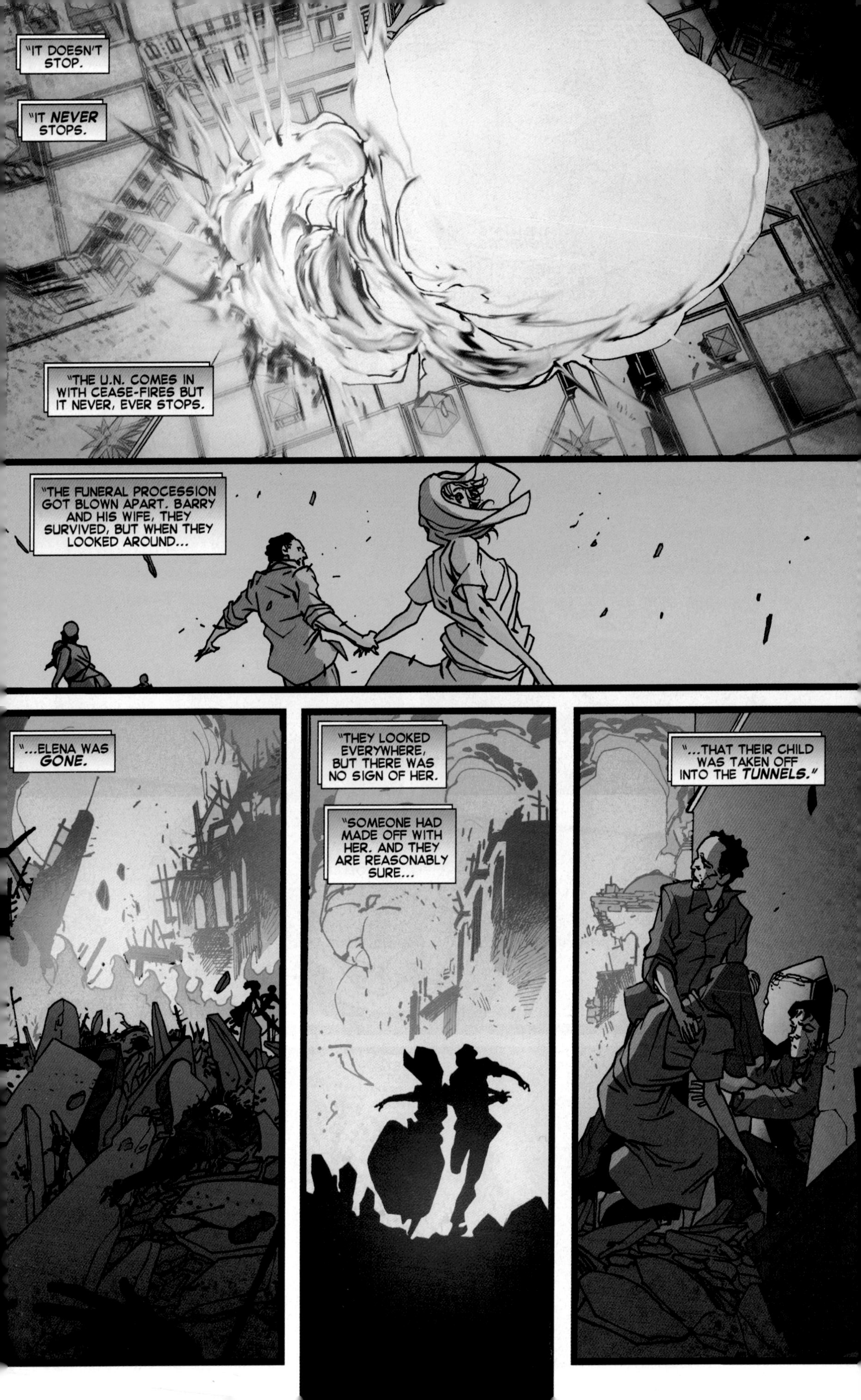
"IT DOESN'T STOP.
"IT *NEVER* STOPS.
"THE U.N. COMES IN WITH CEASE-FIRES BUT IT NEVER, EVER STOPS.
"THE FUNERAL PROCESSION GOT BLOWN APART. BARRY AND HIS WIFE, THEY SURVIVED, BUT WHEN THEY LOOKED AROUND...
"...ELENA WAS *GONE.*
"THEY LOOKED EVERYWHERE, BUT THERE WAS NO SIGN OF HER.
"SOMEONE HAD MADE OFF WITH HER. AND THEY ARE REASONABLY SURE...
"...THAT THEIR CHILD WAS TAKEN OFF INTO THE *TUNNELS.*"

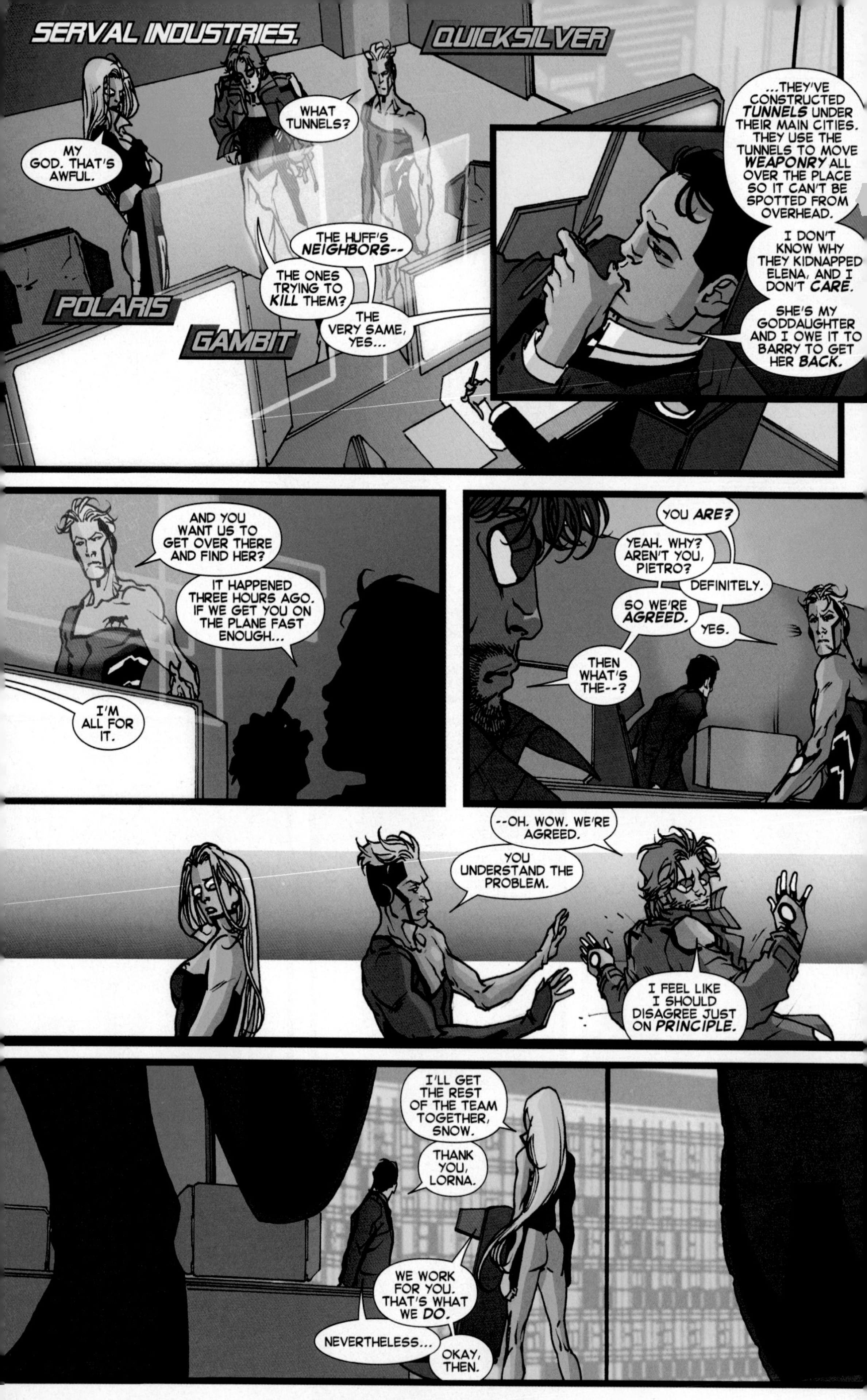
SERVAL INDUSTRIES.
QUICKSILVER
POLARIS
GAMBIT
...THEY'VE CONSTRUCTED TUNNELS UNDER THEIR MAIN CITIES. THEY USE THE TUNNELS TO MOVE WEAPONRY ALL OVER THE PLACE SO IT CAN'T BE SPOTTED FROM OVERHEAD.
MY GOD. THAT'S AWFUL.
WHAT TUNNELS?
THE HUFF'S NEIGHBORS--
THE ONES TRYING TO KILL THEM?
THE VERY SAME, YES...
I DON'T KNOW WHY THEY KIDNAPPED ELENA, AND I DON'T CARE.
SHE'S MY GODDAUGHTER AND I OWE IT TO BARRY TO GET HER BACK.
AND YOU WANT US TO GET OVER THERE AND FIND HER?
IT HAPPENED THREE HOURS AGO. IF WE GET YOU ON THE PLANE FAST ENOUGH...
I'M ALL FOR IT.
YOU ARE?
YEAH. WHY? AREN'T YOU, PIETRO?
DEFINITELY.
SO WE'RE AGREED.
YES.
THEN WHAT'S THE--?
--OH. WOW. WE'RE AGREED.
YOU UNDERSTAND THE PROBLEM.
I FEEL LIKE I SHOULD DISAGREE JUST ON PRINCIPLE.
I'LL GET THE REST OF THE TEAM TOGETHER, SNOW.
THANK YOU, LORNA.
WE WORK FOR YOU. THAT'S WHAT WE DO.
NEVERTHELESS...
OKAY, THEN.

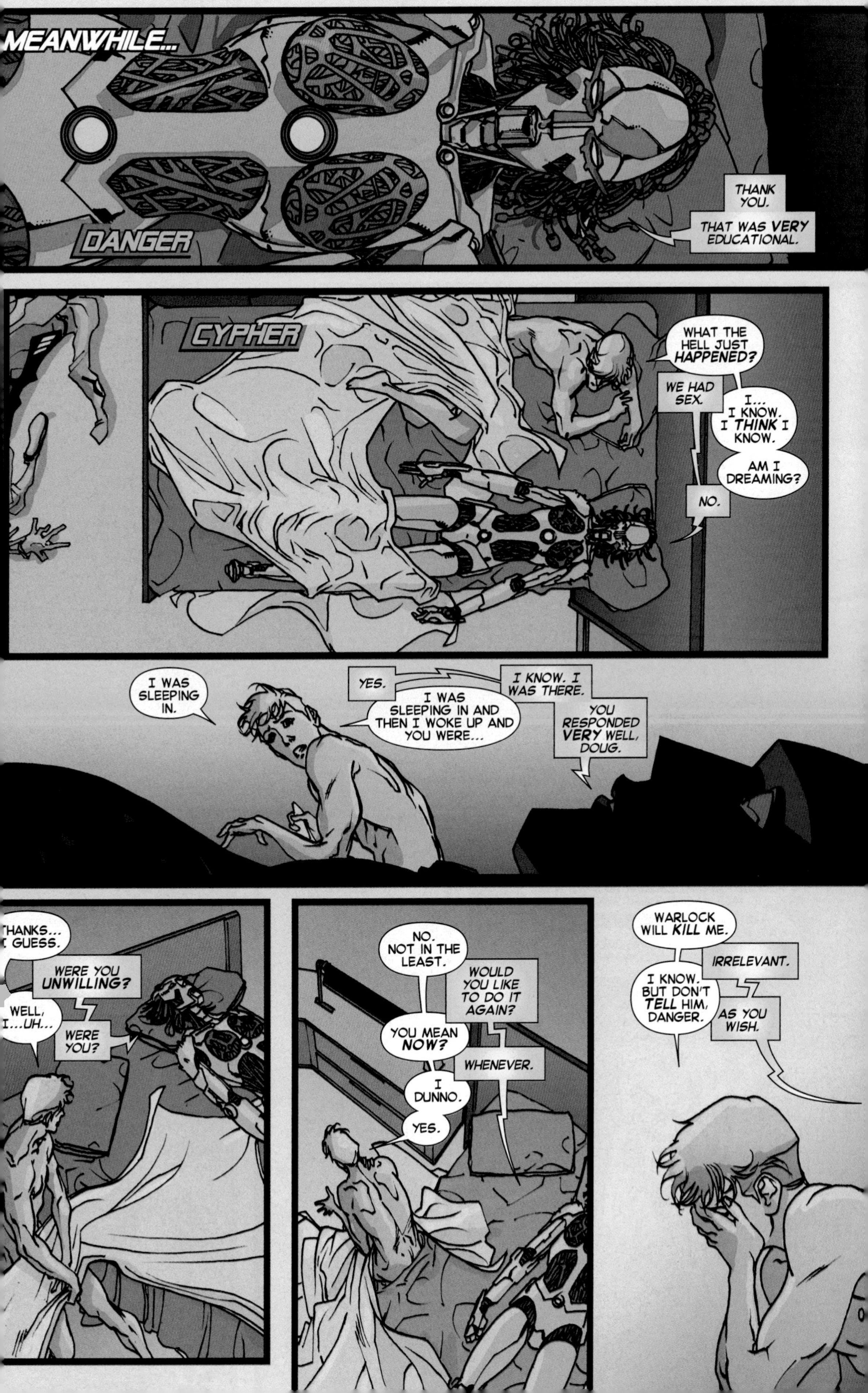
MEANWHILE...
DANGER
THANK YOU.
THAT WAS VERY EDUCATIONAL.
CYPHER
WHAT THE HELL JUST HAPPENED?
WE HAD SEX.
I... I KNOW. I THINK I KNOW.
AM I DREAMING?
NO.
I WAS SLEEPING IN.
I WAS SLEEPING IN AND THEN I WOKE UP AND YOU WERE...
YES.
I KNOW. I WAS THERE.
YOU RESPONDED VERY WELL, DOUG.
THANKS... I GUESS.
WERE YOU UNWILLING?
WELL, I...UH...
WERE YOU?
NO. NOT IN THE LEAST.
WOULD YOU LIKE TO DO IT AGAIN?
YOU MEAN NOW?
WHENEVER.
I DUNNO.
YES.
WARLOCK WILL KILL ME.
IRRELEVANT.
I KNOW. BUT DON'T TELL HIM, DANGER.
AS YOU WISH.

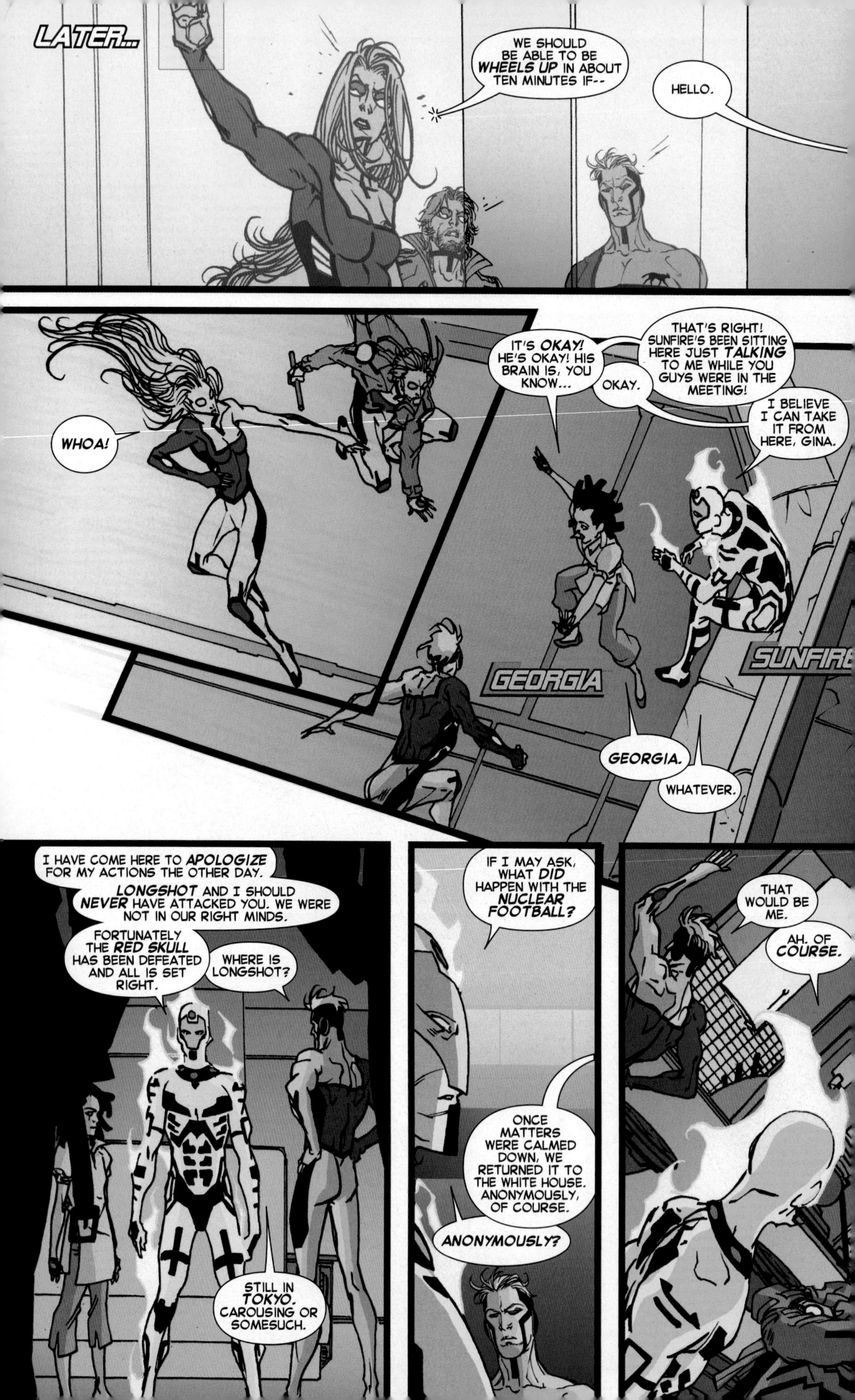
LATER...
WE SHOULD BE ABLE TO BE WHEELS UP IN ABOUT TEN MINUTES IF--
HELLO.
WHOA!
IT'S OKAY! HE'S OKAY! HIS BRAIN IS, YOU KNOW...
THAT'S RIGHT! SUNFIRE'S BEEN SITTING HERE JUST TALKING TO ME WHILE YOU GUYS WERE IN THE MEETING!
OKAY.
I BELIEVE I CAN TAKE IT FROM HERE, GINA.
GEORGIA
SUNFIRE
GEORGIA.
WHATEVER.
I HAVE COME HERE TO APOLOGIZE FOR MY ACTIONS THE OTHER DAY.
LONGSHOT AND I SHOULD NEVER HAVE ATTACKED YOU. WE WERE NOT IN OUR RIGHT MINDS.
FORTUNATELY THE RED SKULL HAS BEEN DEFEATED AND ALL IS SET RIGHT.
WHERE IS LONGSHOT?
STILL IN TOKYO. CAROUSING OR SOMESUCH.
IF I MAY ASK, WHAT DID HAPPEN WITH THE NUCLEAR FOOTBALL?
ONCE MATTERS WERE CALMED DOWN, WE RETURNED IT TO THE WHITE HOUSE. ANONYMOUSLY, OF COURSE.
ANONYMOUSLY?
THAT WOULD BE ME.
AH. OF COURSE.

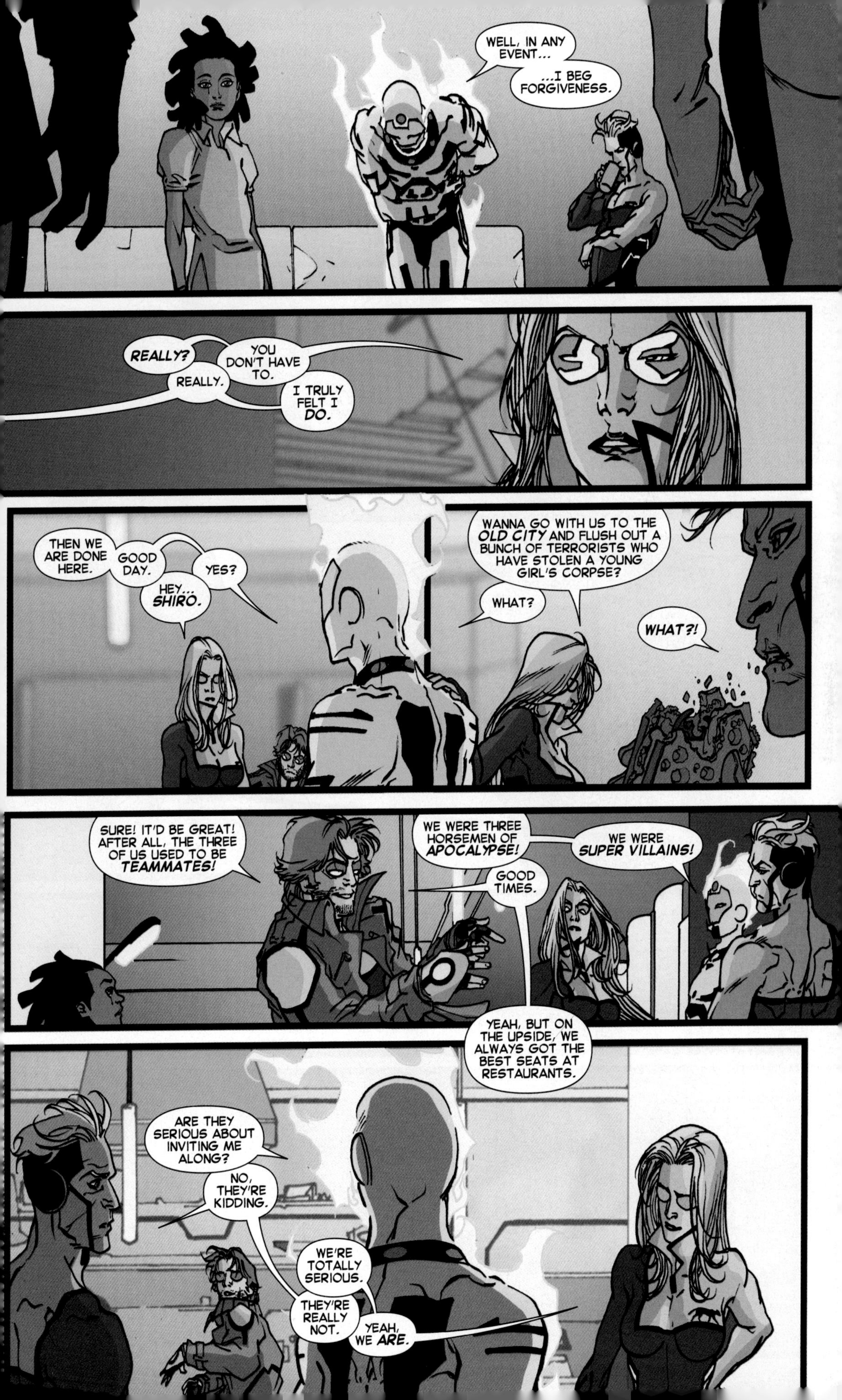
WELL, IN ANY EVENT...
...I BEG FORGIVENESS.
REALLY?
YOU DON'T HAVE TO.
REALLY.
I TRULY FELT I DO.
THEN WE ARE DONE HERE.
GOOD DAY.
YES?
HEY... SHIRO.
WANNA GO WITH US TO THE OLD CITY AND FLUSH OUT A BUNCH OF TERRORISTS WHO HAVE STOLEN A YOUNG GIRL'S CORPSE?
WHAT?
WHAT?!
SURE! IT'D BE GREAT! AFTER ALL, THE THREE OF US USED TO BE TEAMMATES!
WE WERE THREE HORSEMEN OF APOCALYPSE!
WE WERE SUPER VILLAINS!
GOOD TIMES.
YEAH, BUT ON THE UPSIDE, WE ALWAYS GOT THE BEST SEATS AT RESTAURANTS.
ARE THEY SERIOUS ABOUT INVITING ME ALONG?
NO, THEY'RE KIDDING.
WE'RE TOTALLY SERIOUS.
THEY'RE REALLY NOT.
YEAH, WE ARE.

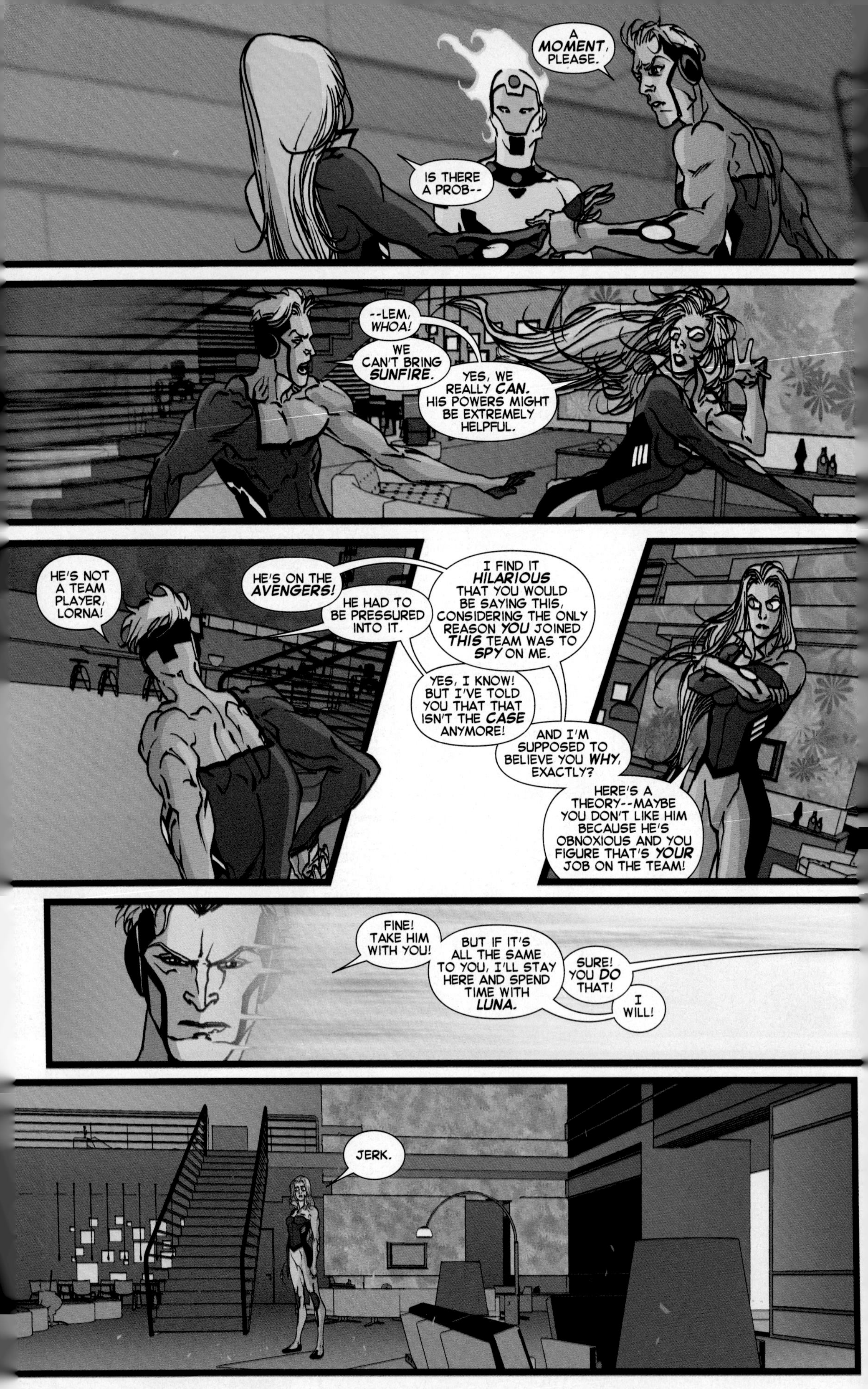
A MOMENT, PLEASE.
IS THERE A PROB--
--LEM, WHOA!
WE CAN'T BRING SUNFIRE.
YES, WE REALLY CAN. HIS POWERS MIGHT BE EXTREMELY HELPFUL.
HE'S NOT A TEAM PLAYER, LORNA!
HE'S ON THE AVENGERS!
HE HAD TO BE PRESSURED INTO IT.
I FIND IT HILARIOUS THAT YOU WOULD BE SAYING THIS, CONSIDERING THE ONLY REASON YOU JOINED THIS TEAM WAS TO SPY ON ME.
YES, I KNOW! BUT I'VE TOLD YOU THAT THAT ISN'T THE CASE ANYMORE!
AND I'M SUPPOSED TO BELIEVE YOU WHY, EXACTLY?
HERE'S A THEORY--MAYBE YOU DON'T LIKE HIM BECAUSE HE'S OBNOXIOUS AND YOU FIGURE THAT'S YOUR JOB ON THE TEAM!
FINE! TAKE HIM WITH YOU!
BUT IF IT'S ALL THE SAME TO YOU, I'LL STAY HERE AND SPEND TIME WITH LUNA.
SURE! YOU DO THAT!
I WILL!
JERK.

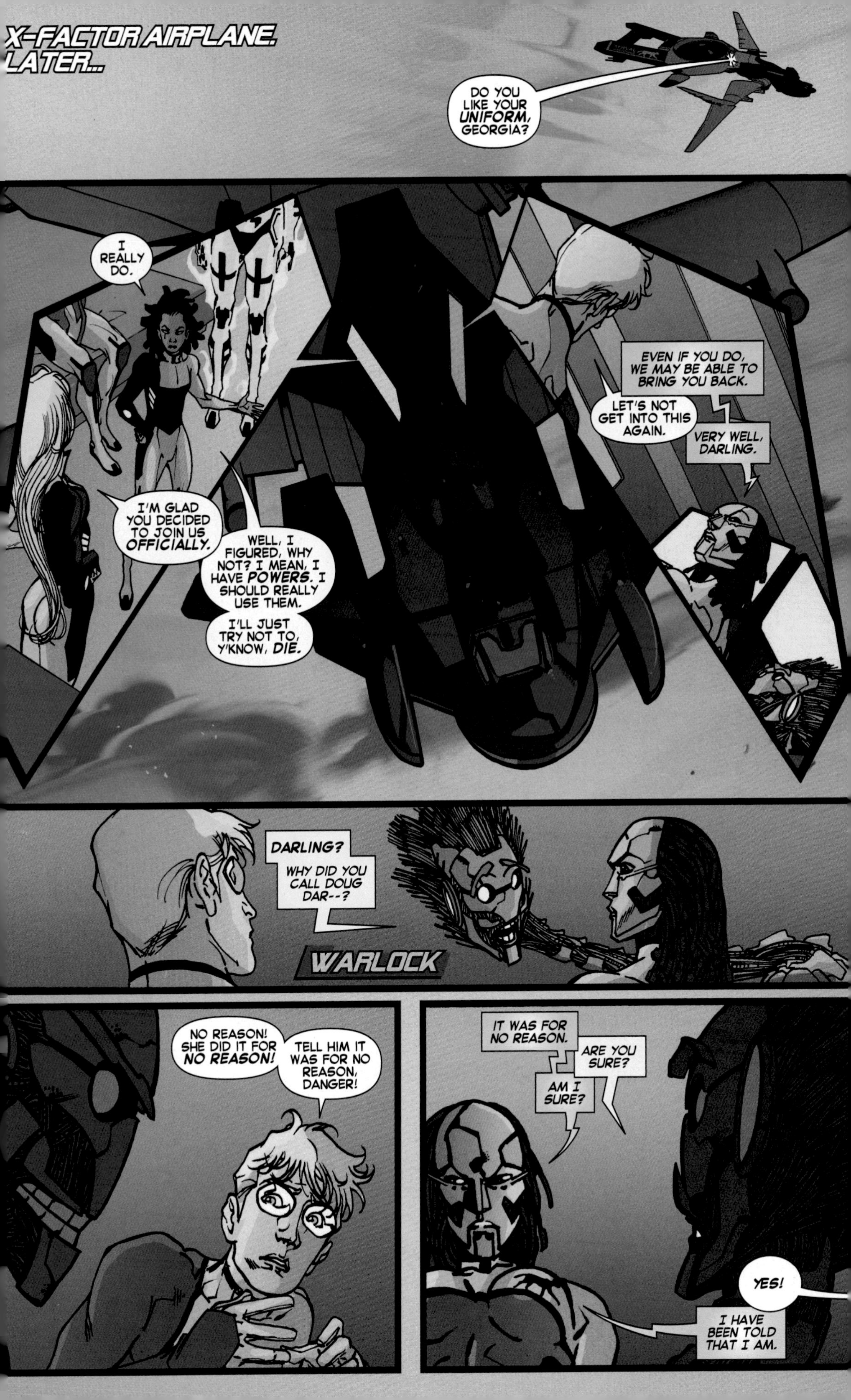
X-FACTOR AIRPLANE. LATER...
DO YOU LIKE YOUR UNIFORM, GEORGIA?
I REALLY DO.
I'M GLAD YOU DECIDED TO JOIN US OFFICIALLY.
WELL, I FIGURED, WHY NOT? I MEAN, I HAVE POWERS. I SHOULD REALLY USE THEM.
I'LL JUST TRY NOT TO, Y'KNOW, DIE.
EVEN IF YOU DO, WE MAY BE ABLE TO BRING YOU BACK.
LET'S NOT GET INTO THIS AGAIN.
VERY WELL, DARLING.
DARLING?
WHY DID YOU CALL DOUG DAR--?
WARLOCK
NO REASON! SHE DID IT FOR NO REASON!
TELL HIM IT WAS FOR NO REASON, DANGER!
IT WAS FOR NO REASON.
ARE YOU SURE?
AM I SURE?
YES!
I HAVE BEEN TOLD THAT I AM.

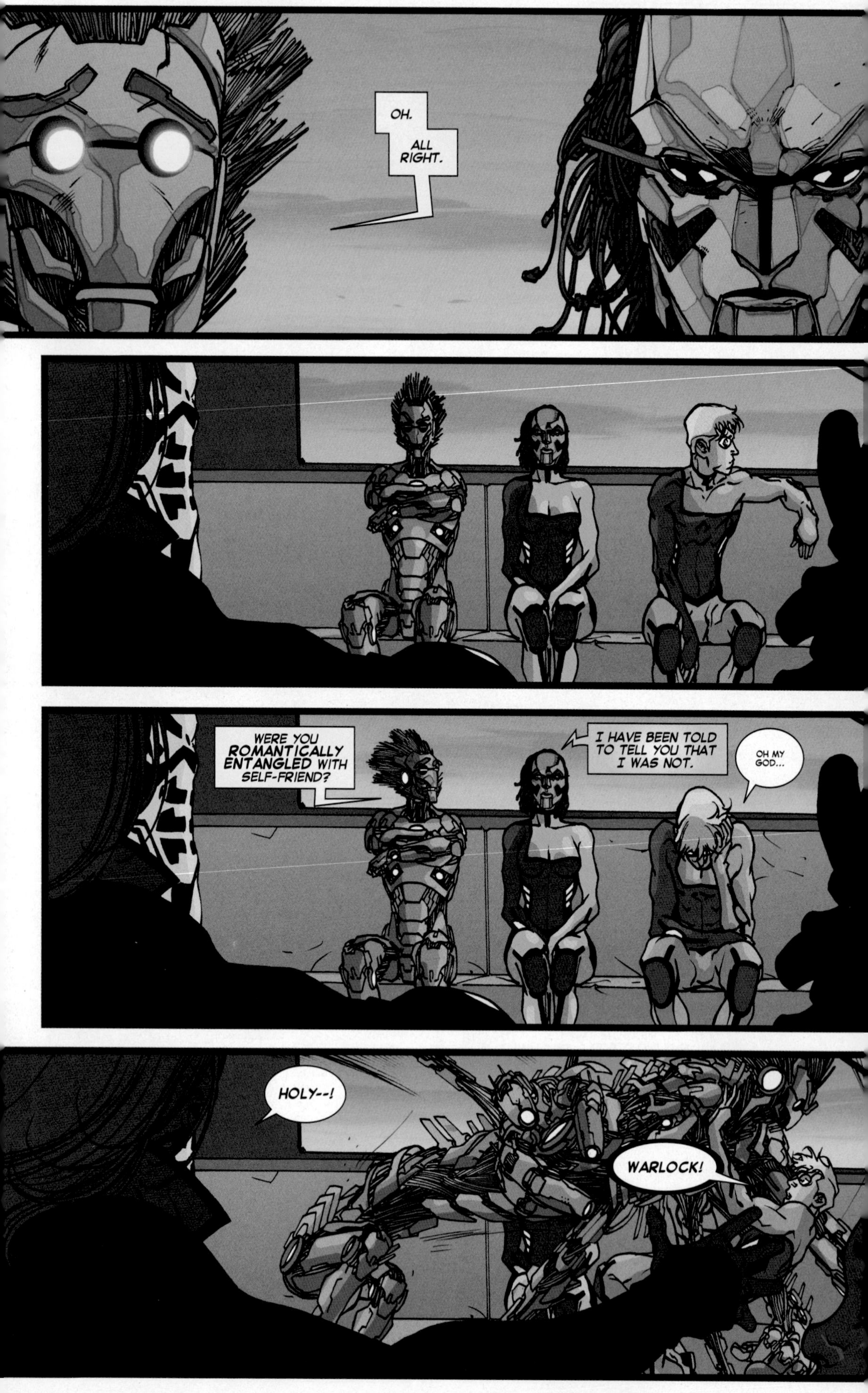
OH.
ALL RIGHT.
WERE YOU ROMANTICALLY ENTANGLED WITH SELF-FRIEND?
I HAVE BEEN TOLD TO TELL YOU THAT I WAS NOT.
OH MY GOD...
HOLY--!
WARLOCK!

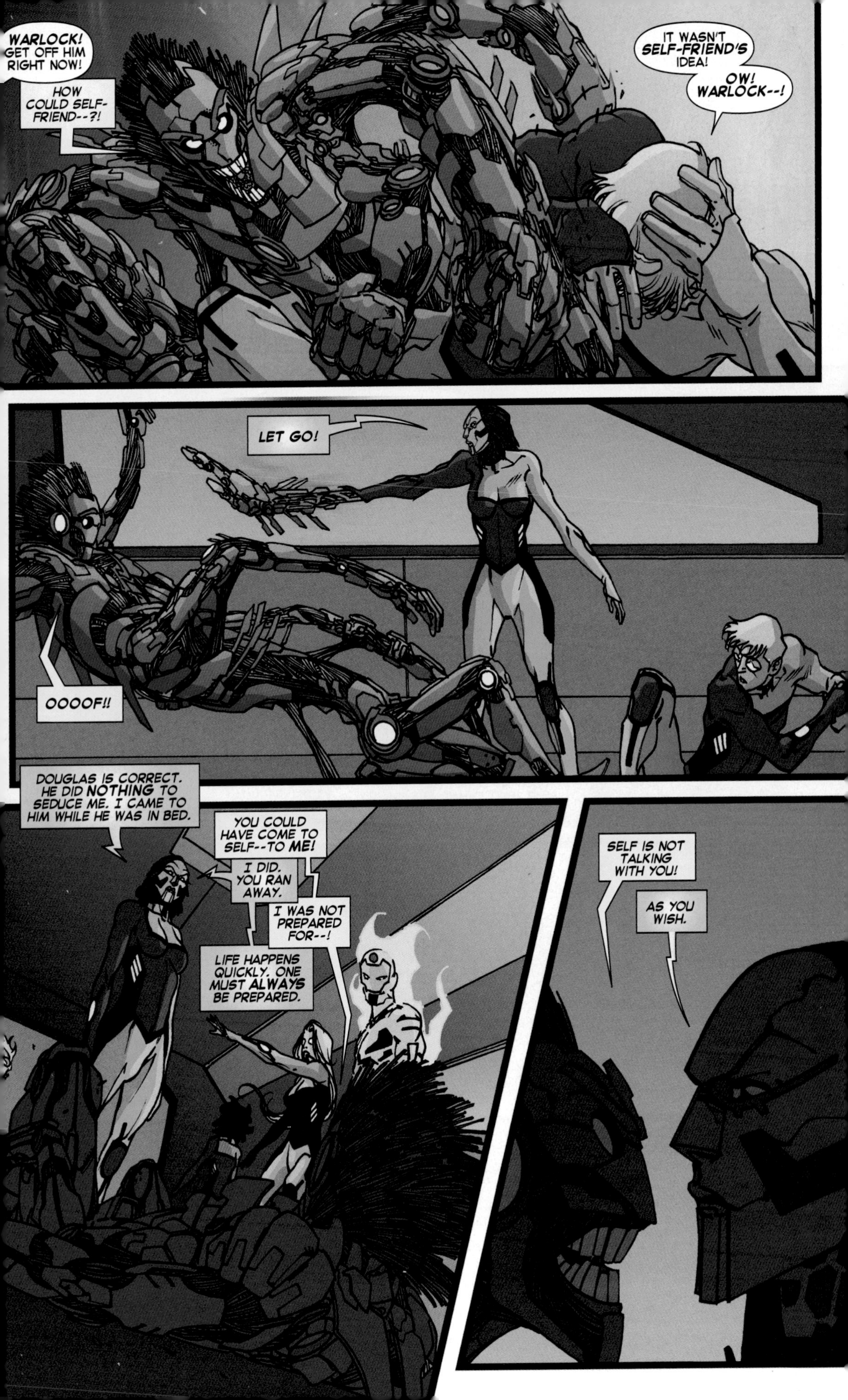

WARLOCK! GET OFF HIM RIGHT NOW!
HOW COULD SELF-FRIEND--?!
IT WASN'T SELF-FRIEND'S IDEA!
OW! WARLOCK--!
LET GO!
OOOOF!!
DOUGLAS IS CORRECT. HE DID NOTHING TO SEDUCE ME. I CAME TO HIM WHILE HE WAS IN BED.
YOU COULD HAVE COME TO SELF--TO ME!
I DID. YOU RAN AWAY.
I WAS NOT PREPARED FOR--!
LIFE HAPPENS QUICKLY. ONE MUST ALWAYS BE PREPARED.
SELF IS NOT TALKING WITH YOU!
AS YOU WISH.

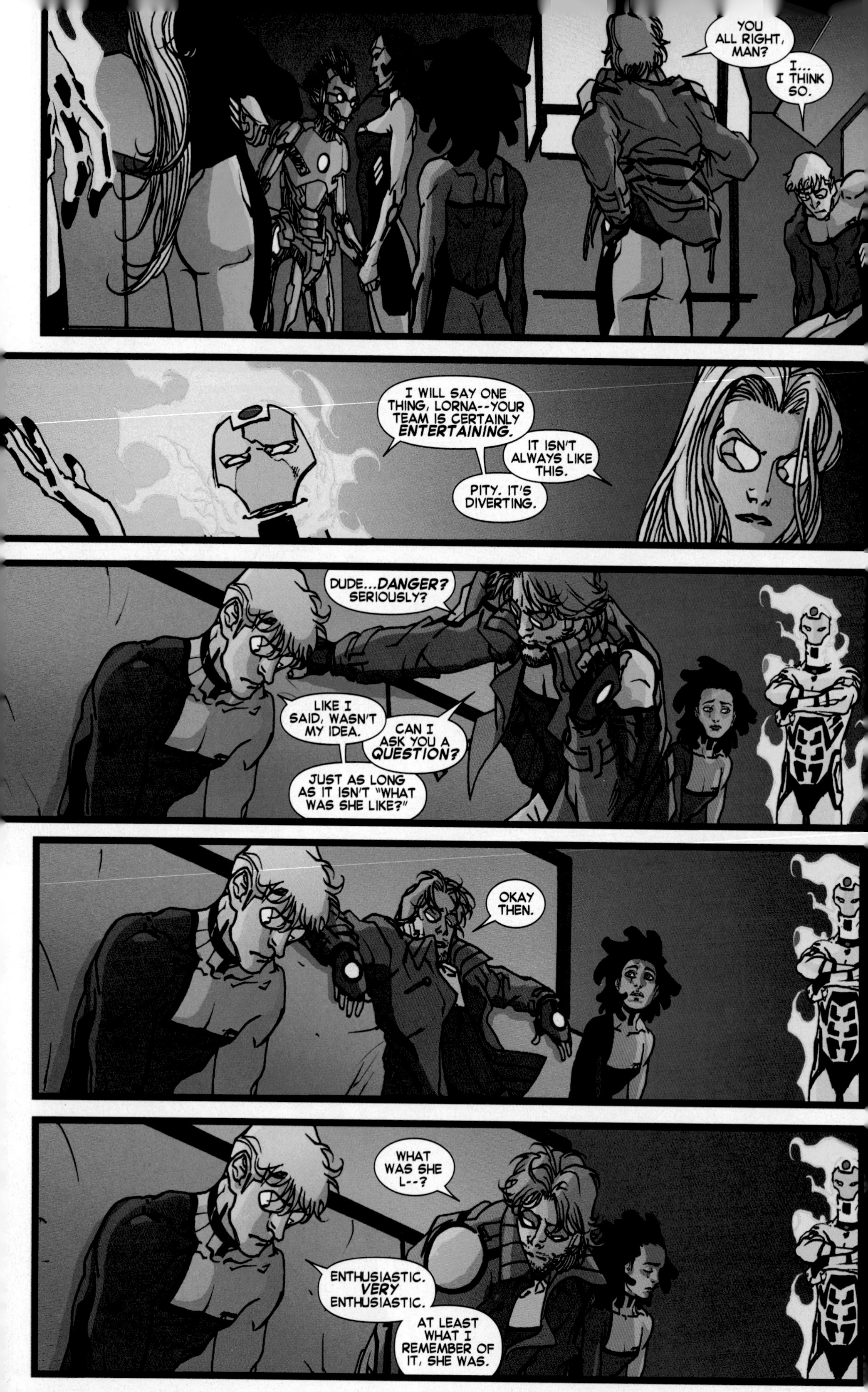
YOU ALL RIGHT, MAN?
I... I THINK SO.
I WILL SAY ONE THING, LORNA--YOUR TEAM IS CERTAINLY ENTERTAINING.
IT ISN'T ALWAYS LIKE THIS.
PITY. IT'S DIVERTING.
DUDE...DANGER? SERIOUSLY?
LIKE I SAID, WASN'T MY IDEA.
CAN I ASK YOU A QUESTION?
JUST AS LONG AS IT ISN'T "WHAT WAS SHE LIKE?"
OKAY THEN.
WHAT WAS SHE L--?
ENTHUSIASTIC. VERY ENTHUSIASTIC.
AT LEAST WHAT I REMEMBER OF IT, SHE WAS.

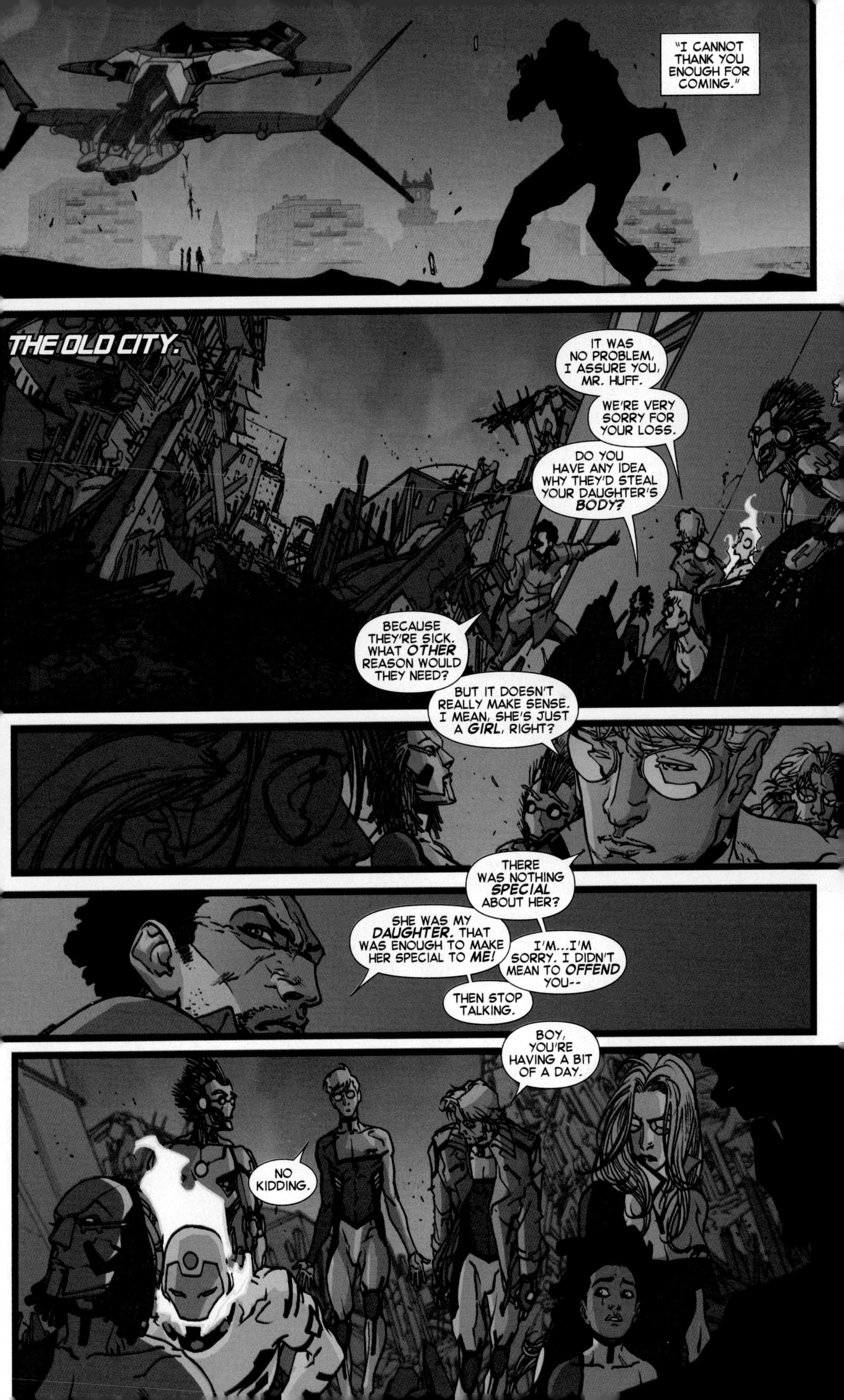
"I CANNOT THANK YOU ENOUGH FOR COMING."
THE OLD CITY.
IT WAS NO PROBLEM, I ASSURE YOU, MR. HUFF.
WE'RE VERY SORRY FOR YOUR LOSS.
DO YOU HAVE ANY IDEA WHY THEY'D STEAL YOUR DAUGHTER'S BODY?
BECAUSE THEY'RE SICK. WHAT OTHER REASON WOULD THEY NEED?
BUT IT DOESN'T REALLY MAKE SENSE. I MEAN, SHE'S JUST A GIRL, RIGHT?
THERE WAS NOTHING SPECIAL ABOUT HER?
SHE WAS MY DAUGHTER. THAT WAS ENOUGH TO MAKE HER SPECIAL TO ME!
I'M...I'M SORRY. I DIDN'T MEAN TO OFFEND YOU--
THEN STOP TALKING.
BOY, YOU'RE HAVING A BIT OF A DAY.
NO KIDDING.

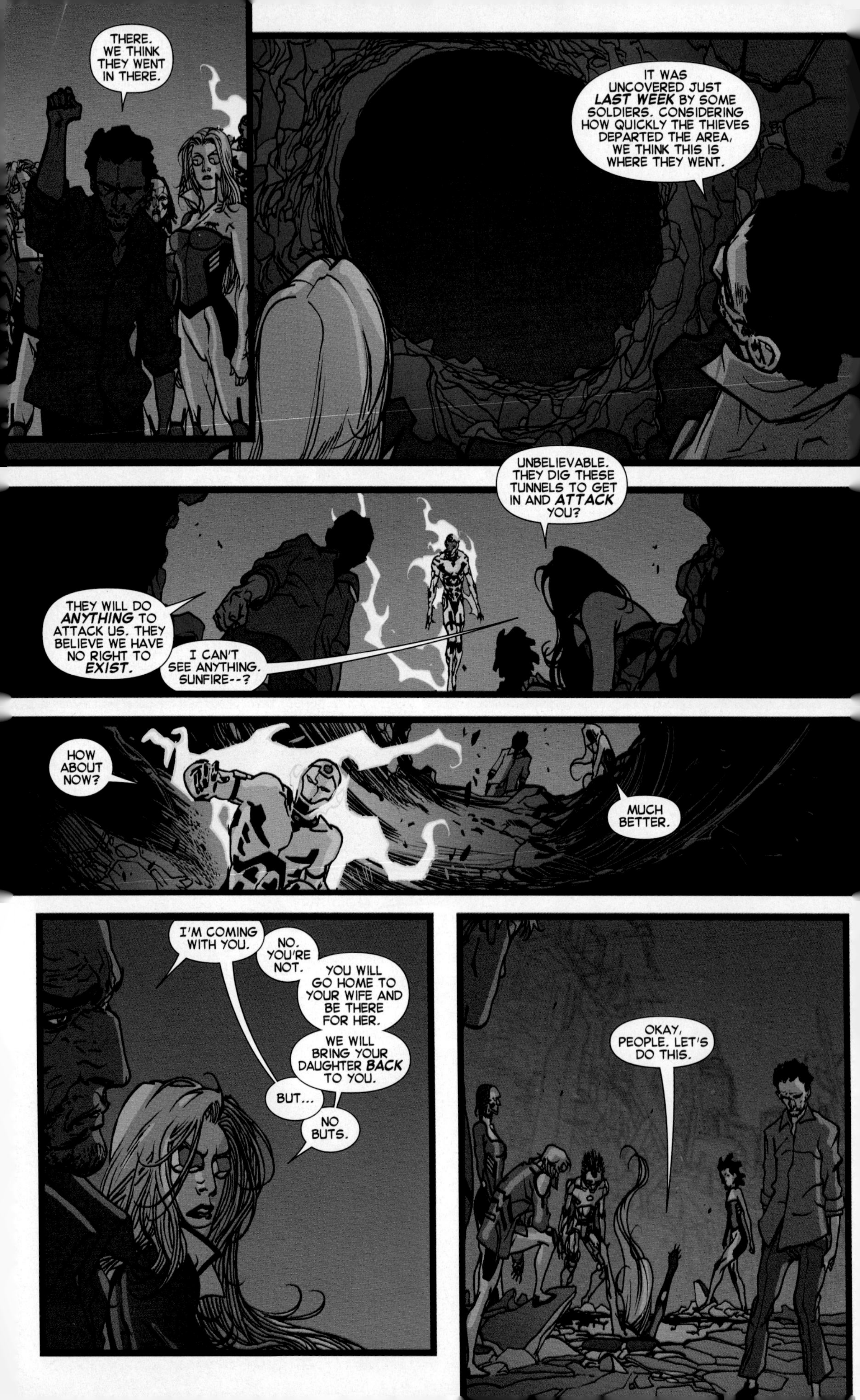
THERE. WE THINK THEY WENT IN THERE.
IT WAS UNCOVERED JUST LAST WEEK BY SOME SOLDIERS. CONSIDERING HOW QUICKLY THE THIEVES DEPARTED THE AREA, WE THINK THIS IS WHERE THEY WENT.
UNBELIEVABLE. THEY DIG THESE TUNNELS TO GET IN AND ATTACK YOU?
THEY WILL DO ANYTHING TO ATTACK US. THEY BELIEVE WE HAVE NO RIGHT TO EXIST.
I CAN'T SEE ANYTHING. SUNFIRE--?
HOW ABOUT NOW?
MUCH BETTER.
I'M COMING WITH YOU.
NO. YOU'RE NOT.
YOU WILL GO HOME TO YOUR WIFE AND BE THERE FOR HER.
WE WILL BRING YOUR DAUGHTER BACK TO YOU.
BUT...
NO BUTS.
OKAY, PEOPLE. LET'S DO THIS.

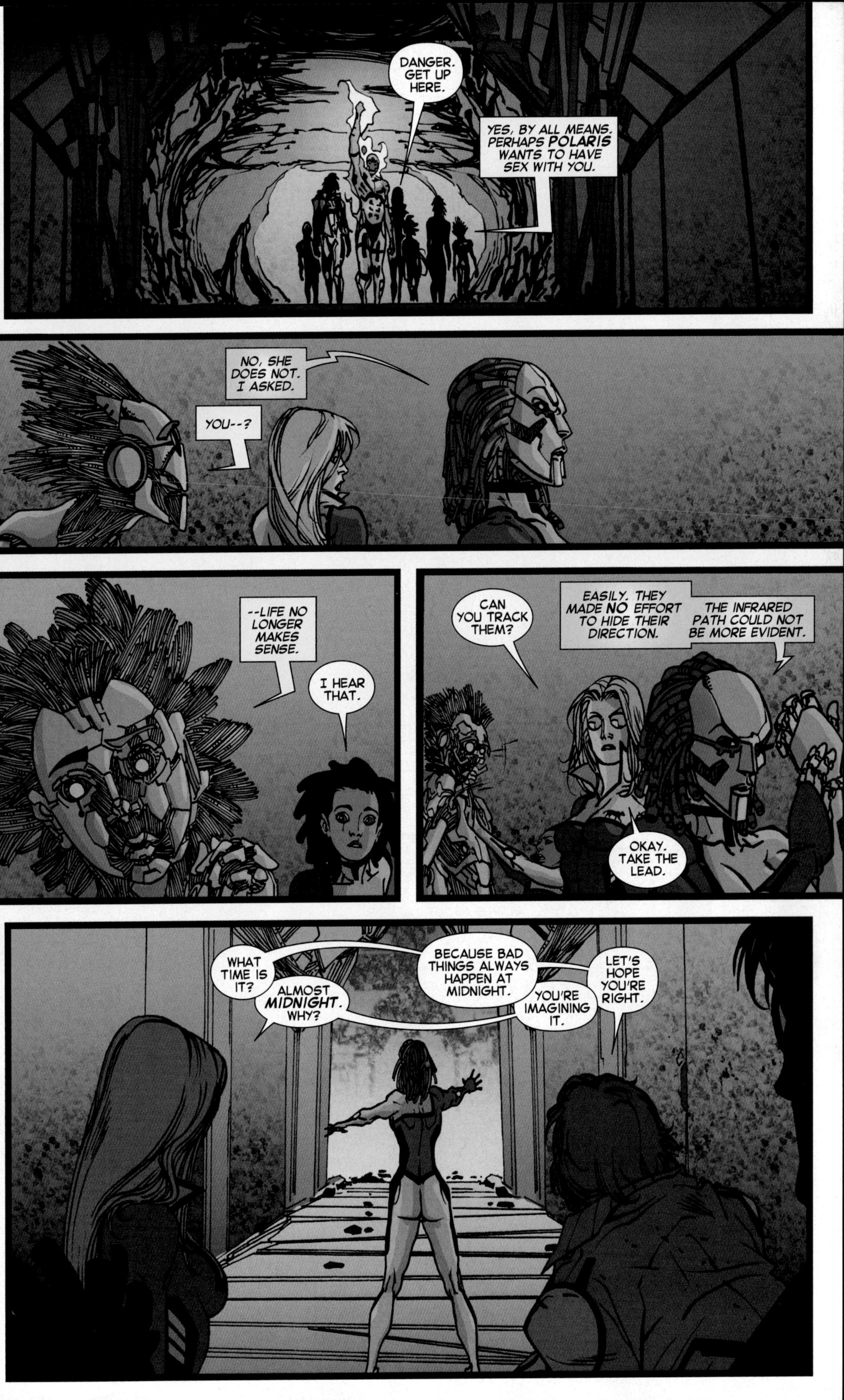
DANGER. GET UP HERE.
YES, BY ALL MEANS. PERHAPS POLARIS WANTS TO HAVE SEX WITH YOU.
NO, SHE DOES NOT. I ASKED.
YOU--?
--LIFE NO LONGER MAKES SENSE.
I HEAR THAT.
CAN YOU TRACK THEM?
EASILY. THEY MADE NO EFFORT TO HIDE THEIR DIRECTION.
THE INFRARED PATH COULD NOT BE MORE EVIDENT.
OKAY. TAKE THE LEAD.
WHAT TIME IS IT?
ALMOST MIDNIGHT. WHY?
BECAUSE BAD THINGS ALWAYS HAPPEN AT MIDNIGHT.
YOU'RE IMAGINING IT.
LET'S HOPE YOU'RE RIGHT.

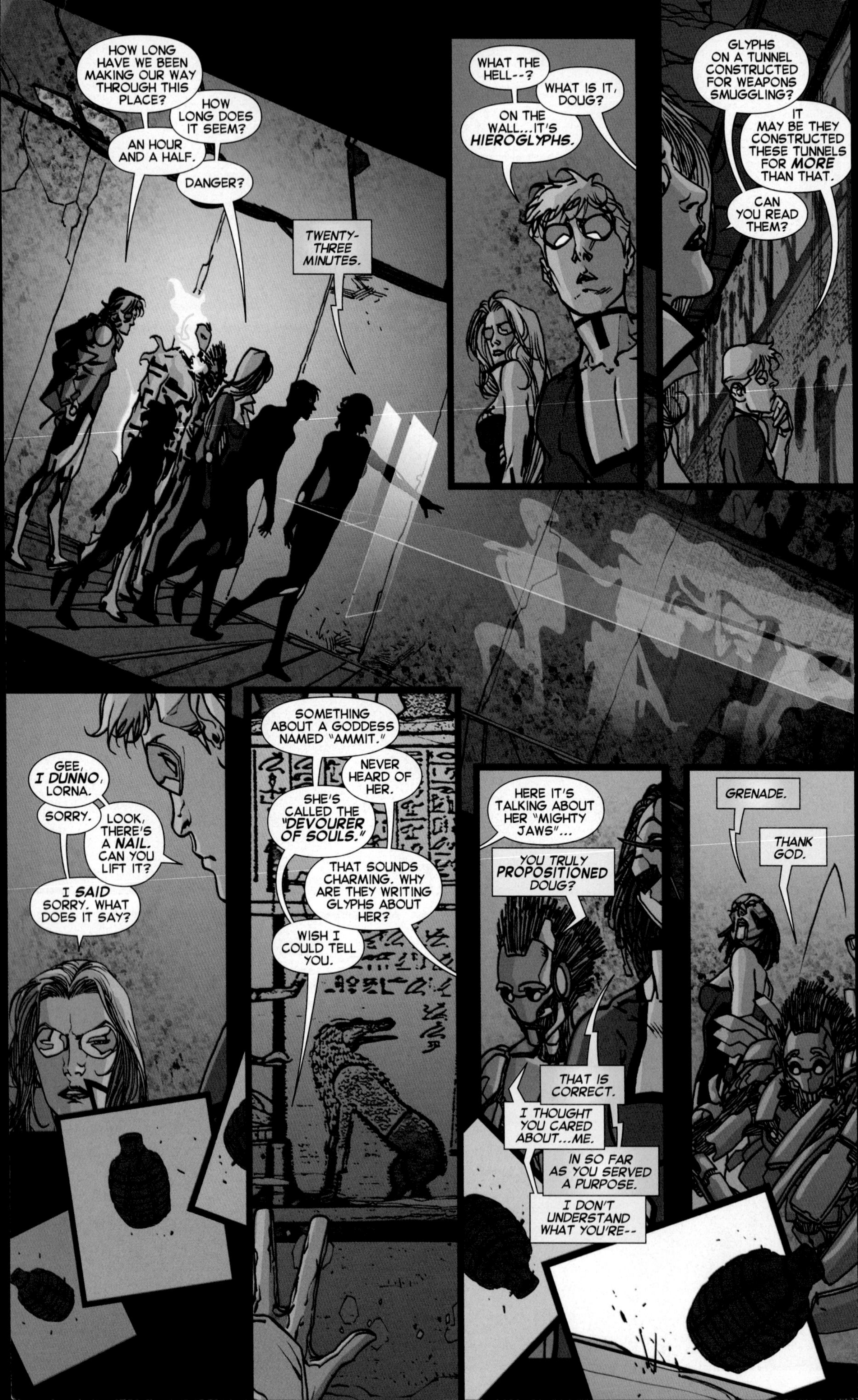

HOW LONG HAVE WE BEEN MAKING OUR WAY THROUGH THIS PLACE?
HOW LONG DOES IT SEEM?
AN HOUR AND A HALF.
DANGER?
TWENTY-THREE MINUTES.
WHAT THE HELL--?
WHAT IS IT, DOUG?
ON THE WALL...IT'S HIEROGLYPHS.
GLYPHS ON A TUNNEL CONSTRUCTED FOR WEAPONS SMUGGLING?
IT MAY BE THEY CONSTRUCTED THESE TUNNELS FOR MORE THAN THAT.
CAN YOU READ THEM?
GEE, I DUNNO, LORNA.
SORRY.
LOOK, THERE'S A NAIL. CAN YOU LIFT IT?
I SAID SORRY. WHAT DOES IT SAY?
SOMETHING ABOUT A GODDESS NAMED "AMMIT."
NEVER HEARD OF HER.
SHE'S CALLED THE "DEVOURER OF SOULS."
THAT SOUNDS CHARMING. WHY ARE THEY WRITING GLYPHS ABOUT HER?
WISH I COULD TELL YOU.
HERE IT'S TALKING ABOUT HER "MIGHTY JAWS"...
YOU TRULY PROPOSITIONED DOUG?
THAT IS CORRECT.
I THOUGHT YOU CARED ABOUT...ME.
IN SO FAR AS YOU SERVED A PURPOSE.
I DON'T UNDERSTAND WHAT YOU'RE--
GRENADE.
THANK GOD.

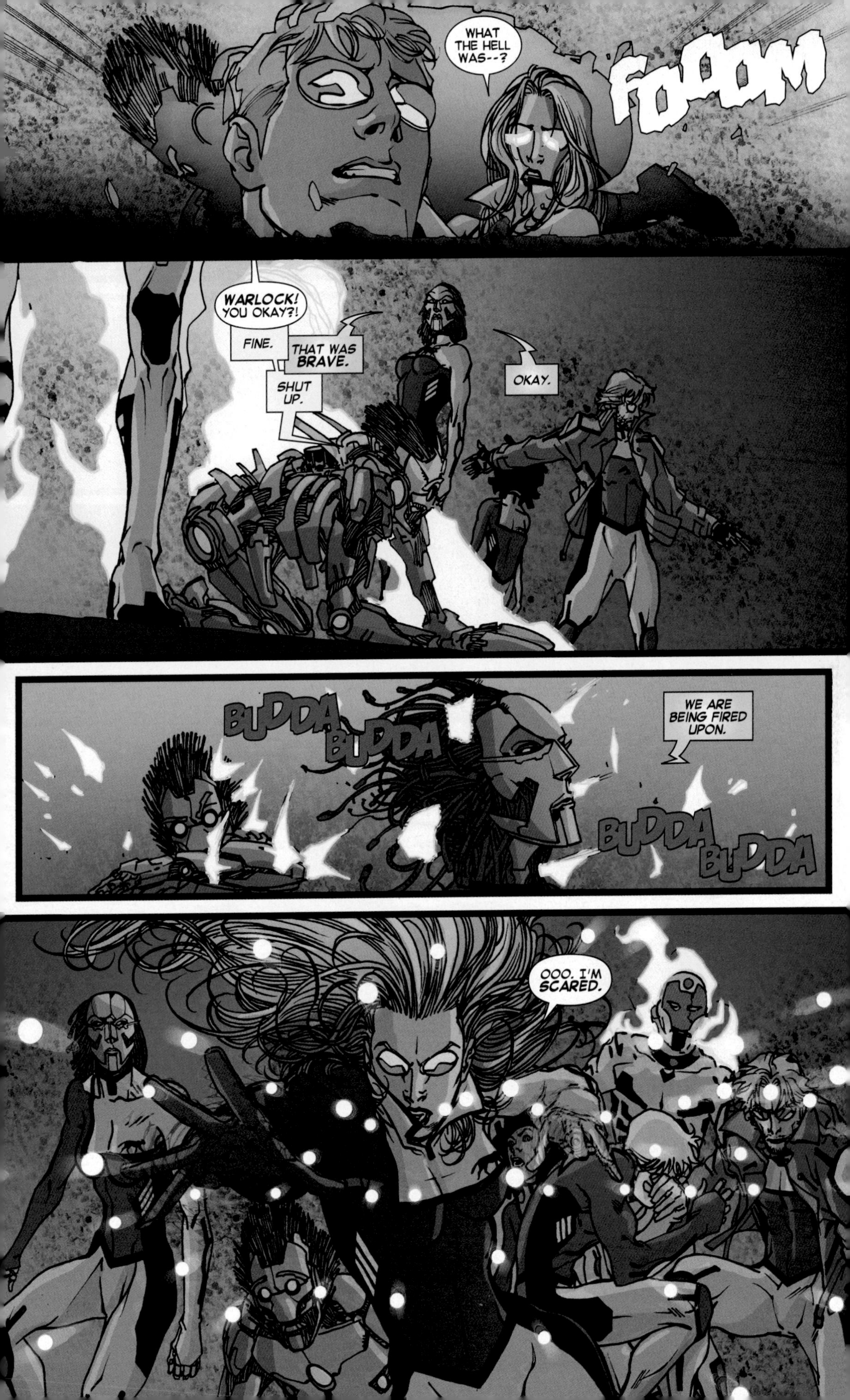
WHAT THE HELL WAS--?
FOOOM
WARLOCK! YOU OKAY?!
FINE.
THAT WAS BRAVE.
SHUT UP.
OKAY.
BUDDA BUDDA
WE ARE BEING FIRED UPON.
BUDDA BUDDA
OOO. I'M SCARED.

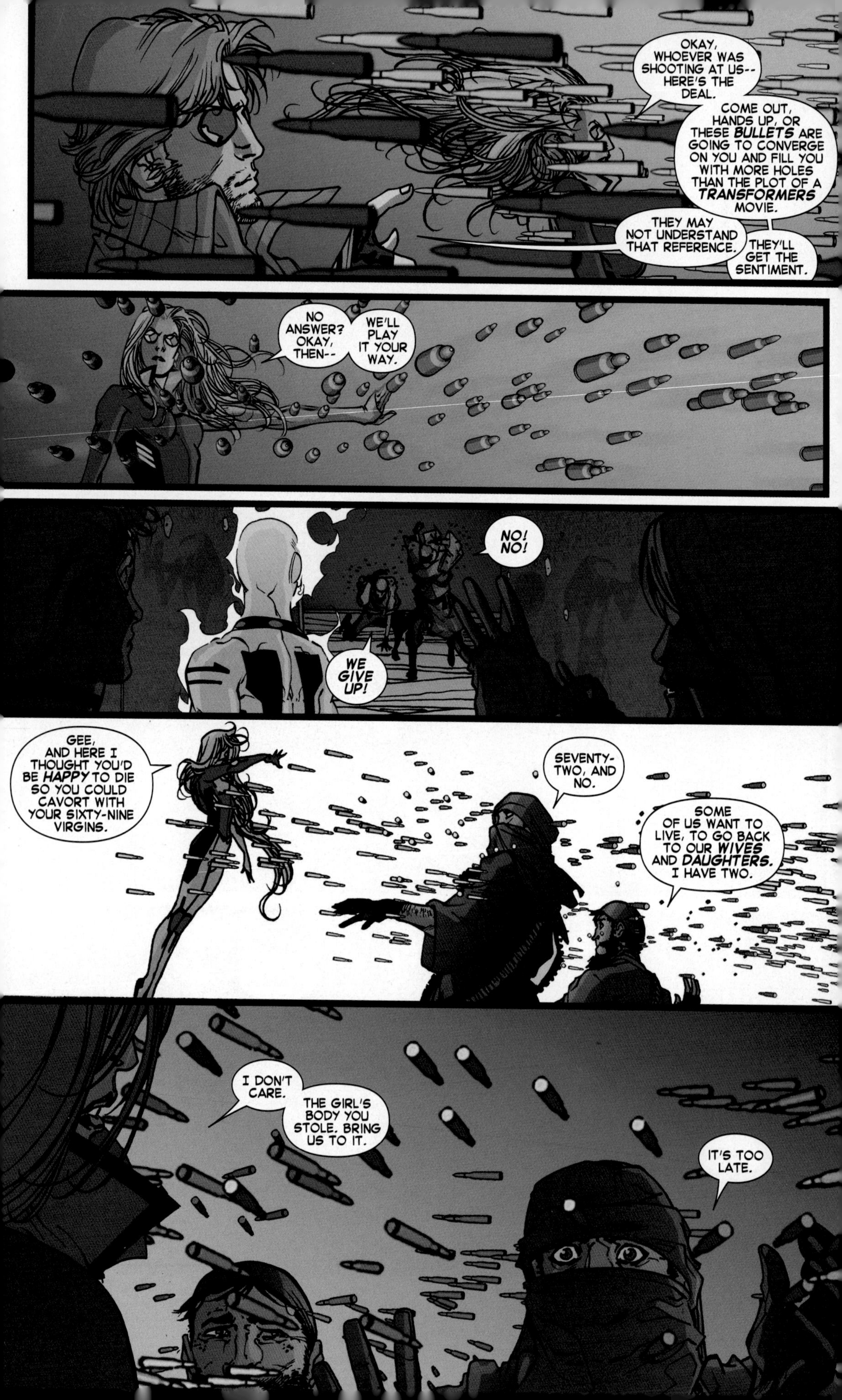
OKAY, WHOEVER WAS SHOOTING AT US-- HERE'S THE DEAL.
COME OUT, HANDS UP, OR THESE BULLETS ARE GOING TO CONVERGE ON YOU AND FILL YOU WITH MORE HOLES THAN THE PLOT OF A TRANSFORMERS MOVIE.
THEY MAY NOT UNDERSTAND THAT REFERENCE.
THEY'LL GET THE SENTIMENT.
NO ANSWER? OKAY, THEN--
WE'LL PLAY IT YOUR WAY.
NO! NO!
WE GIVE UP!
GEE, AND HERE I THOUGHT YOU'D BE HAPPY TO DIE SO YOU COULD CAVORT WITH YOUR SIXTY-NINE VIRGINS.
SEVENTY-TWO, AND NO.
SOME OF US WANT TO LIVE, TO GO BACK TO OUR WIVES AND DAUGHTERS. I HAVE TWO.
I DON'T CARE.
THE GIRL'S BODY YOU STOLE. BRING US TO IT.
IT'S TOO LATE.

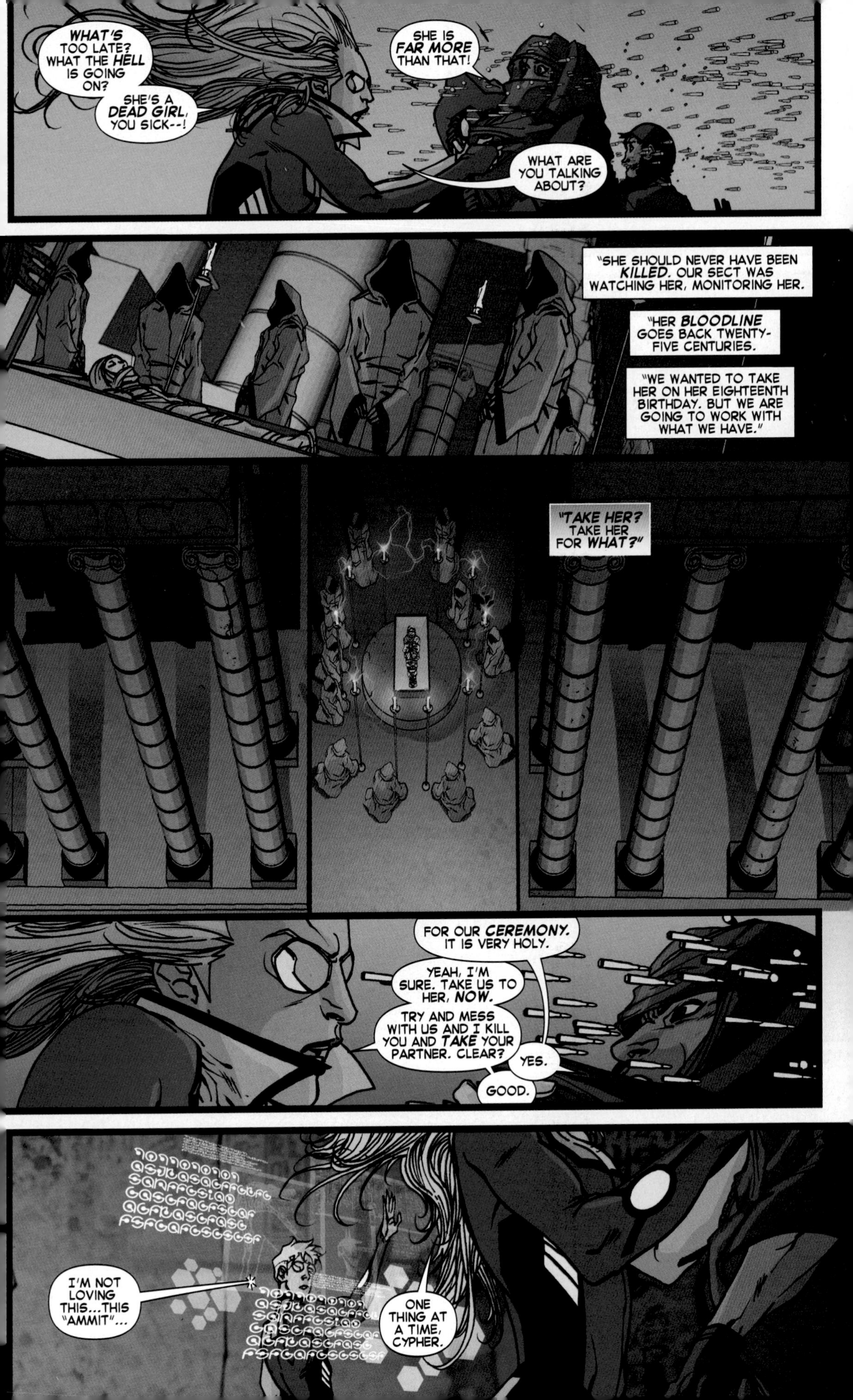
WHAT'S TOO LATE? WHAT THE HELL IS GOING ON?
SHE'S A DEAD GIRL, YOU SICK--!
SHE IS FAR MORE THAN THAT!
WHAT ARE YOU TALKING ABOUT?
"SHE SHOULD NEVER HAVE BEEN KILLED. OUR SECT WAS WATCHING HER, MONITORING HER.
"HER BLOODLINE GOES BACK TWENTY-FIVE CENTURIES.
"WE WANTED TO TAKE HER ON HER EIGHTEENTH BIRTHDAY. BUT WE ARE GOING TO WORK WITH WHAT WE HAVE."
"TAKE HER? TAKE HER FOR WHAT?"
FOR OUR CEREMONY. IT IS VERY HOLY.
YEAH, I'M SURE. TAKE US TO HER, NOW.
TRY AND MESS WITH US AND I KILL YOU AND TAKE YOUR PARTNER. CLEAR?
YES.
GOOD.
I'M NOT LOVING THIS...THIS "AMMIT"...
ONE THING AT A TIME, CYPHER.

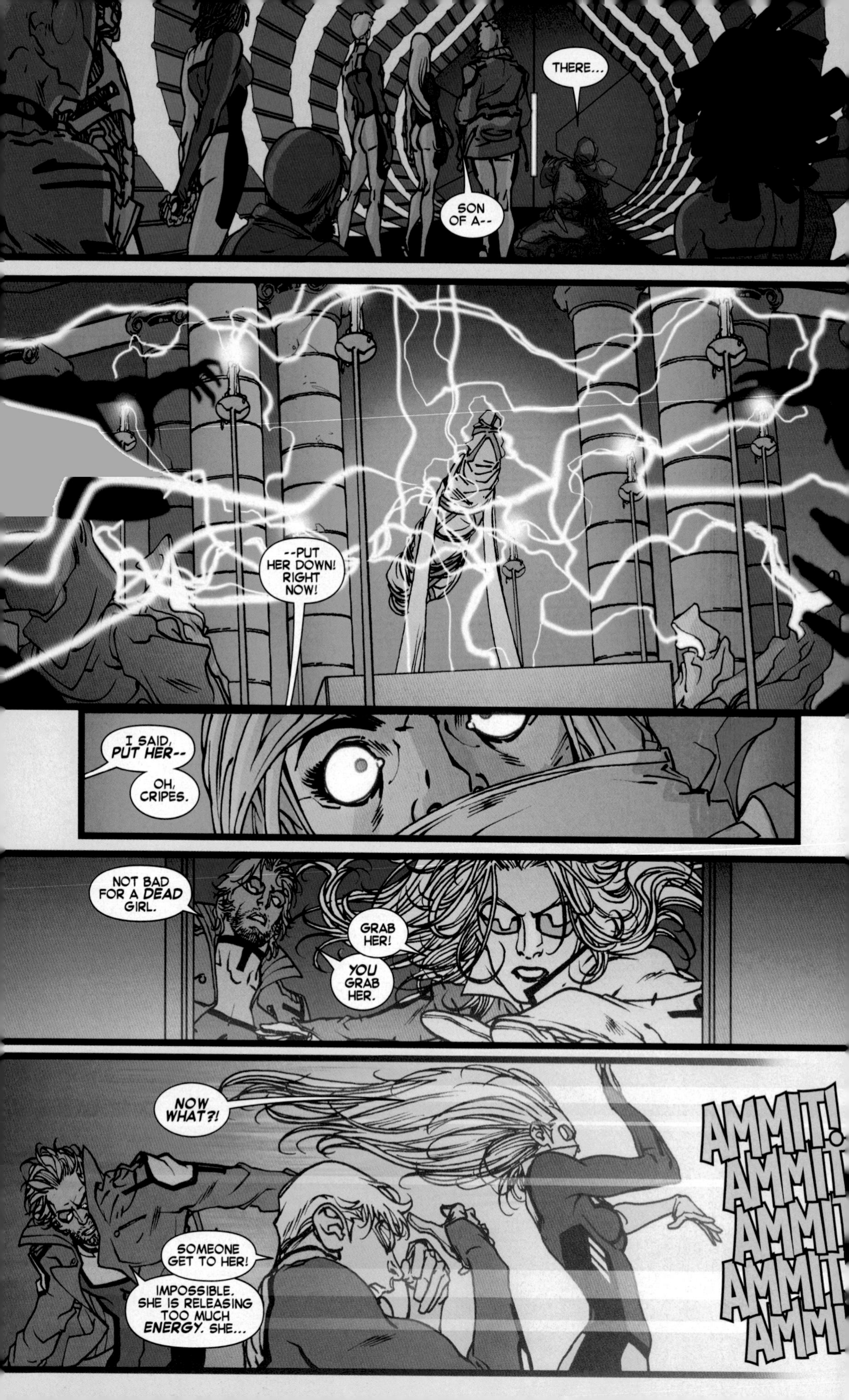
THERE...
SON OF A--
--PUT HER DOWN! RIGHT NOW!
I SAID, PUT HER--
OH, CRIPES.
NOT BAD FOR A DEAD GIRL.
GRAB HER!
YOU GRAB HER.
NOW WHAT?!
SOMEONE GET TO HER!
IMPOSSIBLE. SHE IS RELEASING TOO MUCH ENERGY. SHE...
AMMIT!
AMMIT
AMMI
AMMIT
AMMI

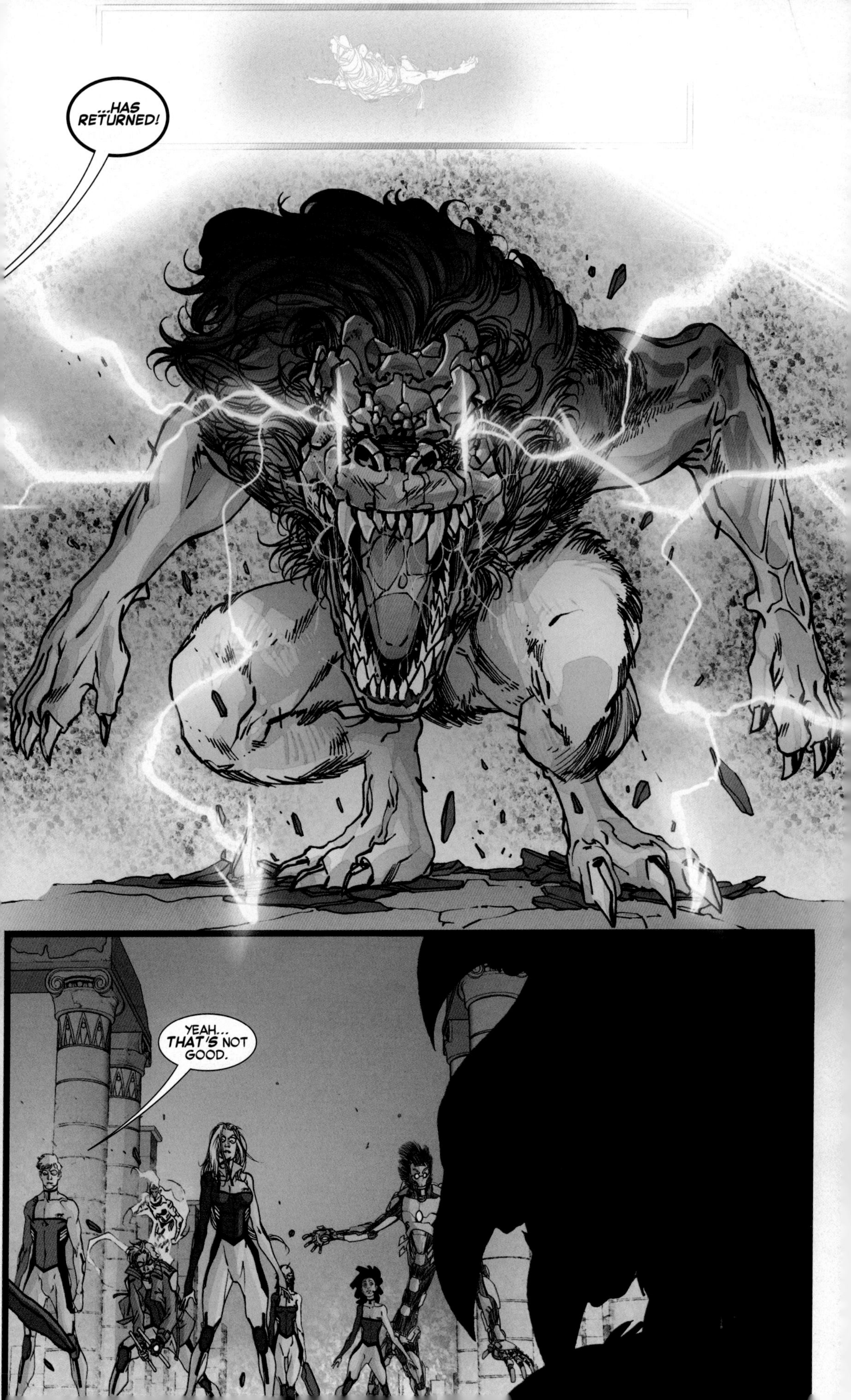
...HAS RETURNED!
YEAH... THAT'S NOT GOOD.

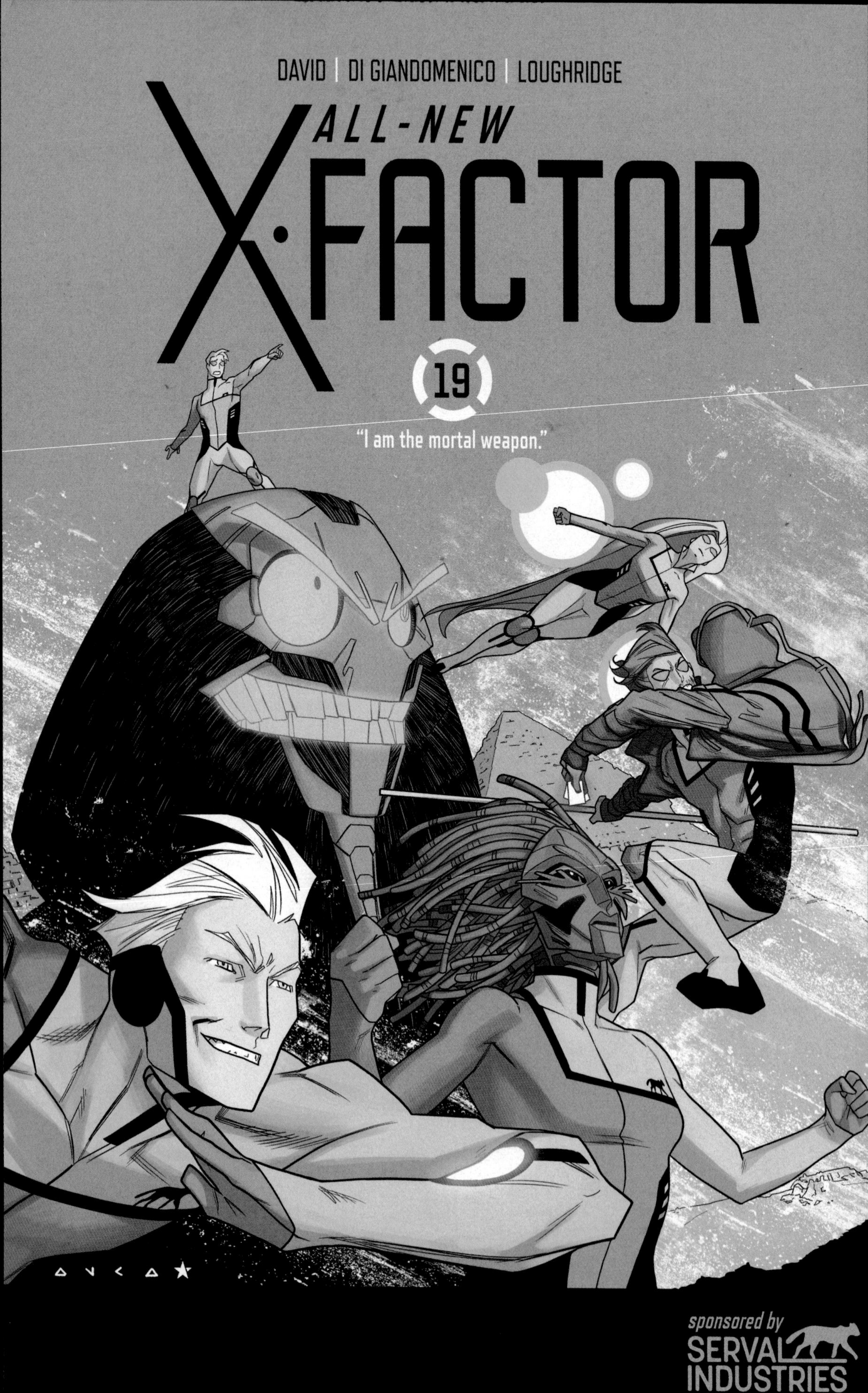

DAVID | DI GIANDOMENICO | LOUGHRIDGE
ALL-NEW
X-FACTOR
19
"I am the mortal weapon."
sponsored by
SERVAL INDUSTRIES

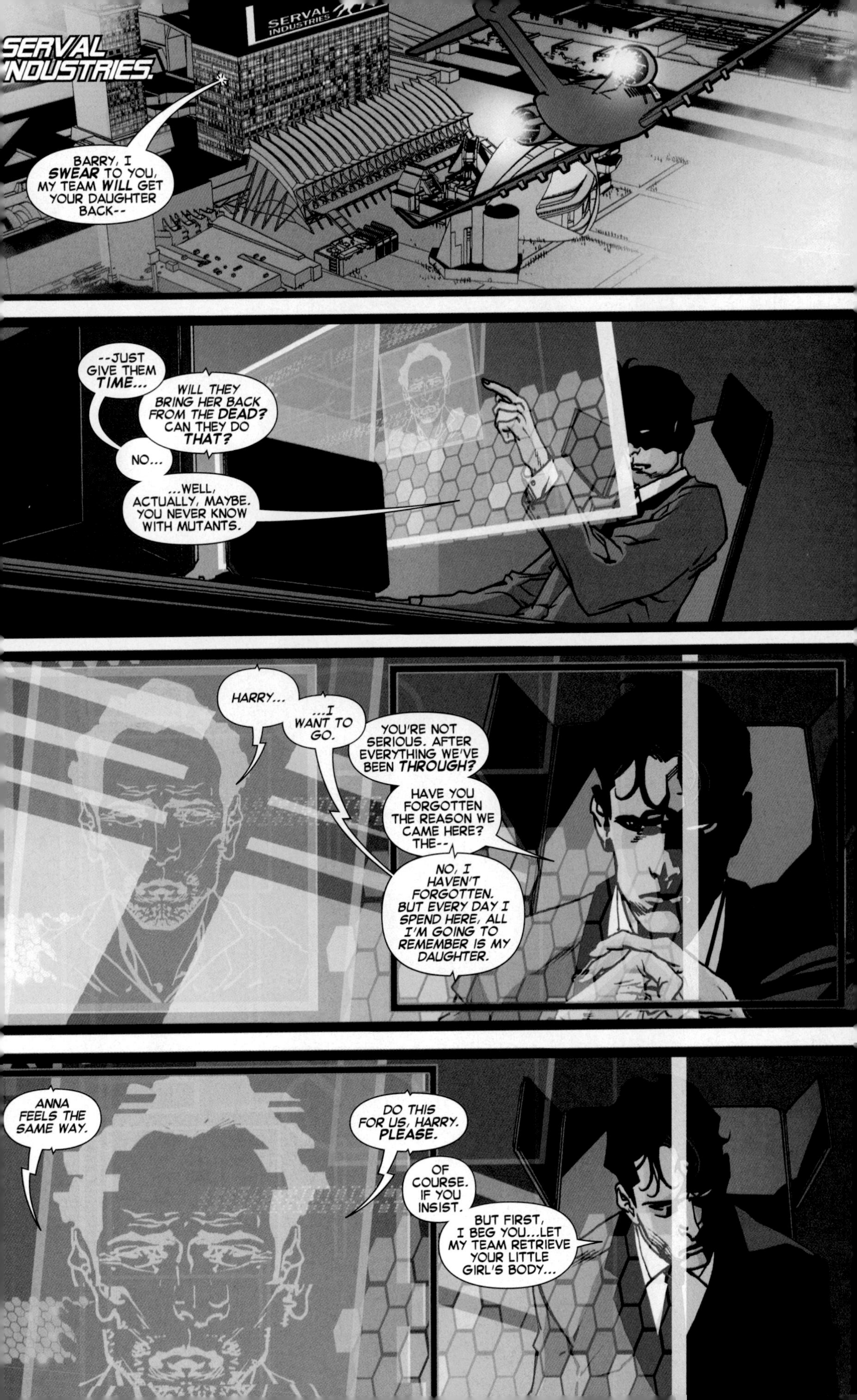
SERVAL INDUSTRIES.
SERVAL INDUSTRIES
BARRY, I SWEAR TO YOU, MY TEAM WILL GET YOUR DAUGHTER BACK--
--JUST GIVE THEM TIME...
WILL THEY BRING HER BACK FROM THE DEAD? CAN THEY DO THAT?
NO...
...WELL, ACTUALLY, MAYBE. YOU NEVER KNOW WITH MUTANTS.
HARRY...
...I WANT TO GO.
YOU'RE NOT SERIOUS. AFTER EVERYTHING WE'VE BEEN THROUGH?
HAVE YOU FORGOTTEN THE REASON WE CAME HERE? THE--
NO, I HAVEN'T FORGOTTEN. BUT EVERY DAY I SPEND HERE, ALL I'M GOING TO REMEMBER IS MY DAUGHTER.
ANNA FEELS THE SAME WAY.
DO THIS FOR US, HARRY. PLEASE.
OF COURSE. IF YOU INSIST.
BUT FIRST, I BEG YOU...LET MY TEAM RETRIEVE YOUR LITTLE GIRL'S BODY...

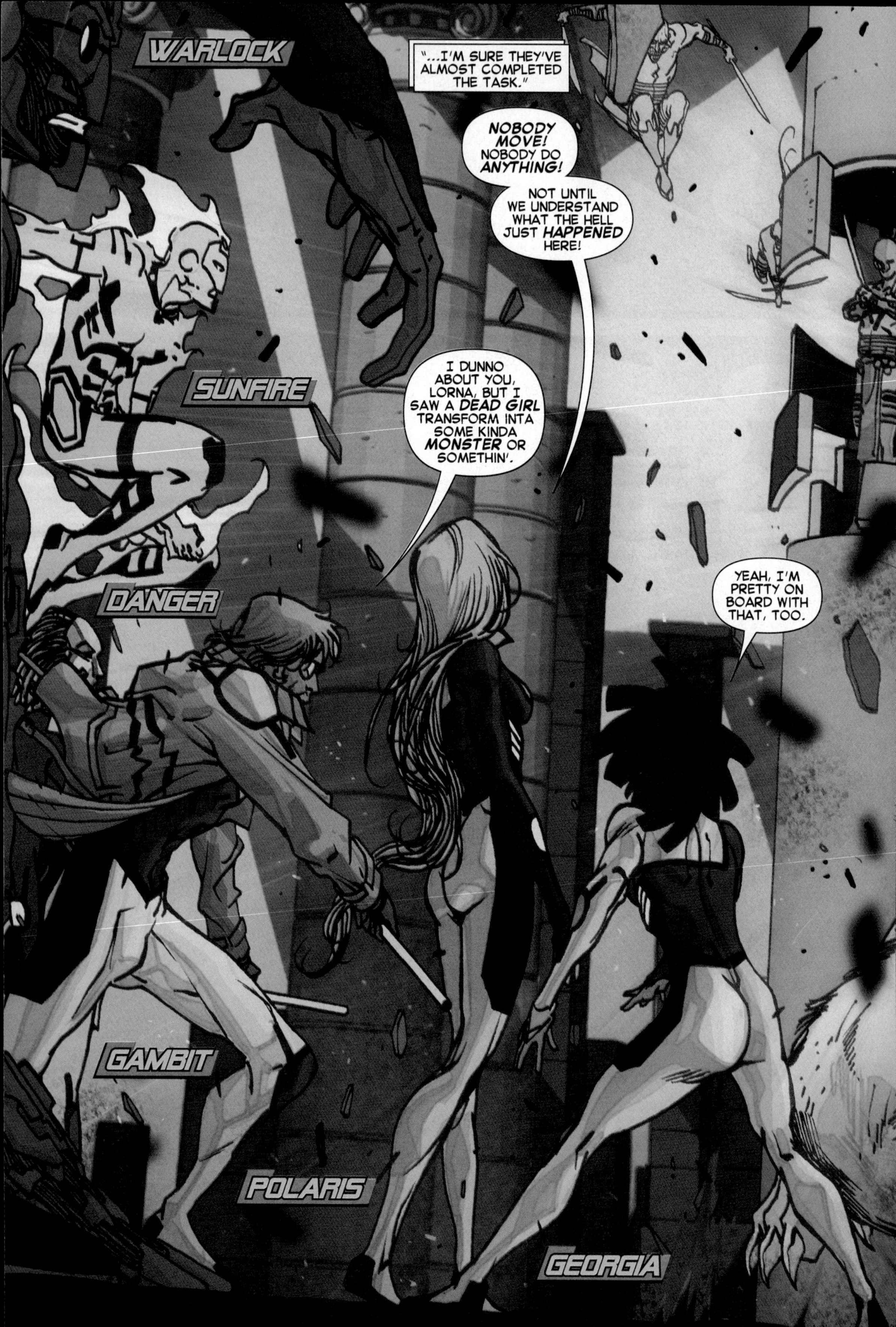
WARLOCK
"...I'M SURE THEY'VE ALMOST COMPLETED THE TASK."
NOBODY MOVE! NOBODY DO ANYTHING!
NOT UNTIL WE UNDERSTAND WHAT THE HELL JUST HAPPENED HERE!
SUNFIRE
I DUNNO ABOUT YOU, LORNA, BUT I SAW A DEAD GIRL TRANSFORM INTA SOME KINDA MONSTER OR SOMETHIN'.
DANGER
YEAH, I'M PRETTY ON BOARD WITH THAT, TOO.
GAMBIT
POLARIS
GEORGIA

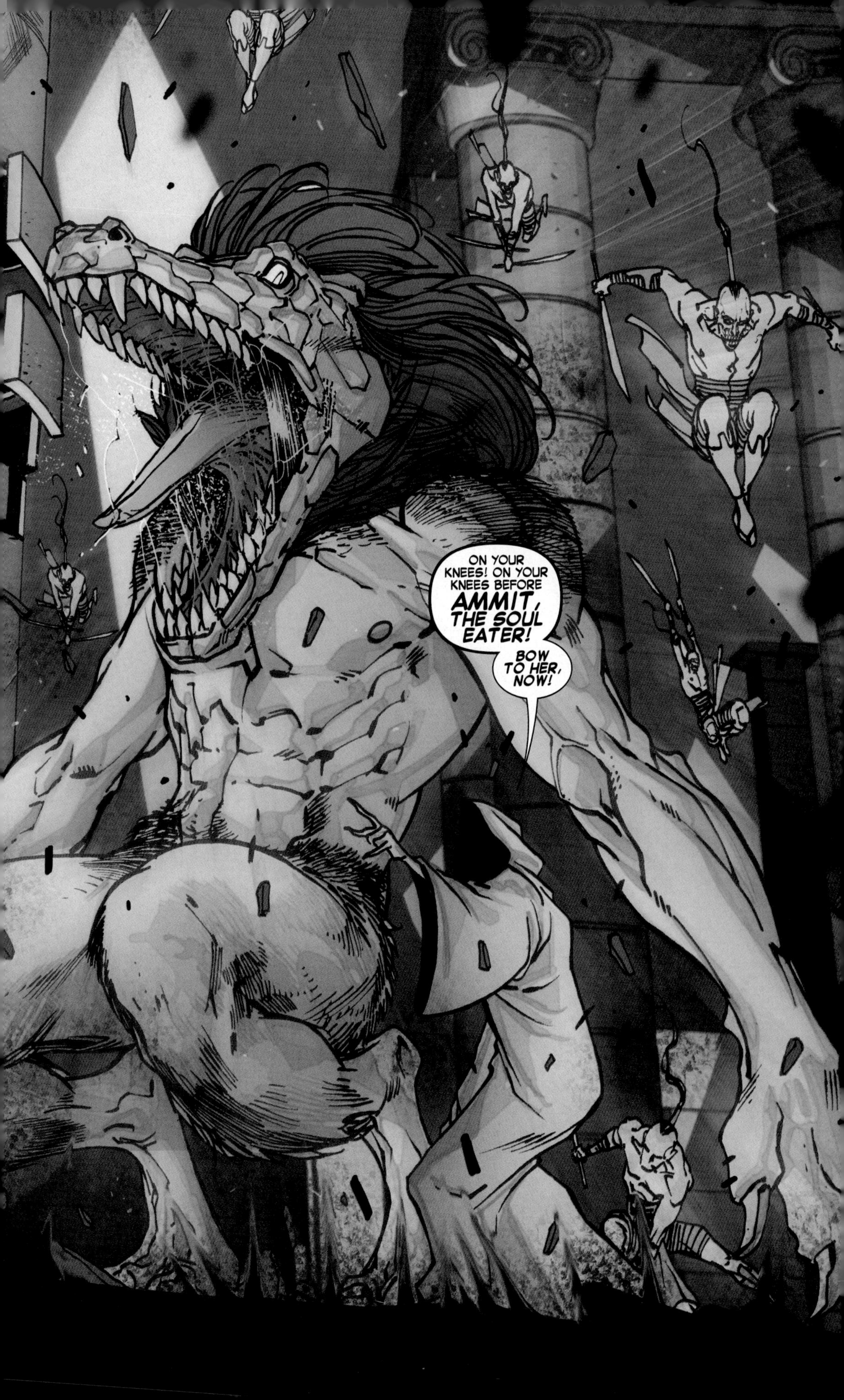
ON YOUR KNEES! ON YOUR KNEES BEFORE AMMIT, THE SOUL EATER!
BOW TO HER, NOW!

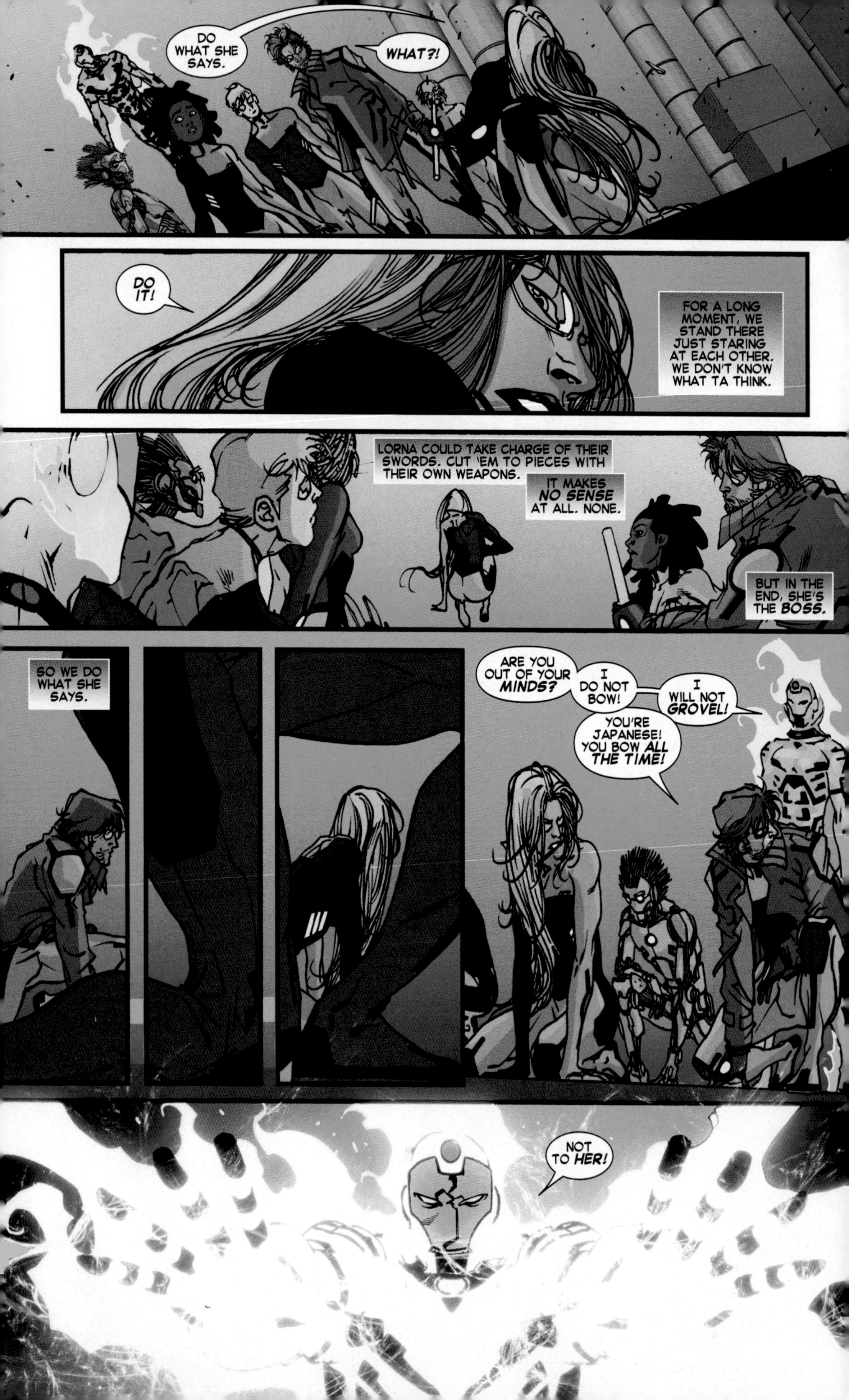
DO WHAT SHE SAYS.
WHAT?!
DO IT!
FOR A LONG MOMENT, WE STAND THERE JUST STARING AT EACH OTHER. WE DON'T KNOW WHAT TA THINK.
LORNA COULD TAKE CHARGE OF THEIR SWORDS. CUT 'EM TO PIECES WITH THEIR OWN WEAPONS.
IT MAKES NO SENSE AT ALL. NONE.
BUT IN THE END, SHE'S THE BOSS.
SO WE DO WHAT SHE SAYS.
ARE YOU OUT OF YOUR MINDS?
I DO NOT BOW!
I WILL NOT GROVEL!
YOU'RE JAPANESE! YOU BOW ALL THE TIME!
NOT TO HER!

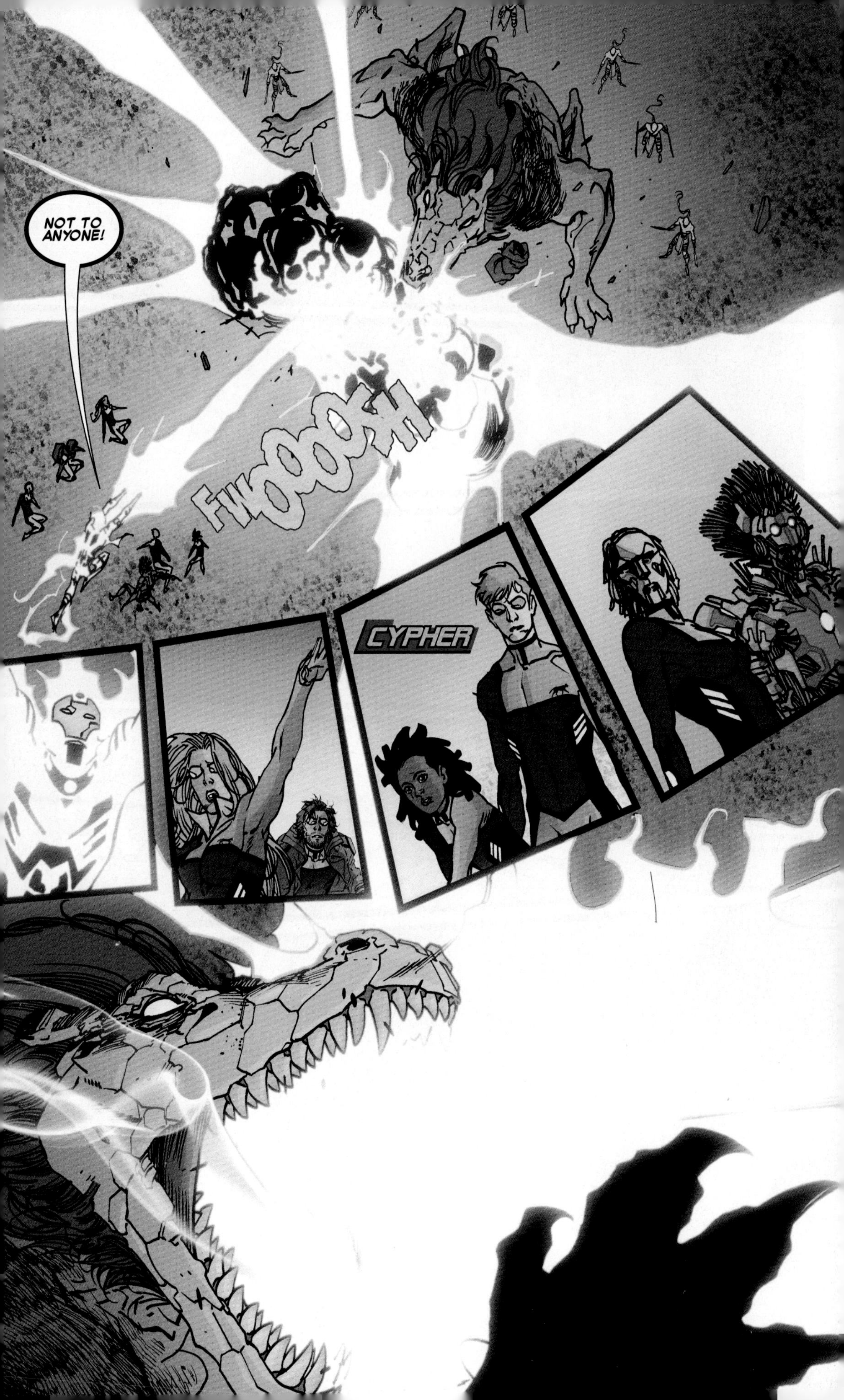
NOT TO ANYONE!
FWOOOSH
CYPHER

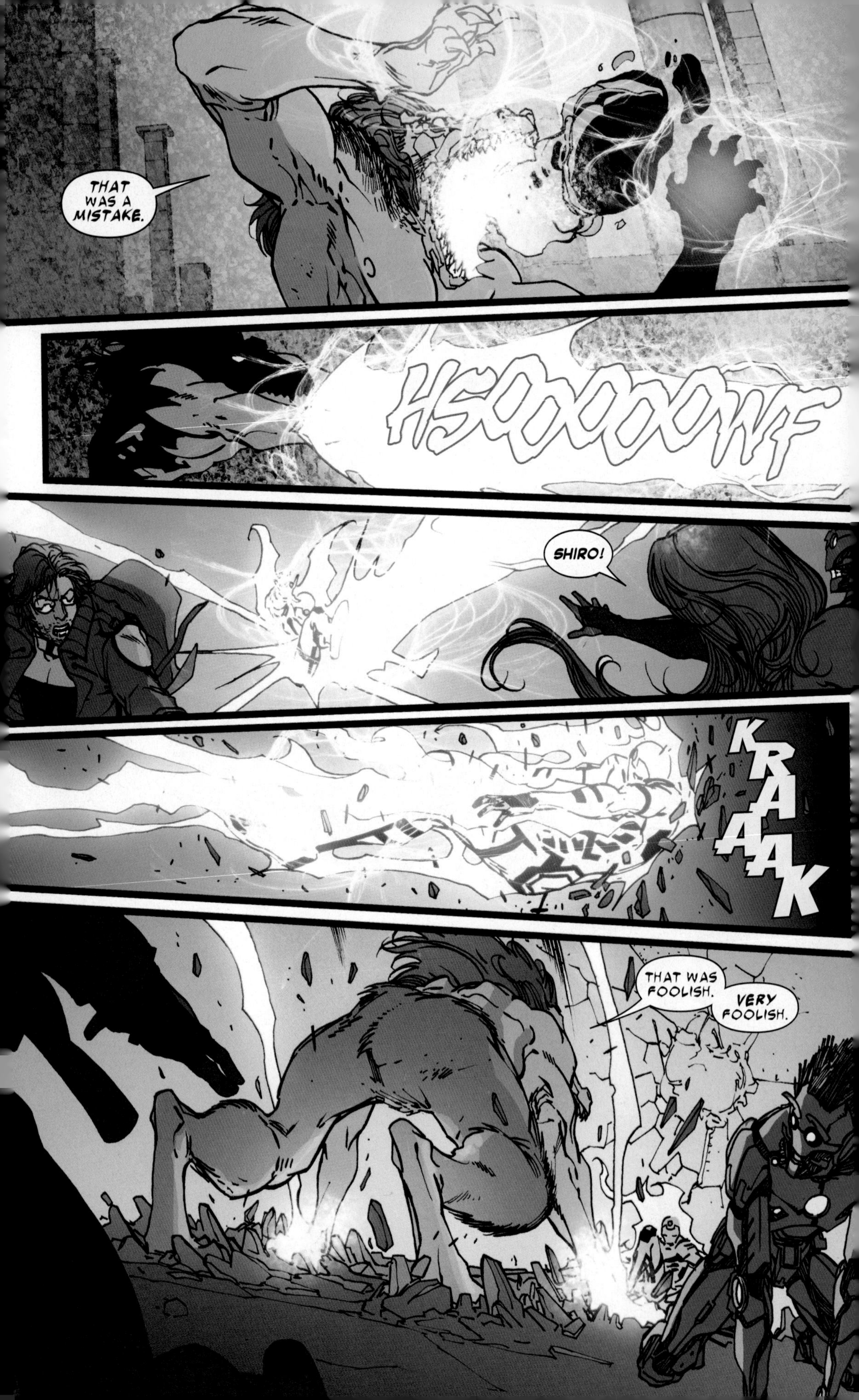
THAT WAS A MISTAKE.
HSOOOOOWF
SHIRO!
KRAAAK
THAT WAS FOOLISH.
VERY FOOLISH.

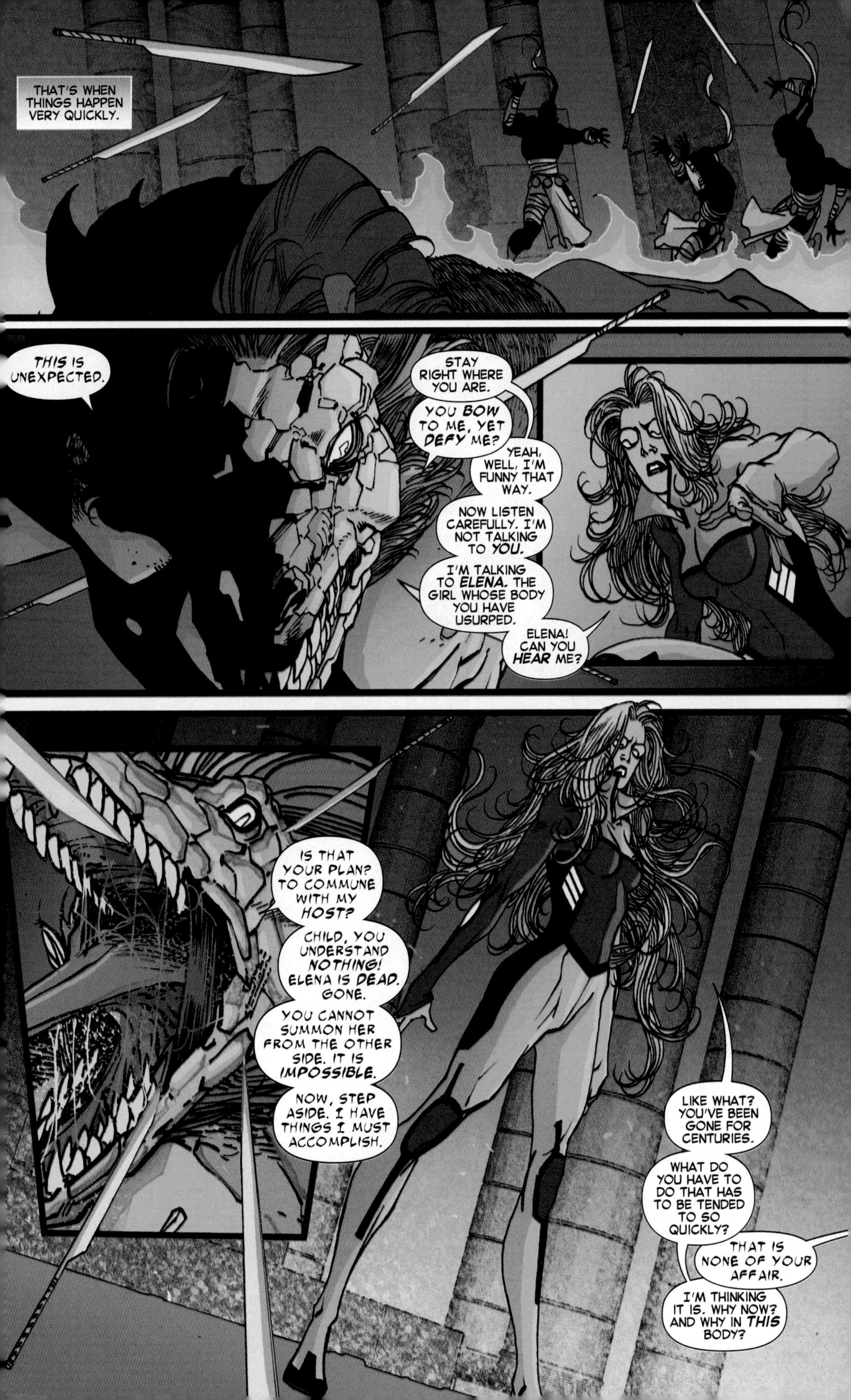
THAT'S WHEN THINGS HAPPEN VERY QUICKLY.
THIS is UNEXPECTED.
STAY RIGHT WHERE YOU ARE.
YOU BOW TO ME, YET DEFY ME?
YEAH, WELL, I'M FUNNY THAT WAY.
NOW LISTEN CAREFULLY. I'M NOT TALKING TO YOU.
I'M TALKING TO ELENA. THE GIRL WHOSE BODY YOU HAVE USURPED.
ELENA! CAN YOU HEAR ME?
IS THAT YOUR PLAN? TO COMMUNE WITH MY HOST?
CHILD, YOU UNDERSTAND NOTHING! ELENA IS DEAD. GONE.
YOU CANNOT SUMMON HER FROM THE OTHER SIDE. IT IS IMPOSSIBLE.
NOW, STEP ASIDE. I HAVE THINGS I MUST ACCOMPLISH.
LIKE WHAT? YOU'VE BEEN GONE FOR CENTURIES.
WHAT DO YOU HAVE TO DO THAT HAS TO BE TENDED TO SO QUICKLY?
THAT IS NONE OF YOUR AFFAIR.
I'M THINKING IT IS. WHY NOW? AND WHY IN THIS BODY?

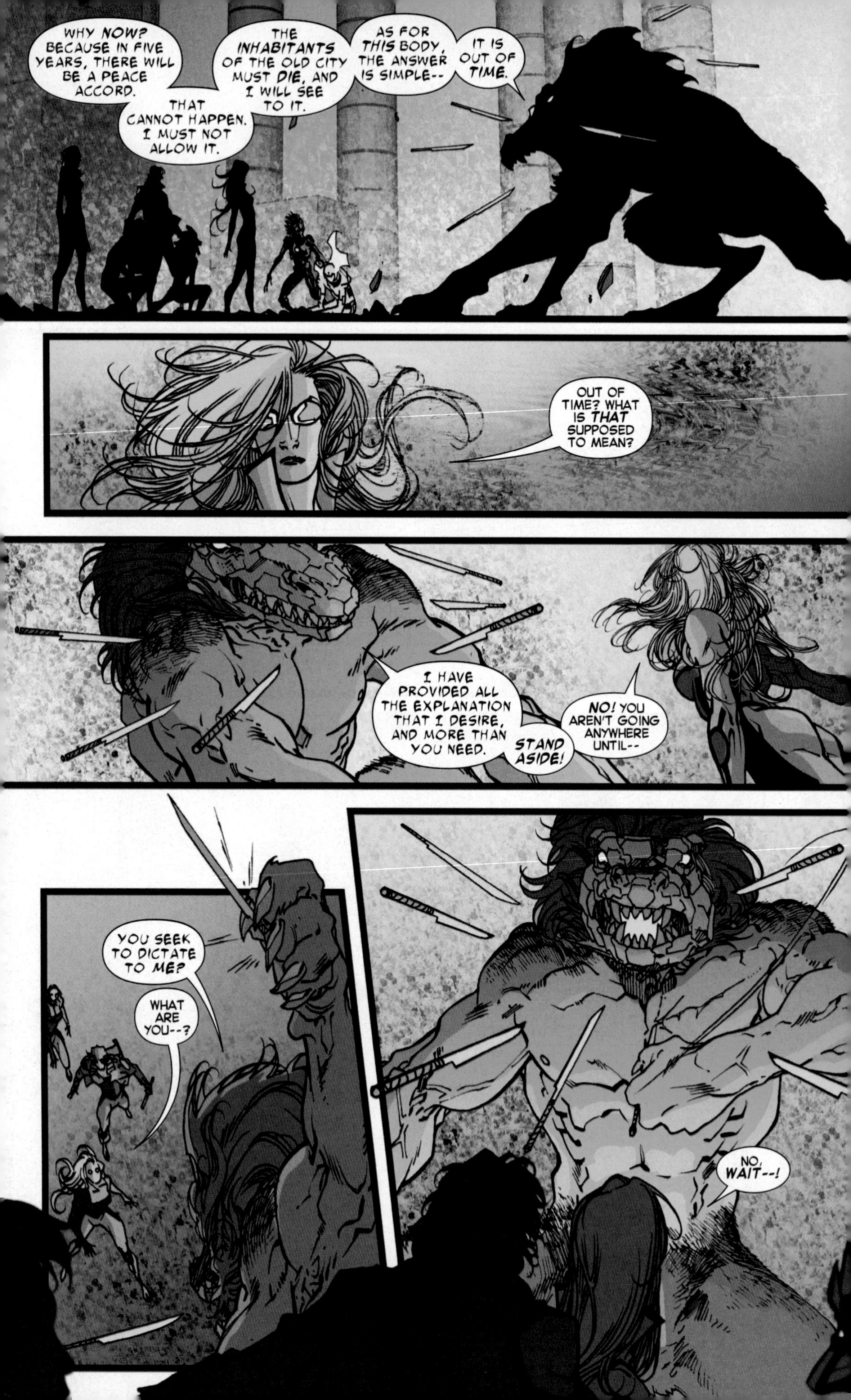

WHY NOW? BECAUSE IN FIVE YEARS, THERE WILL BE A PEACE ACCORD.
THAT CANNOT HAPPEN. I MUST NOT ALLOW IT.
THE INHABITANTS OF THE OLD CITY MUST DIE, AND I WILL SEE TO IT.
AS FOR THIS BODY, THE ANSWER IS SIMPLE--
IT IS OUT OF TIME.
OUT OF TIME? WHAT IS THAT SUPPOSED TO MEAN?
I HAVE PROVIDED ALL THE EXPLANATION THAT I DESIRE, AND MORE THAN YOU NEED.
STAND ASIDE!
NO! YOU AREN'T GOING ANYWHERE UNTIL--
YOU SEEK TO DICTATE TO ME?
WHAT ARE YOU--?
NO, WAIT--!

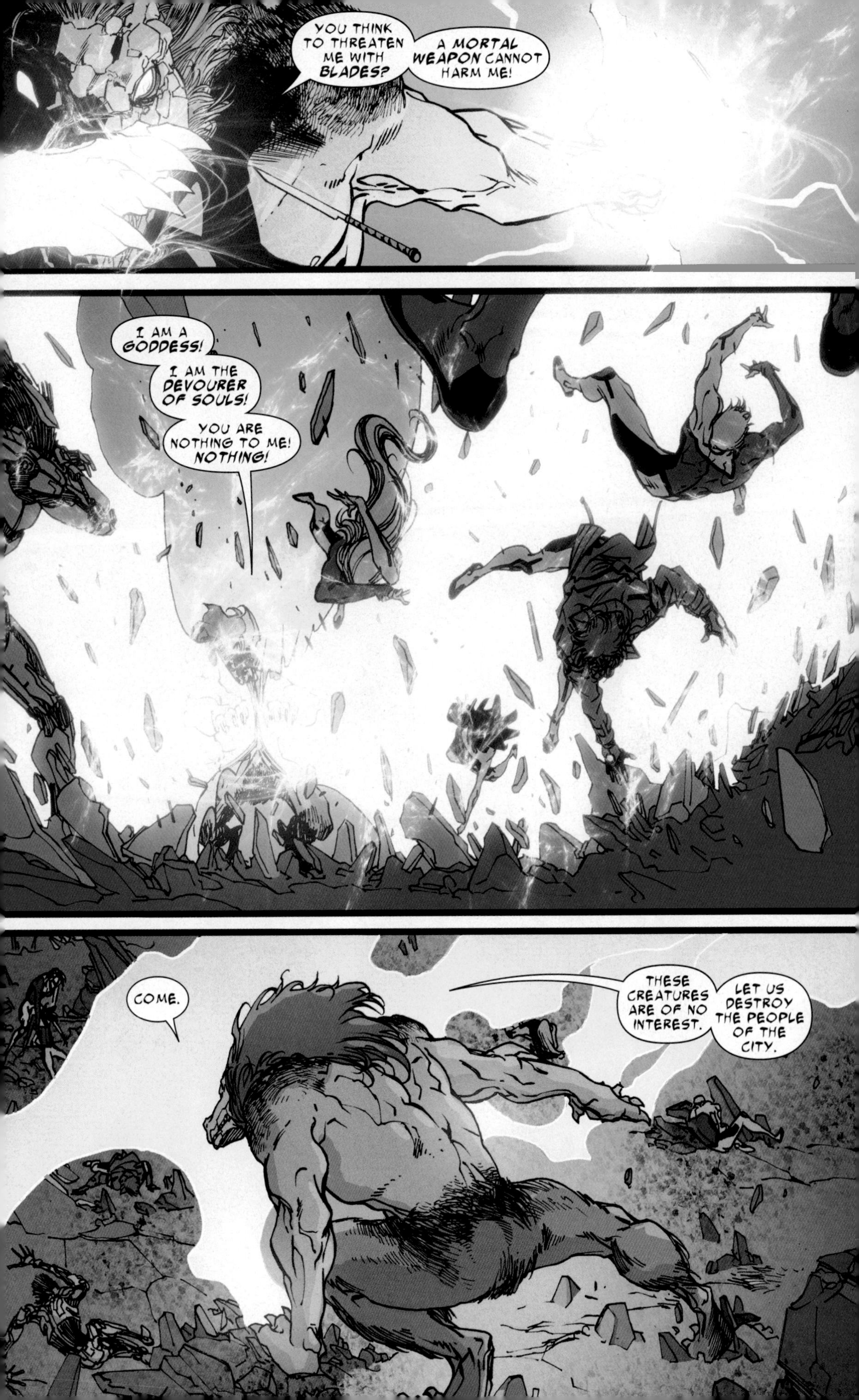
YOU THINK TO THREATEN ME WITH BLADES?
A MORTAL WEAPON CANNOT HARM ME!
I AM A GODDESS!
I AM THE DEVOURER OF SOULS!
YOU ARE NOTHING TO ME! NOTHING!
COME.
THESE CREATURES ARE OF NO INTEREST.
LET US DESTROY THE PEOPLE OF THE CITY.

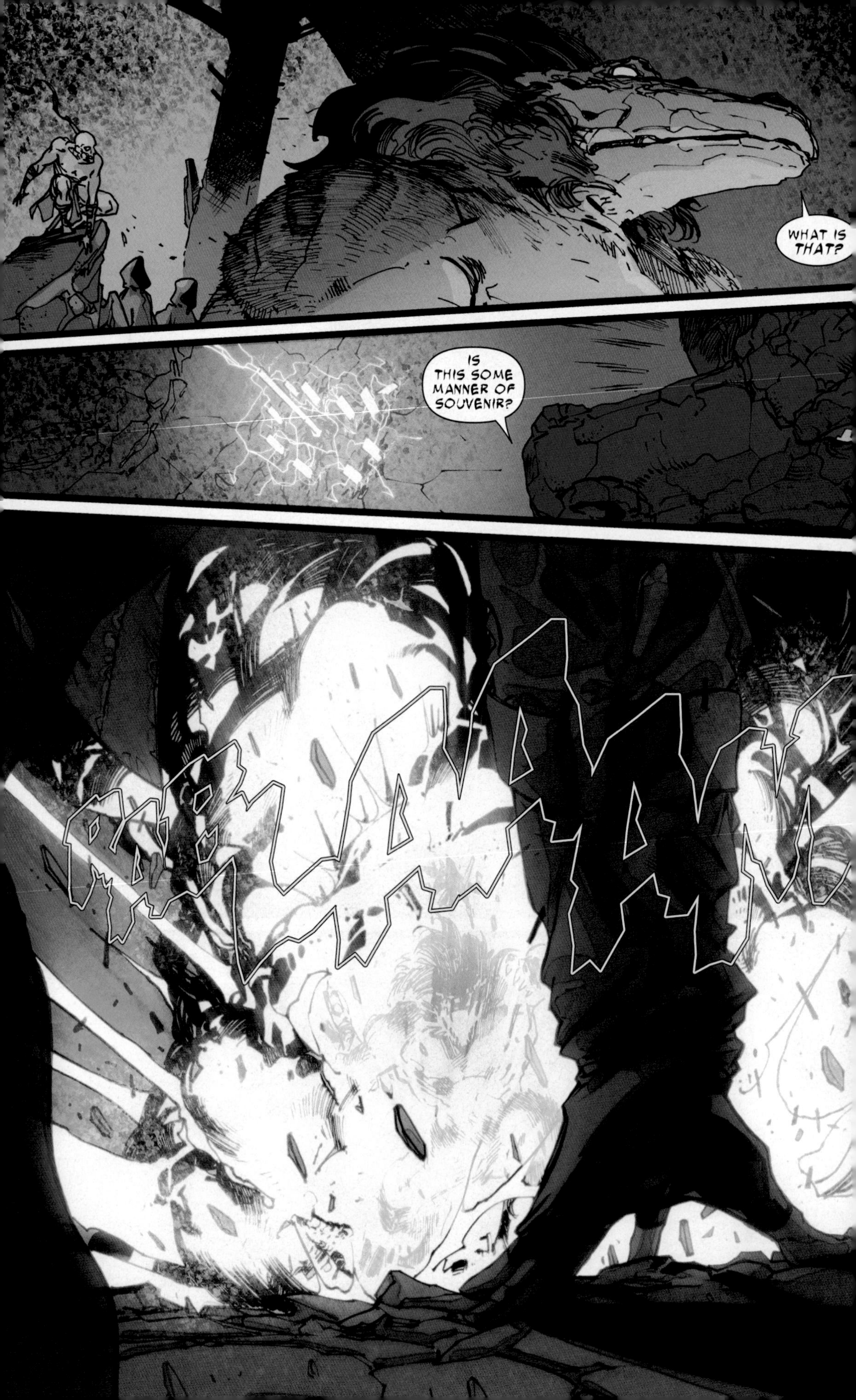
WHAT IS THAT?
IS THIS SOME MANNER OF SOUVENIR?

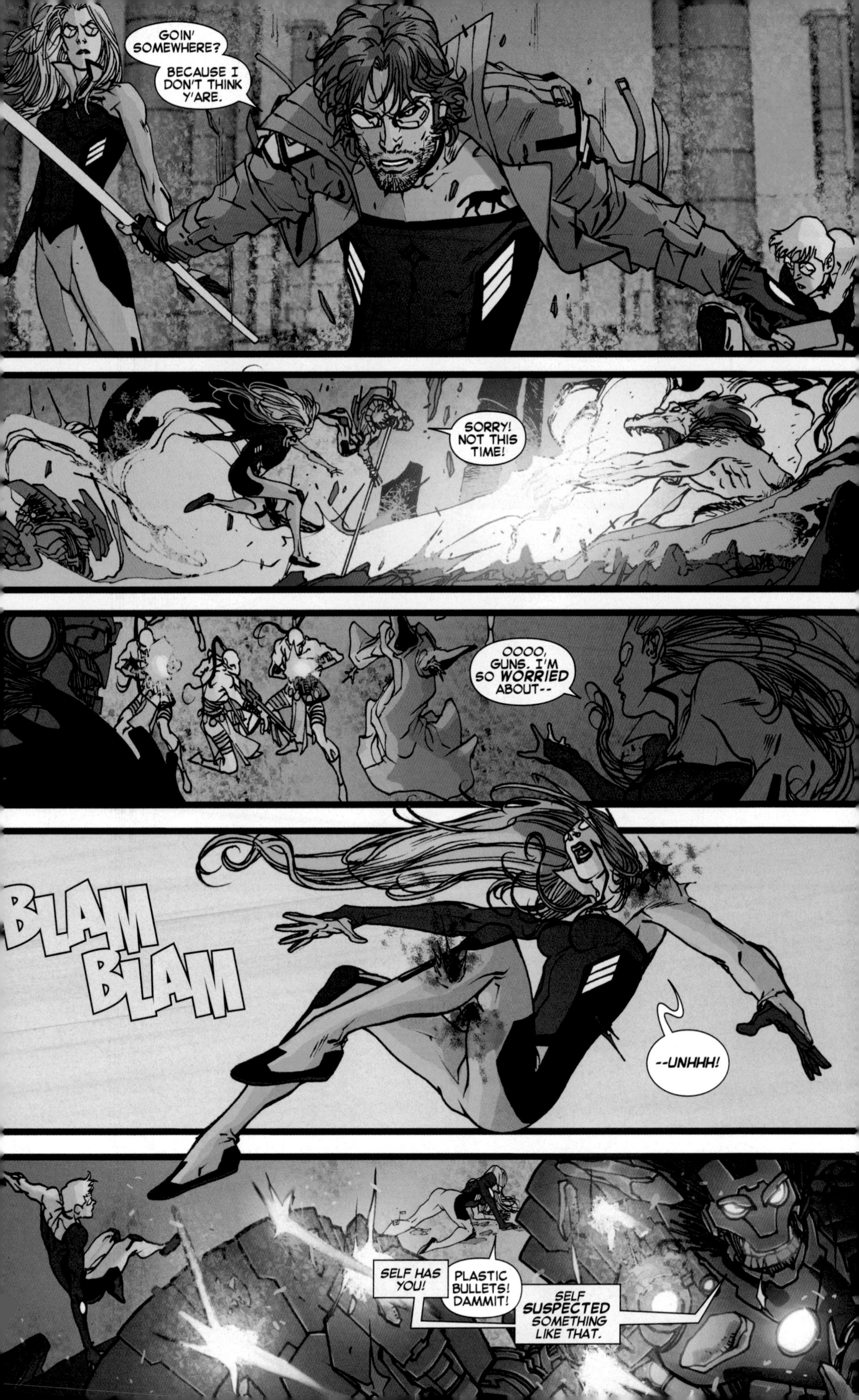
GOIN' SOMEWHERE?
BECAUSE I DON'T THINK Y'ARE.
SORRY! NOT THIS TIME!
OOOO, GUNS. I'M SO WORRIED ABOUT--
BLAM BLAM
--UNHHH!
SELF HAS YOU!
PLASTIC BULLETS! DAMMIT!
SELF SUSPECTED SOMETHING LIKE THAT.

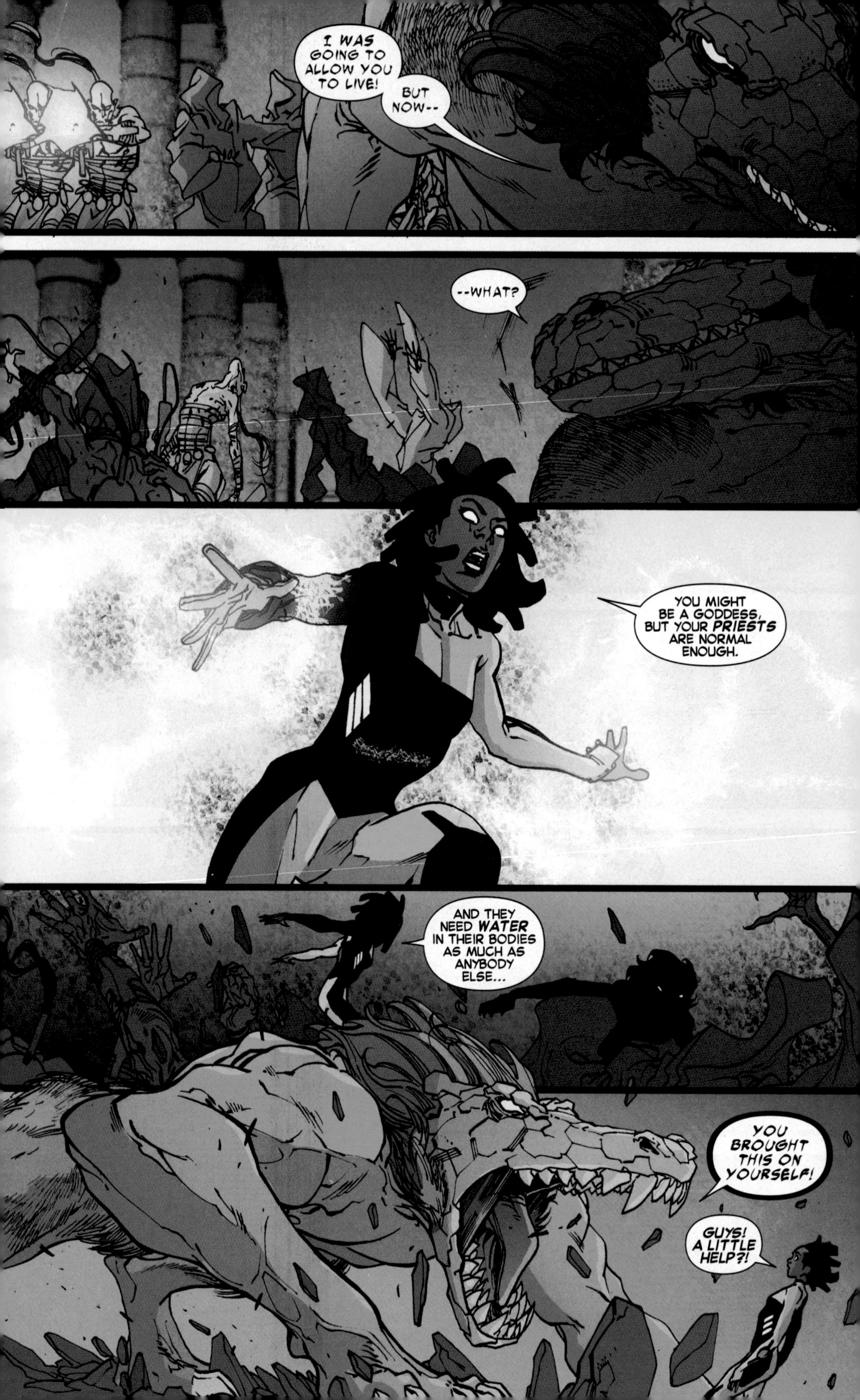
I WAS GOING TO ALLOW YOU TO LIVE!
BUT NOW--
--WHAT?
YOU MIGHT BE A GODDESS, BUT YOUR PRIESTS ARE NORMAL ENOUGH.
AND THEY NEED WATER IN THEIR BODIES AS MUCH AS ANYBODY ELSE...
YOU BROUGHT THIS ON YOURSELF!
GUYS! A LITTLE HELP?!

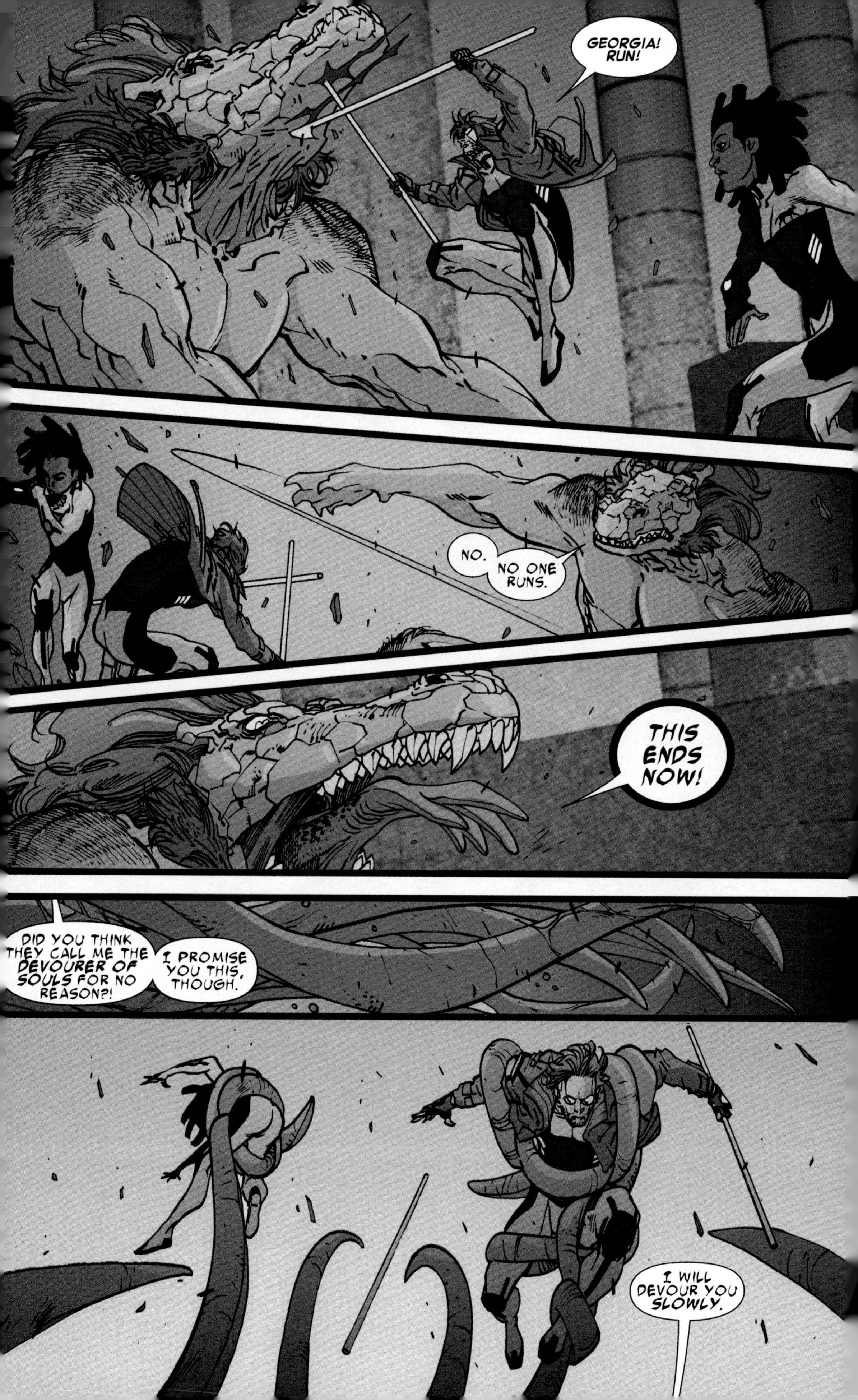
GEORGIA! RUN!
NO.
NO ONE RUNS.
THIS ENDS NOW!
DID YOU THINK THEY CALL ME THE DEVOURER OF SOULS FOR NO REASON?!
I PROMISE YOU THIS, THOUGH.
I WILL DEVOUR YOU SLOWLY.

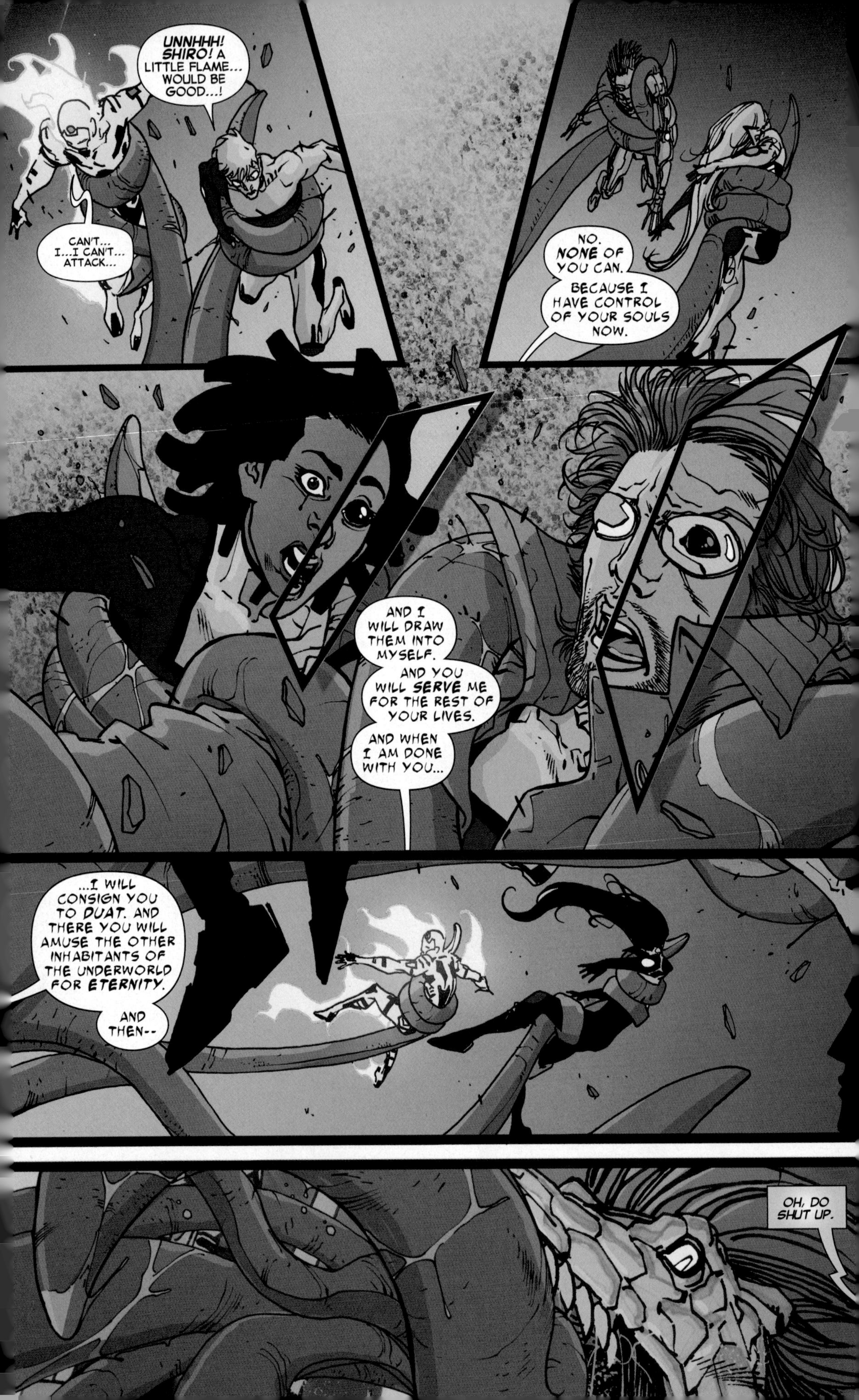
UNNHHH! SHIRO! A LITTLE FLAME... WOULD BE GOOD...!
CAN'T... I...I CAN'T... ATTACK...
NO. NONE OF YOU CAN.
BECAUSE I HAVE CONTROL OF YOUR SOULS NOW.
AND I WILL DRAW THEM INTO MYSELF.
AND YOU WILL SERVE ME FOR THE REST OF YOUR LIVES.
AND WHEN I AM DONE WITH YOU...
...I WILL CONSIGN YOU TO DUAT. AND THERE YOU WILL AMUSE THE OTHER INHABITANTS OF THE UNDERWORLD FOR ETERNITY.
AND THEN--
OH, DO SHUT UP.

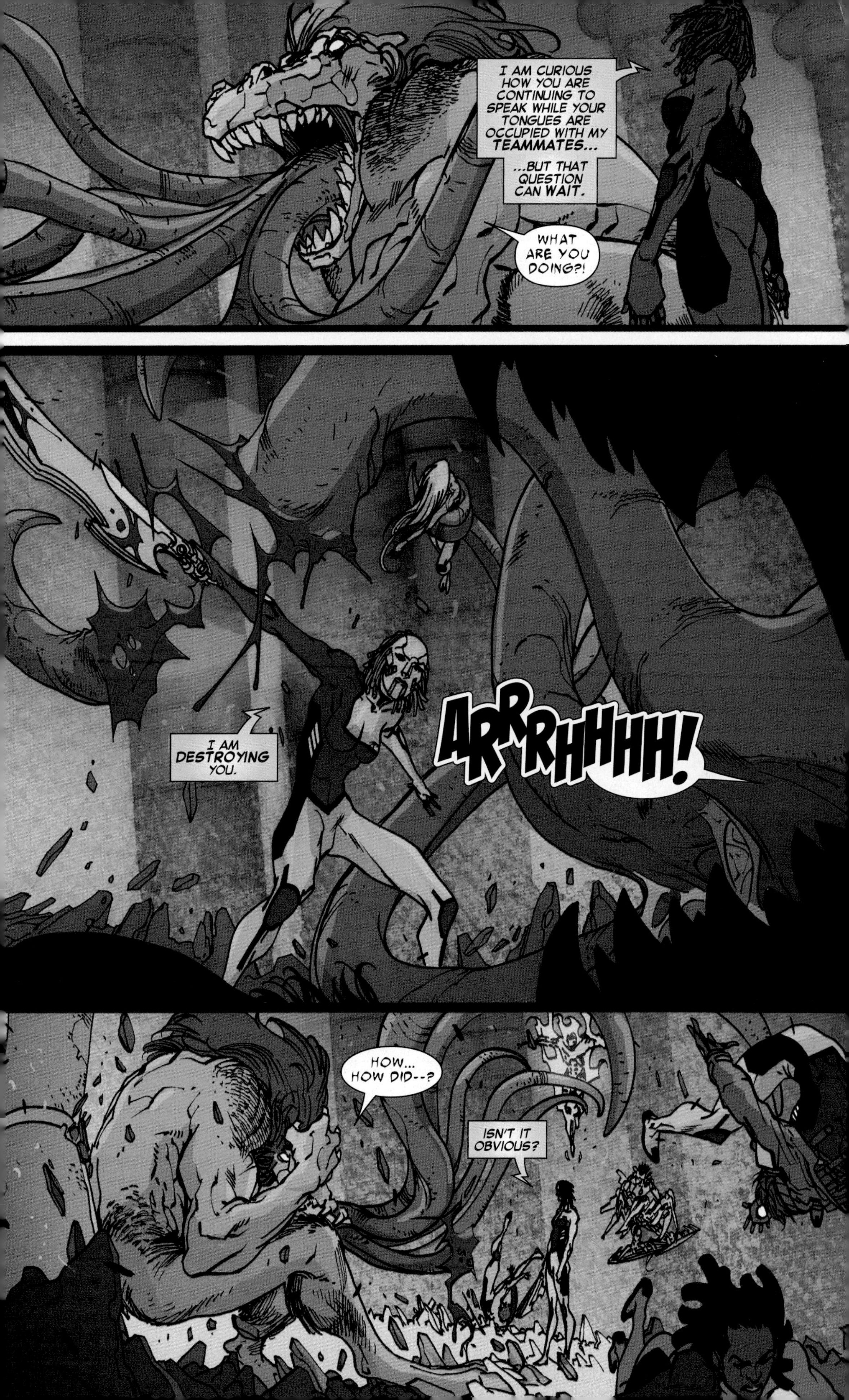
I AM CURIOUS HOW YOU ARE CONTINUING TO SPEAK WHILE YOUR TONGUES ARE OCCUPIED WITH MY TEAMMATES...
...BUT THAT QUESTION CAN WAIT.
WHAT ARE YOU DOING?!
I AM DESTROYING YOU.
ARRRHHHH!
HOW... HOW DID--?
ISN'T IT OBVIOUS?

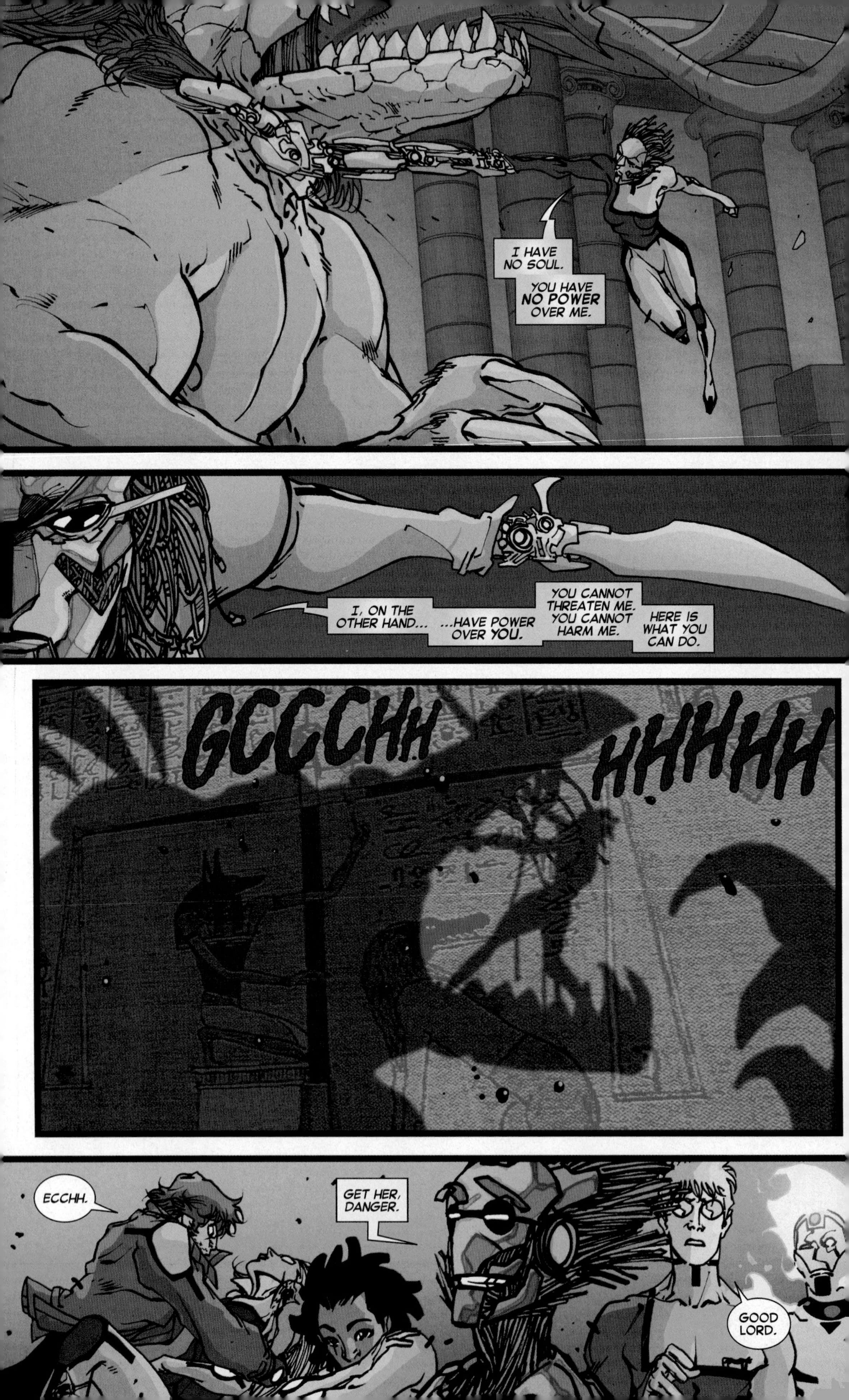
I HAVE NO SOUL.
YOU HAVE NO POWER OVER ME.
I, ON THE OTHER HAND...
...HAVE POWER OVER YOU.
YOU CANNOT THREATEN ME. YOU CANNOT HARM ME.
HERE IS WHAT YOU CAN DO.
GCCCHH HHHHHH
ECCHH.
GET HER, DANGER.
GOOD LORD.

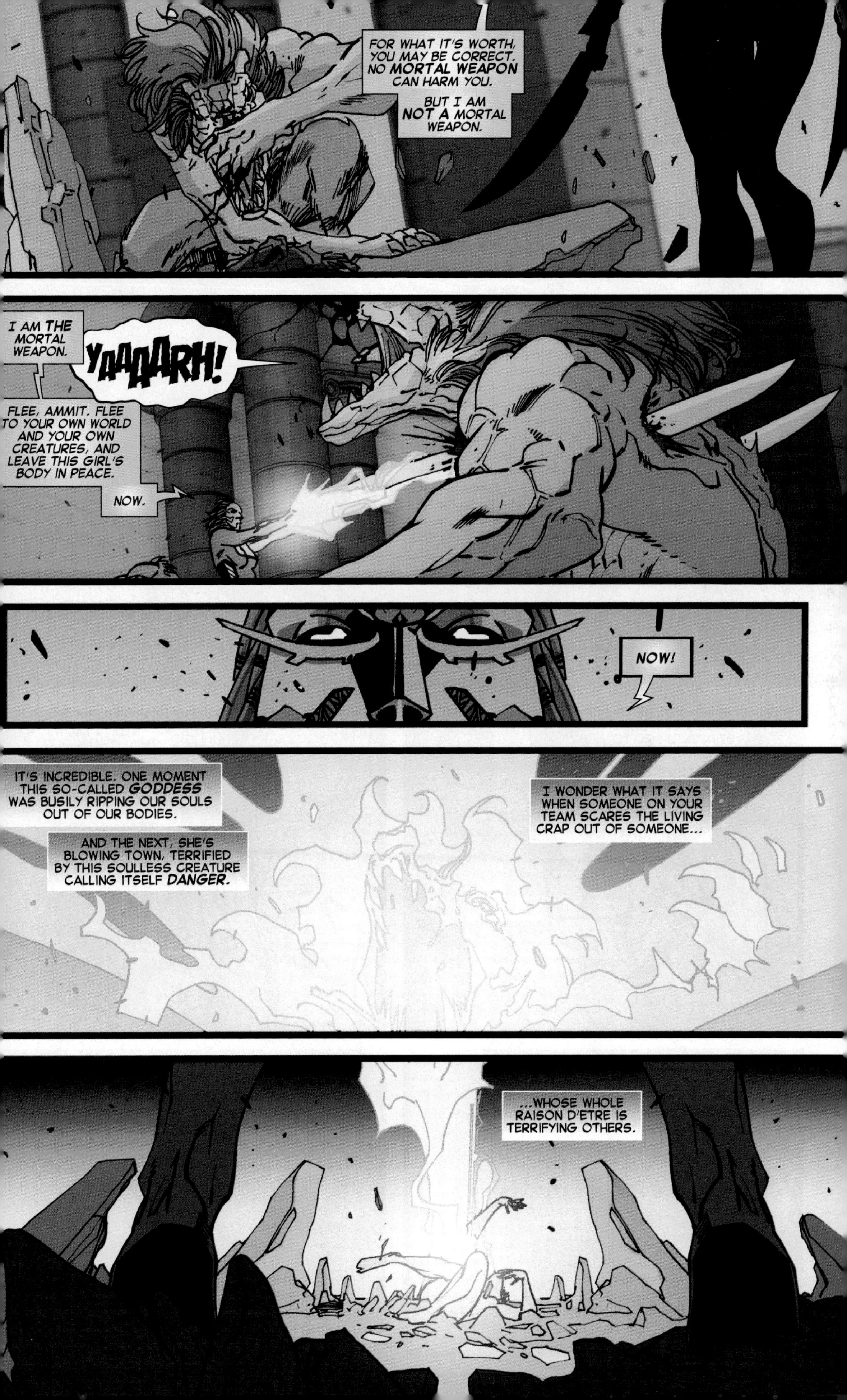

FOR WHAT IT'S WORTH, YOU MAY BE CORRECT. NO MORTAL WEAPON CAN HARM YOU.
BUT I AM NOT A MORTAL WEAPON.
I AM THE MORTAL WEAPON.
YAAAARH!
FLEE, AMMIT. FLEE TO YOUR OWN WORLD AND YOUR OWN CREATURES, AND LEAVE THIS GIRL'S BODY IN PEACE.
NOW.
NOW!
IT'S INCREDIBLE. ONE MOMENT THIS SO-CALLED GODDESS WAS BUSILY RIPPING OUR SOULS OUT OF OUR BODIES.
AND THE NEXT, SHE'S BLOWING TOWN, TERRIFIED BY THIS SOULLESS CREATURE CALLING ITSELF DANGER.
I WONDER WHAT IT SAYS WHEN SOMEONE ON YOUR TEAM SCARES THE LIVING CRAP OUT OF SOMEONE...
...WHOSE WHOLE RAISON D'ETRE IS TERRIFYING OTHERS.

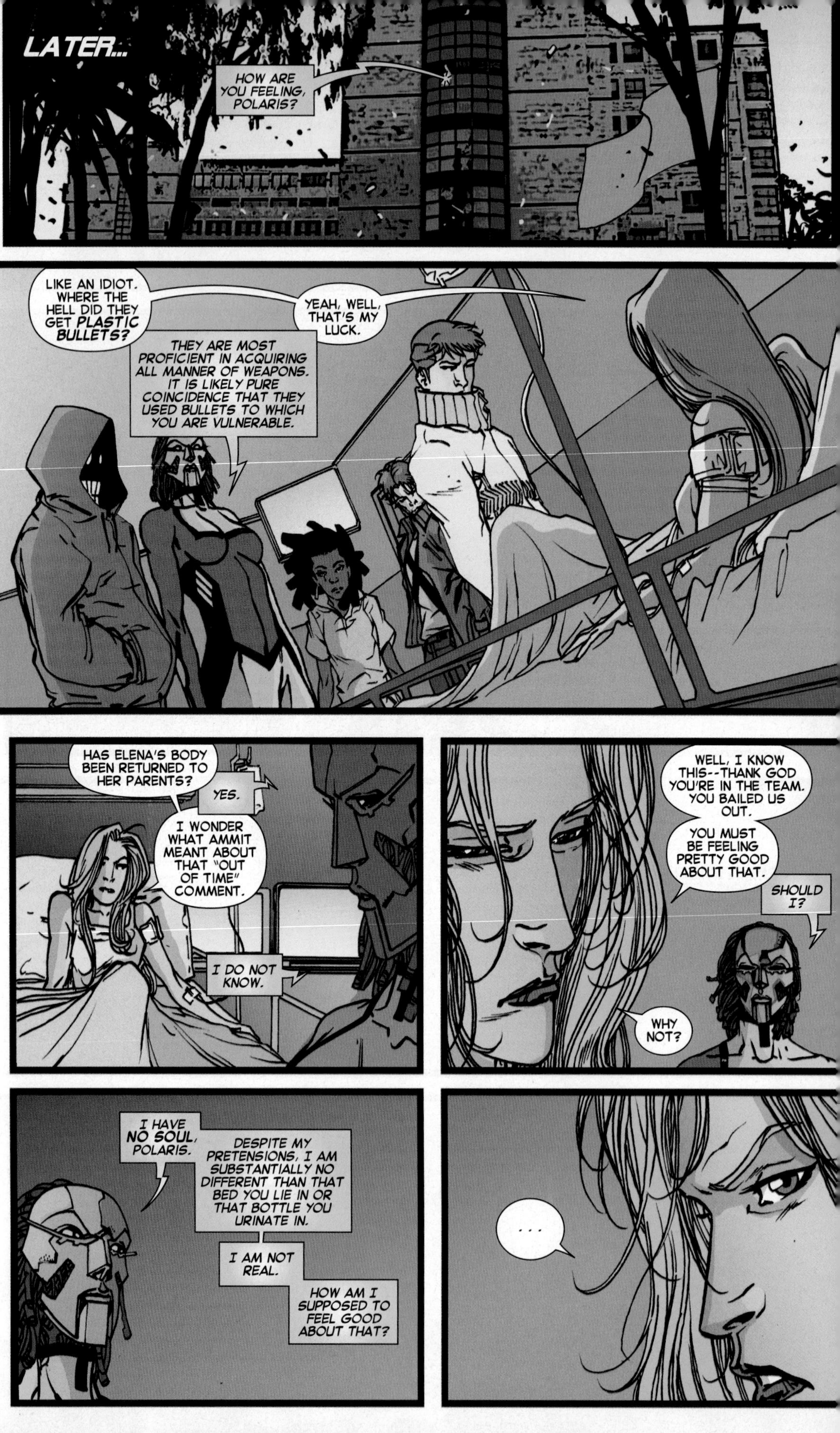
LATER...
HOW ARE YOU FEELING, POLARIS?
LIKE AN IDIOT. WHERE THE HELL DID THEY GET PLASTIC BULLETS?
YEAH, WELL, THAT'S MY LUCK.
THEY ARE MOST PROFICIENT IN ACQUIRING ALL MANNER OF WEAPONS. IT IS LIKELY PURE COINCIDENCE THAT THEY USED BULLETS TO WHICH YOU ARE VULNERABLE.
HAS ELENA'S BODY BEEN RETURNED TO HER PARENTS?
YES.
I WONDER WHAT AMMIT MEANT ABOUT THAT "OUT OF TIME" COMMENT.
I DO NOT KNOW.
WELL, I KNOW THIS--THANK GOD YOU'RE IN THE TEAM. YOU BAILED US OUT.
YOU MUST BE FEELING PRETTY GOOD ABOUT THAT.
SHOULD I?
WHY NOT?
I HAVE NO SOUL, POLARIS.
DESPITE MY PRETENSIONS, I AM SUBSTANTIALLY NO DIFFERENT THAN THAT BED YOU LIE IN OR THAT BOTTLE YOU URINATE IN.
I AM NOT REAL.
HOW AM I SUPPOSED TO FEEL GOOD ABOUT THAT?
...

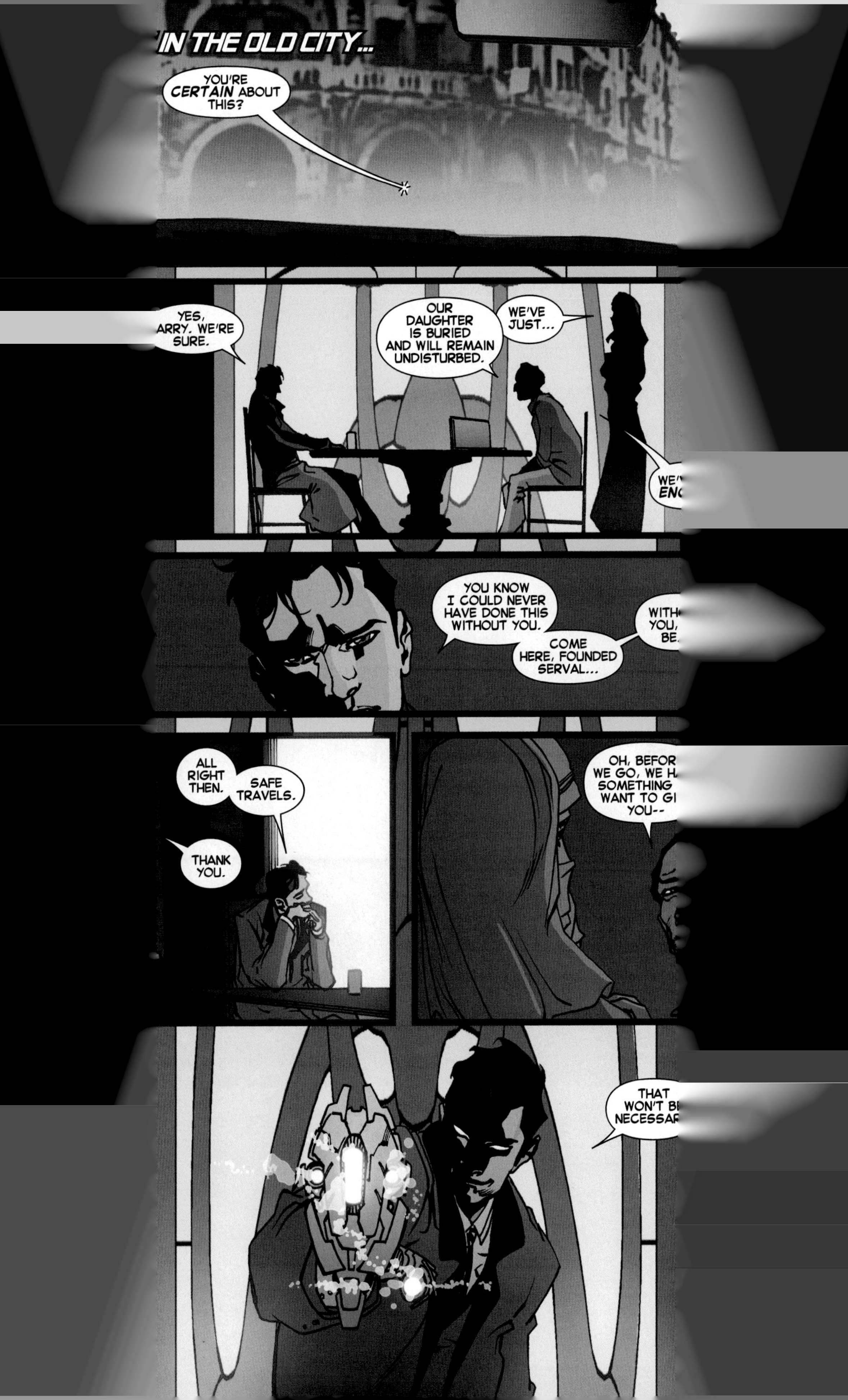

IN THE OLD CITY...
YOU'RE CERTAIN ABOUT THIS?
YES, ARRY. WE'RE SURE.
OUR DAUGHTER IS BURIED AND WILL REMAIN UNDISTURBED.
WE'VE JUST...
YOU KNOW I COULD NEVER HAVE DONE THIS WITHOUT YOU.
COME HERE, FOUNDED SERVAL...
WITH YOU, BE
ALL RIGHT THEN.
SAFE TRAVELS.
THANK YOU.
OH, BEFOR WE GO, WE H SOMETHING WANT TO GI YOU--
THAT WON'T B NECESSAR

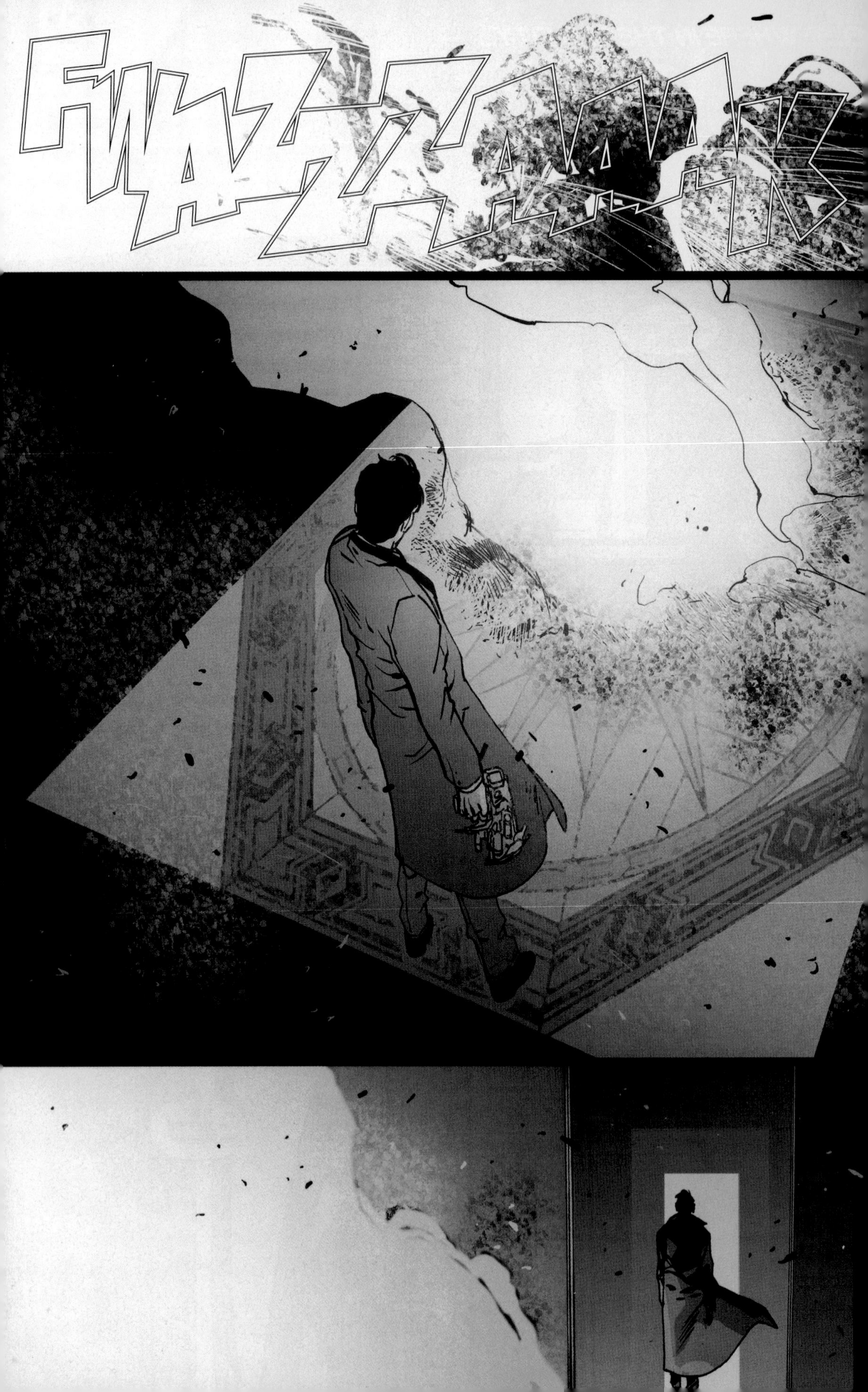
FWAZZZAAAK

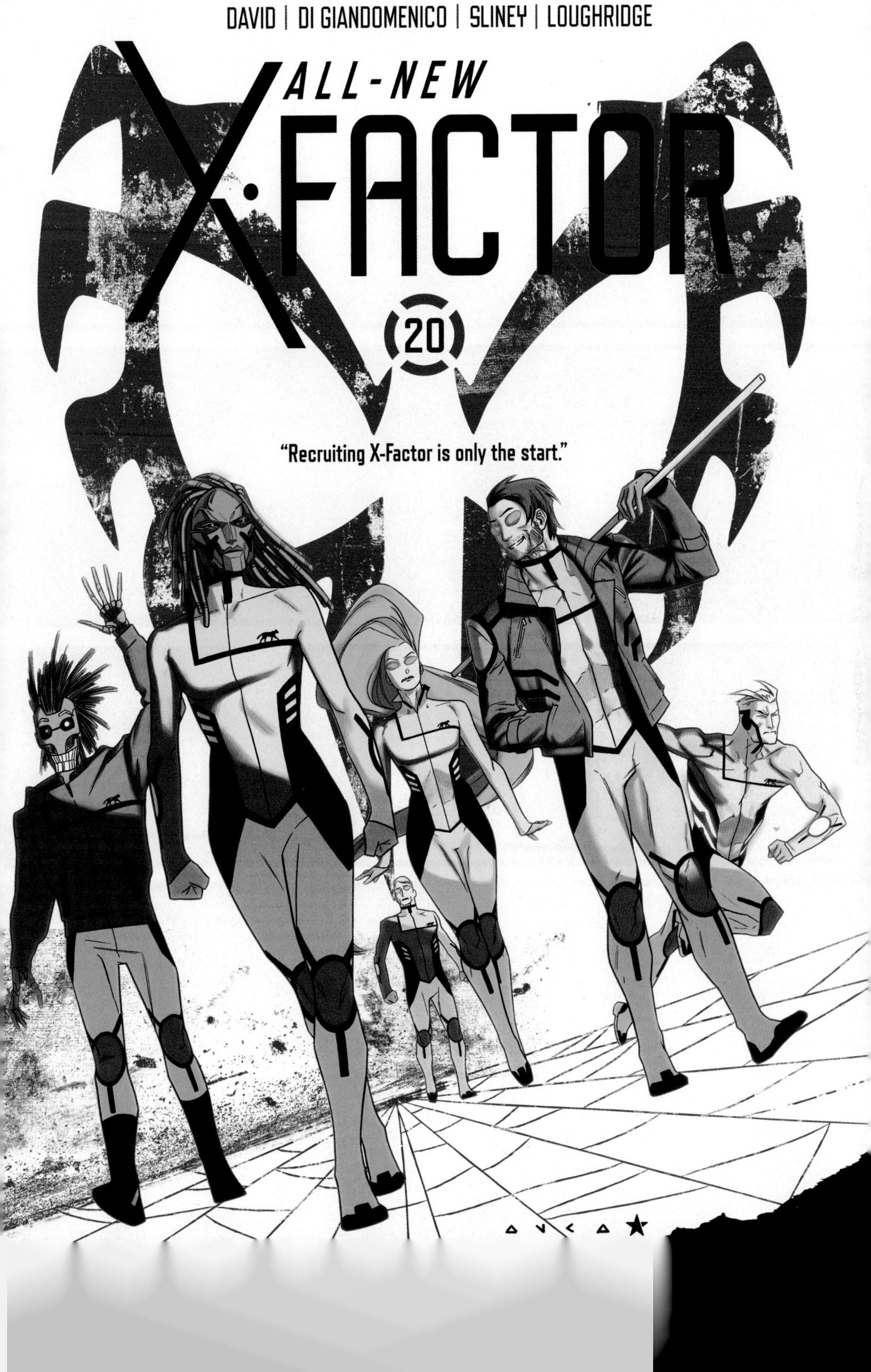
DAVID | DI GIANDOMENICO | SLINEY | LOUGHRIDGE
ALL-NEW
X-FACTOR
20
"Recruiting X-Factor is only the start."

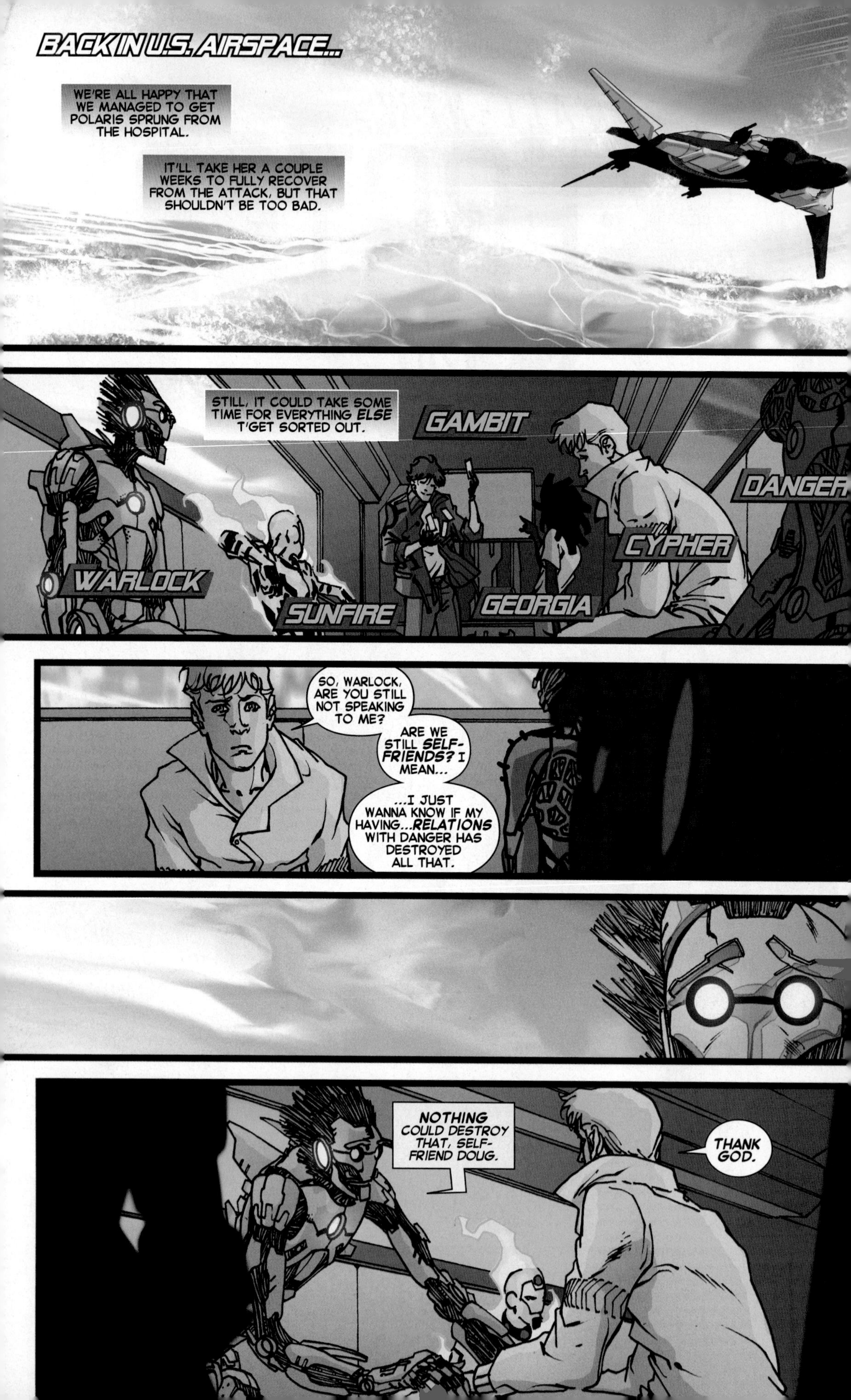

BACK IN U.S. AIRSPACE...
WE'RE ALL HAPPY THAT WE MANAGED TO GET POLARIS SPRUNG FROM THE HOSPITAL.
IT'LL TAKE HER A COUPLE WEEKS TO FULLY RECOVER FROM THE ATTACK, BUT THAT SHOULDN'T BE TOO BAD.
STILL, IT COULD TAKE SOME TIME FOR EVERYTHING ELSE T'GET SORTED OUT.
GAMBIT
DANGER
CYPHER
WARLOCK
SUNFIRE
GEORGIA
SO, WARLOCK, ARE YOU STILL NOT SPEAKING TO ME?
ARE WE STILL SELF-FRIENDS? I MEAN...
...I JUST WANNA KNOW IF MY HAVING...RELATIONS WITH DANGER HAS DESTROYED ALL THAT.
NOTHING COULD DESTROY THAT, SELF-FRIEND DOUG.
THANK GOD.

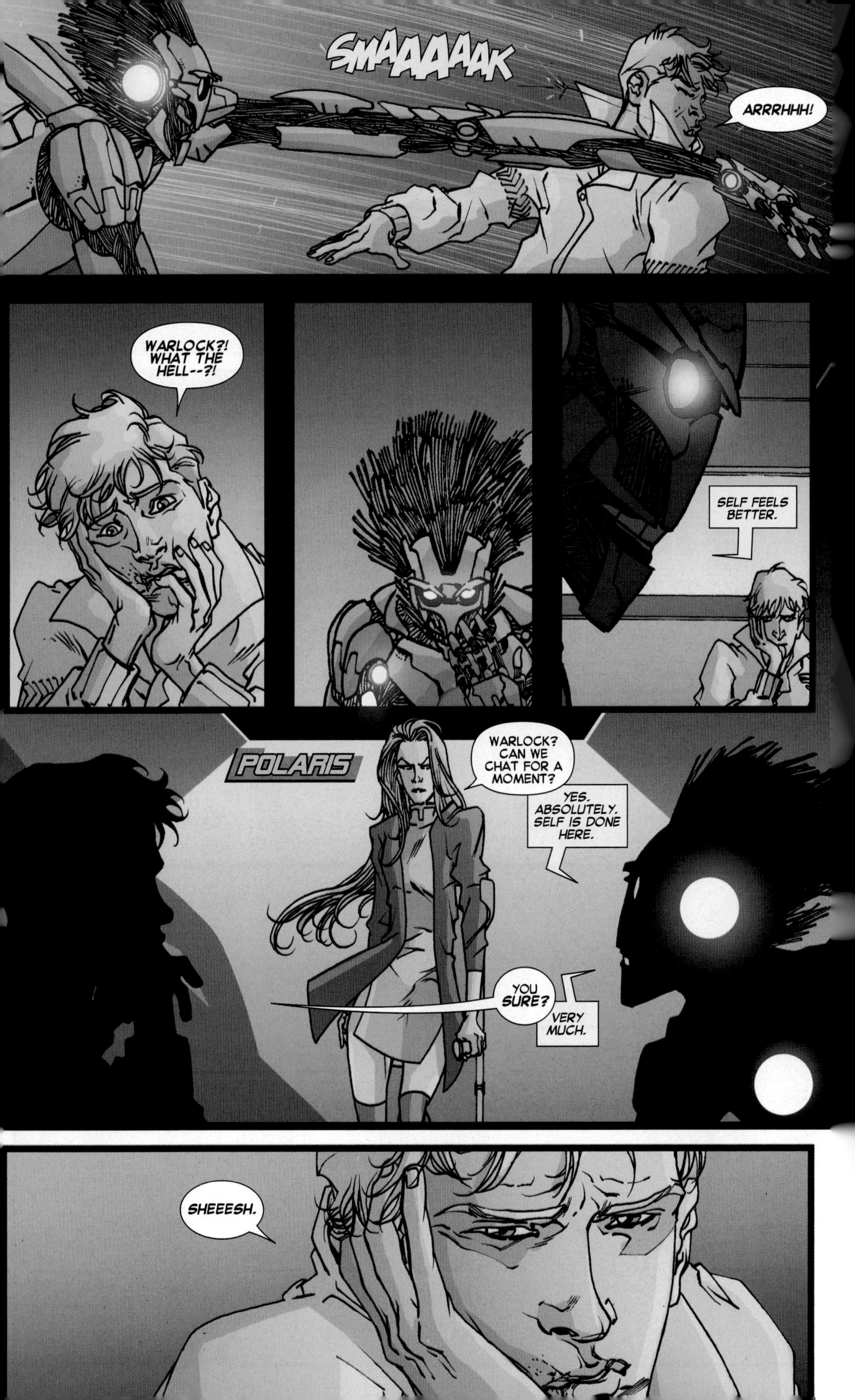
SMAAAAAK
ARRRHHH!
WARLOCK?! WHAT THE HELL--?!
SELF FEELS BETTER.
POLARIS
WARLOCK? CAN WE CHAT FOR A MOMENT?
YES. ABSOLUTELY. SELF IS DONE HERE.
YOU SURE?
VERY MUCH.
SHEEESH.

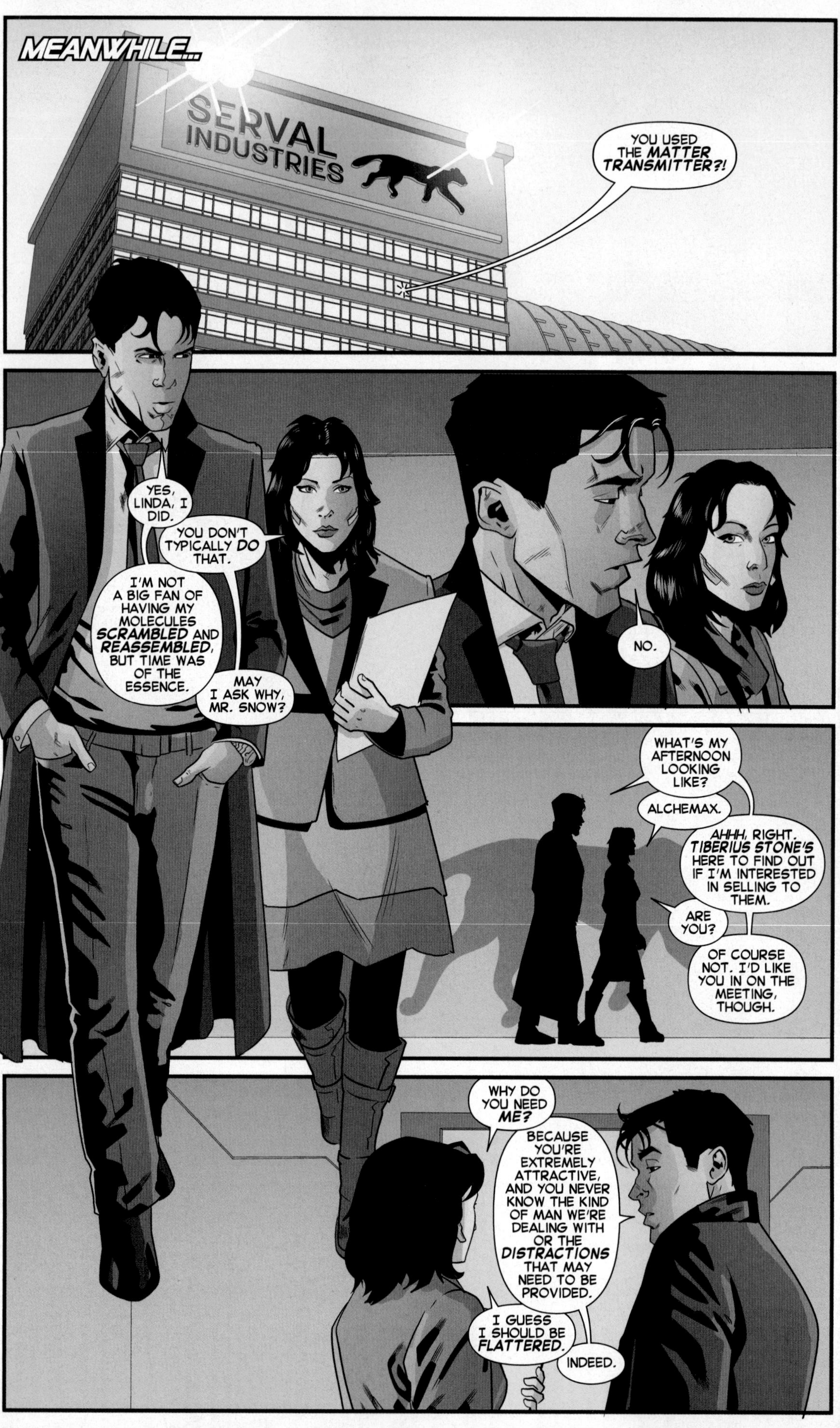
MEANWHILE...
SERVAL INDUSTRIES
YOU USED THE MATTER TRANSMITTER?!
YES, LINDA, I DID.
YOU DON'T TYPICALLY DO THAT.
I'M NOT A BIG FAN OF HAVING MY MOLECULES SCRAMBLED AND REASSEMBLED, BUT TIME WAS OF THE ESSENCE.
MAY I ASK WHY, MR. SNOW?
NO.
WHAT'S MY AFTERNOON LOOKING LIKE?
ALCHEMAX.
AHHH, RIGHT. TIBERIUS STONE'S HERE TO FIND OUT IF I'M INTERESTED IN SELLING TO THEM.
ARE YOU?
OF COURSE NOT. I'D LIKE YOU IN ON THE MEETING, THOUGH.
WHY DO YOU NEED ME?
BECAUSE YOU'RE EXTREMELY ATTRACTIVE, AND YOU NEVER KNOW THE KIND OF MAN WE'RE DEALING WITH OR THE DISTRACTIONS THAT MAY NEED TO BE PROVIDED.
I GUESS I SHOULD BE FLATTERED.
INDEED.

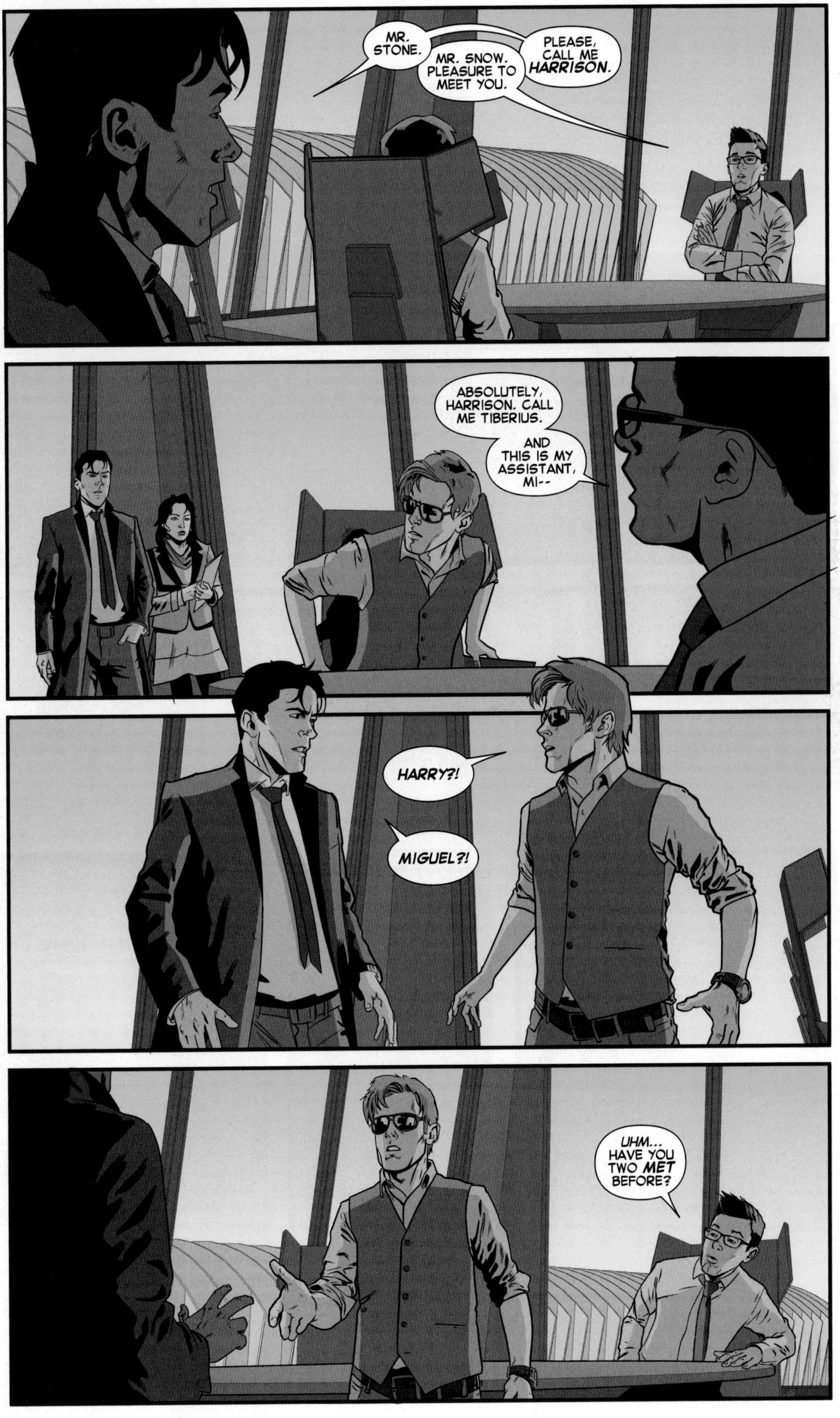
MR. STONE.
MR. SNOW. PLEASURE TO MEET YOU.
PLEASE, CALL ME HARRISON.
ABSOLUTELY, HARRISON. CALL ME TIBERIUS.
AND THIS IS MY ASSISTANT, MI--
HARRY?!
MIGUEL?!
UHM... HAVE YOU TWO MET BEFORE?

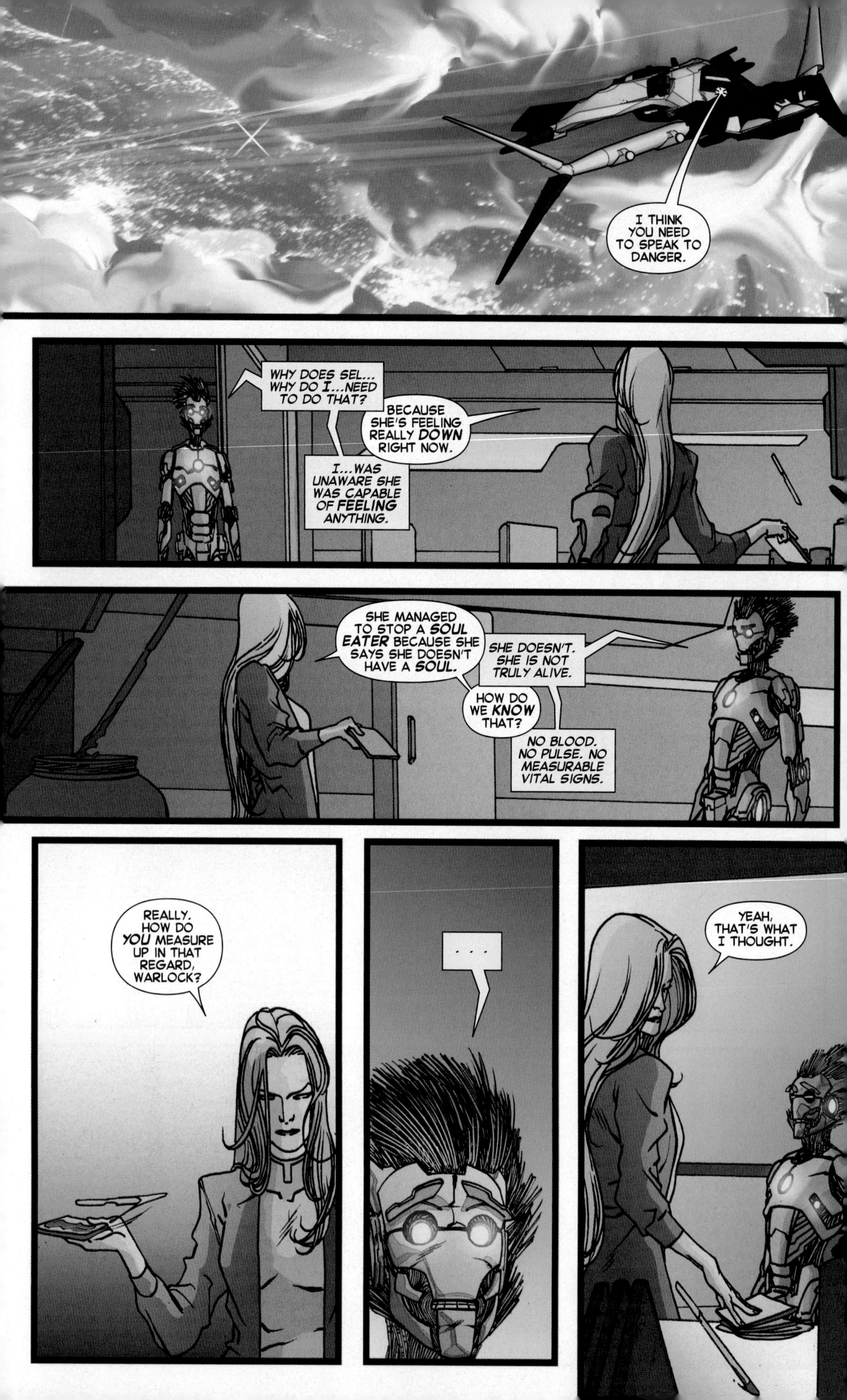
I THINK YOU NEED TO SPEAK TO DANGER.
WHY DOES SEL... WHY DO I...NEED TO DO THAT?
BECAUSE SHE'S FEELING REALLY DOWN RIGHT NOW.
I...WAS UNAWARE SHE WAS CAPABLE OF FEELING ANYTHING.
SHE MANAGED TO STOP A SOUL EATER BECAUSE SHE SAYS SHE DOESN'T HAVE A SOUL.
SHE DOESN'T. SHE IS NOT TRULY ALIVE.
HOW DO WE KNOW THAT?
NO BLOOD. NO PULSE. NO MEASURABLE VITAL SIGNS.
REALLY. HOW DO YOU MEASURE UP IN THAT REGARD, WARLOCK?
. . .
YEAH, THAT'S WHAT I THOUGHT.

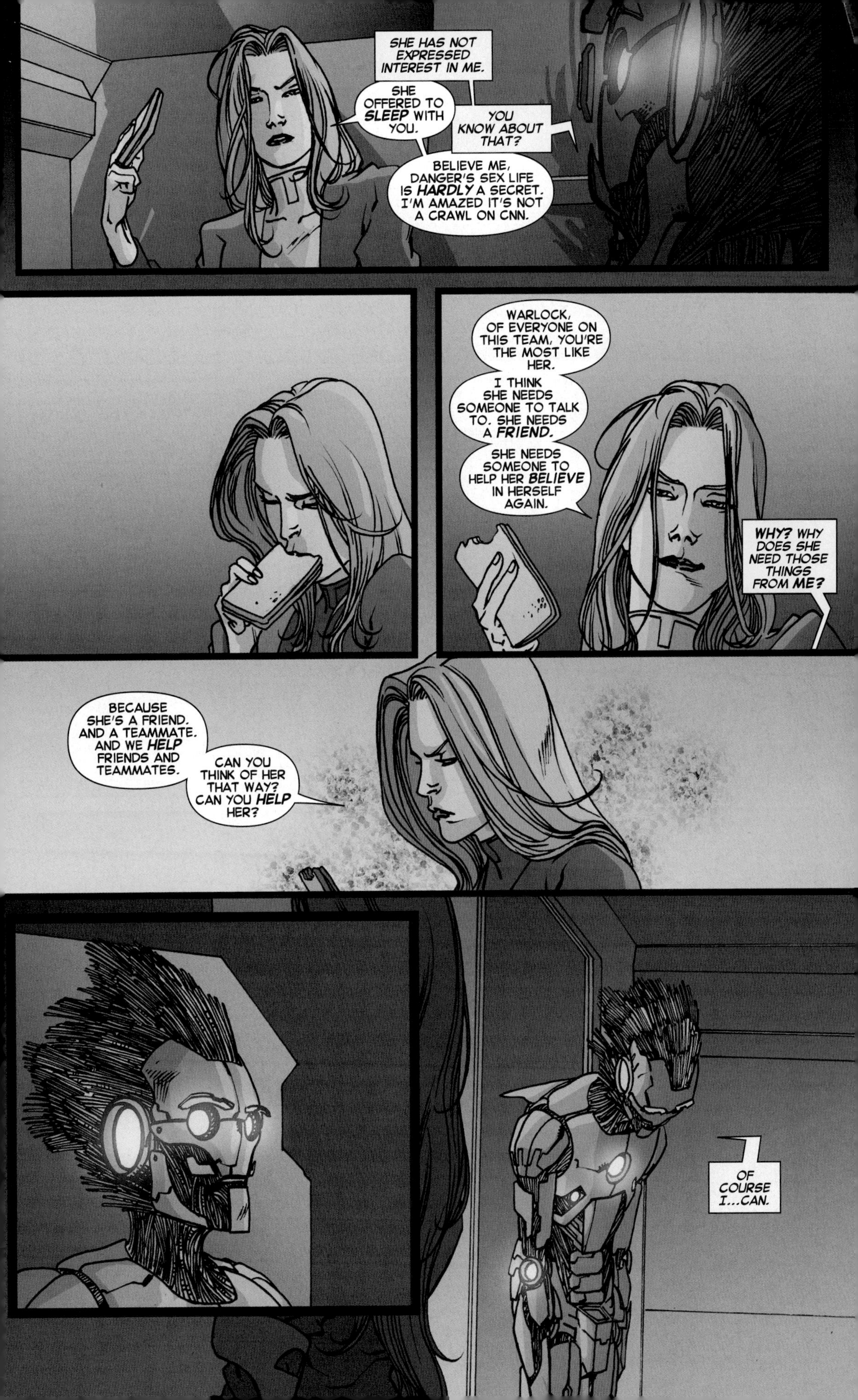
SHE HAS NOT EXPRESSED INTEREST IN ME.
SHE OFFERED TO SLEEP WITH YOU.
YOU KNOW ABOUT THAT?
BELIEVE ME, DANGER'S SEX LIFE IS HARDLY A SECRET. I'M AMAZED IT'S NOT A CRAWL ON CNN.
WARLOCK, OF EVERYONE ON THIS TEAM, YOU'RE THE MOST LIKE HER.
I THINK SHE NEEDS SOMEONE TO TALK TO. SHE NEEDS A FRIEND.
SHE NEEDS SOMEONE TO HELP HER BELIEVE IN HERSELF AGAIN.
WHY? WHY DOES SHE NEED THOSE THINGS FROM ME?
BECAUSE SHE'S A FRIEND. AND A TEAMMATE. AND WE HELP FRIENDS AND TEAMMATES.
CAN YOU THINK OF HER THAT WAY? CAN YOU HELP HER?
OF COURSE I...CAN.

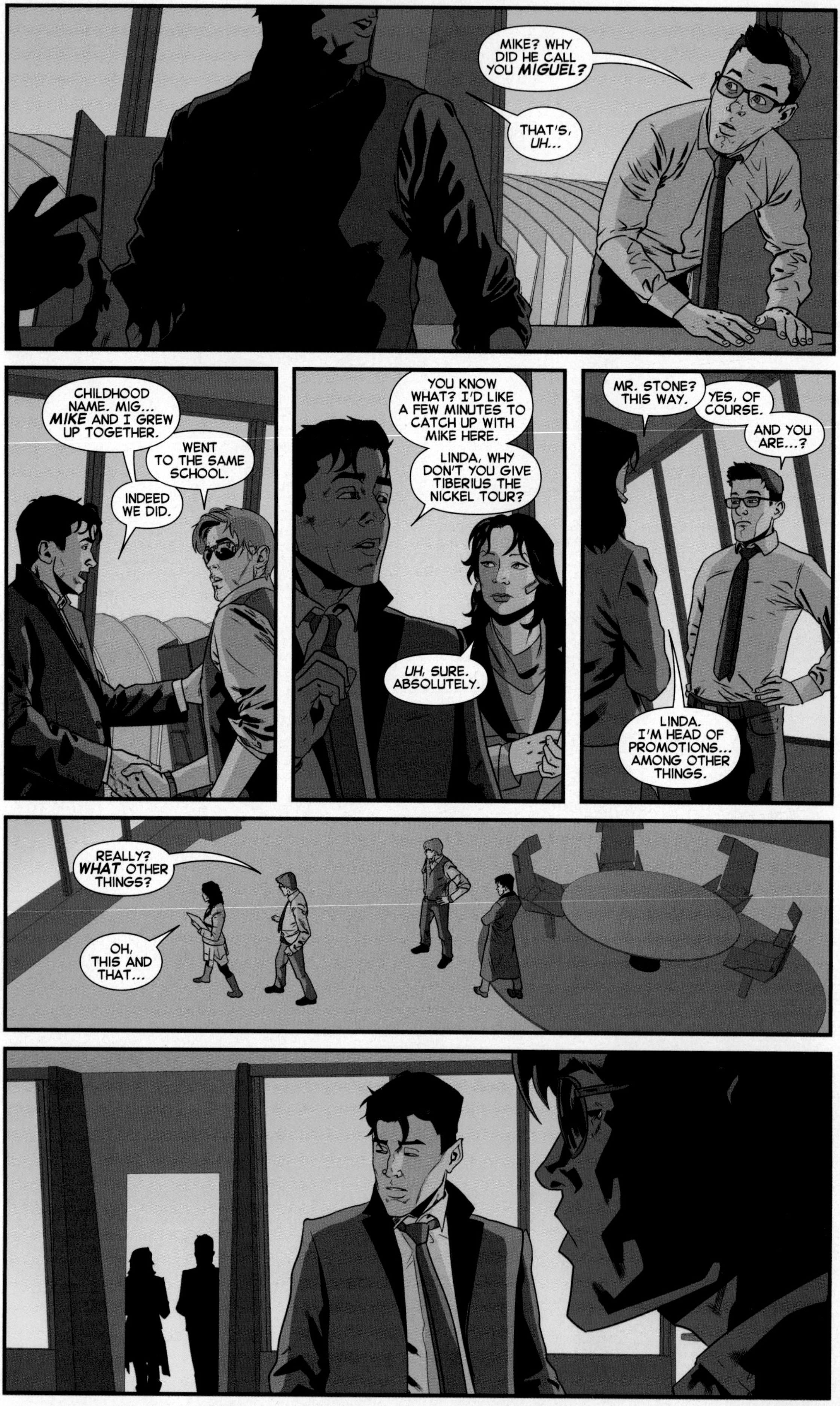
MIKE? WHY DID HE CALL YOU MIGUEL?
THAT'S, UH...
CHILDHOOD NAME. MIG... MIKE AND I GREW UP TOGETHER.
INDEED WE DID.
WENT TO THE SAME SCHOOL.
YOU KNOW WHAT? I'D LIKE A FEW MINUTES TO CATCH UP WITH MIKE HERE.
LINDA, WHY DON'T YOU GIVE TIBERIUS THE NICKEL TOUR?
UH, SURE. ABSOLUTELY.
MR. STONE? THIS WAY.
YES, OF COURSE.
AND YOU ARE...?
LINDA. I'M HEAD OF PROMOTIONS... AMONG OTHER THINGS.
REALLY? WHAT OTHER THINGS?
OH, THIS AND THAT...

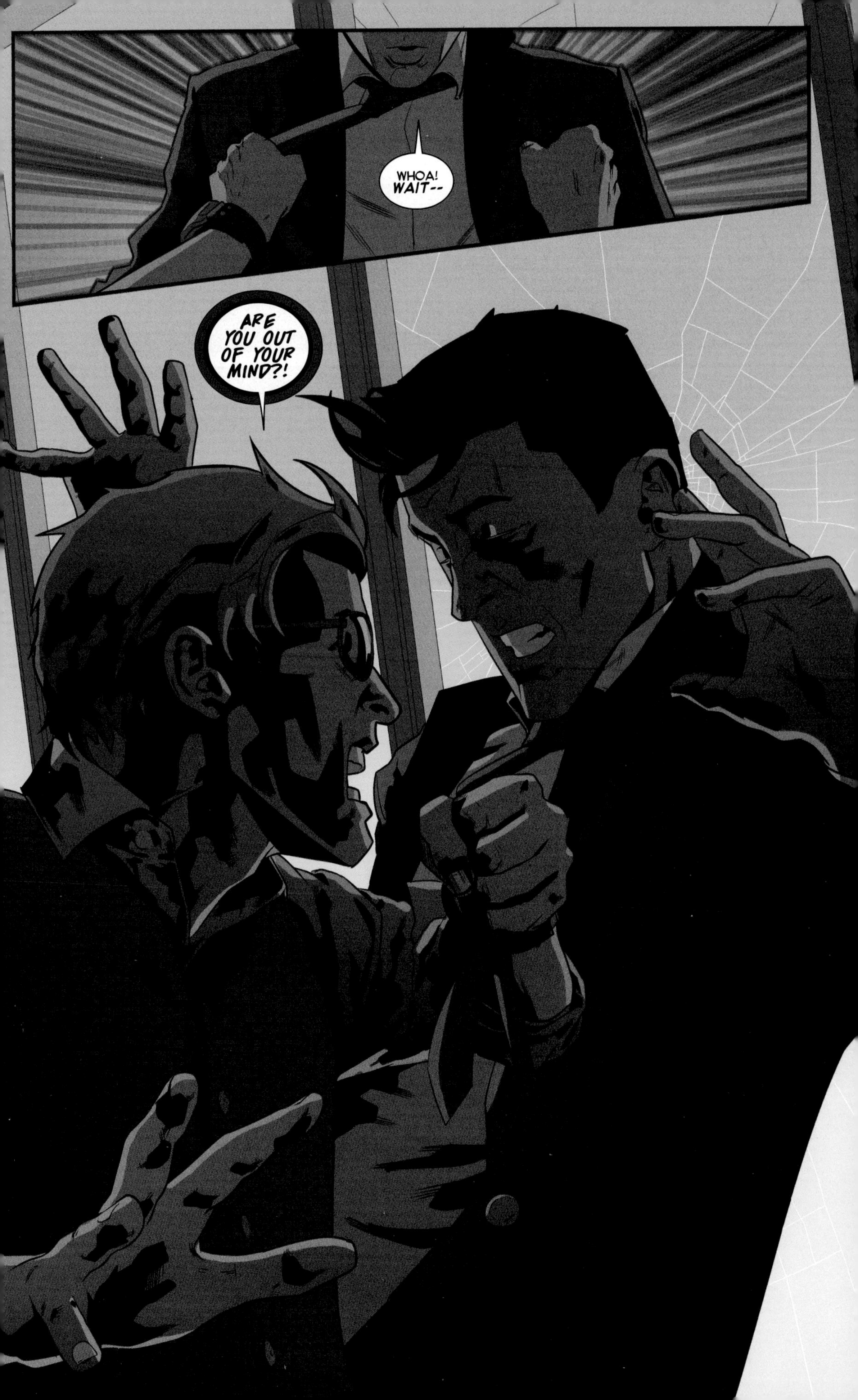
WHOA! WAIT--
ARE YOU OUT OF YOUR MIND?!

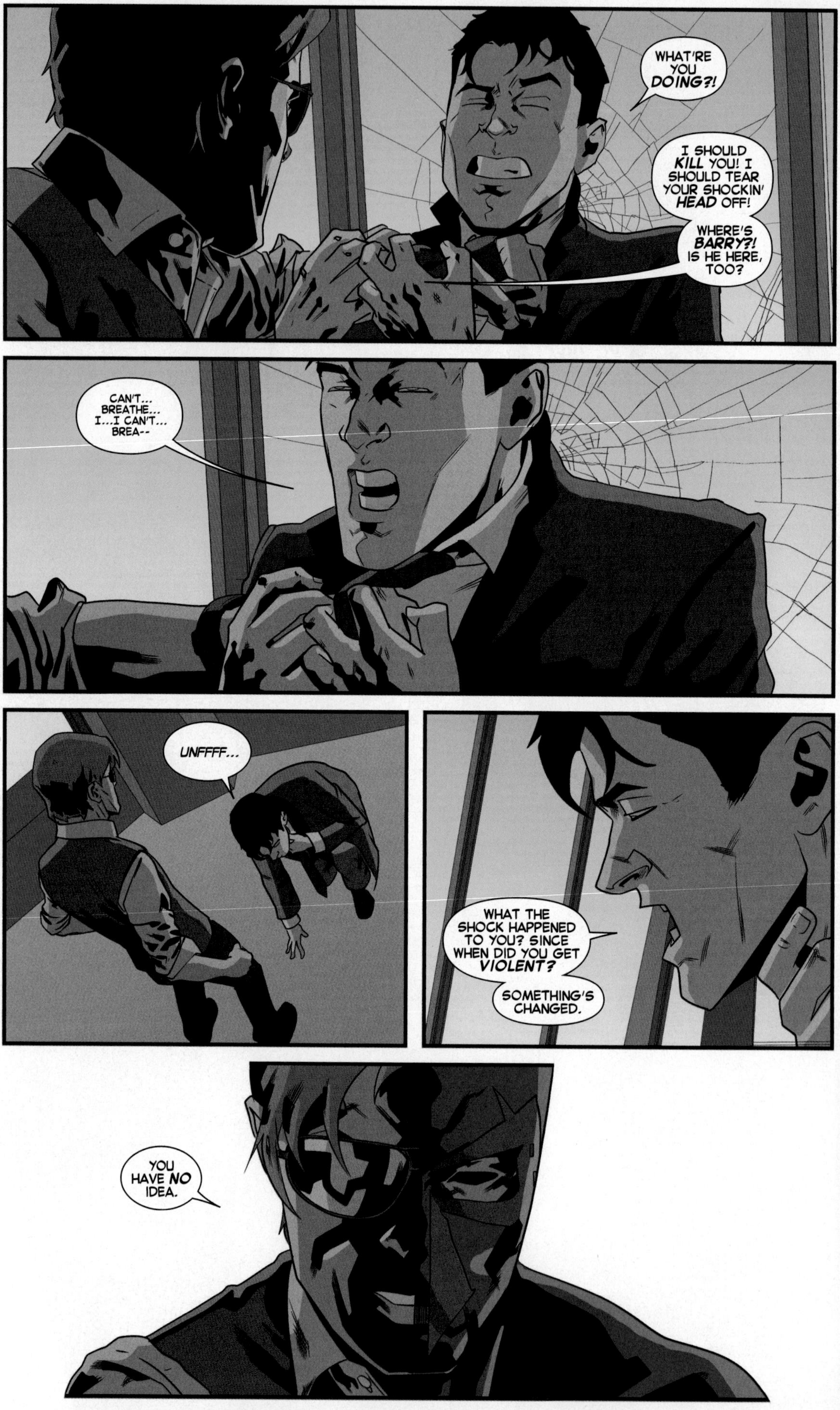
WHAT'RE YOU DOING?!
I SHOULD KILL YOU! I SHOULD TEAR YOUR SHOCKIN' HEAD OFF!
WHERE'S BARRY?! IS HE HERE, TOO?
CAN'T... BREATHE... I...I CAN'T... BREA--
UNFFFF...
WHAT THE SHOCK HAPPENED TO YOU? SINCE WHEN DID YOU GET VIOLENT?
SOMETHING'S CHANGED.
YOU HAVE NO IDEA.

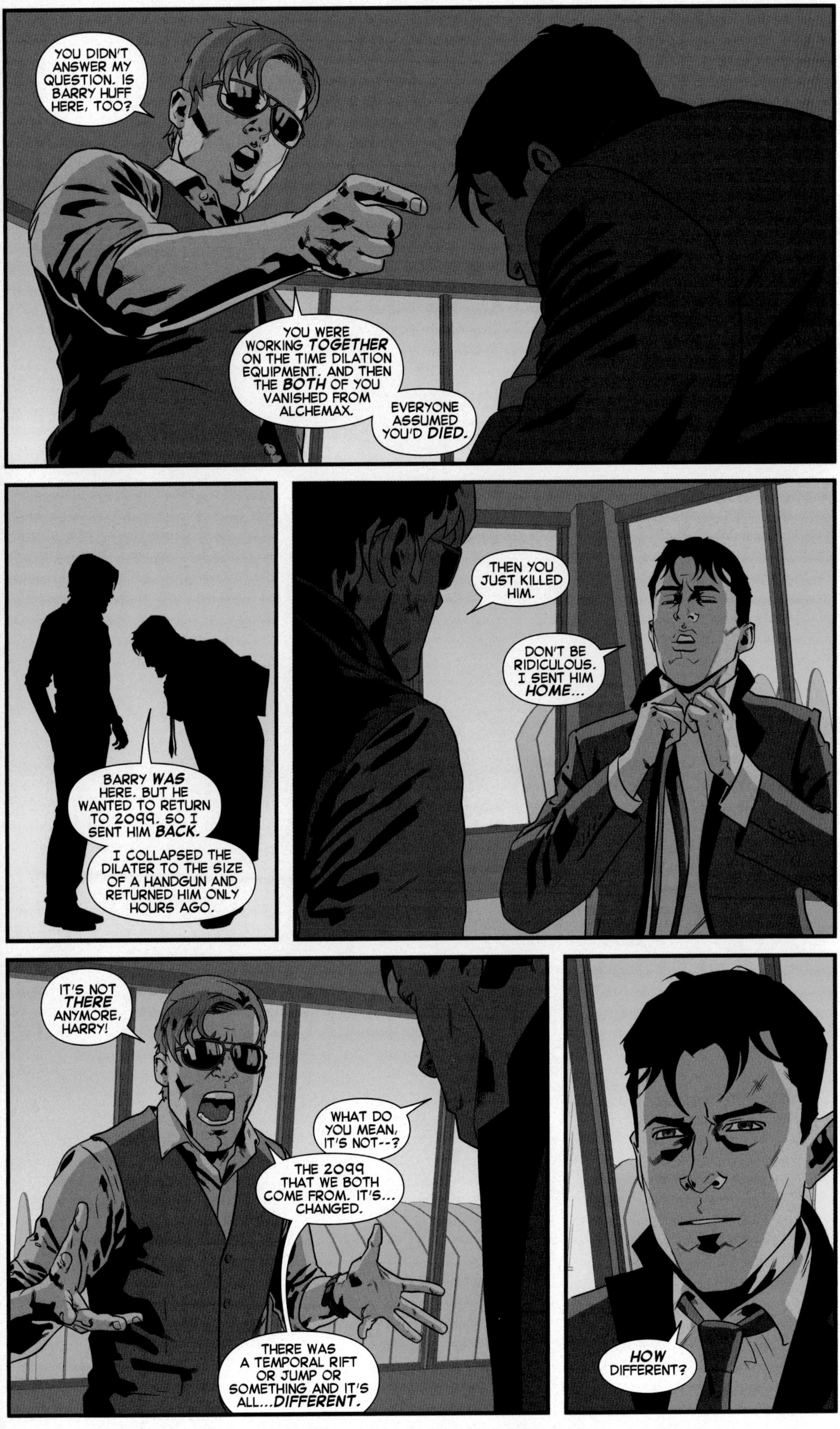
YOU DIDN'T ANSWER MY QUESTION. IS BARRY HUFF HERE, TOO?
YOU WERE WORKING TOGETHER ON THE TIME DILATION EQUIPMENT. AND THEN THE BOTH OF YOU VANISHED FROM ALCHEMAX.
EVERYONE ASSUMED YOU'D DIED.
BARRY WAS HERE. BUT HE WANTED TO RETURN TO 2099. SO I SENT HIM BACK.
I COLLAPSED THE DILATER TO THE SIZE OF A HANDGUN AND RETURNED HIM ONLY HOURS AGO.
THEN YOU JUST KILLED HIM.
DON'T BE RIDICULOUS. I SENT HIM HOME...
IT'S NOT THERE ANYMORE, HARRY!
WHAT DO YOU MEAN, IT'S NOT--?
THE 2099 THAT WE BOTH COME FROM. IT'S... CHANGED.
THERE WAS A TEMPORAL RIFT OR JUMP OR SOMETHING AND IT'S ALL...DIFFERENT.
HOW DIFFERENT?

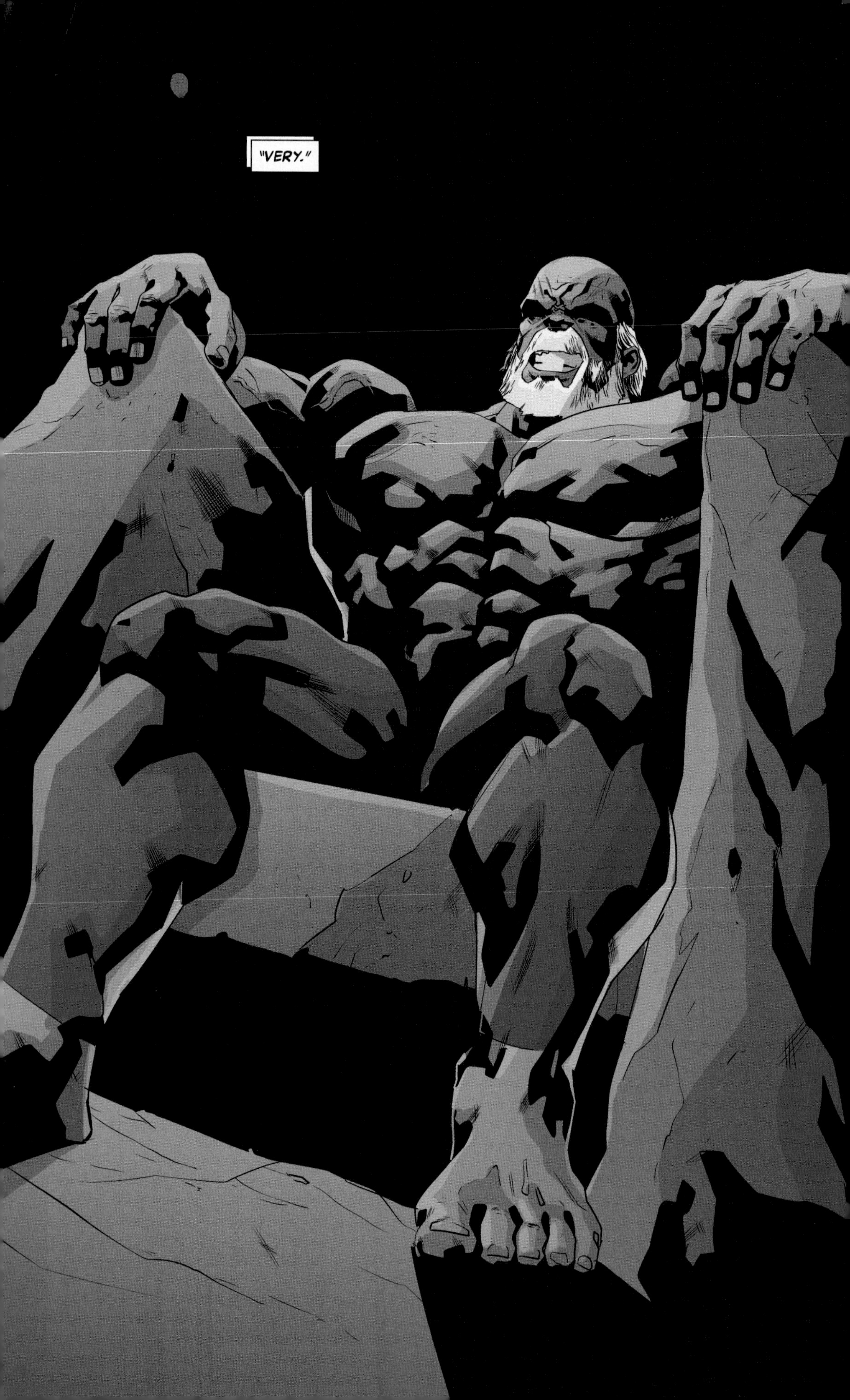
"VERY."

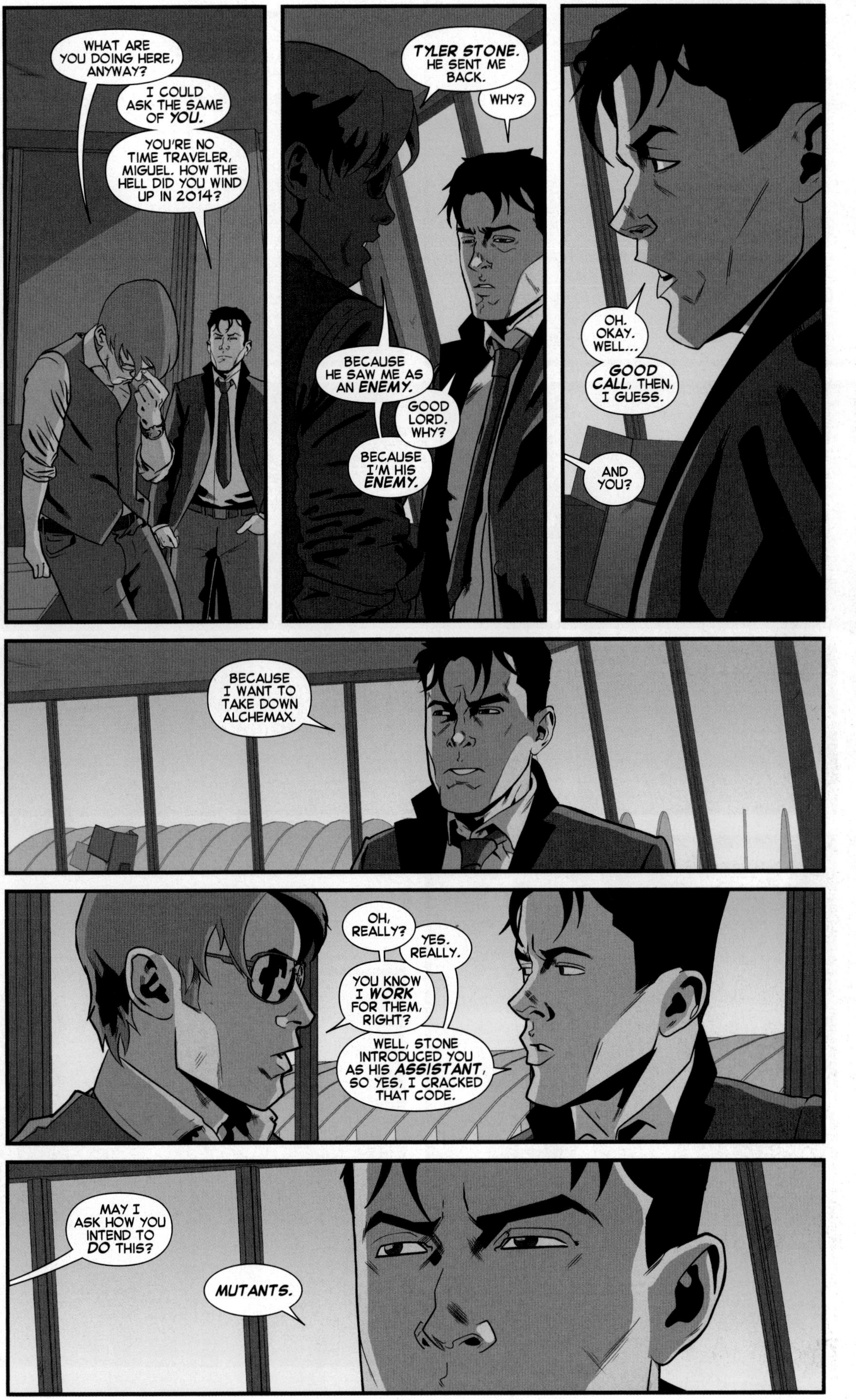
WHAT ARE YOU DOING HERE, ANYWAY?
I COULD ASK THE SAME OF YOU.
YOU'RE NO TIME TRAVELER, MIGUEL. HOW THE HELL DID YOU WIND UP IN 2014?
TYLER STONE. HE SENT ME BACK.
WHY?
BECAUSE HE SAW ME AS AN ENEMY.
GOOD LORD. WHY?
BECAUSE I'M HIS ENEMY.
OH. OKAY. WELL... GOOD CALL, THEN, I GUESS.
AND YOU?
BECAUSE I WANT TO TAKE DOWN ALCHEMAX.
OH, REALLY?
YES. REALLY.
YOU KNOW I WORK FOR THEM, RIGHT?
WELL, STONE INTRODUCED YOU AS HIS ASSISTANT, SO YES, I CRACKED THAT CODE.
MAY I ASK HOW YOU INTEND TO DO THIS?
MUTANTS.

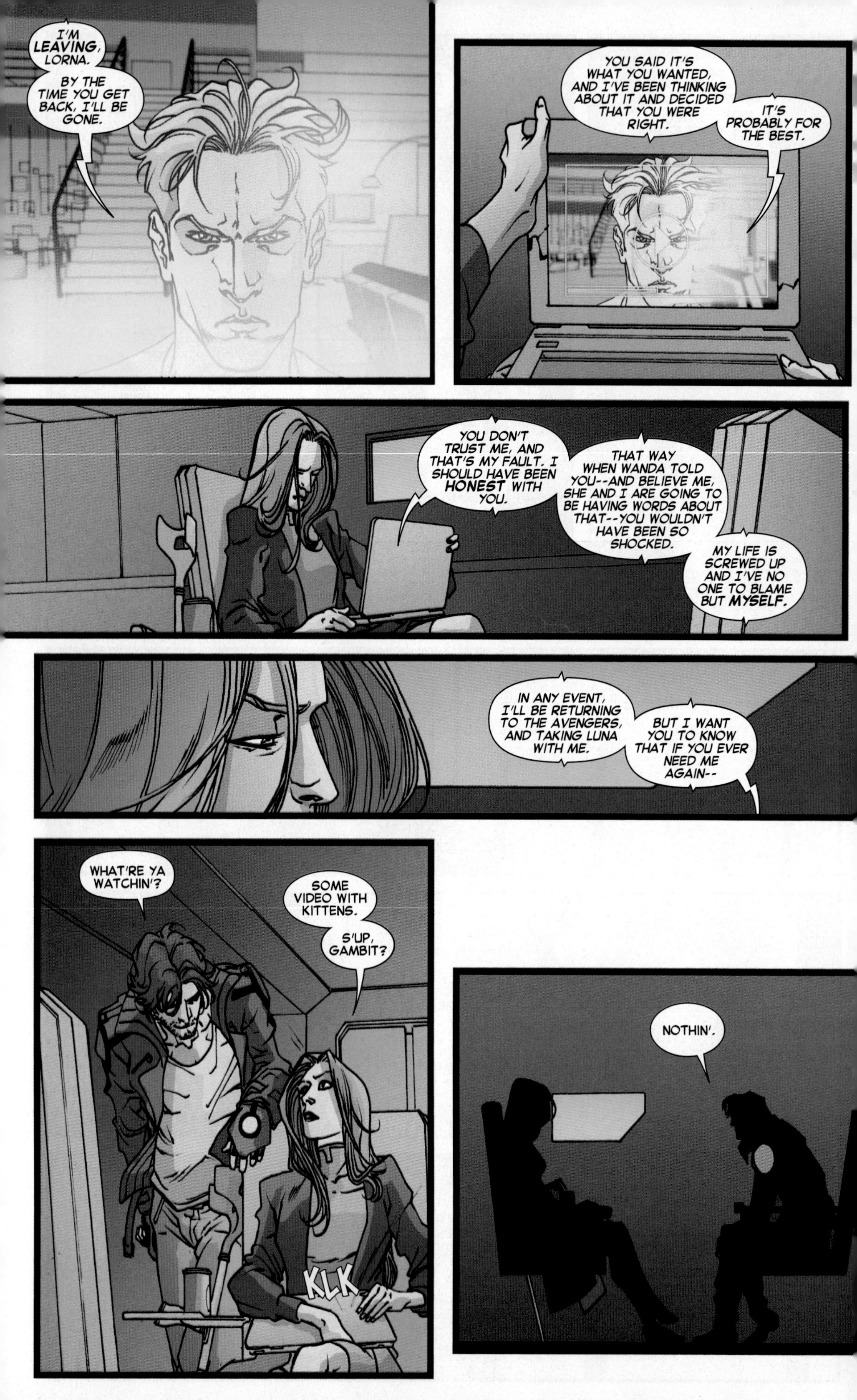
I'M LEAVING, LORNA.
BY THE TIME YOU GET BACK, I'LL BE GONE.
YOU SAID IT'S WHAT YOU WANTED, AND I'VE BEEN THINKING ABOUT IT AND DECIDED THAT YOU WERE RIGHT.
IT'S PROBABLY FOR THE BEST.
YOU DON'T TRUST ME, AND THAT'S MY FAULT. I SHOULD HAVE BEEN HONEST WITH YOU.
THAT WAY WHEN WANDA TOLD YOU--AND BELIEVE ME, SHE AND I ARE GOING TO BE HAVING WORDS ABOUT THAT--YOU WOULDN'T HAVE BEEN SO SHOCKED.
MY LIFE IS SCREWED UP AND I'VE NO ONE TO BLAME BUT MYSELF.
IN ANY EVENT, I'LL BE RETURNING TO THE AVENGERS, AND TAKING LUNA WITH ME.
BUT I WANT YOU TO KNOW THAT IF YOU EVER NEED ME AGAIN--
WHAT'RE YA WATCHIN'?
SOME VIDEO WITH KITTENS.
S'UP, GAMBIT?
KLK
NOTHIN'.

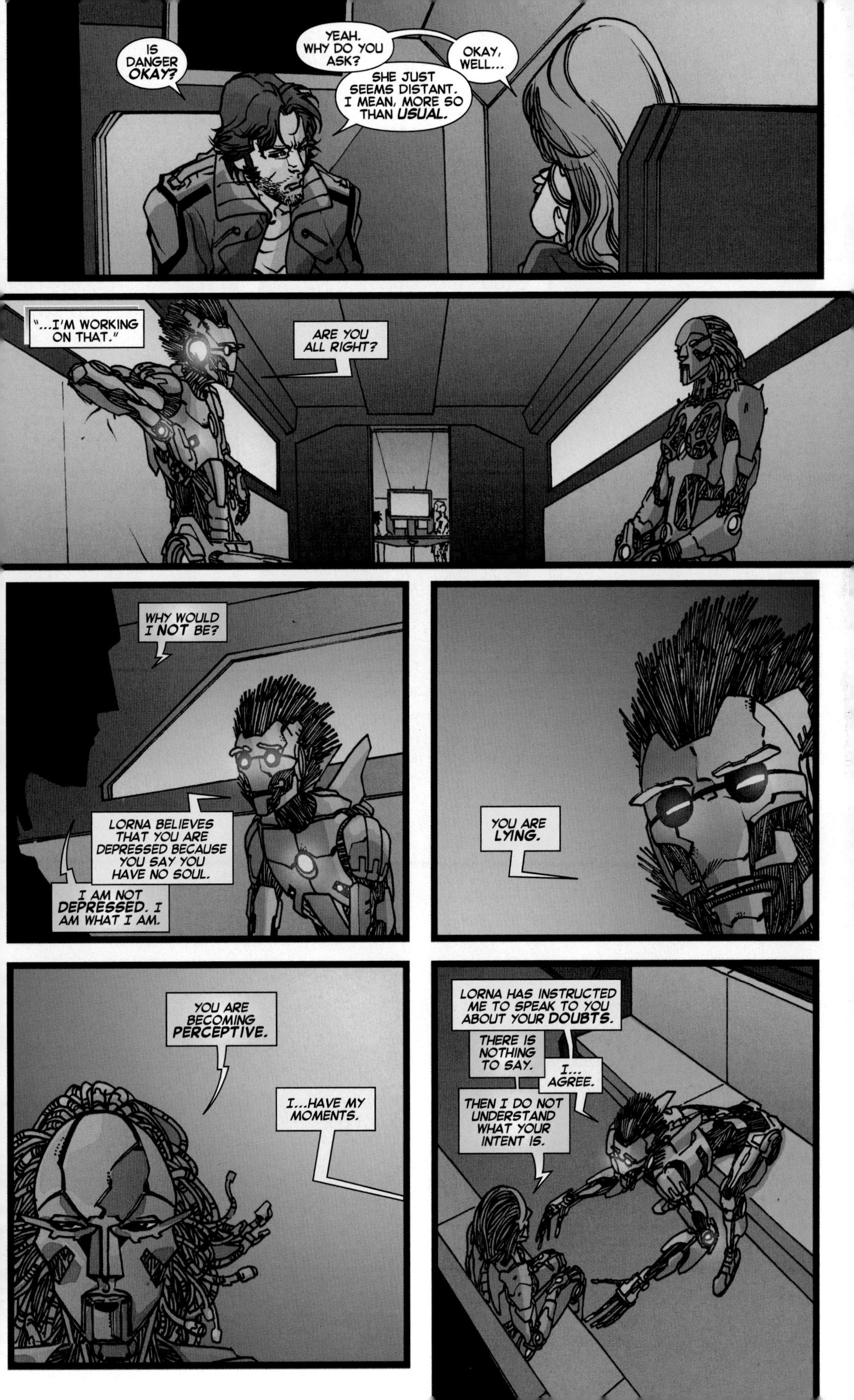

IS DANGER OKAY?
YEAH. WHY DO YOU ASK?
SHE JUST SEEMS DISTANT. I MEAN, MORE SO THAN USUAL.
OKAY, WELL...
"...I'M WORKING ON THAT."
ARE YOU ALL RIGHT?
WHY WOULD I NOT BE?
LORNA BELIEVES THAT YOU ARE DEPRESSED BECAUSE YOU SAY YOU HAVE NO SOUL.
I AM NOT DEPRESSED. I AM WHAT I AM.
YOU ARE LYING.
YOU ARE BECOMING PERCEPTIVE.
I...HAVE MY MOMENTS.
LORNA HAS INSTRUCTED ME TO SPEAK TO YOU ABOUT YOUR DOUBTS.
THERE IS NOTHING TO SAY.
I... AGREE.
THEN I DO NOT UNDERSTAND WHAT YOUR INTENT IS.

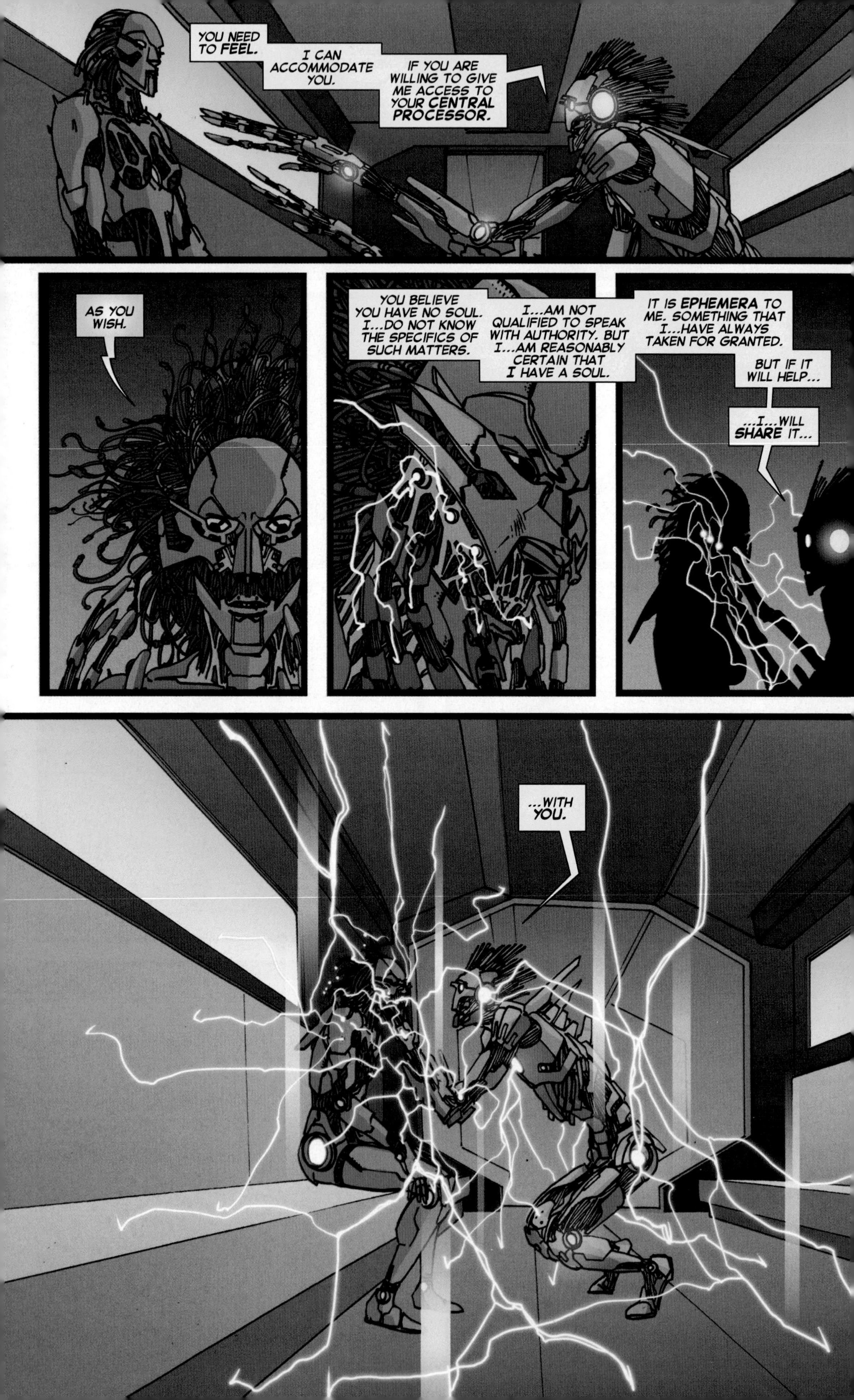
YOU NEED TO FEEL.
I CAN ACCOMMODATE YOU.
IF YOU ARE WILLING TO GIVE ME ACCESS TO YOUR CENTRAL PROCESSOR.
AS YOU WISH.
YOU BELIEVE YOU HAVE NO SOUL. I...DO NOT KNOW THE SPECIFICS OF SUCH MATTERS.
I...AM NOT QUALIFIED TO SPEAK WITH AUTHORITY. BUT I...AM REASONABLY CERTAIN THAT I HAVE A SOUL.
IT IS EPHEMERA TO ME. SOMETHING THAT I...HAVE ALWAYS TAKEN FOR GRANTED.
BUT IF IT WILL HELP...
...I...WILL SHARE IT...
...WITH YOU.

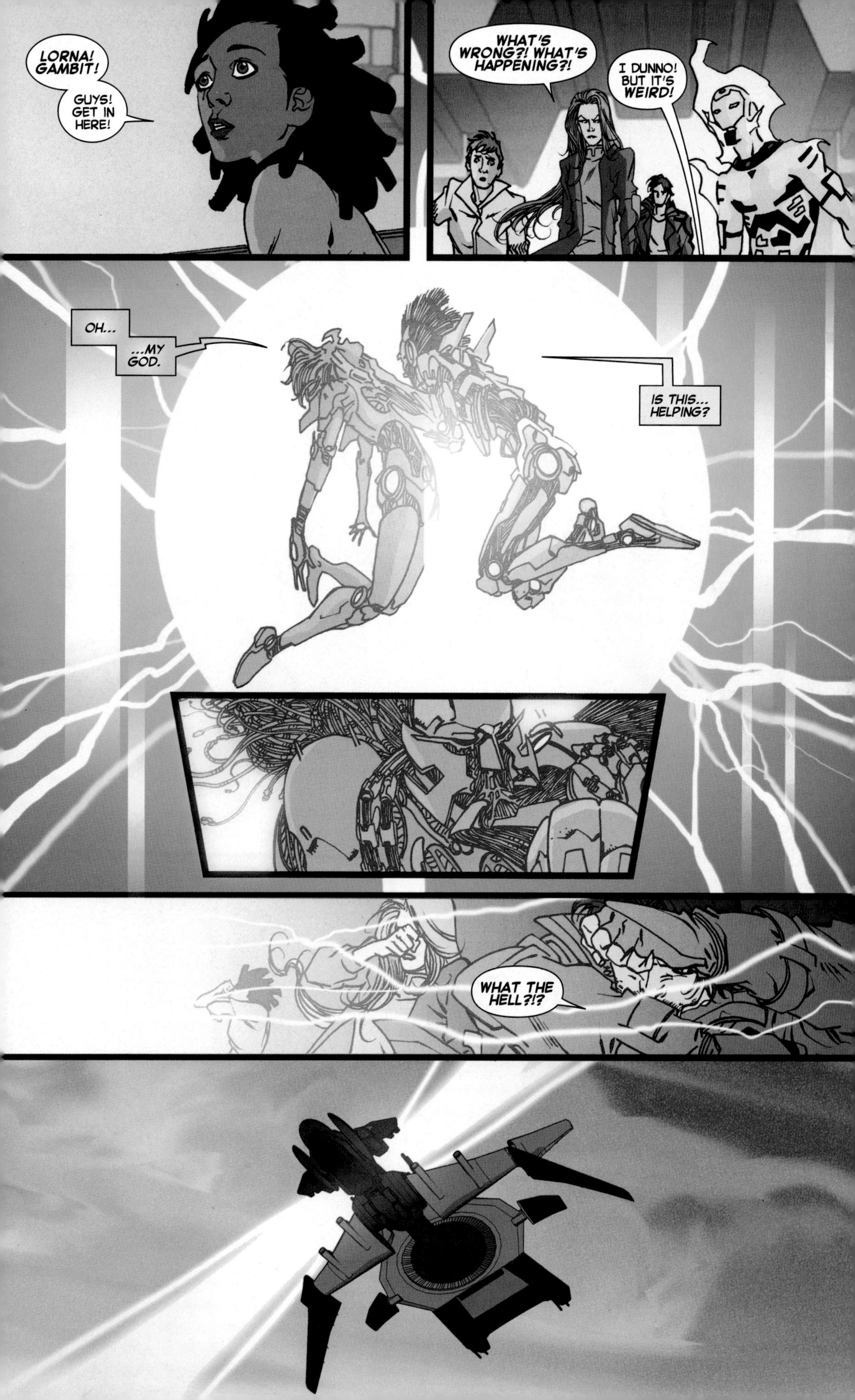
LORNA! GAMBIT!
GUYS! GET IN HERE!
WHAT'S WRONG?! WHAT'S HAPPENING?!
I DUNNO! BUT IT'S WEIRD!
OH...
...MY GOD.
IS THIS... HELPING?
WHAT THE HELL?!?

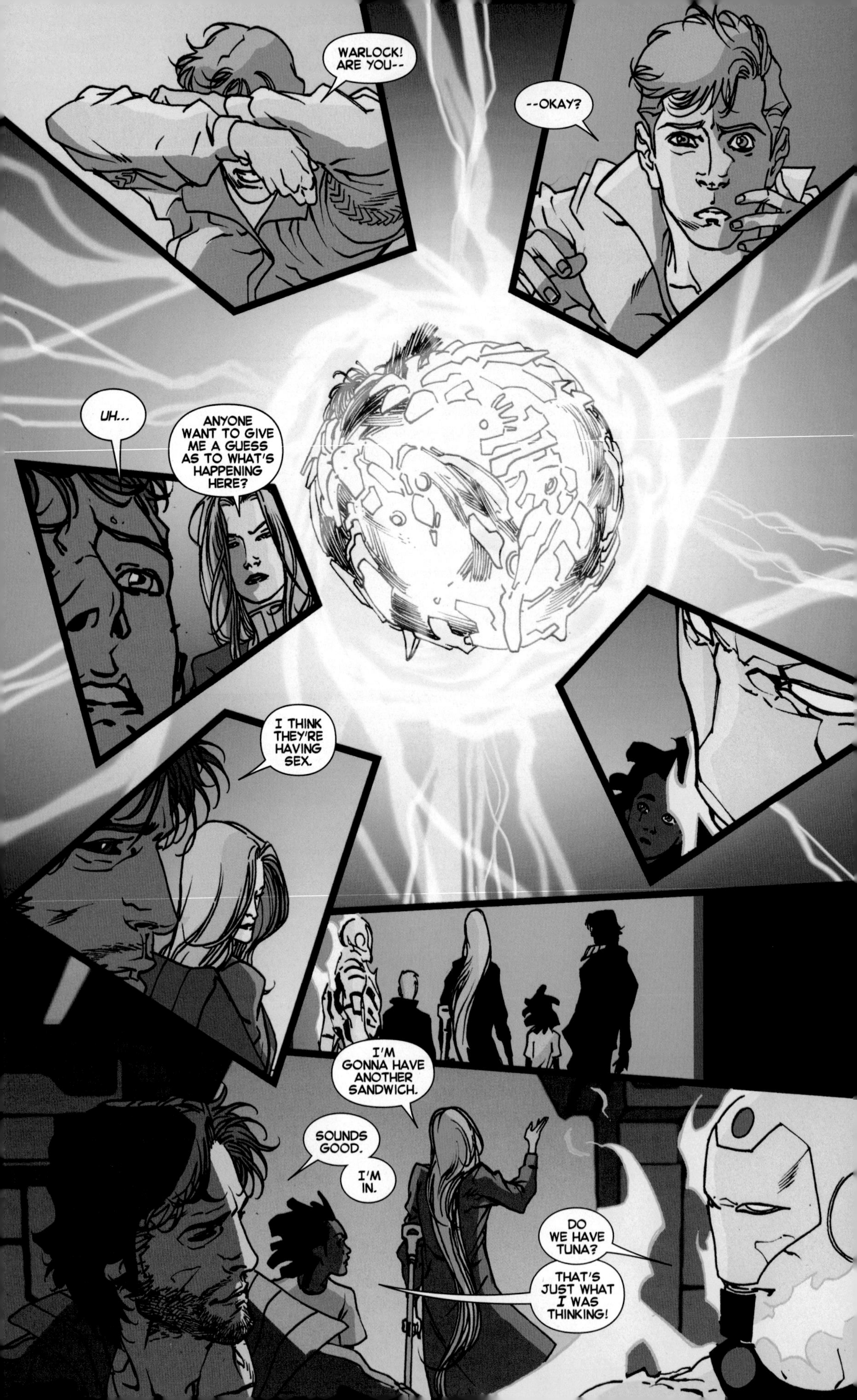
WARLOCK! ARE YOU--
--OKAY?
UH...
ANYONE WANT TO GIVE ME A GUESS AS TO WHAT'S HAPPENING HERE?
I THINK THEY'RE HAVING SEX.
I'M GONNA HAVE ANOTHER SANDWICH.
SOUNDS GOOD.
I'M IN.
DO WE HAVE TUNA?
THAT'S JUST WHAT I WAS THINKING!

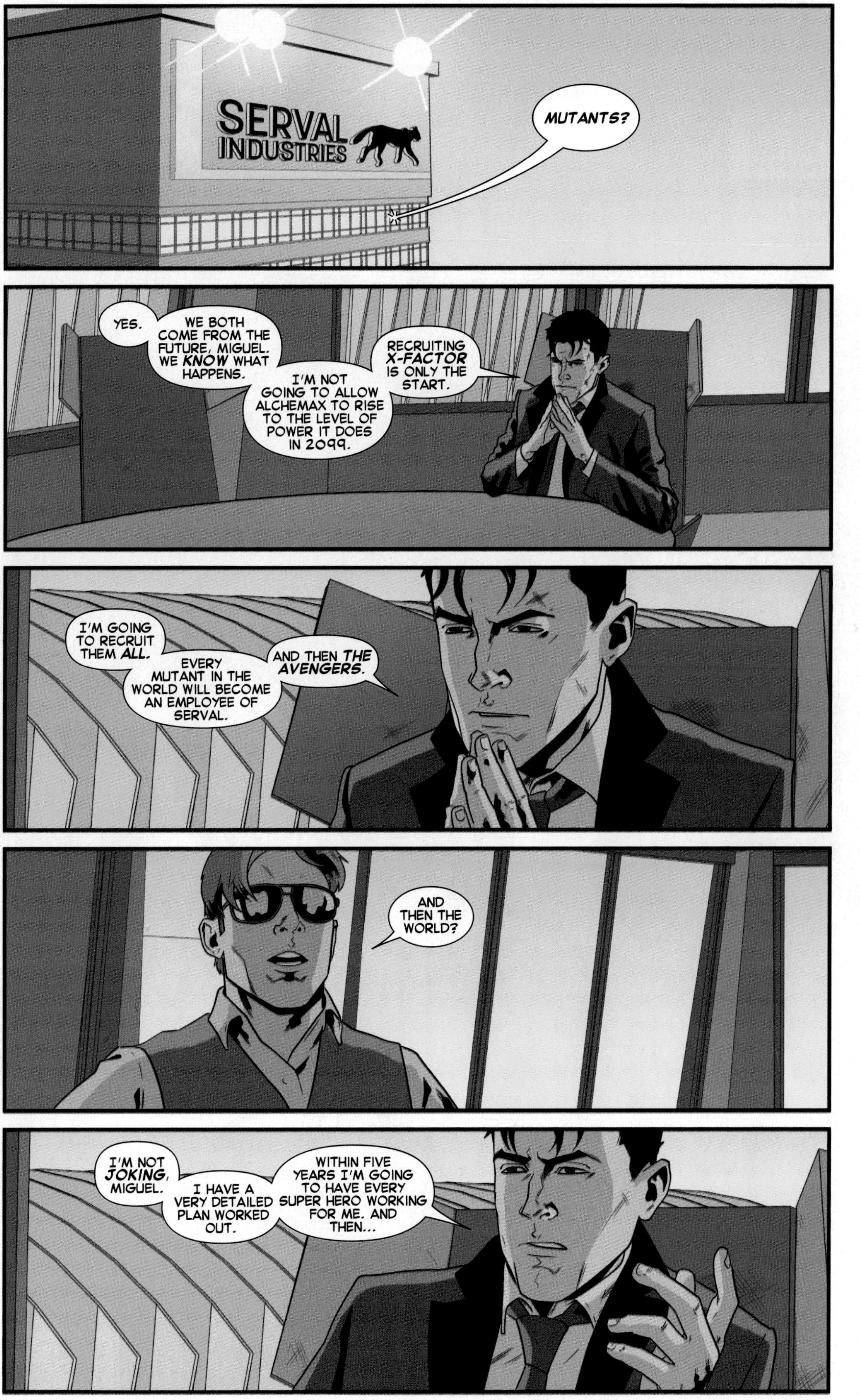
SERVAL INDUSTRIES
MUTANTS?
YES.
WE BOTH COME FROM THE FUTURE, MIGUEL. WE KNOW WHAT HAPPENS.
I'M NOT GOING TO ALLOW ALCHEMAX TO RISE TO THE LEVEL OF POWER IT DOES IN 2099.
RECRUITING X-FACTOR IS ONLY THE START.
I'M GOING TO RECRUIT THEM ALL.
EVERY MUTANT IN THE WORLD WILL BECOME AN EMPLOYEE OF SERVAL.
AND THEN THE AVENGERS.
AND THEN THE WORLD?
I'M NOT JOKING, MIGUEL.
I HAVE A VERY DETAILED PLAN WORKED OUT.
WITHIN FIVE YEARS I'M GOING TO HAVE EVERY SUPER HERO WORKING FOR ME. AND THEN...

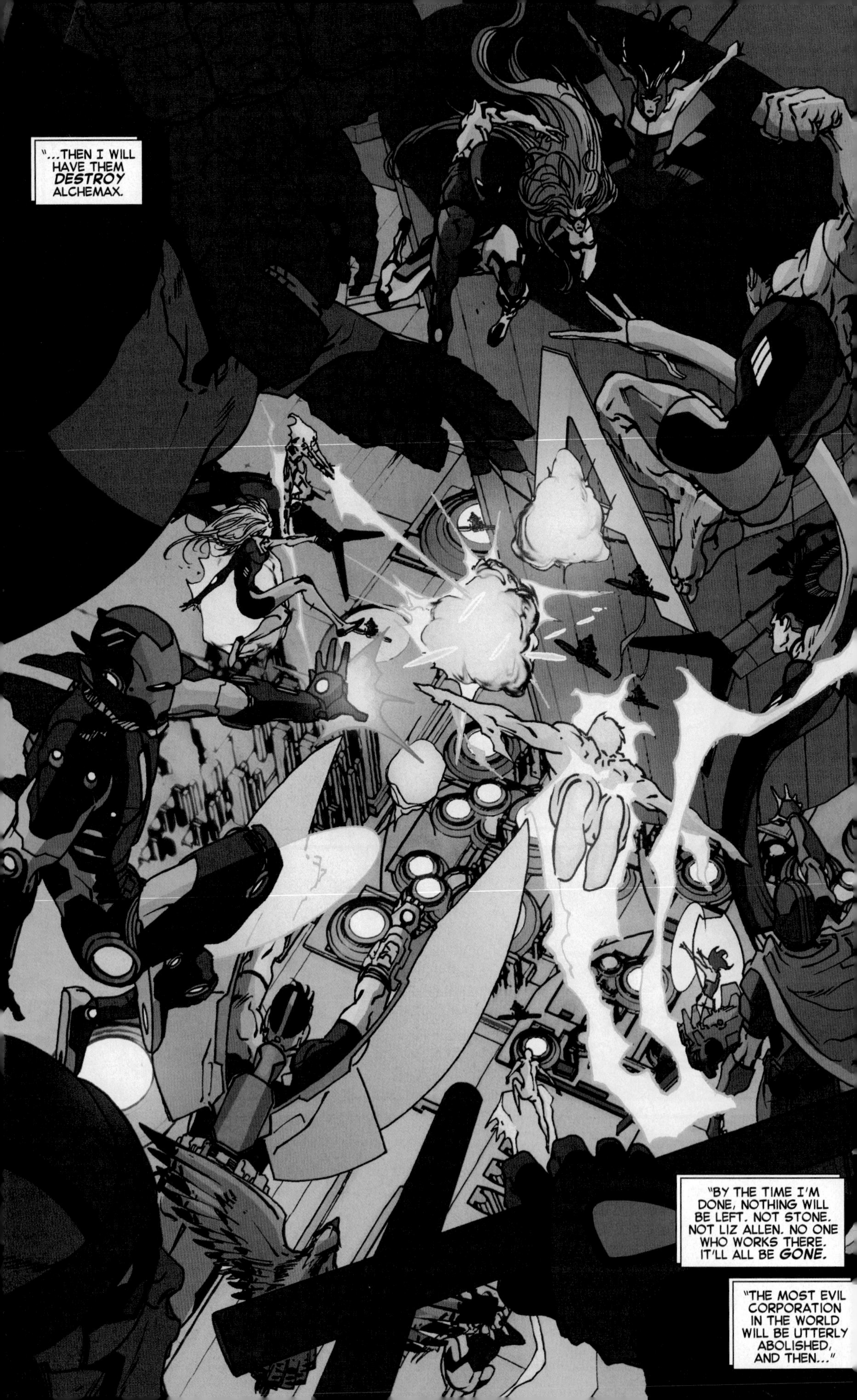
"...THEN I WILL HAVE THEM *DESTROY* ALCHEMAX.
"BY THE TIME I'M DONE, NOTHING WILL BE LEFT. NOT STONE. NOT LIZ ALLEN. NO ONE WHO WORKS THERE. IT'LL ALL BE *GONE*.
"THE MOST EVIL CORPORATION IN THE WORLD WILL BE UTTERLY ABOLISHED, AND THEN..."

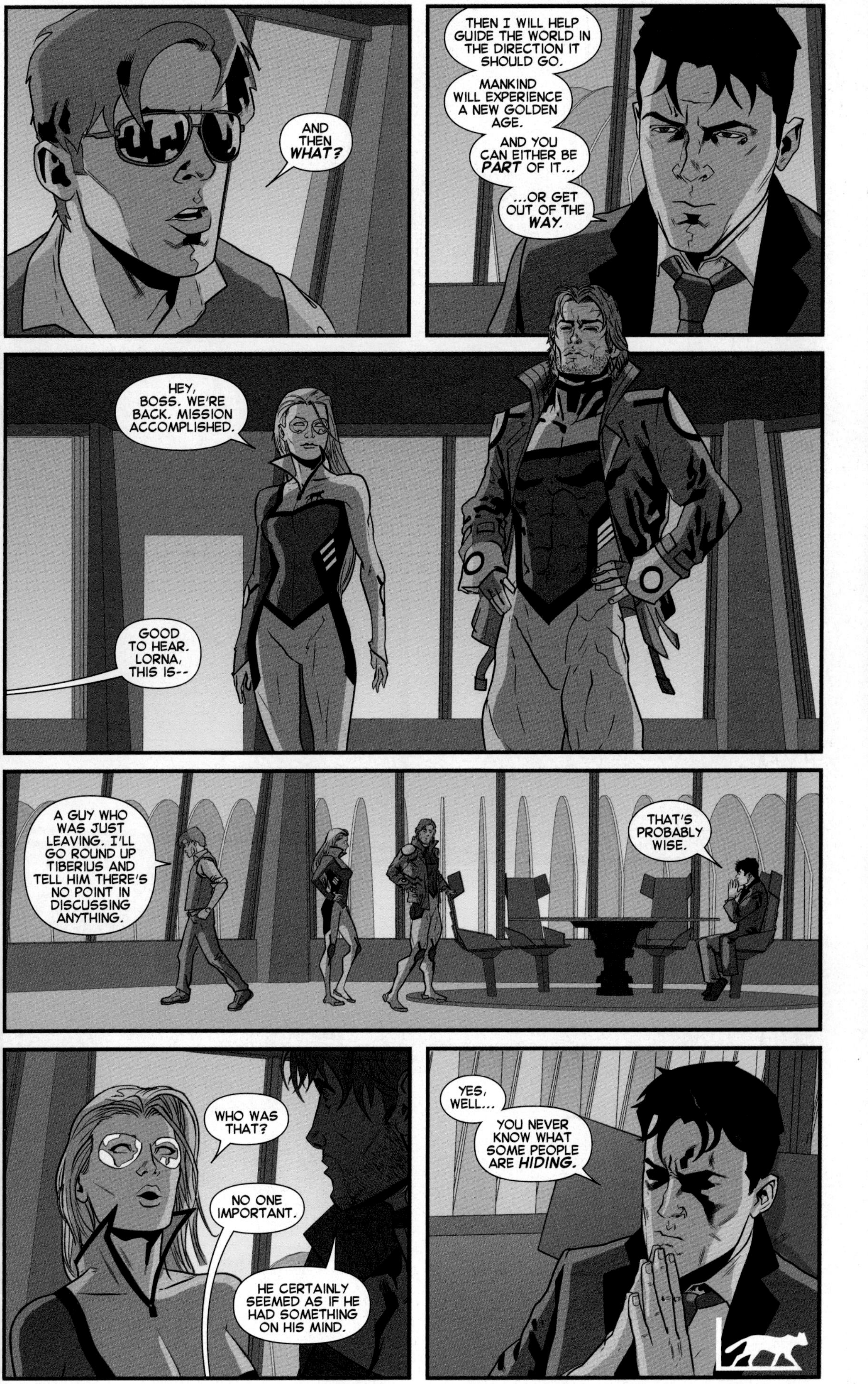
AND THEN WHAT?
THEN I WILL HELP GUIDE THE WORLD IN THE DIRECTION IT SHOULD GO.
MANKIND WILL EXPERIENCE A NEW GOLDEN AGE.
AND YOU CAN EITHER BE PART OF IT...
...OR GET OUT OF THE WAY.
HEY, BOSS. WE'RE BACK. MISSION ACCOMPLISHED.
GOOD TO HEAR. LORNA, THIS IS--
A GUY WHO WAS JUST LEAVING. I'LL GO ROUND UP TIBERIUS AND TELL HIM THERE'S NO POINT IN DISCUSSING ANYTHING.
THAT'S PROBABLY WISE.
WHO WAS THAT?
NO ONE IMPORTANT.
HE CERTAINLY SEEMED AS IF HE HAD SOMETHING ON HIS MIND.
YES, WELL...
YOU NEVER KNOW WHAT SOME PEOPLE ARE HIDING.

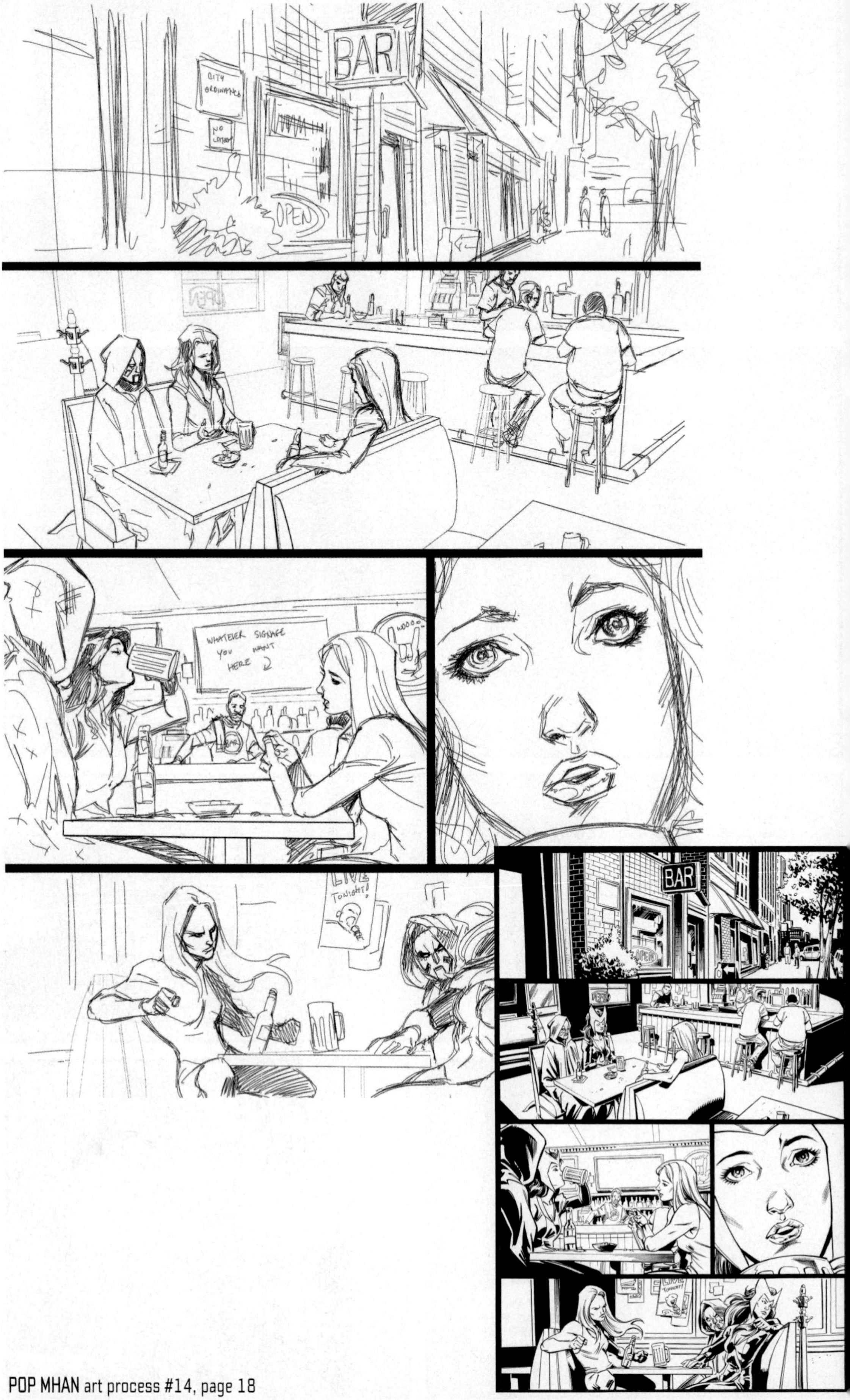
BAR
OPEN
WHATEVER SIGNAGE YOU WANT HERE
LIVE TONIGHT!

POP MHAN art process #14, page 18

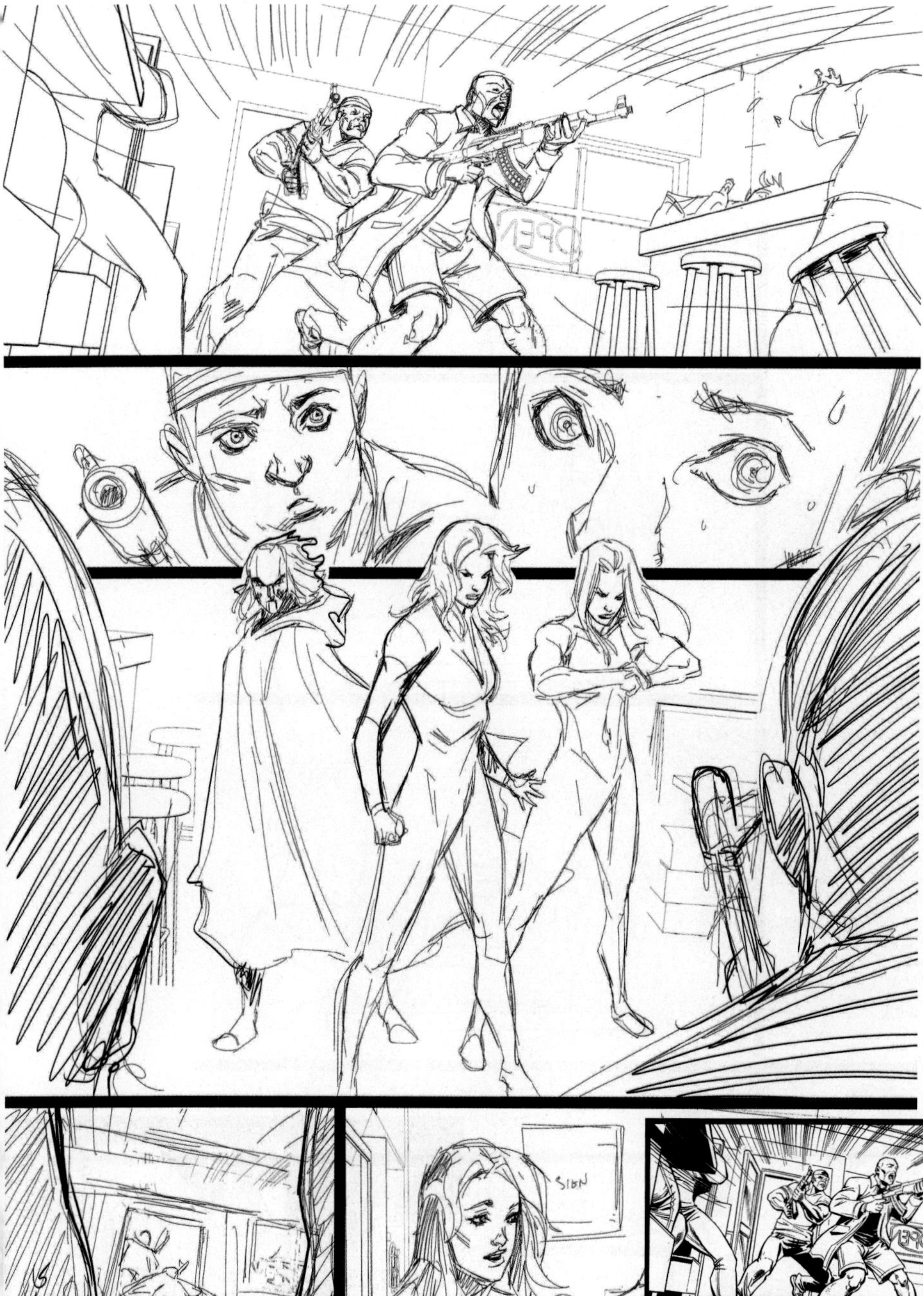
SIGN

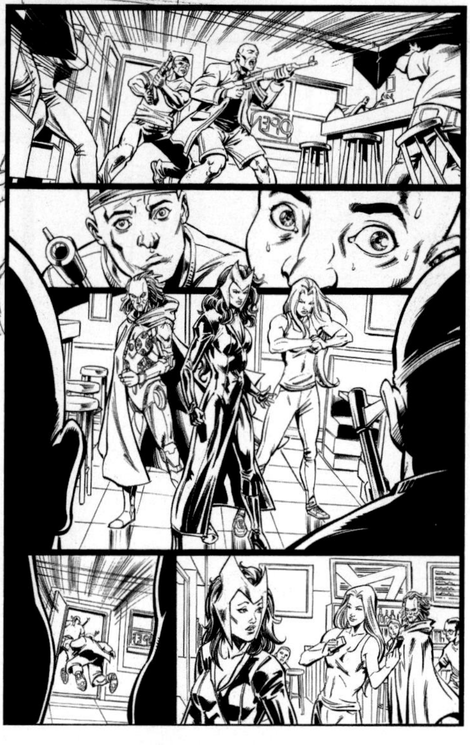

POP MHAN art process #14, page 19

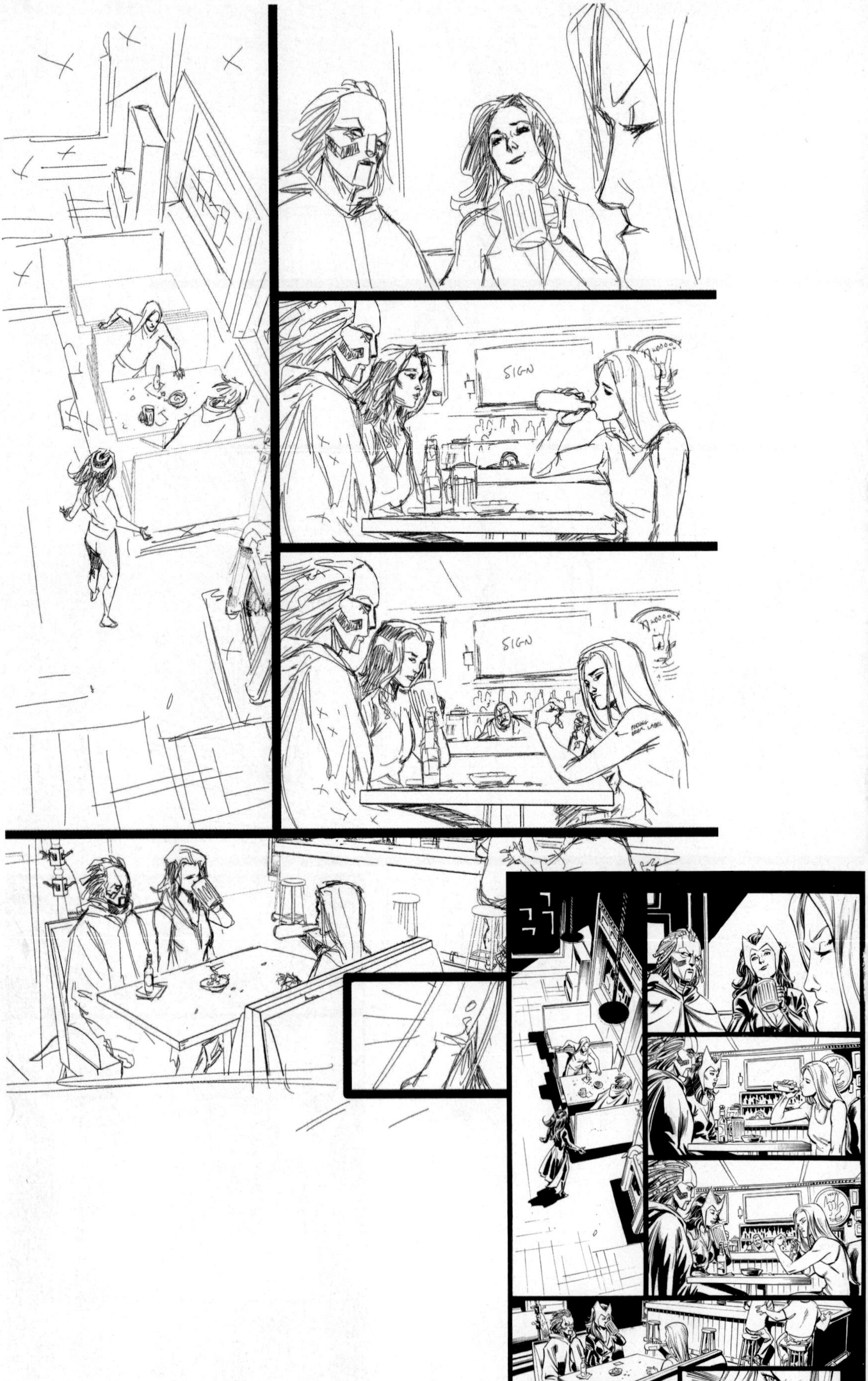
SIGN
SIGN

POP MHAN art process #14, page 20